Struggle for the Land

Indigenous Resistance to Genocide, Ecocide and Expropriation in Contemporary North America

Ward Churchill

Foreword by John Trudell
Preface by Winona LaDuke

Common Courage Press Monroe, Maine

Cover by Norma Whitman
Cover photo by Kevin Barry McKiernan
Manufactured in the United States
This edition not for sale in Canada

Library of Congress Cataloging in Publication Data
Churchill, Ward.
Struggle for the land: indigenist resistance to genocide, ecocide, and expropriation in contemporary North America / Ward Churchill ; foreword by John Trudell ; preface by Winona LaDuke.
p. cm.
Includes bibliographical references and index.
ISBN 1-56751-001-9 (cloth). -- ISBN 1-56751-000-0 (paper)
1. Indians of North America--Land tenure. 2. Indians of North America--Claims. 3. Indians of North America--Government relations. 4. Human ecology--North America. I. Title.
E98.L3C48 1993
[342.643208997] 92-22676

Common Courage Press
Box 702
Monroe, ME 04951
207-525-0900

Preface

Succeeding Into Native North America: A Secessionist View

Winona LaDuke

The map on the previous page could be called the indigenous North American view of bioregional secession. Although the scale in which it is presented prevent the details from being clear, the treaty and land claim areas involved are not exactly how it was B.C. (Before Columbus). They are instead the basic outlines of the legacy—defined land areas of native nations.[1] The map, even through its general contours, may help correct some of the basic miseducation with which most non-Indian residents of the continent have been afflicted.

- First, the map shows how North America's indigenous peoples lived in what amounted to natural, bioregional configurations;

- Second, it shows that North America's reigning nation-state governments—those of the United States and Canada—are, according to the indigenous "host" nations, on shaky ground, both legally and environmentally. Very little land in North America should rightly fall outside native jurisdiction, administered under indigenous rather than immigrant values.

Back to the first point. When I was in grade school, I was taught there were Plains Indians (warlike), Woodland Indians (democratic), and Pueblo Indians (pacifistic), and that's about all. What was left out was that the treaty areas and treaty rights of indigenous people in North America are ongoing, and that they accrue to recognized nations, demonstrating distinct sociocultural and linguistic patterns. Also omitted from my education was the fact that these nations had lived quite well within these defined territories since time immemorial; there was/is trade between each of the indigenous areas, but each was also essentially self-sufficient.

Today, a lot of people question the necessity and utility of centralized nation-state governances and economics.[2] They find the status quo to be increasingly absurd and are seeking alternatives to the values and patterns of consumption presently dominating not only North America, but the rest of the planet as well. The living reality of Native North America, and the bioregionally-determined redefinition of polity it represents, offers the model for an alternative arrangement.[3] And, if Leopold Kohr and the Euskadi (Basque) say such a naturally-grounded structure could work in Europe, why not here?[4] It is obviously important that everyone learn as much as possible about American Indian realities, rather than the self-serving junk usually taught in school.

The map also points out the legal basis for protecting the environment and its inhabitants. The native struggle in North America today can only be properly understood as a pursuit of the recovery of land rights which are guaranteed through treaties. What Indians ask—what we really expect—from those who claim to be our friends and allies is respect and support for these treaty rights.

What does this mean? Well, it starts with advocating that Indians regain use of and jurisdiction over what the treaties define as being our lands. It means direct support to Indian efforts to recover these lands, but not governmental attempts to "compensate" us with money for lands we never agreed to relinquish. This, in turn, means that those indigenous governments which traditionally held regulatory and enforcement power within Indian Country—not the "more modern" and otherwise non-traditional "tribal councils" imposed upon Indians by the federal government under the Indian Reorganization Act of 1934—should have the right to resume their activities now.[5] By extension, this would mean that much land which is currently taxed, regulated, strip-mined, militarized, drowned by hydroelectric generation or over-irrigation, and nuked by the U.S. and Canadian governments would no longer be under their control or jurisdiction. Surely, this is a prospect which all progressive and socially-conscious people can embrace.

What is perhaps most important about Indian treaty rights is the power of the documents at issue to clarify matters which would otherwise be consigned by nation-state apologists to the realm of "opinion" and "interpretation." The treaties lay things out clearly, and they are instruments of international law.[6] In this sense, the violation of the treaty rights of any given people represents a plain transgression against the rights of all people everywhere. This can be a potent weapon in the organization of struggles for justice and sanity in every corner of the globe. And it should be appreciated as such by those who champion causes ranging from protection of the environment to universal human rights.

Native North America is struggling to break free of the colonialist, industrialist, militarist nation-state domination in which it is now engulfed. It is fighting to "secede" from the U.S. and Canada. But, because of the broader implications of this, we refer to the results we seek not as "secession," but as "success." This is true, not just for Indians, but for all living beings and the earth itself. Won't you help us succeed into a full-scale re-emergence of our Natural World?

Notes

1. For fuller details, see Charles C. Royce, *Eighteenth Annual Report of the American Bureau of Ethnography: Indian Land Cessions tn the United States* (Smithsonian Institution, Washington, DC: U.S. Government Printing Office, 1899).
2. A good reading in this regard is Pierre Clastres, *Society Against the State* (New York: Urizen Books, 1977).
3. For orientation to the principles at issue within the rubric of "bioregionalism," see Alexandra Hart, ed., *North American Bioregional Congress II: Proceedings, August 25-29, 1986* (Forestville, CA Hart Publishing, 1987).
4. Leopold Kohr, *The Breakdown of Nations* (New York: E.P. Dutton Publishers, 1957) and *The Overdeveloped Nations: The Diseconomies of Scale* (New York Schoken Books, 1978). On the struggles of the indigenous peoples of Iberia, see Kenneth Medhurst, *The Basques and Catalans*, Minority Rights Group Report No. 9, September 1977.
5. For parallel analysis centered in a practical contemporary application, see Gudmundur Alfredson, "Greenland and the Law of Political Decolonization" (Bonn: *German Yearbook on International Law*, 1982).
6. See Zed Nanda, "Self-Determination Under International Law: Validity of Claims to Secede," *Case Western Reserve Journal of International Law*, No. 13, 1981.

Introduction

Land Theft and the Mechanisms of Genocide and Ecocide

The history of 500 years of warfare directed against the indigenous inhabitants of the Americas is gradually coming to light. Even those who acknowledge the genocidal nature of European and Euroamerican policies regarding American Indians, however, tend to see them as the extremes of a different era: the brutality of the Conquistadores or the massacres permeating the saga of the "Winning of the West." The underlying motivation prompting the genocide of Native Americans, the lust for their territories and the resources within them, is typically hidden behind a rhetoric extolling the "settlement" of essentially vacant and "undiscovered" lands. To admit otherwise risks revealing that the past motive for genocide exists as much today, and in some ways more so.

This volume of the series on Genocide and Resistance illustrates through a sequence of case studies that the destruction of indigenous peoples through the expropriation and/or destruction of their land bases is very much an ongoing phenomenon in both the United States and Canada. The processes are not simply genocidal; they are increasingly ecocidal in their implications.[1] Not only the people of the land are being destroyed, but, more and more, the land itself. The nature of native resistance to the continuing onslaught of the invading industrial culture is shaped accordingly. It is a resistance forged in the crucible of a struggle for survival.

As "Perversions of Justice" demonstrates, the philosophical/legalistic rationalization of such circumstances is not new. Rather, the present situation is simply the outgrowth of a juridical doctrine which has been evolving in the U.S. since before the very earliest moments of the republic. This ideology of expansionism—popularly known as "Manifest Destiny"—has ongoing direct impacts upon the indigenous peoples of North America. The ideology also supported philosophical developments elsewhere. A salient example is Adolf Hitler's concept of *lebensraumpolitik* ("politics of living space"). The ideology stipulated that Germans were innately entitled, by virtue of an imagined racial and cultural superiority, to land belonging to others. This rendered Germany morally free in its own mind to take such lands through the aggressive use of military force.[2]

In Part II, "Struggle for the Land," a series of examples demonstrate how U.S. juridical doctrine and its Canadian counterpart have been applied as a means to justify the continuing encroachment of these nation-states upon the residual territories of native peoples. Connections between the policies and techniques of expropriation and other problematic aspects of U.S. and Canadian actions become clear. For instance, in "The Struggle for Newe Segobia," the interrelationship between the taking of the Western Shoshone homeland in Nevada and the ability of the U.S. military to engage in a massive and sustained program of nuclear weapons testing is made clear. Similarly, in "Last Stand at Lubicon Lake," there is a link between Canada's denial of Cree land rights, and governmental/corporate plans to clearcut vast expanses of northern forest. The undertaking is in many ways just as ecologically dangerous as the cutting of the Amazon rain forest in Brazil, though few recognize this to be the case.[3]

Part III, "Other Battles," pursues such themes with even greater emphasis. It examines the uses to which Indian lands and resources have been put by the colonizing powers, the effects of such use, and the means by which the system of utilization is administered. In "Radioactive Colonization" the connection between U.S. domination, the mining and milling of uranium, and the resulting scale of nuclear contamination not only of the Indian reservations and the habitat of the broader society is revealed. In "The Water Plot," Canada's disregard for native land rights is leading to another environmental catastrophe of the first magnitude. "American Indian Self-Governance" explores how colonialism has deformed indigenous governments so that they act against the interests of their ostensible constituents, "legitimating" the very forces which seek to destroy them.

The essays collected here return again and again to the resistance of native people against the horrors visited unrelentingly upon them. In the final essay—the text of a recent lecture entitled "I Am Indigenist"—the meanings of these struggles are drawn together. Focusing on workable solutions to the most pressing dimensions of indigenous land claims on this continents, a philosophical alternative to what can be described as the "predatory" world view of the status quo is offered. Within this, it is to be hoped, lie the seeds of an alternative perspective, "a truly American radical vision," one which is "anchored in the wisdom and experience of those who acquired their knowledge directly from the land itself."[4] Such an outlook provides the basis for a wholly different way of relating to one another, and with the world we inhabit, than that which was imported to this hemisphere from the "Old World."

Struggle for the Land is not meant as an exhaustive or definitive treatment. The essays are in each case illustrative of larger trends. Other land rights struggles might have been selected, from the efforts of the native peoples of Alaska to retain the forty-four million acres of their territory currently being stripped away under provision of the Alaska Native Claims Settlement Act,[5] to the efforts of the Anishinabe in Minnesota to recover their treaty-guaranteed reservation land base,[6] to the partially-successful battles recently fought by the Penobscot in Maine to recover some portion of their lost homeland.[7] Other examples of environmental devastation could have served equally well to make the points raised in this volume. These might have included a much more detailed examination of the James Bay II Project in northern Quebec,[8] the destruction of the Everglades in the Seminole territories of southern Florida,[9] or the rapid depletion of groundwater beneath the O'Odham Nation in southern Arizona.[10]

Struggle for the Land is intended as a point of departure, a tool in the process of reforging popular consciousness of things Indian in modern North America, and thereby to facilitate the emergence of genuine alliances between Indians and non-Indians. Readers are urged to follow up with readings from the abundant notes. In this way, perhaps we can at last arrive at a common understanding of our common situation, the common peril which confronts us all, and a common strategy by which to eliminate it. It is, after all, our collective future which is at stake.

Ward Churchill
September 1992

Notes

1. The concept of ecocide—the deliberate extermination of natural habitat as a matter of state policy—arose in response to the U.S. performance in Southeast Asia during the Vietnam war. See Barry Weisberg, ed., *Ecocide in Indochina: The Ecology of War* (San Francisco: Canfield Press, 1970).
2. See Frank Parrella's *Lebensraum and Manifest Destiny: A Comparative Study in the Justification of Expansion* (Washington, DC, 1950). This important 124 page work has never been exactly popular among "responsible" scholars, and is therefore extremely rare. Perhaps the most

accessible remaining copy may be found in the library of the University of California at Santa Barbara.

3. Alexander Cockburn and Susanna Hecht, *The Fate of the Forest: Developers, Destroyers, and Defenders of the Amazon,* (New York: HarperCollins, 1990).
4. Ward Churchill, "Journeying Toward a Debate," in his *Marxism and Native Americans* (Boston: South End Press, 1983, pp. 3, 10, 16).
5. See Jerry Mander, *In the Absence of the Sacred: The Failure of Technology and the Survival of the Indian Nations* (San Francisco: Sierra Club Books, 1991, pp. 287-302.)
6. See Winona LaDuke, "The White Earth Land Struggle," in Ward Churchill, ed., *Critical Issues in Native North America* (Copenhagen: International Work Group on Indigenous Affairs, Document 62, 1989, pp. 55-71).
7. The Pennobscot settlement is covered in Jack Campisi, "The Trade and Intercourse Acts: Indian Land Claims on the Eastern Seaboard," In Imre Sutton, ed., *Irredeemable America: The Indians' Estate and Land Claims* (Albuquerque: University of New Mexico Press, 1985, pp. 337-62).
8. See Boyce Richardson, *Strangers Devour the Land* (Post Mills, VT: Chelsea Green Publishing Co., 1991).
9. See Robert T. Coulter, "Seminole Land Rights in Florida and the Award of the Indian Claims Commission," *American Indian Journal* Vol. 4, No. 3, August 1978, p. 227.
10. See Marianna Guerrero, "American Indian Water Rights: The Blood of Life In Native North America," in M. Annette Jaimes, ed., *The State of Native America: Genocide, Colonization, and Resistance* (Boston: South End Press, 1992, pp. 189-216).

Part I
American "Justice"

At times
They were kind
They were polite
in their sophistication
smiling but never too loudly

acting in a civilized manner
an illusion of gentleness
always fighting to get their way

While the people see
            the people know
            the people wait
            the people say

The closing of your doors
will never shut us out
The closing of your doors
can only shut you in

We know the predator
we see them feed
on us
We are aware
to starve the beast
is our destiny

The times
they were kind
they were polite
but never honest.

—John Trudell—
from *Living in Reality*

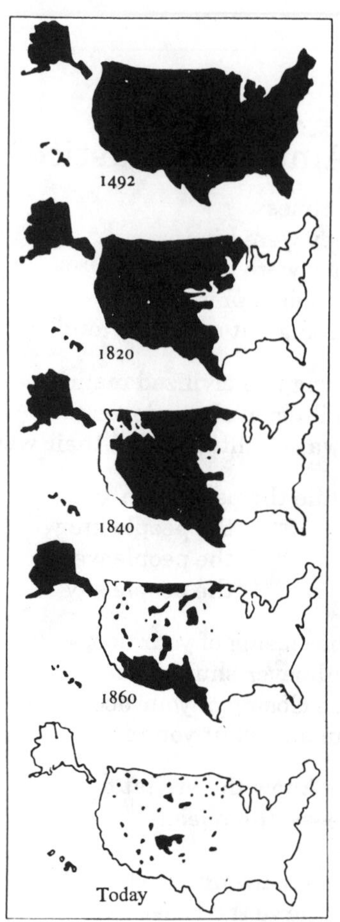

INDIAN LAND WITHIN THE UNITED STATES:1492 to Today.

American Indian Lands

The Native Ethic Amid Resource Development

The Europeans who began taking over the New World in the sixteenth and seventeenth centuries were not ecologists. Although they were compelled to realize that the Americas were not quite *un*inhabited, they were not prepared to recognize that these new lands really were, in an ecological sense, much more than "sparsely" inhabited. This second hemisphere was, in fact, essentially "full."

—William R. Catton, Jr.—
Overshoot

The general conception of Native Americans before European contact holds that they wandered perpetually in scattered bands, grubbing out a marginal subsistence from hunting and gathering, without developing serious apprehensions of art, science, mathematics, governance, and so on. Aside from the Indians' utilization of furs and hides for clothing, the manufacture of stone implements, use of fire, and domestication of the dog, there is little in this view to distinguish Indians from the higher orders of mammalian life surrounding them in "the American wilderness."[1]

This essay is developed from a presentation entitled "The Indigenous Peoples of North America: A Struggle Against Internal Colonialism" given at the *II Seminario sobre la situation de las negras, chicanas, cubana, nativa noorteamericanas, puertorriquena, carbena y asiatica en los Estadas Unidas,* Havana, Cuba, December 1984.

The conclusions reached by those who idealize "Indianness" are no different at base from the findings of those who denigrate it: Native Americans were able to inhabit the hemisphere for tens of thousands of years without causing appreciable ecological disruption only because they lacked the intellectual capacity to create social forms and technologies that would substantially alter their physical environment. In effect, a sort of sociocultural retardation on the part of Indians is typically held to be responsible for the pristine quality of the Americas at their point of "discovery" by the Europeans.[2]

In contrast to this perspective, it has recently been demonstrated that, far from living hand-to-mouth, "Stone Age" American Indians adhered to an economic structure that not only met their immediate needs but provided considerable surplus of both material goods and leisure time.[3] It has also been established that most traditional Native American economies were based in agriculture rather than in hunting and gathering—a clear implication of a stationary, not nomadic, way of life—until Europeans dislocated the native populations in North America.[4]

It is often argued that indigenous Americans' long-term co-existence with the environment was possible only because of the extremely low population level before European contact. However, serious historians have lately documented that statistics on native population levels in North America were deliberately set low during the nineteenth century to lessen the implications of genocide bound up in U.S. policy.[5] A noted ecological demographer has recently determined that, rather than being dramatically underpopulated at the point of European contact, North America was in fact saturated with people in 1500. The feasible carrying capacity of the continent, however, was outstripped by the European influx by 1840, despite massive reductions of native populations and numerous mammal groups.[6]

Another myth is contained in the suggestion that

indigenous governmental forms were less advanced than their European counterparts. However, the enlightened republicanism established by the United States during the late 1700s—usually considered a great advance over European norms—was lifted directly from the model of the Haudenosaunee (Iroquois) confederacy which functions to this day.[7] In many ways the Haudenosaunee were indicative of the native political status quo across North America.[8] Native Americans made similar achievements in preventive medicine,[9] mathematics,[10] astronomy,[11] architecture and engineering all without engendering appreciable environmental disruption.[12] Such a juxtaposition of advanced sociocultural matrices and sustained ecological equilibrium is inexplicable from the vantage point of conventional European-derived assumptions.

Unlike Europeans, Native Americans long ago achieved a profound intellectual apprehension that human progress must be measured as an integral aspect of the natural order, rather than as something apart from and superior to it. Within this structure, elaborated and perfected through oral tradition and codified as "law" in ceremonial and ritual forms, the indigenous peoples of this hemisphere lived comfortably and in harmony with the environment, the health of which they recognized as an absolute requirement for their continued existence.[13]

In simplest terms, the American Indian world view may be this: Human beings are free (indeed, encouraged) to develop their innate capabilities, but only in ways that do not infringe upon other elements—called "relations," in the fullest dialectical sense of the word—of nature. Any activity going beyond this is considered as "imbalance," a transgression, and is strictly prohibited. For example, engineering was and is permissible, but only insofar as it does not permanently alter the earth itself. Similarly, agriculture was widespread, but only within norms that did not supplant natural vegetation.[14]

Key to the indigenous American world view is the firm acknowledgement that the human population may expand only to the point, determined by natural geographical and environmental circumstances, where it begins to displace other animal species and requires the permanent substitution of cropland for normal vegetation in any area. Indian populations never entered a trajectory of excessive growth, and even today, many Native American societies practice a self-regulation of population size that allows the substance of their traditional world view with its interactive environmental relationship to remain viable.[15]

Within the industrial wasteland of the late twentieth century, the traditional Native American relationship to the environment has become the stuff of pop mythology. A television public-service announcement features an aging Indian, clad in beads and buckskins, picking his way carefully among mounds of rusting junk along a well-polluted river. He concludes his walk through the modern world by shedding a tragic tear induced by the panorama of rampant ecological devastation surrounding him.

The undergirding message is clear enough: The common good requires that we clean up the habitat before it becomes uninhabitable. The use of an archaic Indian image is intended not only to stir the country's sense of survival but also to strum the strings of collective guilt as well. Having slaughtered the native population as a means to expropriate its land base, the new North Americans now have an obligation to make things right by preserving and protecting that which was stolen.

Contemporary Circumstances

The contemporary situation of the indigenous peoples of the United States (American Indians, Native Americans, Amerindians, etc. in the popular vernacular) is generally misunderstood to be that of ethnic or racial minorities. This is a fundamental misconception in at least two primary ways.

First, there is no given ethnicity which encompasses those who are indigenous to what is now construed as U.S. territory. Rather, there are at least 400 distinctly identifiable ethnicities comprising what is lumped into the catch-all category of "Native American." Similarly, at least three noticeably different racial divisions prevail within the overall group: persons of the so-called "Athabascan stock" (such as Navajos, Apaches and the Dene of Northern Canada) are as physically different from Iroquoian peoples (Mohawks and Cherokees, for example) as Mongolians are from Arabs.[16]

Second, notions of ethnic or racial minority status fail profoundly to convey the sense of national identity by which most or all North American indigenous populations define themselves. It is this national identity, not the factor of ethnicity, that is most important in understanding the reality of native North America today. It is this sense of themselves as coherent and viable nations which lends substance and logic to the forms of struggle undertaken by these peoples over the past quarter-century.

When we speak of North American indigenous peoples as nationalities, it is essential to understand that the term is not being employed rhetorically, metaphorically, or symbolically. To the contrary, there is a precise meaning. We contend that the indigenous peoples of the North have constituted and continue to constitute nations in the strictest definition of this term. We assert this on the basis of three major premises.

First, there is a doctrine within modern international law known as "the right of inherent sovereignty." This principle holds that a people constitute a nation simply because "since time immemorial," it has always done so. That is, from the point of its earliest contact with other peoples or nations the people in question have been known to possess: a given territory; a means of providing its own subsistence; a common language; a structure of self-governance; a form of legality; and means to determine its own membership and social composition.[17]

Second, the conventional understanding of international law and custom is that treaty-making and treaty relationships are only entered into between nations. This is reflected in U.S. domestic law at the highest level. Articles I and VI of the U.S. Constitution clearly restrict U.S. treaty-making prerogatives to the federal rather than state, local or individual levels. It asserts that the federal government is itself forbidden from entering into treaty relationships with other than *fully* sovereign entities (i.e., the U.S. federal government is not empowered to legally enter into treaty relations with provincial, state or local governments, or with individuals).[18]

The U.S. government's willing entry into 371 treaty relationships with various indigenous peoples in North America between the years 1790 and 1870 corroborates their claim to status as sovereign national entities under the right of inherent sovereignty.[19] It also established beyond any reasonable doubt that these peoples enjoy valid legal claims to sovereign national status under both international and U.S. domestic law.[20]

Ironically, the United States, above all nations or even groups of nations, has gone to the greatest lengths to formally recognize the full legitimacy of the sovereign status of the indigenous nations of North America. Of such paradoxes are modern international relations born.

Some U.S. officials and others assert that although North American indigenous nations present an impeccable case on moral grounds, and a technically valid legal case as well, pragmatic considerations of "the real world of the twentieth century" preclude actualization of their national autonomy and self-determination. Within this perspective indigenous nations are too small, both in terms of landbase (and accompanying resources) and in size of population(s), to survive in the contemporary international context.[21]

At first glance, such thinking seems plausible enough, even humane. But it overlooks the examples of tiny European nations such as Monaco and Liechtenstein which have survived for decades in the midst of the greediest and most warlike continental context in the history of the world. Further, it ignores the fact of even smaller national entities among the islands of the Pacific whose current sovereignty the United States not only is willing to acknowledge, but whose recent admission to the United nations the United States endorses. The contradictions here are readily apparent.[22] The excuses for U.S. actions are really a veneer, the rationalization "justifying" colonialism and "assimilation" (the contemporary U.S. euphemism for genocide, where indigenous North Americans are concerned).

Closer examination reveals further inaccuracy within the posture of apologists for present-day U.S. "Indian policy." The Navajo Nation, for example, holds a landbase considerably larger than a number of Caribbean islands—such as Grenada—each of which hold an obvious and unquestionable right to sovereignty and self-determination. The Navajo population is also greater than that of Grenada and a number of other smaller Caribbean islands. In addition, the Navajo Nation possesses an estimated 150 billion tons of low-sulphur coal, approximately 40 percent of all known "U.S." reserves of uranium, substantial deposits of oil and natural gas, and assets in zeolites, gold, silver, copper, gypsum and bauxite. (Overall indigenous holdings in what the United States terms its "energy resource reserves" include some 60 percent of uranium, 40 percent of readily strippable low-sulphur coal and perhaps 15 percent of known oil and natural gas.)[23]

This is aside from a limited, but real grazing and agricultural capability. By any standard of conventional economic definition, the Navajo people have a relatively wealthy resource base as compared to most Third and Fourth World nations, and some capitalist ones. To say that the Navajo lack the ability to survive in the modern context while simultaneously postulating that Grenada had assumed proportions of being a threat to U.S. "national security" as late as 1984 is the height of cynicism and absurdity.[24]

While Navajo is perhaps the clearest example of the potential for complete autonomy on the part of indigenous nations internal to the United States, it is by no means the only one. The combined Lakota reservations possess an aggregate landbase exceeding that of the Navajo and, although they exhibit a somewhat less spectacular range of mineral assets, this seems largely offset by their greater agricultural/grazing potential in combination with a considerably smaller population size.[25]

Other, smaller indigenous nations possess landbases entirely adequate to their population sizes and many possess rich economic potentials which vary from mineral assets and agricultural grazing lands to timbering and fishing/aquaculture. Small manufacturing enterprises and even tourism are also viable options in a number of instances.[26]

Moreover, possession of all this natural wealth exists even without a just resolution of current claims lodged by indigenous nations against the U.S. government that relate to tracts of land and resources which were expropriated (in direct violation of domestic and international law).

The Lakota Nation alone, were its 1868 treaty with the United States to be honored, would find itself in possession of an area amounting to nearly 5 percent of the 48 contiguous states.[27] Naturalization of persons residing within the various treaty areas (and those wishing to place themselves or willing to relocate for purposes of coming under indigenous governance and jurisdiction) might well increase the citizenry of Native North America by several millions.[28]

In combination, these three points explain why the

indigenous peoples of North America retain every right, not only by virtue of ethics and morality, but in terms of legality and current viability to conduct their affairs as sovereign nations.

Internal Colonialism

One of the major problems confronting those attempting to articulate the status of the indigenous nations of this continent has to do with the specific form of imperialism imposed upon us: "internal colonialism."[29] The idea of internal colonialism is undoubtedly somewhat unorthodox. The conventional analysis of colonization ranges from that adopted by the United Nations (which requires by strict definition that an ocean separate the colonizer from the colonized in order for a "true" condition of colonization to exist) to that of conventional socialist thinking which, with certain exceptions, subscribes to a less specific though similar interpretation.[30]

Internal colonialism is the result of a peculiarly virulent form of socioeconomic penetration wherein the colonizing country literally exports a sufficient proportion of its population to supplant (rather than enslave) the indigenous population of the colony. Elsewhere, this method has been termed "settler colonialism."[31]

Often under such conditions, the settler population itself revolts at a certain point against the mother country regime and establishes itself as an independent or quasi-independent sovereignty; the indigenous peoples/nations consequently become colonized entities within a given national territory rather than subject to the more classic form of colonization from abroad.

Aside from the United States and Canada, the modern world witnesses several other leading examples of this state of affairs. Among these are Australia, Northern Ireland, New Zealand, Bolivia, Peru, Guatemala, Ecuador, South Africa and Israel. Until liberated by African revolutionary forces, Rhodesia (now Zimbabwe) at least aspired to this model. Current indications are that the phenomenon of internal colonialism has been dramatically underestimated as a global condition. It requires serious study on the part of progressive intellectuals and governments, as well as the development/implementation of effective ways and means of supporting impacted nationalities as soon as possible.

The liberation struggle we wage is not extended against the discrimination and class exploitation visited by a dominant society and its bourgeoisie upon ethnic and racial minorities within the United States, although we staunchly oppose these conditions and fully support those who actively resist them. Rather, as colonized nations we are pursuing strategies and courses of action designed to lead to decolonization *within* the colonizing "mother country."

Hence, while we share a common oppressor with our brothers and sisters of African, Latin and Asian origins within the United States, the goals, objectives and many of the means of our struggle must be understood in terms necessarily different from theirs. We "the Indians" of the North and "Indios" of the South—of all the people of the Americas—struggle for the liberation of our homelands rather than for the liberation of land upon which to build our homes. We, of all the people of the Americas, engage in our struggles from the basis of our cultures—our freely collective societies, born in, and long since integral to, this hemisphere—rather than struggling to create liberatory cultures allowing the expression of human freedom.[32]

It is from this perspective that the recent history of North American indigenous struggle—the occupation of Alcatraz Island, the Bureau of Indian Affairs Building in Washington, D.C. and Wounded Knee, the armed resistance demonstrated on the Pine Ridge Reservation and all the rest—must be viewed.[33]

With this understanding the sacrifices of our warriors—brothers and sisters, such as Buddy Lamont, Byron DeSersa, Pedro Bissonette, Anna Mae Aquash, Joe Stuntz, Tina Trudell, Richard Oaks (all fatalities of the Movement), Leonard Peltier (prisoner of war), and many others—takes on its true meaning.[34] And it is from this meaning that one can appreciate the substance of the struggles in which we engage at this very moment: the unswerving resistance of some 10,000 traditional Navajo people in the Big Mountain area of Arizona (headed by the true tribal leadership composed of elder women) to U.S. plans to forcibly relocate them from their land in order to stripmine the coal underlying the area.[35]

This understanding of sovereignty underlies our struggles in the Black Hills area of South Dakota, the occupation of Yellow Thunder Camp, a part of an effort undertaken by traditional Lakota elders and the American Indian Movement to recover Lakota treaty territories.[36] It is also the basis for the ongoing efforts in the states of Washington and Wisconsin by traditional indigenous people to retain their treaty-guaranteed livelihood based upon fishing.[37] It informs the struggles, including armed resistance, of the Mohawk people of New York to retain control of their communities and to implement alternative technologies leading to greater self-sufficiency (and corresponding independence from the United States).[38]

At a level broader than the specific and localized confrontations mentioned above, the American Indian Movement continues to wage its struggle against the various mechanisms by which the U.S. government asserts its doctrine of "plenary power" over all North American indigenous nations. This effort is a campaign to reinforce and protect indigenous sovereignties from a range of U.S. juridical instruments and accompanying policies.[39]

At the present juncture, the fully sovereign status of American Indian nations has been reduced by federal fiat to a point where it falls roughly between the level of counties and that of municipalities.[40] This has occurred despite Indian nations' nominal retention, on paper, of considerable land and resource holdings.

At another level still, several indigenous Non-Governmental Organizations (NGOs) work continuously within the United Nations to acquaint other nations with the realities of Native American sovereignty.[41] Their role is not only educational/informative in the international community, but to establish alliances and other forms of working relationships with governments around the world.

This goal of creating government-to government relations is pursued with the utmost seriousness because, in the end, it is through recognition of themselves as fully sovereign entities within the international arena that indigenous people in the Americas perceive the sole possibilities of a just and permanent resolution of the difficulties they now confront.

Notes

1. References in this regard are legion. In general, we might say that the views initiated with Christopher Columbus' reports to the Spanish Crown upon his "discovery of the New World," were well codified by the time of John Smith's and other British colonial journals and reports and were academically perfected in the works of Mooney, Kroeber and other seminal American anthropologists. By the present day, it amounts to "scholarly" doctrine.
2. For a particularly virulent exposition of this view, and from an ostensibly radical source, see Revolutionary Communist Party, U.S.A., "Searching for the Second Harvest: Russell Means Attack on Revolutionary Marxism," in Ward Churchill, ed., *Marxism and Native Americans* (Boston: South End Press, 1983), pp. 35-58.
3. See, for example, Marshall Sahlins, *Stone Age Economics* (Chicago: Aldine Publishing Co., 1972), pp. 1-40. Also see the survey material contained in Jack Weatherford, *In-*

dian Givers: How the Indians of the Americas Transformed the World (New York, Crown Publishers, 1988).

4. With regard to the indigenous American agricultural forms which created approximately two-thirds of the vegetal foodstuffs currently consumed by humanity, a deeply flawed but nonetheless useful study is R. Douglas Hurt, *Indian Agriculture in America: Prehistory to the Present* (Lawrence: University Press of Kansas, 1987). Probably the best synthesis of this material overall will be found in M. Annette Jaimes, "The Stone Age Revisited: An Indigenist View of Primitivism, Industrialism and the Labor Process," *New Studies on the Left*, Vol. XiV, No. 3 (1989).
5. The apparently willful manipulation of demographic data pertaining to precontact Native North America by anthropologists such as James Mooney and Alfred Kroeber in order to arrive at absurdly low estimates of indigenous population is well-covered in Francis Jennings, *The Invasion of America: Indians, Colonialism and the Cant of Conquest* (New York: W.W. Norton & Co., 1976), pp. 15-31. For further analysis of the implications of the procedure, see Lenore Stiffar, and Phil Lane, Jr., "The Demography of Native North America: A Question of Indigenous Survival," in M. Annette Jaimes, ed., *The State of Native America: Genocide, Colonization and Resistance* (Boston: South End Press, 1992), pp. 23-46.
6. William R. Catton Jr., *Overshoot: The Ecological Basis of Revolutionary Change* (Urbana: University of Illinois Press, 1981). The most comprehensive assessment of aggregate precontact population figures in North America will be found in Russell Thornton, *American Indian Holocaust and Survival: A Population History Since 1492* (Norman: University of Oklahoma Press, 1987).
7. For a detailed and excellent accounting of the Haudenosaunee influence on the Founding Fathers' conceptualization of the U.S. Constitution, see Donald A. Grinde, Jr., and Bruce Johansen, *Exemplar of Liberty: Native America and the Founding of Democracy* (Los Angeles: UCLA American Indian Studies Center, 1991). Also see Donald A. Grinde, Jr., *The Iroquois and the Founding of the American Nation* (San Francisco: Indian Historian Press, 1977), and Bruce Johansen, *Forgotten Founders:*

How the American Indian Helped Shape Democracy (Boston: Harvard Common Press, 1982).

8. For a very good survey of indigenous governmental forms, see Rebecca L. Robbins, "Self-Determination and Subordination: The Past, Present, and Future of American Indian Governance," in *The State of Native America, op. cit.*, pp. 87-112.
9. See Virgil Vogel, *American Indian Medicine* (Norman: University of Oklahoma Press, 1970). Also see Miguel Guzmá Peredo, *Medical Practices in Ancient America* (Mexico City: Ediciones Euroamericanas, 1985). Other good readings are Clark Wissler, Willton M. Krogman and Walter Krickerber, *Medicine Among the American Indians* (Ramona, CA: Acoma Press, 1939), and Alma R. Hutchins, *Indian Herbology of North America* (Ontario: Merco Publishers, 1969).
10. The Maya of present-day Guatemala, for example, had developed the concepts of zero and prime numbers, both unknown to medieval Europe, long before the Columbian arrival; see Sylvanus C. Morley and George W. Bainerd, *The Ancient Maya* (Stanford: Stanford University Press, [4th edition] 1983). Obviously, as is witnessed by, among other things, the precision of their calendar, the Aztecs of Mexico had evolved comparable mathematical knowledge; see Peter Thompkins, *Mysteries of the Mexican Pyramids* (New York: Harper and Row Publishers, 1976). It is clear that the Incas of the Andean highlands had done likewise; see Garcilasco de la Vega, *The Incas: Royal Commentaries of the Inca* (New York: Avon Books, 1961). There is no reason to believe that conceptual elements of these mathematics had not spread among other peoples of the Americas as well.
11. See Guillermo Céspedes, *América Indigena* (Madrid: Alianza Publishers, 1985). Also see Mary W. Helms, *Middle America* (New York: University Press of America, 1982).
12. Overall, see Peter Nabokov and Robert Easton, *American Indian Architecture* (London/New York: Oxford University Press, 1988). Also see Buddy Mays, *Ancient Cities of the Southwest* (San Francisco: Chronicle Books, 1982), which points out that the surface water transportation system presently in use by the city of Phoenix is actually a 400

mile complex of irrigation canals—virtually perfect in engineering terms—constructed by the Hohokam centuries before Columbus. Again, see Victor Wolfgang von Hagen, *The Royal Road of the Inca* (London: Gordon and Cremonesi Publishers, 1976) for a detailed exposition on this spectacular 2,500 mile engineering feat, constructed at an even twenty-four foot width, complete with curbs, gutters, graded slopes, banked curves and suspension bridges. Such sophisticated road-building—upon which the contemporary Peruvian highway system is built in part—extended at least as far northward as Chaco Canyon (New Mexico) in precontact times. Not bad for "peoples without wheels."

13. One example of this practice, that of the Haudenosaunee is delineated in Paul A. W. Wallace, *The White Roots of Peace* (Philadelphia: University of Pennsylvania Press, 1946). For interpretation, see Christopher Vecsey and Robert W. Venables, eds., *Native American Environments: Ecological Issues in American History* (Syracuse, NY: Syracuse University Press, 1980).
14. A detailed examination of the application of these principles in one region may be found in William Cronon, *Changes in the Land: Indians, Colonists, and the Ecology of New England* (New York: Hill and Wang Publishers, 1983).
15. See Catton, *op. cit.* Also see Henry F. Dobyns, *Their Numbers Became Thinned: Native American Population Dynamics in Eastern North America* (Nashville: University of Tennessee Press, 1983).
16. This is brought out clearly enough in Jesse D. Jennings, *Prehistory of North America* (New York: McGraw-Hill Publishers, 1974).
17. For a fuller elaboration, see Aureliu, Cristescu, *The Historical and Current Development of the Right to Self-Determination on the Basis of the Charter of the United Nations and Other Instruments adopted by United Nations Organs, With Particular Reference to the Promotion and Protection of Human Rights and Fundamental Freedoms* (U.N. Doc. E/CN.4/Sub.2/404, 2 June 1978).
18. Article I, Section 10, specifically precludes the States of the Union and their subordinate components (i.e., coun-

ties, municipalities, corporations, or individuals) from entering into treaties. Reciprocally, the federal government is prohibited from entering into treaties with them, or their correspondents abroad.

19. For the complete texts of 371 ratified treaties with American Indian peoples, see Charles J. Kappler, ed., *Indian Treaties, 1778-1883* (New York: Interland Publishing Co., [second printing] 1973).
20. See Glenn T. Morris, "International Law and Politics: Toward a Right to Self-Determination for Indigenous Peoples," in *The State of Native America, op. cit.*, pp. 55-79.
21. As illustration of such sentiments, see the quotations from various U.S. officials before the U.N. Working Group on Indigenous Populations deployed by Jimmie Durham in his *Columbus Day* (Minneapolis: West End Press, 1983).
22. This would certainly pertain to the Marshall, Caroline, and Solomon Islands, for example. See Norman Meller, *The Congress of Micronesia: Development of the Legislative Process in the Trust Territory of the Pacific Islands* (Honolulu: University of Hawaii Press, 1969). This is not to say that the U.S. posture in regard to recognizing the identity of Micronesian nations is not cooptive or imperialistic; see, for instance, Micronesia Support Committee, *Palau: Self-Determination vs. U.S. Military Plans* (Honolulu: Micronesia Support Committee, 1983).
23. On Navjo landbase and demography, see Francisco Paul Prucha, *Atlas of American Indian Affairs* (Lincoln: University of Nebraska, 1990). On resource distribution and political status, see U.S. Commission on Civil Rights, *The Navajo Nation: An American Colony* (Washington, DC: U.S. Government Printing Office, 1975).
24. See Hugh O'Shaugnessy, *Grenada: Revolution, Invasion and Aftermath* (London: Zed Press, 1984).
25. Prucha, *op. cit.*
26. See the relevant material in Teresa L. Ammott and Julie A. Matthei, *Race, Gender and Work: A Multicultural Economic History of Women in the United States* (Boston: South End Press, 1991).
27. Nick Meinhart and Diane Payne, *Reviewing U.S. Commitments to the Lakota Nation* (Rapid City, SD: Pine Ridge Education/Action Project, 1978). More broadly, see the

testimony included in Roxanne Dunbar Ortiz, ed., *The Great Sioux Nation: Sitting in Judgement on America* (New York/San Francisco: International Indian Treaty Council/Moon Books, 1977).

28. This principle was incorporated into an actual political agenda on the Pine Ridge Reservation during the early 1980s. See *TREATY: The Campaign of Russell Means for the Presidency of the Oglala Sioux Tribe* (Porcupine, SD: TREATY Campaign, 1983).
29. The concept of internal colonialism seems to have been initially developed to explain the subordination of the Welsh and Scots to British imperialism; see Michael Hector, *Internal Colonialism: The Celtic Fringe in British National Development, 1536-1966* (Berkeley: University of California Press, 1975). It was first applied to the situation of American Indians by the pioneering Cherokee anthropologist Robert K. Thomas; see his "Colonialism: Classic and Internal," *New University Thought,* Vol 4, No. 4, Winter 1966-67).
30. The "Blue Water" or "Salt Water" thesis is embodied in U.N. Resolution 1541 (XV) 1960. For analysis, see Gordon Bennett, *Aboriginal Rights in International Law* (London: Royal Anthropological Society of Great Britain, 1978). Further background may be found in *The Belgian Thesis: Sacred Mission of Civilization, To Which Peoples Should the Benefit be Extended?* (New York: Belgian Government Information Center, 1953).
31. One of the clearer articulations of the "settler state" concept may be found in J. Sakai, *Settlers: The Mythology of the White Proletariat* (Chicago: Morningstar Press, 1983). For a less doctrinaire application of the theory, see Ronald Weitzer, *Transforming Settler States: Communal Conflict and Internal Security in Northern Ireland and Zimbabwe* (Berkeley: University of California Press, 1992).
32. Firm indication of this is provided in Sadruddin Aga Khan and Hassan bin Talal, *Indigenous Peoples: A Global Quest for Justice* (London: Zed Books, 1987). Also see Julian Burger, *Report from the Frontier: The State of the World's Indigenous Peoples* (London: Zed Books, 1987).
33. One of the better readings on these topics is Peter

Matthiessen's *In the Spirit of Crazy Horse* (New York: Viking Press, [second edition] 1991). Also see his *Indian Country* (New York: Viking Press, [second edition] 1990).

34. See Ward Churchill and Jim Vanderwall, *Agents of Repression: The FBI's Secret Wars Against the Black Panther Party and the American Indian Movement* (Boston: South End Press, [second edition] 1990).
35. See Anita Parlow, *Cry, Sacred Ground: Big Mountain U.S.A.* (Washington, DC: Christic Institute, 1988).
36. On the Yellow Thunder occupation, see Rex Wyler, *Blood of the Land: The U.S. Government and Corporate War Against the American Indian Movement* (New York: Everest House Publishers, 1982).
37. See The Institute for Natural Progress, "In Usual and Accustomed Places: Contemporary American Indian Fishing Rights Struggles," in *The State of Native America, op. cit.*, pp. 217-36.
38. See Rick Horning, *One Nation Under the Gun: Inside the Mohawk Civil War* (New York: Pantheon Books, 1991).
39. See Douglas Sanders, "The Re-Emergence of Indigenous Questions in International Law" (Toronto: *Canadian Human Rights Yearbook,* No. 3, 1983).
40. For analysis, see Carole E. Goldberg, "Public Law 280: The Limits of State Law over Indian Reservations" *(UCLA Law Review,* No. 22, February 1975).
41. A good survey of this phenomenon may be found in Douglas Sanders, "The U.N. Working Group on Indigenous Populations," *Human Rights Quarterly,* No. 11, 1989.

Perversions of Justice

Examining the Doctrine of U.S. Rights to Occupancy in North America

For the nation, there is an unrequited account of sin and injustice that sooner or later will call for national retribution.

—George Catlin—
1844

Recognition of the legal and moral rights by which a nation occupies its land base is a fundamental issue of its existence. Typically, such claims to sovereign and proprietary interest in national territories rest on its citizenry being composed of direct descendants of peoples who have dwelt within the geographical area claimed since "time immemorial."[1] But when the dominating population is comprised either of the representatives of a foreign power or of immigrants ("settlers") who can offer no such assertion of "aboriginal" lineage to justify their presence or ownership of property in the usual sense, the issue is vastly more complicated.[2]

History is replete with philosophical, theological and juridical arguments of one people's alleged entitlement to the homelands of others, only to be rebuffed by the community of nations as lacking both moral force and sound legal principle. International rejection of "imperial" pretensions has often interfered with imperialist designs.[3] Modern illustrations include the dissolution of the classic European empires—those of France, Netherlands, Portugal and Great Britain in particular—during the post-World War II period, as well as the resounding defeat of the Axis powers' territorial ambitions during the war itself. Even more recent examples may be found in the breakup of the Soviet (Great Russian) and Yugoslavian (Serbian) states. Controversy continues in the maintenance of such settler states as Northern Ireland, Israel and South Africa.

What is the basis for the contemporary U.S. settler state to claim legitimate—indeed, inviolate—rights to approximately two and a quarter billion acres of territory in North America?[4] Such scrutiny will provide insight, on both issues of territorial rights and the logic and morality of the state. Frequent pronouncements extol this country as essentially "peaceful," uniquely enlightened in its commitments to the rule of law and concept of liberty, and that it is the natural leader of a "New World Order" in which the conquest and occupation of any nation by another "cannot and will not stand."[5] How the United States justifies its territorial claims is a good test of this rhetoric.

Setting the International Legal Standards for Territorial Acquisition

From the outset of the "Age of Discovery" precipitated by the Columbian voyages, the European powers, eager to obtain uncontested title to at least some portion of the lands their emissaries were encountering, quickly recognized the need to establish a formal code of juridical standards to legitimate what they acquired.[6] This lent a patina of "civilized" legality to the actions of the European Crowns. More importantly, the system was envisioned to resolve disputes between the Crowns themselves, each vying with the others in a rapacious battle over the wealth accruing through ownership of given regions in the "New World."[7]

In order for any such regulatory code to be considered effectively binding by all Old World parties, it was vital that it be sanctioned by the Church.[8] A theme begun with a series of Papal Bulls begun by Pope Innocent IV during the late thirteenth century First Crusade[9] were used to define the proper ("lawful") relationship between Christians and "Infidels" in worldly matters such as property rights. Beginning in the early sixteenth century, Spanish jurists in particular did much to develop this theory into what have come to be known as the "Doctrine of Discovery" and an attendant dogma, the "Rights of Conquest."[10] Through the efforts of legal scholars such as Franciscus de Vitoria and Matías de Paz, Spanish articulations of Discovery Doctrine, endorsed by the Pope, rapidly evolved to hold the following as primary tenets of international law:[11]

- Outright ownership of land accrued to the Crown represented by a given Christian (European) discoverer only when the land discovered proved to be uninhabited *(territorium res nullius).*[12]

- Title to inhabited lands discovered by Crown representatives was recognized as belonging inherently to the indigenous people encountered, but rights to acquire land from, and to trade with the natives of the region accrued exclusively to the discovering Crown *vis-à-vis* other European powers. In exchange for this right, the discovering power committed itself to proselytizing the Christian gospel among the natives.[13]

- Acquisition of land title from indigenous peoples could occur only by their consent—by an agreement usually involving purchase—rather than through force of arms, so long as the natives did not arbitrary decline to trade with Crown representatives, refuse to admit missionaries among them, or inflict gratuitous violence upon citizens of the Crown.

- Absent these last three conditions, utilization of armed force to acquire aboriginally held territory was considered unjust and claims to land title accruing there from to be correspondingly invalid.

- Should one or more of the three conditions be present, then the Crown had a legal right to use whatever force was required to subdue native resistance and impound their property as compensation. Land title gained by prosecution of such "Just Wars" was considered valid.[14]

Although this legal perspective was hotly debated at the time (it still is, in certain quarters), and saw considerable violation by European colonists, it was generally acknowledged as the standard against which international conduct would be weighed.[15] By the early seventeenth century, the requirements of the Discovery Doctrine had led the European states, England in particular, to adopt a policy of entering into formal treaties with native nations. These full-fledged international instruments officially recognized the sovereignty of the indigenous parties to such agreements as equivalent to that of the respective Crowns. They became an expedient to obtaining legally valid land titles from American Indian peoples, first in what is now the state of Virginia, and then in areas further north. Treaties concerning trade, professions of peace and friendship, and to consummate military alliances were also quite common.[16]

Undeniably, there is a certain overweening arrogance imbedded in the proposition that Europeans were somehow intrinsically imbued with an authority to unilaterally restrict the range of those to whom Native Americans might sell their property, assuming they wished to sell it at all. Nonetheless, the legal posture of early European colonialism in recognizing that indigenous peoples constituted bona fide nations holding essentially the same rights to land and sovereignty as any other, seems rather advanced and refined in retrospect. In these respects, the Doctrine of Discovery is widely viewed as one of the more important cornerstones of modern international law and diplomacy.[17]

With its adoption of Protestantism, however, Britain had already begun to mark its independence from papal regulation by adding an element of its own to the doctrine. Usually termed the "Norman Yoke," land rights were said to rest in large part upon the extent to which owners demonstrate a willingness and ability to "develop" their territories in accordance with a scriptural obligation to exercise "dominium" over nature. Thus, entitlement is restricted to the quantity of real estate which the individual or people can convert from "wilderness" to a "domesticated" state.[18] This criterion bestowed on English settlers an inherent right to dispossess native people of all land other than that which the latter might be "reasonably expected" to put to such "proper" uses as cultivation.[19] More importantly at this time, this doctrinal innovation automatically placed the British Crown on a legal footing from which it could contest the discovery rights of any European power not adhering to the requirement of "overcoming the wilderness."

This allowed England to simultaneously "abide by the law" and directly confront Catholic France for ascendancy in the Atlantic regions of North America. After a series of "French and Indian Wars" beginning in the late 1600s and lasting nearly a century, the British were victorious, but at a cost greater than the expected financial benefits to the Crown of launching its colonial venture in the first place. As one major consequence, King George

II, in a move intended to preclude further warfare with indigenous nations, issued the Proclamation of 1763. This royal edict stipulated that all settlement or other forms of land acquisition by British subjects west of a line running along the Allegheny and Appalachian Mountains from Canada to the Spanish colony of Florida would be suspended indefinitely, and perhaps permanently. English expansion on the North American continent was thereby brought to an abrupt halt.[20]

Treaties as Tools of the State

The new British proclamation conflicted sharply with the desires for personal gain growing among a voracious elite within the seaboard colonial population. Most of the colonies held some pretense of title to "western" lands, much of it conveyed by earlier Crown grant, and had planned to use it as a means of bolstering their respective economic positions. Similarly, members of the landed gentry such as George Washington, Thomas Jefferson, John Adams, James Madison and Anthony Wayne all possessed considerable speculative interests in land parcels on the far side of the 1763 demarcation line. The only way in which these could be converted into profit was for the parcels to be settled and developed. Vociferous contestation and frequent violation of the proclamation, eventually enforced by George III, became quite common.[21] This dynamic became a powerful precipitating factor in the American Revolution, during which many rank and file rebels were convinced to fight against the Crown by promises of western land grants "for services rendered" in the event their revolt was successful.[22]

But successful revolt does not necessarily bring legitimacy. The United States emerged from its decolonization struggle against Britain—perhaps the most grievous offense which could be perpetrated by any subject people under then prevailing law—as a pariah, an outlaw state

from indigenous nations through treaties, the U.S. was simultaneously admitting not only that Indians ultimately owned virtually all of the territory coveted by the U.S., but that they were also under no obligation to part with it. As William Wirt, an early attorney general, put it in 1821:

> [Legally speaking,] so long as a tribe exists and remains in possession of its lands, its title and possession are sovereign and exclusive. We treat with them as separate sovereignties, and while an Indian nation continues to exist within its acknowledged limits, we have no more right to enter upon their territory than we have to enter upon the territory of a foreign prince."[29]

A few years later, Wirt amplified his point:

> The point, once conceded, that the Indians are independent to the purpose of treating, their independence is to that purpose as absolute as any other nation. Being competent to bind themselves by treaty, they are equally competent to bind the party that treats with them. Such party cannot take benefit of [a] treaty with the Indians, and then deny them the reciprocal benefits of the treaty on the grounds that they are not independent nations to all intents and purposes...Nor can it be conceded that their independence as a nation is a limited independence. Like all other independent nations, they have the absolute power of war and peace. Like all other independent nations, their territories are inviolate by any other sovereignty...They are entirely self-governed, self-directed. They treat, or refuse to treat, at their pleasure; and there is no human power that can rightly control them in the exercise of their discretion in this respect.[30]

For twenty years following the revolution (roughly 1790 to 1810), such acknowledgement of these genuine indigenous soveriegn rights and status considerably retarded the acquisition of land grants by revolutionary soldiers, as well as consummation of the plans of the elite caste of prerevolutionary land speculators. Over the next two decades (1810 to 1830), the issue assumed an ever increasing policy importance: native sovereignty replaced Crown policy as the preeminent barrier to U.S. territorial consolidation east of the Mississippi.[31] Worse, as Chief Justice John Marshall pointed out in 1822, any real adherence to the rule of law in regard to native rights might not only block U.S. expansion, but—since not all the territory therein had been secured through Crown treaties—cloud title to significant portions of the original thirteen states as well.[32] Perhaps predictably, it was perceived in juridical circles that the only means of circumventing this dilemma was through construction of a legal theory—a subterfuge, as it were—by which the more inconvenient implications of international law might be voided even while the republic maintained an appearance of holding to its doctrinal requirements.

The Marshall Doctrine: "Legal" Justification of an Outlaw State

The task of forging the required "interpretation" of existing law fell to Chief Justice Marshall, widely considered one of the great legal minds of his time. Whatever his scholarly qualifications, the Chief Justice was hardly a disinterested party. His ideological advocacy of the rebel cause before and during the revolution was vociferous. More important, both he and his father were consequent recipients of 10,000 acre grants west of the Appalachians, in what is now the state of West Virginia.[33] His first serious foray into land rights law thus centered in devising a conceptual basis to secure title for his own and similar grants. In the 1810 *Fletcher v. Peck* case, he invoked the Norman Yoke tradition in a manner which far exceeded previous British applications, advancing the patently absurd contention that the areas involved were effectively "vacant" even though very much occupied—

and in many instances stoutly defended—by indigenous inhabitants. On this basis, he declared individual Euroamerican deeds within recognized Indian territories might be considered valid whether or not native consent was obtained.[34]

While *Peck* was obviously useful from the U.S. point of view, resolving a number of short-term difficulties in meeting obligations already incurred by the government with regard to individual citizens, it was a tactical opinion, falling far short of accommodating the country's overall territorial goals and objectives. In the 1823 *Johnson v. McIntosh* case, however, Marshall followed up with a more clearly strategic enunciation, reaching to the core issues. Here, he opined that, because Discovery Rights purportedly constricted native discretion in disposing of property, the sovereignty of discoverers was to that extent inherently superior to that of indigenous nations. From this point of departure, he then proceeded to invert all conventional understandings of the Discovery Doctrine, ultimately asserting that native people occupied land within discovered regions at the sufferance of their discoverers rather than the other way around. A preliminary rationalization was thus contrived by which to explain the fact that the U.S. had already begun depicting its borders as encompassing vast portions of unceded Indian Country.[35]

Undoubtedly aware that neither *Peck* nor *McIntosh* was likely to withstand the gaze of even minimal international scrutiny, Marshall next moved to bolster the logic undergirding his position. In the two so-called "Cherokee Cases" of the early 1830s, he hammered out the thesis that native nations within North America were "nations like any other" in the sense that they possessed both territories they were capable of ceding, and recognizable governmental bodies empowered to cede these areas through treaties.[36] However, he argued on the basis of the reasoning deployed in *McIntosh*, they were nations of a "peculiar type," both "domestic to" and "dependent upon" the United States, and therefore possessed of a degree of sovereignty intrinsically less than that enjoyed by the U.S. itself.[37] Thus while native peoples are entitled to exercise some range of autonomy in managing their affairs within their own territories, both the limits of that autonomy and the extent of the territories involved can be "naturally" and unilaterally established by the federal government. At base, this is little more than a judicial description of the classic relationship between colonizer and colonized,[38] put forth in such a way as to seem at first glance to be the exact opposite.

While it might be contended (and has been, routinely enough) that Marshall's framing of the circumstances pertaining to the Cherokee Nation, already completely surrounded by the territorality of the United States by 1830, bore some genuine relationship to then prevailing reality,[39] he did not confine his observations to the situation of the Cherokees, or even to native nations east of the Mississippi. Rather, he purported to articulate the legal status of *all* indigenous nations, including those west of the Mississippi—the Lakota, Cheyenne, Arapaho, Comanche, Kiowa, Navajo and Chiricahua Apache, to name but a few—which had not yet encountered the U.S. in any appreciable way. Self-evidently, these nations could not have been described with the faintest accuracy as domestic to or dependent upon the United States. The clear intent belied by Marshall's formulation was that they be *made so* in the future. The doctrine completed with elaboration of the Cherokee Cases was thus the pivotal official attempt to rationalize and legitimate the future campaign of conquest and colonization which was absolutely contrary to the customary law of the period.[40]

The doctrine was not complete without a final inversion of accepted international legal norms and definitions of "Just" and "Unjust" warfare.[41] Within Marshall's convoluted and falsely premised reasoning, it became arguable that indigenous nations acted unlawfully whenever and wherever they attempted to physically prevent exercise of the U.S. "right" to expropriate their property. Resistance to invasion of indigenous homelands could then be construed as "aggression" against the United States. In this sense, the U.S. could declare itself to be waging a "Just"—and therefore lawful—War against native people on any occasion where force of arms was required to realize its territorial ambitions. *Ipso facto,* all efforts of native people to defend themselves against systematic dispossession and subordination could thereby be categorized as "unjust"—and thus unlawful—by the United States.[42]

In sum, the Marshall Doctrine shredded significant elements of the existing Laws of Nations. Given the historical records of federal judicial officials such as Attorney General Wirt and Marshall himself, and the embodiment of such understandings in the Constitution and formative federal statutes, this breach was not unintentional or inadvertent. Instead, with calculated juridical cynicism, the Chief Justice deliberately confused and deformed accepted legal principles to "justify" his country's pursuit of a thoroughly illegitimate course of territorial acquisition. Insofar as federal courts and policymakers elected to adopt his doctrine as the predicate to all subsequent relations with American Indians, the posture of the United States as an outlaw state was rendered permanent.

From Treaty Violation to Extermination

The Cherokee Cases were followed by a half-century hiatus in important judicial determinations regarding American Indians. On the foundation provided by the Marshall Doctrine, the government felt confident in entering into the great bulk of the more than 370 treaties with indigenous nations by which it professed to have gained the consent of Indians in ceding huge portions of the native land base. With its self-anointed position of superior sovereignty, it would be under "no legal obligation" to live up to its end of the various bargains struck.[43] Well before the end of the nineteenth century, the United States stood in default on virtually every treaty agreement it had made with native people, and there is considerable evidence in many instances that this was intended from the outset.[44] Aside from the fraudulent nature of U.S. participation in the treaty process, there is an ample record that many of the instruments of cession were militarily coerced while the government implemented Marshall's version of Just Wars against Indians. As the U.S. Census Bureau put it in 1894:

> The Indian wars under the United States government have been about 40 in number [most of them occurring after 1835]. They have cost the lives of...about 30,000 Indians [at a minimum]...The actual number of killed and wounded Indians must be very much greater than the number given, as they conceal, where possible, their actual loss in battle...Fifty percent additional would be a safe number to add to the numbers given.[45]

The same report noted that some number "very much more" than 8,500 Indians were known to have been killed by government-sanctioned private citizen action—dubbed "individual affairs"—during the course of U.S./Indian warfare. In fact, such citizen action was primarily responsible for reducing the native population of Texas from about 100,000 in 1828 to less than 10,000 in 1880.[47] Similarly, in California, an aggregate indigenous population which still numbered approximately 300,000 had been reduced to fewer than 35,000 by 1860, mainly because of "the cruelties and wholesale massacres perpetrated by [American] miners and early settlers."[48] Either of these illustrations offers a death toll several times the total number officially recognized as accruing through individual affairs in the 48 contiguous states.

Even while this slaughter was occurring, the government was conducting, by its own admission, a "policy of extermination" in its conduct of wars against those indigenous nations which proved "recalcitrant" in giving up their land and liberty.[49] This manifested itself in a lengthy series of massacres of native people—men, women, children, and old people alike—at the hands of U.S. troops. Among the worst were those at Blue River (Nebraska, 1854), Bear River (Idaho, 1863), Sand Creek (Colorado, 1864), Washita River (Oklahoma, 1868), Sappa Creek (Kansas, 1875), Camp Robinson (Nebraska, 1878), and Wounded Knee (South Dakota, 1890).[50] Somewhat different, but comparable, methods of destroying indigenous peoples included the forced march of the entire Cherokee Nation along the "Trail of Tears" to Oklahoma during the 1830s (55 percent did not survive),[51] and the internment of the bulk of the Navajo Nation under abysmal conditions at the Bosque Redondo from 1864 to 1868 (35 to 50 percent died).[52] Such atrocities were coupled with an equally systematic extermination of an entire animal species, the buffalo or North American Bison, as part of a military strategy to starve resistant Indians into submission by "destroying their commissary."[53]

It is probable that more than a quarter-million Indians perished as a direct result of U.S. extermination campaigns.[54] By the turn of the century, only 237,196 native people were recorded by census as still being alive with the United States,[55] perhaps 2 percent of the total indigenous population of the U.S. portion of North America at the point of first contact with Europeans.[56] Correlating rather precisely with this genocidal reduction in the number of native inhabitants was an erosion of Indian land holdings to approximately 2.5 percent of the "lower 48" states.[57] Admiring its effectiveness, barely fifty years later, Adolf Hitler would explicitly anchor his concept of *lebensraumpolitik* ("politics of living space") directly upon U.S. practice against American Indians.[58]

Justice as a "Pulverizing Engine"

Even as the 1890 census figures were being tallied, the United States had already moved beyond the "Manifest Destiny" embodied in the conquest phase of its continental expansion, and was emphasizing the development of colonial administration over residual indigenous land and lives through the Bureau of Indian Affairs (BIA), a subpart of the War Department which had been reassigned for this purpose to the Department of Interior.

This was begun as early as 1871, when Congress—having determined that the military capacity of indigenous nations had finally been sufficiently reduced by incessant wars of attrition—elected to consecrate Marshall's description of their "domestic" status by suspending further treaty making with them.[59] In 1885, the U.S. began for the first time to directly extend its internal jurisdiction over reserved Indian territories ("reservations") through passage of the Major Crimes Act.[60] When this was immediately challenged as a violation of international standards, Supreme Court Justice Samuel F. Miller rendered an opinion which consolidated and extended Marshall's earlier assertion of federal plenary power over native nations, contending that the government held an "incontrovertible right" to exercise authority over Indians as it saw fit and "for their own good."[61] Miller also concluded that Indians lacked legal recourse in matters of federal interest, their sovereignty being defined as whatever Congress did not remove through specific legislation. This decision opened the door to enactment of more than 5,000 statutes regulating affairs in Indian Country by the present day.[62]

One of the first of these was the General Allotment Act of 1887, "which unilaterally negated Indian control over land tenure patterns within the reservations, forcibly replacing the traditional mode of collective use and occupancy with the Anglo-Saxon system of individual property ownership."[63] The Act also imposed for the first time a formal eugenics code—dubbed "blood quantum"—by which American Indian identity would be federally defined on racial grounds rather than by native nations themselves on the basis of group membership/citizenship.[64]

The Allotment Act stipulated that each officially recognized American Indian would receive an allotment of land according to the following formula: 160 acres for family heads, eighty acres for single persons over eighteen years of age and orphans under eighteen, and forty acres for [non-orphan] children under eighteen. "Mixed blood" Indians received title by fee simple patent; "full bloods" were issued "trust patents," meaning they had no control over their property for a period of 25 years. Once each person recognized by the government as belonging to a given Indian nation had received his or her allotment, the "surplus" acreage was "opened" to non-Indian homesteading or conversion into the emerging system of national parks, forests, and grasslands.[65]

There proved to be far fewer identifiable Indians under federal eugenics criteria than land parcels within the reserved areas of the 1890s. Hence, "not only was the cohesion of indigenous society dramatically disrupted by allotment, and traditional government prerogatives preempted, but it led to the loss of some two-thirds of all the acreage [about 100 million of 150 million acres] still held by native people at the time it was passed."[66] Moreover, the land assigned to individual Indians during the allotment process fell overwhelmingly within arid and semiarid locales considered to be the least productive in North America. Without exception, the best watered and otherwise useful portions of the reservations were declared surplus and quickly stripped away.[67] This, of course, greatly reinforced the "dependency" aspect of the Marshall thesis, and led U.S. Indian Commissioner Francis Leupp to conclude with approval that allotment should be considered as "a mighty pulverizing engine for breaking up [the last vestiges of] the tribal mass" which stood as a final barrier to complete Euroamerican hegemony on the continent.[68]

As with the Major Crimes Act, native people attempted to utilize their treatied standing in federal courts to block the allotment process and corresponding erosion of the reservation land base. In the 1903 *Lonewolf v. Hitchcock* case, however, Justice Edward D. White extended the concept of federal plenary power to hold that the government possessed a right to unilaterally abrogate whatever portion of any treaty with Indians it found inconvenient while continuing to consider the remaining terms and provisions binding upon the Indians.[69] In essence, this meant that the U.S. could point to the treaties as being the instruments which legally validated much of its North American land title while simultaneously avoiding whatever reciprocal obligations it had incurred. White also opined that the government's plenary power over Indians lent it a "trust responsibility" over residual native property such that it might opt to "change the form" of this property—from land, say, to cash or "services"—whenever and however it chose to do so. This final consolidation of the Marshall Doctrine effectively left native people with no true national rights under U.S. law while voiding the remaining pittance of conformity to international standards the United States had exhibited with regard to its Indian treaties.[70]

Sovereignty: the Great Disappearing Act

A little discussed aspect of the Allotment Act is that it required each Indian, as a condition of receiving the deed to his or her land parcel, to accept U.S. citizenship. By the early 1920s, when most of the allotment the U.S. wished to accomplish had been completed, there were still a significant number of native people who still had not been "naturalized," either because they'd been left out of the process for one reason or another, or because they'd refused to participate. Consequently, in 1924 the Congress passed a "clean up bill," the Indian Citizenship Act, which imposed citizenship upon all remaining indigenous people within U.S. borders whether they wished it or not.[71]

The Indian Citizenship Act greatly confused the circumstances even of many of the blooded and federally-certified Indians, and imposed legal obligations of citizenship upon them. As for the noncertified, mixed-blood people, their status was finally "clarified": they had been absorbed into the American mainstream at the stroke of the congressional pen. Despite the act having technically left certified Indians occupying the status of citizenship within their own indigenous nation as well as the U.S. (a "dual form" of citizenship so awkward as to be sublime), the juridical door had been opened by which the weight of Indian obligations would begin to accrue more to the U.S. than to themselves.[72]

Juaneño/Yaqui scholar M. Annette Jaimes has revealed that the U.S. government is engaged in "a sort of statistical extermination" whereby the government seeks to eventually resolve its "Indian problem" altogether. As historian Patrick Nelson Limerick frames it: "Set the blood quantum at one-quarter, hold to it as a rigid definition of Indians, let intermarriage proceed as it has for centuries, and eventually Indians will be defined out of existence." Such assertions are based on solid statistics: In 1900, about half of all Indians in this country were "full bloods"; by 1990 it stood at about 20 percent and is dropping steadily. Among certain populations, such as the Chippewas of Minnesota and Wisconsin, only about 5 percent of all tribal members are full-blooded Indians. One-third of all recognized Indians in this country are at the quarter-blood cut-off point. Cherokee demographer Russell Thornton estimates that, given continued imposition of purely racial definitions, Native America as a whole will have disappeared by the year 2080.

All of this—suspension of treatymaking, extension of federal jurisdiction, plenary power and "trust" prerogatives, blood quantum and allotment, and the imposition of citizenship—was bound up in a policy officially designated as being the compulsory assimilation of American Indians into the dominant (Euroamerican) society.[73] Put another way, U.S. Indian policy was carefully (and openly) designed to bring about the disappearance of all recognizable Indian groups, as such.[74] The methods used included the general proscription of native languages[75] and spiritual practices,[76] the systematic and massive transfer of Indian children into non-Indian settings via mandatory attendance at boarding schools remote from their communities,[77] and the deliberate suppression of reservation economic structures.[78] As Indian Commissioner Charles Burke put it at the time, "It is not consistent with the general welfare to promote [American Indian national] characteristics and organization."[79]

The assimilationist policy trajectory peaked during the 1950s with the passage of House Concurrent Resolution 108, otherwise known as the "Termination Act of 1953," a measure through which the U.S. moved to unilaterally dissolve 109 indigenous nations within its borders.[80] Termination was coupled to the "Relocation Act," a statute passed in 1956 and designed to coerce reservation residents to disperse to various urban centers around the country.[81] The ensuing programmatic emphasis upon creating an American Indian diaspora has resulted, by 1990, in over half of all Indians inside the U.S. being severed from their respective land bases and generally acculturated to non-Indian mores.[82] Meanwhile, the enactment of Public Law 280, placed many reservations under the jurisdiction of individual States of the Union, thereby reducing the level of native sovereignty to that held by counties or municipalities.[83] This voided one of the last federal pretenses that the government acted as if Indians retained "certain characteristics of sovereign nations."

Given the contours of federal policy towards American Indians, how is it that the indigenous nations were not obliterated long ago? The answer is ironic. Unbeknownst to the policymakers who implemented allotment policy against Indians during the late nineteenth century, much of the ostensibly useless land to which native people were consigned turned out to be some of the most mineral rich on earth. It is presently estimated that as much as two-thirds of all known U.S. "domestic" uranium reserves lie beneath reservation lands, as well as perhaps a quarter of the readily accessible low sulphur coal and about a fifth of the oil and natural gas. In addition, the reservations are now known to hold substantial deposits of copper, zinc, iron, nickel, molybdenum, bauxite, zeolite and gold.[84]

Such matters were becoming known by the early 1920s.[85] Federal economic planners quickly discerned a distinct advantage in retaining these abundant resources within the framework of governmental trust control. In contrast to land held privately, this arrangement was an expedient to awarding extractive leases, mining licenses and the like to preferred corporate entities. Granting these rights might have proven impossible had the reservations been liquidated altogether. Hence, beginning in 1921, it was determined that selected indigenous nations should be maintained. Washington began to experiment with the creation of "tribal governments" intended to administer what was left of Indian Country on behalf of an emerging complex of interlocking federal/corporate interests.[86] In 1934, this resulted in the passage of the Indian Reorganization Act (IRA), a bill which served to supplant virtually every remaining traditional indigenous government in the country, replacing them with federally-designed "Tribal Councils" structured along the lines of corporate boards and empowered primarily to sign off on mineral leases and similar instruments.[87]

The arrangement led to a recapitulation of the Marshall Doctrine's principle of indigenous "quasi-sovereignty" in slightly revised form: now, native nations were cast as being sovereign enough to legitimate Euroamerican mineral exploitation on their reservations, never sovereign enough to prevent it. Predictably, under such circumstances the BIA negotiated mining leases, duly endorsed by the puppet governments it had installed, "on behalf of" its "Indian wards" which have typically paid native people 15 percent or less of market royalty rates on minerals taken from their lands.[88] The "super profits" thus generated for major corporations have had a significant positive effect on U.S. economic growth since 1950, a matter amplified by the BIA "neglecting" to include land restoration and other environmental cleanup clauses into contracts pertaining to reservation land. (Currently, Indians are construed as sovereign enough to waive environmental protection regulations but never sovereign enough to enforce them).[89] One consequence of this trend is that, on reservations where uranium mining has occurred, Indian Country has become so contaminated by radioactive substances that the government has actively considered designating them as "National Sacrifice Areas" unfit for human habitation.[90] Planning is also afoot to utilize several reservations as dump sites for high level nuclear wastes and toxic chemical substances which cannot be otherwise disposed of conveniently.[91]

Your Wealth is Our Poverty

Further indication of the extent and virulence of the colonial system by which the United States has come to rule Native America is easily found. For instance, dividing the 50 million-odd acres of land still nominally reserved for Indian use and occupancy in the U.S. by the approximately 1.6 million Indians the government recognized in its 1980 census, reveals that native people—on paper, at least—remain the largest landholders on a per capita basis of any population sector on the continent.[92] In combination with the resources known to lie within their land and the increasingly intensive "development" of these resources over the past forty years, simple arithmetic suggests they should also be the wealthiest of all aggregate groups.[93] Instead, according to the federal government's own data, Indians are far and away the poorest in terms of both annual and lifetime per capita income. Correspondingly, we suffer all the standard indices of dire poverty: North America's highest rates of infant mortality and teen suicide, death from malnutrition, exposure, and plague disease.[94] Overall, we consistently experience the highest rate of unemployment, lowest level of educational attainment, and one of the highest rates of incarceration of any group. The average life expectancy of a reservation-based American Indian male is currently less than forty-five years; that of a reservation-based female, barely over forty-seven.[95]

In Latin America, there is a core axiom which guides understanding of the interactive dynamics between the northern and southern continents of the Western Hemisphere. "Your wealth," ladino analysts point out to their Yanqui counterparts, "is our poverty."[96] Plainly, the structure of the relationship forged by the United States *vis-à-vis* the indigenous nations of the northern continent itself follows exactly the same pattern of parasitic domination. The economic veins of the prostrate Native North American host have been carefully opened, their lifeblood drained for consumption by the predatory creature which applied the knife. Such are the fruits of John Marshall's doctrine after a century and a half of continuous application to the "real world" context.

International Sleight of Hand

The U.S. has attempted in various ways to mask the face of this reality. In the wake of World War II, even as the United States was engaged in setting a "moral example" to all of humanity by assuming a lead role in prosecuting former nazi leaders for having ventured down much the same road of continental conquest the U.S. itself had pioneered.[97] Congress passed the Indian Claims Commission Act,[98] its premise being that all nonconsensual—and therefore illegal—takings of native property which had transpired during the course of American history had been "errors," sometimes "tragic" ones.[99] As a means, at least figuratively, of separating U.S. historical performance and expansionist philosophy from the more immediate manifestations of nazism, the new law established a commission empowered to review the basis of U.S. land title in every quarter of the country, and to award retroactive monetary compensation to indigenous nations shown to have been unlawfully deprived of their territory. But the commission was authorized to set compensation amounts only on the basis of the estimated per acre value of illegally taken property at the time it was taken (often a century or more before), and was specifically disempowered from restoring land to Indian control, no matter how it had been taken or what the desires of the impacted native people might be.[100] These restrictions make clear that the law was to save face, not restore justice.

Although the life of the commission was originally envisioned as being only ten years, the magnitude of the issues it encountered, and the urgency with which its mission to "quiet title" to aboriginal land rights came to be viewed by the Euroamerican status quo, caused it to be repeatedly extended.[101] When it was finally suspended on September 30, 1978, it still had sixty-eight cases docketed for review, despite having heard and ostensibly "disposed of" several hundred others over a period of three decades.[102] In the end, while its intent had been the exact opposite, it had accomplished nothing more than to establish with graphic clarity how little of North America the United States legally owned:

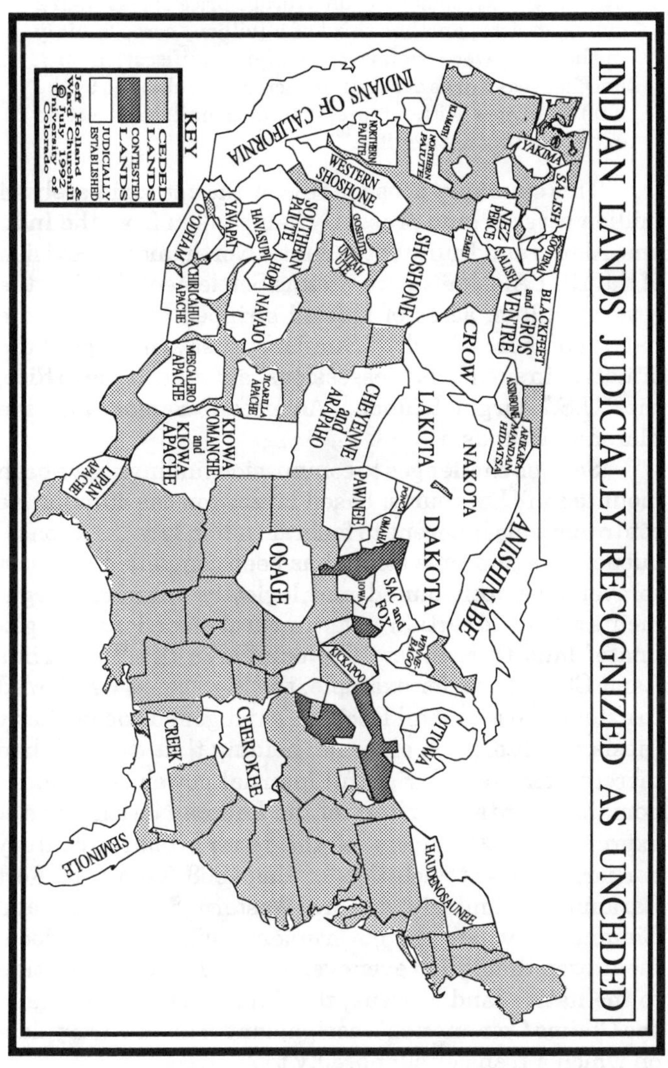
INDIAN LANDS JUDICIALLY RECOGNIZED AS UNCEDED
KEY
CEDED LANDS
CONTESTED LANDS
JUDICIALLY ESTABLISHED
Jeff Holland & Ward Churchill
© July 1992 University of Colorado
INDIANS OF CALIFORNIA
KLAMATH
NORTHERN PAIUTE
NORTHERN PAIUTE
YAKIMA
SALISH
WESTERN SHOSHONE
NEZ PERCE
SALISH
KOOTENAI
LEMHI
GOSHUTE
UINTAH UTE
SHOSHONE
BLACKFEET and GROS VENTRE
SOUTHERN PAIUTE
HAVASUPI
YAVAPAI
O'ODHAM
HOPI
NAVAJO
CHIRICAHUA APACHE
CROW
ASSINIBOINE
ARIKARA MANDAN HIDATSA
CHEYENNE and ARAPAHO
LAKOTA
NAKOTA
JICARILLA APACHE
MESCALERO APACHE
KIOWA COMANCHE and KIOWA APACHE
LIPAN APACHE
PAWNEE
PONCA
OMAHA
DAKOTA
ANISHINABE
OSAGE
IOWA
SAC and FOX
WINNEBAGO
KICKAPOO
OTTOWA
CHEROKEE
CREEK
SEMINOLE
HAUDENOSAUNEE

> ...about half the land area of the country was purchased by treaty or agreement at an average price of less than a dollar an acre; another third of a [billion] acres, mainly in the west, were confiscated without confiscation *[sic]*; another two-thirds of a [billion] acres were claimed by the United States without pretense of a unilateral action extinguishing native title.[103]

This summary does not review the approximately 44 million acres of land presently being taken from the Indians, Aleuts and Inuits of the Arctic North under provision of the 1971 Alaska Native Claims Settlement Act[104] or the several million acres of Hawaii stripped away from the natives of those islands.[105] Similarly, it says nothing of the situation in such U.S. "possessions" as Guam, Puerto Rico, the "U.S." Virgin Islands, "American" Samoa, and the Marshall Islands.

Serious challenges to commission findings have been mounted in U.S. courts, based largely on the cumulative contradictions inherent to federal Indian law. As a consequence, the Supreme Court has been compelled to resort to ever more convoluted and logically untenable arguments to uphold certain governmental assertions of "legitimate" land title. In its 1980 opinion in the Black Hills Land Claim case, for example, the high court was forced to extend the Marshall Doctrine's indigenous domesticity thesis to a ludicrous extreme, holding that the U.S. had merely exercised its rightful internal power of "eminent domain" over the territory of the Lakota Nation when it expropriated 90 percent of the latter's land a century earlier, in direct violation of the 1868 Treaty of Fort Laramie.[106] Similarly, in the Western Shoshone Land Claim case, where the government could show no documentation that it had ever even pretended to assume title to the native land at issue, the Supreme Court let stand the Claims Commission's assignment of an arbitrary date on which a transfer supposedly took place.[107]

A Legal Raft in Blue Water

During the 1970s, the American Indian Movement (AIM), an organization militantly devoted to the national liberation of Native North America, emerged in the United States. In part, the group attempted the physical decolonization of the Pine Ridge Reservation in South Dakota (home of the Oglala Lakota people), but was met with a counterinsurgency war waged by federal agencies such as the FBI and U.S. Marshals Service, and surrogates associated with the reservation's IRA Council.[108] Although unsuccessful in achieving a resumption of indigenous self-determination at Pine Ridge, the tenacity of AIM's struggle (and the ferocity of the government's repression of it) attracted considerable international attention. This led, in 1980, to the establishment of a United Nations Working Group on Indigenous Populations, under auspices of the U.N. Economic and Social Council (ECOSOC), an entity mandated to assess the situation of native peoples globally and produce a universal declaration of their rights as a binding element of international law.[109]

Within this arena, the United States, joined by Canada, has consistently sought to defend its relations with indigenous nations by trotting out the Marshall Doctrine's rationalization that the U.S. has assumed a trust responsibility rather than outright colonial domination over Native North America.[110] American Indian delegates have countered, correctly, that trust prerogatives, in order to be valid under international law, must be tied to some clearly articulated time interval after which the subordinate nations resume independent existence. This has been successfully contrasted to the federal (and Canadian) government's presumption that it enjoys a permanent trust authority over indigenous nations; assumption of *permanent* plenary authority over another nation's affairs and property is the essential definition of colonialism, it is argued, and is illegal under a number of international covenants.[111]

The U.S. and Canada have responded with prevarication, contending that their relationship to Native North America cannot be one of colonialism insofar as United Nations Resolution 1541 (XV), the so-called "Blue Water Thesis," specifies that in order to be defined as a colony a nation must be separated from its colonizer by at least thirty miles of open ocean.[112] The representatives of both countries have also done everything in their power to delay or prevent completion of the Universal Declaration of the Rights of Indigenous Peoples, arguing, among other things, that the term "peoples," when applied to native populations, should not carry the force of law implied by its use in such international legal instruments as the Universal Declaration of Human Rights (1948), Covenant on Civil and Political Rights (1978), and the International Convention on Elimination of All Forms of Racial Discrimination (1978).[113] The United States in particular has implied that it will not abide by any declaration of indigenous rights which runs counter to what it perceives as its own interests, a matter which would replicate its posture with regard to the authority of the International Court of Justice (the "World Court")[114] and elements of international law such as the 1948 Convention on Prevention and Punishment of the Crime of Genocide.[115]

Meanwhile, the U.S. has set out to "resolve things internally" through what may be intended as a capstone extrapolation of the Marshall Doctrine. This has assumed the shape of a drive to convince Indians to accept the premise that, rather than struggling to regain the self-determining rights to separate sovereign existence embodied in their national histories and treaty relationships, they should voluntarily merge themselves with the U.S. polity. In this scenario, the IRA administrative apparatus created during the 1930s would assume a position as a "third level of the federal government," finally making indigenous rights within the U.S. inseparable from those of the citizenry as a whole. This final assimilation of native people into the "American sociopolitical mainstream" would obviously void most (or perhaps all) potential utility for Indian rights which exist in or might emerge from international law over the next few years. The option is therefore being seriously pursued by a Senate Select Committee on Indian Affairs, chaired by Hawaii Senator Daniel Inouye (who has already done much to undermine the last vestiges of rights held by the native people of his own state).[116]

The Marshall Doctrine on a Global Scale

During the fall of 1990, President George Bush stepped onto the world stage beating the drums for what he termed a "Just War" to roll back what he described as the "naked aggression" of Iraq's invasion and occupation of neighboring Kuwait. Claiming to articulate "universal principles of international relations and human decency," Bush stated that such aggression "cannot stand," that "occupied territory must be liberated, legitimate governments must be reinstated, the benefits of their aggression must be denied to aggressive powers."[117] Given the tone and tenor of this Bushian rhetoric—and the undeniable fact that Iraq had a far better claim to Kuwait (its nineteenth province, separated from the Iraqis by the British as an administrative measure following World War I), than the U.S. has to virtually any part of North America[118]—one might logically expect the American president to call airstrikes in upon his own capitol as a means of forcing his government to withdraw from Indian Country. Since he did not, the nature of his "New World Order" is clear: it is based on the rule of force, not on the rule of law.

The United States does not now possess, nor has it ever had, a legitimate right to occupancy in at least half the territory it claims as its own on this continent. It began its existence as an outlaw state and, given the nature of its expansion to its present size, it has adamantly remained so through the present moment. In order to make things appear otherwise, its legal scholars and its legislators have persistently and often grotesquely manipulated and deformed accepted and sound legal principles, both internationally and domestically. They have done so in precisely the same fashion, and on the same basis, as the nazi leaders they stood at the forefront in condemning for Crimes Against Humanity at Nuremberg.

In no small part because of its past achievements in consolidating its position on other peoples' land in North America, the United States may well continue to succeed where the nazis failed. With the collapse of the Soviet Union, it has emerged as the ascendant military power on the planet during the late twentieth century. As the sheer margin of its victory over Iraq has revealed, it now possesses the capacity to extend essentially the same sort of relationships it has already imposed upon American Indians to the remainder of the world. And, given the experience it has acquired in Indian Affairs over the years, it is undoubtedly capable garbing this process of planetary subordination in a legalistic attire symbolizing its deep-seated concern with international freedom and dignity, the sovereignty of other nations, and the human rights of all peoples. At a number of levels, the Marshall Doctrine reckons to become truly globalized in the years ahead.

This is likely to remain the case, unless and until significant numbers of people within and without the United States recognize the danger and the philosophical system underpinning it for what they are. More importantly, any genuine alternative to a consummation of the Bushian vision of world order is predicated upon these same people acting upon their insights, opposing the order implicit to the U.S. status quo both at home and abroad. Ultimately, the dynamic represented by the Marshall Doctrine must be reversed, the structure it fostered dismantled, within the territorial corpus of the United States itself. In this, nothing can be more central than the restoration of indigenous land and indigenous national rights in the fullest sense of the term. The U.S.—at least as it has come to be known, and in the sense that it knows itself—must be driven from North America. In its stead resides the possibility, likely the only possibility, of a truly just and liberatory future for all humanity.

Notes

1. This, in essence, is the legal concept of "aboriginal" land rights. One of the strongest and clearest articulations of the doctrine may be found In Jeze, Gaston, *Etud Theoretique et Pratique Sur L'occupation Comme Mode d'Acquerir les Territoires en Droit International,* Paris, 1896.
2. For a very solid analysis of the various problems at issue in this regard, see Taylor, Robert, *International Public Law,* Metheun Publishers, London, 1901. Also see Lindley, Mark Frank, *The Acquisition and Government of Backward Country In International Law: A Treatise on the Law and Practice Relating to Colonial Expansion,* Longmans, Green Publishers, London, 1926.
3. This principle is plainly embodied in the United Nations Declaration on the Granting of Independence to Colonial Countries and Peoples (14 Dec. 1960). The complete text of the declaration will be found in Brownlie, Ian, *Basic Documents on Human Rights,* Clarendon Press, Oxford, 1981, pp. 28-30.
4. The comprehensive elaboration of the U.S. position may be found in Cohen, Felix S., *Handbook on Federal Indian Law,* University of New Mexico Press, Albuquerque, (reprint of 1942 U.S. Government Printing Office edition) n.d.
5. Broad analysis of such rhetoric by President George Bush during the 1990-91 Gulf War may be found in Bates, Greg (ed.), *Mobilizing Democracy: Changing the U.S. Role in the Middle East,* Common Courage Press, Monroe, ME, 1991. Also see Peters, Cynthia (ed.), *Collateral Damage: The "New World Order" at Home and Abroad,* South End Press, Boston, 1992.

6. See Truyol y Serra, Antonio, "The Discovery of the New World and International Law," *Toledo Law Review*, No. 43, 1971.
7. Probably the best delineation of these issues may be found in Williams, Robert A. Jr., *The American Indian in Western Legal Thought: The Discourses of Conquest*, Oxford University Press, London/New York, 1990.
8. The first solid evidence that the Church had become engaged in this process comes on May 3 and May 5, 1493, with the signing of two Bulls by Pope Alexander VI which endorsed the rights of the sovereigns of Castille and Aragon to acquire the lands of newly-discovered portions of America while spreading Christianity among the natives thereof. See Gottshalk, Paul, *The Earliest Diplomatic Documents of America*, New York, 1978, p. 21.
9. On the Bulls of Innocent IV (Sinibaldo Fiesco), see Nys, Ernest, *Les Origins du Troit International*, Brussels/Paris, 1984, esp. Chapter Seven. It is worth noting that Innocent himself was heavily influenced by the treatise of Thomas Aquinas in *Summa Theologica Secunda Secundae*, written around 1250; see Deane, Herbert Andrew, *The Political and Social Ideals of St. Augustine*, Columbia University Press, New York, 1963.
10. See Nussbaum, Alfred, *A Concise History of the Laws of Nations*, Macmillan Publishers, New York, (revised edition) 1954. Also see Hanke, Lewis, *The Spanish Struggle for Justice in the Conquest of America*, University of Pennsylvania Press, Philadelphia, 1949.
11. Vitoria's formulation of the doctrine is available under the title *De Indis et De Jure Belli Reflectiones*, published by the Carnegie Institution in 1917. The pivotal international legal theorist Emer Vattel drew heavily on Vitoria's discourse when drafting his *The Laws of Nations* (T. & J.W. Johnson Publishers, Philadelphia, 1855). Overall, see Parry, John Horace, *The Spanish Theory of Empire in the Sixteenth Century*, Cambridge University Press, Cambridge, MA, 1940.
12. This principle derives directly from Roman law promulgated at least a century before Christ; see Maine, Henry (ed.), *Ancient Law*, London, (thirteenth edition) 1850.
13. This thinking is embodied in the Bull *Inter Caetera* of May

4, 1493: Gottshalk *op. cit.*, p. 21. The matter is also taken up about thirty years later by the renowned jurist John Mair, in his *Commentary on the Sentences of Pater Lombard;* see Truyol y Serra, *op. cit.*, p. 313.

14. Matías de Paz took the lead, in his *Concerning the Rule of the Kings of Spain Over the Indians,* in reflecting Aristotelian logic and formulating the concepts of Just and Unjust Wars as applied to the Americas; see Díaz, Jorge, "Los Doctrinas de Palacios Rubios y Matías de Paz ante la Conquista America," in *Memoria de El Colegio Nacional,* Burgos, 1950, pp. 71-94. Matías' arguments led to promulgation of the Laws of Burgos, theoretically regulating all aspects of Spanish colonial practice. For an overview of where the discussion led, see Hanke, Lewis, *Aristotle and the American Indians: A Study in Race Prejudice in the Modern World,* Indiana University Press, Bloomington/Indianapolis, 1959. For more on the relevant laws, see Taylor, John, *Spanish Law Concerning Discoveries, Pacifications, and Settlements among the Indians,* University of Utah Press, Salt Lake City, 1980.

15. For a sample of the sort of debates involved, see Hanke, Lewis, *All Mankind Is One: A Study of the Disputation Between Bartolome de Las Casas and Juan Gines de Sepulueda in 1550 on the Intellectual and Religious Capacity of American Indians,* Northern Illinois University, DeKalb, 1950. On general acceptance of the doctrine, see Peckman, Howard, and Charles Cibson (eds.), *Attitudes of the Colonial Powers Towards American Indians,* University of Utah Press, Salt Lake City, 1969. An excellent textual source in the latter regard is Davenport, Francis Gardiner (ed.), *European Treaties Bearing on the History of the United States and Its Dependencies* (2 Vols.), Carnegie Institution of Washington, Washington, D.C., 1917.

16. See Quinn, David Beers, *England and the Discovery of America,* 1481-1620, Alfred A. Knopf Publishers, New York, 1974. Also see Porter, Harry Culverwell, *The Inconstant Savage: England and the American Indian, 1500-1600,* Duckworth Publishers, London, 1979. A more general view may be found in Parry, John Horace, *The Establishment of European Hegemony, 1415-1713,* Harper and Row Publishers, New York, (revised edition) 1966. For

a selection of relevant texts with regard to England, see Vaughn, Alden T., *Early American Indian Documents: Treaties and Laws, 1607-1789,* University Publications of America, Washington, D.C., 1979.

17. See Scott, James Brown, *The Spanish Origin of International Law,* Clarendon Press, Oxford, 1934. Also see Oppenheim, L., *International Law,* Vol. 1, Longmans, Creen and Co., Publishers, London, 1955. That these principles were not unknown to or misunderstood by early U.S. jurists is conclusively demonstrated by Felix S. Cohen in his essay, "The Spanish Origin of Indian Rights in the Law of the United States," *Georgetown Law Review,* Vol. 31, No. 1, Winter 1942.
18. The concept of the Norman Yoke emerged from the idea of "Natural Law"; see von Cierke, Freidrich, *Natural Law and the Theory of Society, 1500-1800,* Cambridge University Press, Cambridge, MA, 1934. For the concept's application in the New World setting, see Knorr, K., *British Colonial Theories, 1570-1850,* University of Toronto Press, Toronto, 1944. Also see Jacobs, Wilbur R., *Dispossessing the American Indian: Indians and Whites on the Colonial Frontier,* (Charles Scribner, Publisher, New York, 1972), Vaughn, Aden T., *The New England Frontier: Puritans and Indians, 1620-1675* (Little, Brown Publishers, New York, 1965), and Williams *(op. cit.).*
19. The seeds of the subsequent "reservation" systems developed by the U.S. and Canada may be seen to be imbedded in this construction. The motivations underlying nearly three centuries of endemic falsification of indigenous American demographic and agricultural realities by Angloamerican "scholars" may also be discerned as residing within the theory of the Norman Yoke. In order to justify, or at least rationalize, the sorts of territorial acquisition undertaken by the British and their U.S. descendants, it was necessary that North America have been very sparsely populated by peoples subsisting primarily on the basis of hunting and gathering. A good job of debunking such patent nonsense is found in Francis Jennings' *The Invasion of America: Indians, Colonialism, and the Cant of Conquest,* W.W. Norton and Co., New York, 1976). Also see Stiffarm, Lenore A., and Phil Lane, Jr., "The Demog-

raphy of Native North America: A Question of American Indian Survival," in M. Annette Jaimes (ed.), *The State of Native America: Genocide, Colonization and Resistance,* South End Press, Boston, 1992, pp. 23-54.

20. It should be noted that Spain conceded title over Florida to England through the 1763 Treaty of Paris. For a good overview and contextualization of the French and Indian Wars, as well as the 1763 Proclamation, see Leach, Douglas Edward, *The Northern Colonial Frontier, 1607-1763, Histories of the American Frontier, New York, 1966.* A focus on the last, and decisive, of these wars will be found in Jacobs, Wilbur R., *Diplomacy and Indian Gifts: Anglo-French Rivalry Along the Ohio and Northwest Frontiers, 1748-1763,* Stanford University Press, Stanford, CA, 1950. Also see Downes, Randolph C., *Council Fires on the Upper Ohio,* University of Pittsburg Press, Pittsburg, 1940.
21. See Jensen, Merrill, *Founding of a Nation: A History of the American Revolution, 1763-1776,* Oxford University Press, London/New York, 1979.
22. See Abernathy, Thomas Perkins, *Western Lands and the American Revolution,* Russell and Russell Publishers, New York, 1959. Also see Wood, Gordon, *Creation of the American Republic, 1776-1787,* University of North Carolina Press, Chapel Hill, 1969.
23. Deloria, Vine Jr., "Sovereignty," In Roxanne Dunbar Ortiz and Larry Emerson (eds.), *Economic Development in American Indian Reservations,* Native American Studies Center, University of New Mexico, Albuquerque, 1979. Also see Mohr, Walter Harrison, *Federal Indian Relations, 1774-1788,* University of Pennsylvania Press, Philadelphia, 1933.
24. For an assessment of the centrality of Indian relations in congressional deliberations concerning the treaty-making provisions found in Article IX of the Articles of Confederation, and Articles I and VI of the Constitution (as well as its so-called "Commerce Clause"), see Jensen, Merril, *The Articles of Confederation: An Interpretation of the Socio-Constitutional History of the American Revolution, 1774-1788,* University of Wisconsin Press, Madison, 1940, esp. pp. 154-62, 190-232. Another useful reading is Schaaf, Gregory, *Wampum Belts and Peace Trees: George Morgan,*

Native Americans and Revolutionary Diplomacy, Fulcrum Publishers, Golden, CO, 1990.

25. 1 Stat. 50, 1789.
26. Quoted in Lazarus, Edward, *Black Hills, White Justice: The Sioux Nation versus the United States, 1775 to the Present,* Harper-Collins Publishers, New York, 1991, p. 158.
27. U.S. contentions that it gained "Discovery Rights" by virtue of the British capitulation are strained at best. Such rights, under both English and Spanish legal understandings, attached themselves solely to monarchies under the doctrine of "Divine Right." In other words, it is dubious that George III could have conveyed such rights upon the rebels, even had he desired to do so (and there is no language in the treaty suggesting that he did). At most, then, the U.S. could claim bona fide rights to only that territory—all of it east of the 1763 demarcation line—which the British Crown could be said to have acquired by prior treaties with indigenous nations. On the relationship between Divine Rights and Discovery Rights, see Ullman, Walter, *The Church and Laws ln the Early Middle Ages,* Metheun Publishers, London, 1975.
28. On Tecumseh, see Edmunds, R. David, *Tecumseh and the Quest for American Indian Leadership,* Little, Brown Publishers, Boston, 1984. On the Red Sticks, see Martin, Joel W., *Sacred Revolt: The Muskogees' Struggle for a New World,* Beacon Press, Boston, 1991.
29. Opinion rendered by the Attorney General (Op. Atty. Gen.), April 26, 1821, p. 345.
30. Op. Patty. Gen., 1828, pp. 623-3. For further background, see Berman, Howard, "The Concept of Aboriginal Rights in the Early Legal History of the United States," *Buffalo Law Review,* No. 28, 1978, pp. 637-67. Also see Cohen, Felix S., "Original Indian Land Title," *Minnesota Law Review,* No. 32,1947,pp.28-59.
31. For context, see Horsman, Reginald, *Expansion and American Policy, 1783-1812,* Michigan State University Press, East Lansing, 1967.
32. *Johnson v. McIntosh,* 21 U.S. 98 Wheat. 543, 1822.
33. Baker, L., John Marshall: *A Life in Law, Macmillan Publishers, New York 1976, p. 80.*

34. *Fletcher v. Peck* 10 U.S. 87 (1810).
35. *Johnson v. McIntosh,* 21 U.S. 98 Wheat. 543 (1823).
36. The cases are *Cherokee Nation v. Georgia* (30 U.S. (5 Pet.) 1 (1831)) and *Worcester v. Georgia* (31 U.S. (6 Pet.) 551 (1832)). In effect, Marshall held that indigenous nations should always be considered sovereign enough to transfer legal title to their lands to the United States, but never sovereign enough to possess a right to prevent U.S. assumption of ownership of those lands. Simultaneously, he denied comparable rights over Indian property to the various states, reserving them exclusively to the federal government. Oddly, this last has led to Marshall being generally considered a "champion" of native rights.
37. This is a constitutional absurdity. The sort of limited sovereignty implied in Marshall's "domestic dependent nation" theory places indigenous nations in essentially the same "quasi-sovereign" status of subordination to the federal government as is possessed by the states of the union or provinces in relationship to the government of Canada. Article 1, Section 10, of the U.S. Constitution specifically prohibits the states from entering into treaty relationships. Conversely, the federal government is prohibited from entering into a treaty relationship with states or provinces (or any entity other than another fully sovereign nation). The unprecedented (and untenable) politico-legal status invented by Marshall to describe the "partial sovereignty" he needed native nations to fulfill has been compared to "the biological impossibility of a woman's being part-pregnant."
38. For penetrating insights into the power relations involved, see Memmi, Albert, *Colonizer and Colonized,* Beacon Press, Boston, 1965.
39. For example, this is the basic argument advanced in Wilkinson, Charles F., *Indians, Time and Law,* Yale University Press, New Haven, CT, 1987.
40. It is interesting to note that the United States, without renouncing its own doctrine, took a leading role in defining the creation of an exactly similar juridical rationalization of expansionist intent by nazi Germany to be a criminal endeavor. See Parella, Frank, *Lebensraum and Manifest Destiny: A Comparative Study in the Justification of Ex-*

pansionism, Washington, D.C., 1950.

41. For a comprehensive survey of the meanings of these terms in the international legal vernacular, see Walzer, Michael, *Just and Unjust Wars: A Moral Argument with Historical Illustrations*, Basic Books, New York, 1977.
42. One indicator of the pervasiveness with which this outlook has been implanted is that armed conflicts between the U.S. and indigenous nations are inevitably described as "Indian Wars" despite the fact that each one was demonstrably initiated by the invasion by American citizens of territory belonging to one or more native peoples. The so-called Indian Wars would thus be accurately depicted as "Settlers' Wars" (or, more appropriately yet, "Wars of Aggression by the United States").
43. The texts of 371 ratified treaties are reproduced verbatim in Kappler, Charles J. (ed.), *Indian Treaties, 1778-1883*, Interland Publishing Co., New York, (second printing) 1973. The Lakota scholar Vine Deloria, Jr., has collected more than thirty additional ratified treaty texts, raising the total to approximately 400. Further, Deloria has compiled several hundred treaty texts never ratified by the Senate, but upon which basis the U.S. nonetheless contends it acquired legal title to specific portions of its current geography (California is a prominent example).
44. There are a number of indicators of this. One of the more salient was a tendency of the Senate to alter the terms and conditions of treaties negotiated with indigenous nations after the native leadership had signed. The modified treaty instruments were then passed into U.S. law, and said to be binding upon the Indians involved, even though they'd never agreed to—or in some cases even beennotified of—the new terms (the 1861 Treaty with the Cheyennes and Arapahoes, otherwise known as the Treaty of Fort Wise, is a good example). For details, see Kappler, Charles J. (ed.), *Indian Laws and Treaties* (5 Vols.), U.S. Government Printing Office, Washington, D.C., 1904.
45. U.S. Bureau of the Census, *Report on Indians Taxed and Indians Not Taxed tn the United States (except Alaska)* at the Eleventh U.S. Census: 1890, U.S. Government Printing Office, Washington, D.C., 1894, pp. 637-8.
46. *Ibid.*

47. See Stiffarm and Lane, *op. cit.*, pp. 35-6. The government of first the Republic, and then the State of Texas maintained a bounty on Indian—any Indian—scalps until well into the 1870s; see Newcome, W.W. Jr., *The Indians of Texas,* University of Texas Press, Austin, 1961.
48. Mooney, James A., "Population," in Frederick W. Dodge (ed.), *Handbook of the Indians North of Mexico,* Vol. 2, Bureau of American Ethnology Bulletin No. 30, Smithsonian Institution, U.S. Government Printing Office, Washington, D.C., 1910, pp. 286-7. Also see Cook, Sherburn F., *The Conflict Between the California Indian and White Civilization,* University of California Press, Berkeley, 1976.
49. For details and analysis, see Svaldi, David, *Sand Creek and the Rhetoric of Extermination: A Case-Study in Indian-White Relations,* University Press of America, Washington, D.C., 1989.
50. Stiffarm and Lane, *op. cit.*, p. 34, plus cites.
51. See Thornton, Russell, "Cherokee Population Losses During the Trail of Tears: A New Perspective and Estimate," *Ethnohistory,* No. 31, 1984, pp. 289-300.
52. See Johansson, S. Ryan, and S.H. Preston, "Tribal Demography: The Navajo and Hopi Populations as Seen Through Manuscripts from the 1900 Census," *Social Science History,* No. 3, 1978, p. 26. Also see Salmon, Roberto Mario, "The Disease Complaint at Bosque Redondo (1864-1868)," *The Indian Historian,* No. 9, 1976.
53. See McHugh, Tom, *The Time of the Buffalo,* University of Nebraska Press, Lincoln, 1972, p. 285. Also see Hutton, Paul Andrew, *Phil Sheridan and His Army,* University of Nebraska Press, Lincoln, 1985, p. 246.
54. Scholarly sources suggest the actual total may have been as high as a half-million. See Thornton, Russell, *American Indian Holocaust and Survival: A Population History Since 1492,* University of Oklahoma Press, Norman, 1987, p. 49.
55. This nadir figure is reported in U.S. Bureau of the Census, *Fifteenth Census of the United States, 1930: The Indian Population of the United States and Alaska,* U.S. Government Printing Office, Washington, D.C., 1937. Barely 101,000 Canadian Indians were estimated as surviving in

the same year.

56. Estimating native population figures at the point of first contact is, at best, a slippery business. Recent demographic work has, however, produced a broad consensus that the standard anthropological estimates of "about one million north of the Río Grande" fashioned by James Mooney and Alfred Kroeber, as well as Harold Driver's subsequent upward revision of their calculations to "approximately two million," are far too low. The late Henry Dobyns, using more appropriate methodologies than his predecessors, computed a probable aggregate precontact North American Indian population of 18.5 million, about fifteen million of them within present U.S. borders (*Their Numbers Become Thinned: Native American Population Dynamics In Eastern North America*, University of Tennessee Press, Knoxville, 1983). A somewhat more conservative successor, the Cherokee demographer Russell Thornton, counters that the figure was more likely about 12.5 million, perhaps 9.5 million of them within the U.S. (*American Indian Holocaust and Survival, op. cit.*). Splitting the difference between Dobyns and Thornton leaves one with an approximate fifteen million North American population total, about 12.5 million in the U.S. No matter which set of the newer estimates one uses, the overall attrition by 1900 is in the upper 90th percentile.
57. The figure is arrived at by relying upon Royce, Charles C., *Indian Land Cessions in the United States* (2 Vols.), Bureau of American Ethnography, 18th Annual Report, 1896-97, Smithsonian Institution, Washington, D.C., 1899.
58. The idea was to destroy the *untermensch* ("subhuman") populations—Slavs, Poles, Jews and Gypsies among them—of eastern Europe, replacing them on the lands thus vacated with "superior" Germanic "settlers," and thereby establishing Germany as a first-class world power. Hitler expressed this rather consistently during his career, beginning with the seminal *Mein Kampf* (Sentry Editions, New York, 1962). For instance, after outlining the necessity of a large continental land base for any country seeking a "world historical" role, he observed that, "Today many European states are like pyramids stood on their

heads. Their European area is absurdly small in comparison to their weight of colonies, foreign trade, etc. We may say: summit in Europe, base in the whole world; contrasting with the American Union which possesses its base in its own continent and touches the rest of the earth only with its summit. And from this comes the immense inner strength of this state and the weakness of most European colonial powers...Nor is England any proof to the contrary, since in consideration of the British empire we forget too easily the Anglo-Saxon world as such. The position of England, if only because of her linguistic and cultural bond with the American Union, can be compared to no other state in Europe...For Germany, consequently, the only possibility for carrying out a healthy territorial policy [lies] in the acquisition of new land in Europe itself...suited for settlement by [Germans]...[S]uch a colonial policy [must be] carried out by means of a hard struggle...not for territories outside of Europe, but for land on the home continent itself...If land [is] desired in Europe, it [can] be obtained by and large only at the expense of Russia, and this [means] that the new Reich must again set itself on the march along the road of the Teutonic Knights of old, to obtain by the German sword sod for the German plow and daily bread for the nation (pp. 139-40)." In *Hitler's Secret Book* (New York, 1961, pp. 44-8) he made it even more clear that, "Neither Spain nor Britain should be models of German expansion, but the Nordics of North America, who had ruthlessly pushed aside an inferior race to win for themselves soil and territory for the future"; see Rich, Norman, *Hitler's War Aims: Ideology, the Nazi State, and the Course of Expansion* (W.W. Norton Publishers, New York, 1973, p. 8). Also see Parella, *op. cit.*, and *Hitler's Secret Conversations, 1941-1944*, New York, 1953. Perhaps the very clearest articulation of the conceptual and practical linkages between nazi performance in eastern Europe and 19th century U.S. Indian policy may be found in a lengthy memorandum prepared by Freidrich Hossbach to record the content of a Führer Conference conducted on November 5, 1937; the relevant portion is contained in *Trial of the Major War Criminals before the International Military Tribunal* (42 Vols.), Nuremberg,

1947-1949, 386-PS, 25:402 ff.

59. Ch. 120, 16 Stat. 544, 566, now codified at 25 U.S.C. 71. According to its authors, the suspension did nothing to impair the standing of existing treaties between the U.S. and native nations.
60. Ch. 341, 24 Stat. 362, 385, now codified at 18 U.S.C. 1153; on context and implementation of the act, see Deloria, Vine Jr., and Clifford M. Lytle, *American Indians, American Justice, University of Texas Press, Austin, 1983.*
61. *United States v. Kagama,* 118 U.S. 375 (1886).
62. Deloria and Lytle, *op. cit.*
63. Ch. 119, 24 Stat. 388, now codified as amended at 25 U.S.C. 331 *et seq.*, better known as the "Dawes Act," after its sponsor, Massachusetts Senator Henry Dawes. The quote is from Robbins, Rebecca L. "Self-Determination and Subordination: The Past, Present and Future of American Indian Governance," in Jaimes, *op. cit,* p. 93.
64. See Jaimes, M. Annette, "Federal Indian Identification Policy: A Usurpation of Indigenous Sovereignty in North America," in Jaimes, *op. cit.*, pp. 123-38. It is noteworthy that official eugenics codes have been employed by very few states, mostly such unsavory examples like nazi Germany (against the Jews), South Africa (against "Coloreds") and Israel (against Palestinian Arabs).
65. Robbins, *op. cit.* Also see McDonnell, Janet A., *The Dispossession of the American Indian, 1887-1934,* Indiana University Press, Bloomington/Indianapolis, 1991.
66. Robbins, *op. cit.* Also see Kicking Bird, Kirk, and Karen Ducheneaux, *One Hundred Million Acres,* Macmillan Publishers, New York, 1973.
67. See Otis, D.S., *The Dawes Act and the Allotment of Indian Land,* University of Oklahoma Press, Norman, 1973. Also see McDonnell, *op. cit.*
68. Leupp, Francis E., *The Indian and His Problem,* Charles Scribner's Sons, New York, 1910, p. 93.
69. 187 U.S.553 (1903).
70. Customary international law *(Jus cogens)* with regard to treaty relations was not formally codified until the Vienna Convention on the Law of Treaties was produced in 1969. However, all parties—including the United States, which has yet to ratify it—concur that its major provisions have

been in practical effect for two centuries or more. Article 27 of the Convention states categorically that no state can invoke its own internal laws (including its constitution) as a basis to avoid meeting its treaty obligations. *Lonewolf* plainly defies this principle. On the Vienna Convention, see Sinclair, Sir Ian, *The Vienna Convention on the Law of Treaties,* (Manchester University Press, Dover, [second edition] 1984). On U.S. acknowledgement that its terms are valid and legally binding, see U.S. Senate, Committee on the Judiciary, Subcommittee on the Constitution, *Hearing on Constitutional Issues Relating to the Proposed Genocide Convention Before the Subcommittee on the Constitution of the Senate Committee on the Judiciary,* 99th Cong., 1st Sess., U.S. Government Printing Office, Washington, D.C., 1985.

71. Ch. 233, 43 Stat. 25.
72. Jaimes, "Federal Indian Identification Policy," *op. cit.*, pp. 127-8.
73. For the origins of this policy, see Fritz, Henry E., *The Movement for Indian Assimilation, 1860-1890,* University of Pennsylvania Press, Philadelphia, 1963.
74. This is a clinically genocidal posture within the meaning of the term offered by Raphael Lemkin, the man who coined it: "Generally speaking, genocide does not necessarily mean the immediate destruction of a nation, except when accomplished by mass killing of all the members of a nation. It is intended rather to signify a coordinated plan of different actions aimed at destruction of the essential foundations of the life of national groups, with the aim of annihilating the groups themselves. The objective of such a plan would be disintegration of the political and social institutions, of culture, language, national feelings, religion, and the economic existence of national groups, and the destruction of personal security, liberty, health, dignity, and the lives of individuals belonging to such groups. Genocide is the destruction of the national group as an entity, and the actions involved are directed against individuals, not in their individual capacity but as members of the national group;" see Lemkin, Raphael, *Axis Rule in Occupied Europe,* Carnegie Endowment for International Peace/Rumford Press, Concord, NH, 1944, p. 79.

75. As the Commissioner of Indian Affairs put it in his 1886 *Annual Report* (pp. xxiii-iv): "I [have] expressed very decidedly the idea that Indians should be taught the English language only...There is not an Indian pupil whose tuition is paid for by the United States Government who is permitted to study any other language than our own vernacular—the language of the greatest, most powerful, and enterprising nationalities under the sun. The English language as taught in America is good enough for all her people of all races."
76. Central Indian spiritual practices such as the Potlatch of the nations of the Pacific Northwest and the Sun Dance of the Lakota were prohibited under pain of criminal law. See Cole, Douglas, and Ira Chaikan, *An Iron Hand Upon the People: The Law Against Potlatch on the Northwest Coast* (University of Washington Press, Seattle, 1990) and Jackson, Curtis E., and Marcia J. Galli, *A History of the Bureau of Indian Affairs and Its Activities Among Indians* (R&E Research Associates, San Francisco, 1977).
77. On the boarding school system and its effects, see Noriega, Jorge, "American Indian Education in the United States: Indoctrination for Subordination to Colonialism," in Jaimes, *op. cit., pp.* 371-402. It should be noted that such systematic transfer of the children of a targeted racial or ethnic group to the targeting group is defined as a genocidal act under Article II(e) of the 1948 Convention on the Prevention and Punishment of the Crime of Genocide.
78. The Lakota, for example, rapidly developed a basis for reservation self-sufficiency predicated in livestock during the quarter-century following the 1890 Wounded Knee Massacre. During World War I, however, the U.S. appealed to Lakota "patriotism" to engage in a near-total and cut-rate sell-off of their cattle to provide rations for American troops fighting in France. After the war, when the Lakota requested assistance in replenishing their herds, the government declined. Lakota grazing lands were then leased by the BIA to non-Indian ranchers, while the Indians assumed a position of permanent destitution. See Lazarus, Edward, *Black Hills, White Justice: The Sioux Nation versus the United States, 1775 to the Present,* Harper-Collins Publishers, 1991, pp. 150-2.

79. Letter, Charles Burke to William Williamson, September 16, 1921; William Williamson Papers, Box 2, File—Indian Matters, Miscellaneous, I.D. Weeks Library, University of South Dakota, Vermillion. Such articulation of official sensibility was hardly isolated; see Kvasnicka, Robert M., and Herman J. Viola (eds.), *The Commissioners of Indian Affairs, 1824-1977,* University of Nebraska Press, Lincoln, 1979.
80. The method was to withdraw federal recognition of the existence of specific indigenous nations, converting large reservations into counties, or incorporating smaller reservations into existing counties. Examples of legislation enacted pursuant to House Resolution 108 which implemented such practices include the Menominee Termination Act (ch. 303, 68 Stat. 250 (June 17, 1954)), Klamath Termination Act (ch. 732, 68 Stat. 718 August 13, 1954), codified at 25 U.S.C. 564 *et seq.),* and the Act Terminating the Tribes of Western Oregon (ch. 733, 68 Stat. 724 august 13, 1954), codified at 25 U.S.C. 691 *et seq.).*
81. Public Law 959. For details of implementation, see Fixico, Donald L., *Termination and Relocation: Federal Indian Policy, 1945-1960,* University of New Mexico Press, Albuquerque, 1986.
82. The U.S. Census of 1900 reported almost no Indians (0.4 percent of the native population) living in cities. A half-century later, the 1950 Census showed that proportion had grown to only 13.4 percent. With the implementation of coherent federal relocation programs, however, the number mushroomed to 44.5 percent by 1970. Although relocation was geared down during the 1970s, and finally suspended during the 1980s, it continues to have a lingering effect, with the result that the proportion of urban Indians grew to 49 percent in 1980 and about 52 percent in 1990. See Stiffarm and Lane, *op. cit.,* p. 42, plus cites.
83. Ch. 505, 67 Stat. 588 (August 14, 1954), codified in part at 18 U.S.C. 1162 and 28 U.S.C. 1360. For details of implementation, see Goldberg, Carol E., "Public Law 280: The Limits of State Law over Indian Reservations," *UCLA Law Review,* No. 22, February 1975.
84. On resource distribution, see generally, Garrity, Michael, "The U.S. Colonial Empire is as Close as the Nearest

Reservation," in Holly Sklar (ed.), *Trilateralism: The Trilateral Commission and Elite Planning for World Government,* South End Press, Boston, 1980, pp. 238-68. Also see Jorgensen, Joseph G. (ed.), *Native Americans and Energy Development II,* Anthropology Resource Center/Seventh Generation Funs, Cambridge, MA, 1984.

85. See McDonnell, *op. cit.*

86. The IRA was implemented by referenda, reservation by reservation. In instances where traditionals such as the Hopi manifested their resistance to it through the time-honored means of boycotting the proceedings, however, Indian Commissioner John Collier counted their abstentions as "aye" votes. The same method was used with regard to the Lakota Nation, as well as the inclusion of "aye" votes allegedly cast by long-dead voters. Such fraud permeated implementation of reorganization throughout Indian Country. See the testimony of Rupert Costo in Philip, Kenneth R. (ed.), *Indian Self-Rule: First-Hand Accounts of Indian-White Relations from Roosevelt to Reagan,* Howe Brothers Publishers, Salt Lake City, 1986. Also see Taylor, Graham D., *The New Deal and American Indian Tribalism: The Administration of the Indian Reorganization Act, 1934-45,* University of Nebraska Press, Lincoln, 1980.

87. For further background, see Deloria, Vine Jr., and Clifford M. Lytle, *The Nations Within: The Past and Future of American Indian Sovereignty,* Pantheon Press, New York, 1984.

88. Durham, Jimmie, "Native Americans and Colonialism," *The Guardian,* March 28, 1979. Also see Ammot, Teresa L., and Julie A. Matthei, *Race, Gender and Work: A Multicultural Economic History of Women ln the United States,* South End Press, Boston, 1991.

89. For a somewhat conservative, but nonetheless official acknowledgement of this situation, see U.S. Commission on Civil Rights, *The Navajo Nation: An American Colony,* Washington, D.C., 1976. Also see Garrity, *op. cit.*

90. Primarily at issue are the Navajo Reservation (Arizona/New Mexico), Acoma and Laguna Pueblos (New Mexico), Yakima Reservation (Washington State), and the Pine Ridge Sioux Reservation (South Dakota). For further

information—including the 1972 recommendation by the National Institute of Science that the Black Hills and Four Corners Regions, the areas of the U.S. most heavily populated by native people, be designated as National Sacrifice Areas—see Churchill, Ward, and Winona LaDuke, "Native America: The Political Economy of Radioactive Colonization," in Jaimes, *op. cit.*, pp. 241-66.

91. This idea has been increasingly fronted during the 1980s by the Council of Energy Resource Tribes (CERT), a federally-supported consortium of representatives from IRA Tribal Councils. See LaDuke, Winona, "The Council of Energy Resource Tribes: An Outsider's View In," in Jorgenson, *op. cit.*
92. See U.S. Bureau of the Census, *1980 Census of the Population, Supplementary Reports, Race of the Population by States,* 1980, U.S. Government Printing Office, Washington, D.C., 1981. Also see U.S. Bureau of the Census, Ancestry of the Population by State, 1980, Supp. Rep. PC80- SI-10, U.S. Government Printing Office, Washington, D.C., 1983.
93. This argument is advanced rather well in Seib, Gerald F., "Indians Awaken to their Lands' Energy Riches and Seek to Wrest Development from Companies," *Wall Street Journal* September 20, 1979.
94. See U.S. Bureau of the Census, *General Population Characteristics: United States Summary,* PC80-1-Bl, Pt. 1, U.S. Government Printing Office, Washington, D.C., 1983. Also see U.S. Bureau of the Census, *General Social and Economic Characteristics: United States Summary* (U.S. Government Printing Office, Washington, D.C., 1983) and *1980 Census of the Population, Supplementary Report: American Indian Areas and Alaska Native Villages* (U.S. Government Printing Office, Washington, D.C., 1984).
95. See U.S. Bureau of the Census, Population Division, Racial Statistics Branch, *A Statistical Profile of the American Indian Population, U.S.* Government Printing Office, Washington, D.C., 1984. Also see U.S. Department of Health and Human Services, *Chart Series Book,* Public Health Service, Washington, D.C., 1988 (HE20.9409.988).
96. The quote is taken from Galeano, Eduardo, *The Open Veins of Latin America: Five Centuries of the Pillage of a Conti-*

nent, Monthly Review Press, New York, 1973.

97. For analysis of the U.S. role in formulating the so-called "Nuremberg Doctrine" under which the nazi leadership was tried for violating "customary international law," see Smith, Bradley F., *The American Road to Nuremberg: The Documentary Record,* Stanford University Press, Palo Alto, CA, 1981. On specific aspects of the Second World War German performance which lead to comparison with the earlier American "Winning of the West," see Dallin, Alexander, *German Rule In Russia, 1941-1944,* Macmillan Publishers, London, 1957.
98. 60 Stat. 1049 (1946).
99. See Ehrenfeld, Alice, and Robert W. Barker (comps.), *Legislative Material on the Indian Claims Commission Act of 1946,* unpublished study, Washington, D.C., n.d.
100. For analysis, see Vance, John T., "The Congressional Mandate and the Indian Claims Commission," *North Dakota Law Review,* No. 45, 1969, pp. 325-36.
101. In 1956, the original ten year life-span of the commission was extended for five years. The process was repeated in 1961, 1967, 1972, and 1976. See U.S. Congress, Joint Committee on Appropriations, *Hearings on Appropriations for the Department of Interior,* 94th Cong., 1st Sess., U.S. Government Printing Office, Washington, D.C., 1976.
102. U.S. Department of Interior, *Indian Claims Commission, Final Report,* U.S. Government Printing Office, Washington, D.C., 1978.
103. Barsh, Russel, "Indian Land Claims Policy in the United States," *North Dakota Law Review,* No. 58, 1982, pp. 1-82.
104. Public Law 92-203; 85 Stat. 688, codified at 43 U.S.C. 1601 et seq. For background, see Berry, M.C., *The Alaska Pipeline: The Politics of Oil and Native Land Claims,* Indiana University Press, Bloomington/Indianapolis, 1975.
105. Lecture by Haunani Kay Trask, University of Colorado at Boulder, March 14, 1992 (tape on file). For "official" data, see Cannelora, L., *The Origin of Hawaiian Land Titles and the Rights of Native Tenants,* Security Title Corporation, Honolulu, 1974.
106. *Sioux Nation of Indians v. United States,* 448 U.S. 371 (1980). For analysis, see Hanson, Steven C., *"United States v. Sioux Nation: Political Questions, Moral Imperative and*

National Honor," *American Indian Law Review*, Vol. 8, No. 2, 1980, pp. 459-84.

107. *Western Shoshone Identifiable Group v. United States,* 40 Ind. Cl. Comm. 311 (1977); *United States v. Dann,* 706 F.2d 919, 926 (1983). For background, see Morris, Glenn T., "The Battle for Newe Segobia: The Western Shoshone Land Rights Struggle," in Ward Churchill (ed.), *Critical Issues ln Native North America, Vol. II,* International Work Group on Indigenous Affairs, Copenhagen, 1991, pp. 86-98.
108. For details, see Matthiessen, Peter, *In the Spirit of Crazy Horse,* Viking Press, New York, (2nd edition) 1991. Also see Churchill, Ward, and Jim Vander Wall, *Agents of Repression: The FBI's Secret Wars Against the Black Panther Party and the American Indian Movement,* South End Press, Boston, 1988.
109. The global study has been completed; see Martinez Cobo, Jose R. (Commission on Human Rights), *Study of the Problem of Discrimination Against Indigenous Populations, Final Report: Conclusions, Proposals and Recommendations,* U.N./ID # E/CN.4/Sub.2/ 1983/21 /Add.83, September 1983. At present, an enhancing study covering the extent and nature of treaty relations between indigenous peoples and various states around the world is being completed by the Cuban representative to the Working Group, Miguel Alfonso Martinez. Meanwhile, a draft Universal Declaration of the Rights of Indigenous Peoples has been prepared, and is in the process of revision prior to its submission to the U.N. General Assembly.
110. As the U.S. Department of State put it in its presentation to the Working Group in 1980 (at p. 13): "Actually, the U.S. Government entered into a trust relationship with the separate tribes in acknowledgement...of their political status as sovereign nations"; quoted in Dunbar Ortiz, Roxanne, "Protection of American Indian Territories in the United States: Applicability of International Law," in Imre Sutton (ed.), *Irredeemable America: The Indians' Estate and Land Claims,* University of New Mexico Press, Albuquerque, 1985, pp. 247-70.
111. This jockeying is well summarized in Anaya, S. James, "The Rights of Indigenous Peoples and International Law

in Historical and Contemporary Perspective," in Robert N. Clinton, Neil Jessup Newton and Monroe E. Price (eds.), *American Indian Law: Cases and Materials,* The Michie Co., Law Publishers, Charlottesville, VA, 1991, pp. 1257-76.

112. For analysis, see Dunbar Ortiz, *op. cit., pp. 260-1.*
113. The texts of these instruments may be found in Brownlie, *op. cit.*
114. In October 1985, President Reagan withdrew a 1946 U.S. declaration accepting ICJ jurisdiction in all matters of "international dispute." The withdrawal took effect in April 1986. This was in response to the ICJ determination in *Nicaragua v. United States,* the first substantive case ever brought before it to which the U.S. was a party. The ICJ ruled the U.S. action of mining Nicaraguan harbors in times of peace to be unlawful. The Reagan Administration formally rejected the authority of the ICJ to decide the matter (but removed the mines). It is undoubtedly significant that the Reagan instrument contained a clause accepting continued ICJ jurisdiction over matters pertaining to "international commercial relationships," thus attempting to convert the world court into a mechanism for mere trade arbitration. See *U.S. Terminates Acceptance of ICJ Compulsory Jurisdiction,* Department of State Bulletin No. 86, Washington, D.C., January 1986.
115. The United States declined to ratify the Genocide Convention until 1988, forty years after it became international law (and after more than 100 other nations had ratified it), and then only with an attached "Sovereignty Package" purporting to subordinate the convention to the U.S. Constitution (thereby seeking to protect certain aspects of genocidal conduct). The U.S. stipulation in this regard is, of course, invalid under Article 27 of the 1969 Vienna Convention on the Law of Treaties, and has been protested as such by such countries as Britain, Denmark and the Netherlands. Further, the Genocide Convention is now customary international law, meaning—according the United States' own Nuremberg Doctrine—that it is binding upon the U.S., whether Congress ratifies its terms or not. For further analysis, see LeBlanc, Lawrence J., *The United States and the Genocide Convention,* Duke Univer-

sity Press, Durham (N.C.)/London, 1991.

116. The Inouye Committee is following up on the groundwork laid for such a maneuver by such earlier incorporative legislation as the Indian Civil Rights Act of 1968 (Public Law 90-284; 82 Stat. 77, codified in part at 25 U.S.C. 1301 *et seq.)* and the Indian Self-Determination and Educational Assistance Act of 1975 (Public Law 93-638; 88 Stat. 2203, codified at 25 U.S.C. 450a and elsewhere in Titles 25, 42, and 50, U.S.C.A.). It should be noted that the latter completely inverts international definitions of "self-determination," providing instead for an Indian preference in the hiring of individuals to fill positions within the federal system of administering Indian Country. Critics such as AIM leader Russell Means have therefore dubbed it the "Indian Self Administration Act." For details on the committee itself, see U.S. Senate, Select Committee on Indian Affairs, *Final Report and Legislative Recommendations: A Report of the Special Committee on Investigations,* 101st Cong. 2d Sess., U.S. Government Printing Office, Washington, D.C., 1989.

117. For the context of this rhetoric, see Chomsky, Noam, "'What We Say Goes': The Middle East in the New World Order," in Cynthia Peters (ed.), *Collateral Damage: The "New World Order" At Home and Abroad,* South End Press, Boston, 1992, pp. 49-92.

118. For further information, see Chomsky, Noam, and Eqbal Ahmad, "The Gulf Crisis: How We Got There," in Greg Bates (ed.), *Mobilizing Democracy: Changing the U.S. Role in the Middle East,* Common Courage Press, Monroe, ME, 1991, pp. 3-24.

Part II
In Struggle for the Land

Wandering amongst the opulence
wondering what not to touch
times not knowing
times getting bit
times of temptation
times of seduction
Wandering in the poverty
touched by everything
knowing the bite
no time for temptation
only time for doing
babylon in terror
world run over by machines
the economics of captured dreams
the rich are the poorer
while the poor are waiting
everyone pretending to live
calling exploitation progress
calling submission freedom
calling madness profit
calling earth a plan et
plaguing her

with civilization...

—John Trudell—
from *Living in Reality*

Struggle to Regain a Stolen Homeland

The Iroquois Land Claims in Upstate New York

> The inhabitants of your country districts regard—wrongfully, it is true—Indians and forests as natural enemies which must be exterminated by fire and sword and brandy, in order that they may seize their territory. They regard themselves and their posterity, as collateral heirs to all the magnificent portion of land which God has created from Cumberland and Ohio to the Pacific Ocean.
>
> —Pierre Samuel Du Pont de Nemours—
> letter to Thomas Jefferson
> December 17, 1801

One of the longest fought and more complicated land-claims struggles in the U.S. is that of the Haudenosaunee, or Iroquois Six Nations Confederacy. While the 1782 Treaty of Paris ended hostilities between the British Crown and its secessionist subjects in the thirteen colonies, it had no direct effect upon the state of war existing between those subjects and indigenous nations allied with the Crown. And, while George III had quit-claimed his property rights under the Doctrine of Discovery to the affected portion of North America by treaty, it was the opinion of Thomas Jefferson and others that this action did not vest title to these lands in the newly born United States.[1] On both counts, the Continental Congress found it imperative to enter into treaty arrangements with Indian nations as expeditiously as possible. A very high priority in this regard was accorded the Iroquois Confederacy, four members of which—the Mohawks, Senecas, Cayugas and Onondagas—had fought with the British (the remaining two, the Oneidas and Tuscaroras, had remained largely neutral but occasionally provided assistance to the colonists).[2]

During October 1784, the government conducted extensive negotiations with representatives of the Six Nations at Fort Stanwix. The resulting treaty stipulated that the Indians relinquish claim to all lands lying west of a north-south line running from Niagara to the border of Pennsylvania—territory within the Ohio Valley (a provision reinforced in the 1789 Treaty of Fort Harmar)—and the land on which Fort Oswego had been built. In exchange, the U.S. guaranteed three of the four hostile nations the bulk of their traditional homelands. The Oneida and Tuscarora were also "secured in the possession of the lands on which they are now settled." Altogether, the area in question came to about six million acres, or half of the present state of New York (see map). The agreement, while meeting most of the Indians' needs, was quite useful to the U.S. central government:

> First...in order to sell [land in the Ohio River area] and settle it, the Continental Congress needed to extinguish Indian title, including any claims by the Iroquois of New York. Second, the commissioners wanted to punish the...Senecas. Thus they forced the Senecas to surrender most of their land in New York [and Pennsylvania] to the United States...Third, the United States...wanted to secure peace by confirming to the [Indians] their remaining lands. Fourth, the United States was anxious to protect its frontier from the British in Canada by securing land for forts and roads along lakes Erie and Ontario.[3]

New York state, needless to say, was rather less enthusiastic about the terms of the treaty. It had already attempted, unsuccessfully, to obtain additional land cessions from the Iroquois during meetings conducted prior to arrival of the federal delegation at Fort Stanwix.[4] Arti-

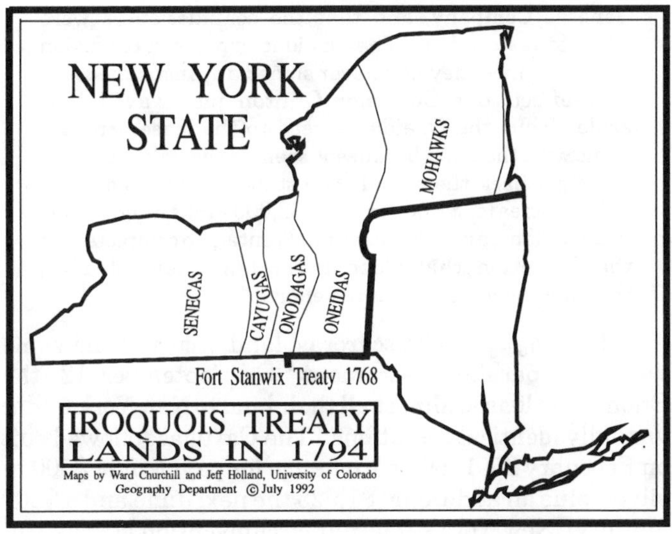

cle IX of the Articles of Confederation—and subsequently Article I (Section 10) and the commerce clause of the Constitution—combined to render treaty-making and outright purchases of Indian land by states illegal. New York then resorted to subterfuge, securing a series of 26 "leases," many of them for 999 years, on almost all native territory within its boundaries. The Haudenosaunee initially agreed to these transactions because of Governor Robert N. Clinton's duplicitous assurances that leases represented a way for them to keep their land, and for his government to "extend its protection over their property against the dealings of unscrupulous white land speculators" in the private sector. The first such arrangement was forged with the Oneidas. In a meeting begun at Fort Schuyler on August 28, 1788:

> The New York commissioners...led them to believe that they had [already] lost all their land to the New York Genesee Company, and that the commissioners were there to restore title. The Oneidas expressed confusion over this since they had never signed any instruments to that effect, but Governor Clinton just waved that aside...Thus the Oneidas agreed to the lease arrangement with the state because it seemed the only way they could get back their land. The state received some five million acres for $2,000 in cash, $2,000 in clothing, $1,000 in provisions, and $600 in annual rental. So complete was the deception that Good Peter [an Oneida leader] thanked the governor for his efforts.[5]

Leasing of the Tuscaroras' land occurred the same day, by a parallel instrument.[6] On September 12, the Onondagas leased almost all their land to New York under virtually identical conditions.[7] The Cayugas followed suit on February 25, 1789, in exchange for payment of $500 in silver, plus an additional $1,625 the next June and a $500 annuity.[8] New York's flagrant circumvention of constitutional restrictions on non-federal acquisitions of Indian land was a major factor in congressional tightening of its mechanisms of control over such activities in the first so-called Indian Trade and Intercourse Act of 1790 (1 Stat. 37).[9] Clinton, however, simply shifted to a different ruse, back-dating his maneuvers by announcing in 1791 that the state would honor a 999 year lease negotiated in 1787 by a private speculator named John Livingston. The lease covered 800,000 acres of mainly Mohawk land, but had been declared null and void by the state legislature in 1788.[10]

The federal government became concerned that such dealings by New York might push the Iroquois, the largely landless Senecas in particular, into joining the Shawnee leader Tecumseh's alliance resisting further U.S. expansion into the Ohio Valley. It sent a new commission to meet with the Haudenosaunee leadership at the principle

Seneca town of Canandaigua in 1794. In exchange for the Indians' pledge not to bear arms against the U.S., their ownership of the lands guaranteed them at Fort Stanwix was reaffirmed, the state's leases notwithstanding, and the bulk of the Seneca territory in Pennsylvania was restored.[11] New York nonetheless began parceling out sections of the leased lands in subleases to the very "unscrupulous whites" it had pledged to guard against. On September 15, 1797, the Holland Land Company—in which many members of the state government had invested—assumed control over all but ten tracts of land, totalling 397 square miles, of the Fort Stanwix Treaty area. The leasing instrument purportedly "extinguished" native title to the land.[12] (See map.)

Expropriation

Tecumseh's 1794 defeat at Fallen Timbers diminished the military importance of the Six Nations. The federal government did nothing to correct the situation despite Iroquois protests. New York was thus emboldened to proceed with its appropriations of native land. In 1810, the Holland Company sold some 200,000 acres of its holdings in Seneca and Tuscarora land to its accountant, David A. Ogden, at a price of 50¢ per acre. Ogden then formed his own company and issued shares against development of this land, many of them to Albany politicians. Thus capitalized, he was able to push through a deal in 1826 to buy a further 1,000 acres of previously unleased reservation land at 58¢ per acre. A federal investigation into the affair was quashed by Secretary of War Peter B. Porter, himself a major stockholder of the Ogden Land Company, in 1828.[13]

Under such circumstances, most of the Oneidas requested in 1831 that what was left of their New York holdings, which they were sure they would lose anyway, be exchanged for a 500,000 acre parcel purchased from the

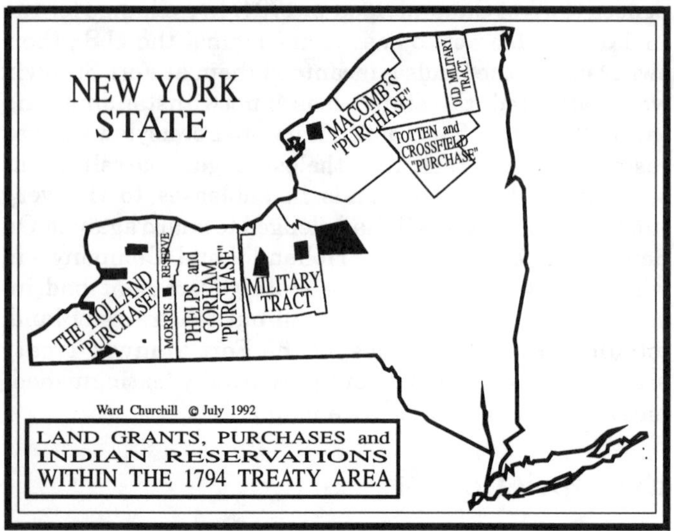

Menominees in Wisconsin. President Andrew Jackson, at the time pursuing his policy of general Indian removal to points west of the Mississippi, readily agreed.[14]

In the climate of removal, U.S. officials actively colluded with the speculators. On January 15, 1838, federal commissioners oversaw the signing of the Treaty of Buffalo Creek, wherein 102,069 acres of Seneca land was "ceded" directly to the Ogden Company. The $202,000 purchase price was divided almost evenly between the government (to be held "in trust" for the Indians), and individual non-Indians seeking to buy and "improve" plots in the former reservation area. At the same time, what was left of the Cayuga, Oneida, Onondaga and Tuscarora holdings were wiped out, at an aggregate cost of $400,000 to Ogden.[15] The Iroquois were told they should relocate en mass to Missouri. Although the Six Nations never consented to the treaty, and it was never properly ratified by the Senate, President Martin Van Buren proclaimed it to be the law of the land on April 4, 1840.[16]

By 1841, Iroquois complaints about the Buffalo Creek Treaty were being joined by increasing numbers of non-Indians outraged not so much by the loss of land to Indians as by the obvious corruption involved in its terms.[17] Consequently, in 1842, a second Treaty of Buffalo Creek was negotiated. Under its provisions, the U.S. again acknowledged the Haudenosaunee right to reside in New York and restored small areas as the Allegany and Cattaraugus Seneca reservations. The Onondaga Reservation was also reconstituted on a 7,300 acre land base, the Tuscarora Reservation on about 2,500 acres. The Ogden Company was allowed to keep the rest.[18] The Tonawanda Seneca Band immediately filed a formal protest of these terms with the Senate, and, in 1857, received a $256,000 "award" of their own money with which to "buy back" a minor portion of its former territory from Ogden.[19]

Beginning in 1855, the Erie Railway Company entered the picture, setting out to lease significant portions of both Cattaraugus and Allegany. Sensing the depth of then prevailing federal support for railroad construction, the state judiciary seized the opportunity to cast an aura of legitimacy upon all of New York's other illicit leasing arrangements:

> Though the leases were ratified by New York, the state's supreme court in 1875 invalidated them. In recognition of this action, the New York legislature passed a concurrent resolution [a century after the fact] that state action was not sufficient to ratify leases because "Congress alone possesses the power to deal with and for the Indians." Instead of setting aside the leases, Congress in 1875 passed an act authorizing [them]. The state now made leases renewable for twelve years, and by an amendment in 1890 the years were extended to ninety-nine. Later the Supreme court of New York deemed them perpetual.[20]

As a result, by 1889, 80 percent of all Iroquois reservation land in New York was under lease to non-Indian interests and individuals. The same year, a commission was appointed by Albany to examine the state's "Indian Problem." Rather than "suggesting that the leasing of four-fifths of their land had deterred Indian welfare, the commission criticized the Indians for not growing enough to feed themselves," thereby placing an "undue burden" on those profiting from their land. Chancellor C.N. Sims of Syracuse University, a commission member, argued strongly that only "obliteration of the tribes, conferral of citizenship, and allotment of lands" would set things right.[21] Washington duly set out to undertake allotment, but was stunned to discover it was stymied by the "underlying title" to much of the reserved Iroquois land it had allowed the Ogden Company to obtain over the years. In 1895, Congress passed a bill authorizing a buy-out of the Ogden interest (again at taxpayer expense), but the company upped its asking price for the desired acreage from $50,000 to $270,000. Negotiations thereupon collapsed, and the Six Nations were spared the trauma (and further land loss) of the allotment process.[22]

In 1900, New York Governor Theodore Roosevelt created a commission to reexamine the matter. This led to introduction of another bill (HR 12270) in 1902 aimed at allotting the Seneca reservations (with 50,000 acres in all, they were by far the largest remaining Iroquois land areas) by paying Ogden $200,000 of the Indians' "trust funds" to abandon its claims on Allegany and Cattaraugus.[23] The Senecas retained attorney John VanVoorhis to argue that the Ogden claim was invalid because, for more than 100 years, the company had not been compelled to pay so much as a nickle of tax on the acreage it professed to "own." By this, VanVoorhis contended, both Ogden and the government had all along admitted—for purposes of federal law— that the land was really still the property of "Indians not taxed." The new bill was withdrawn in some confusion at this point, and allotment was again averted.[24] In 1905, the Senecas carried the tax issue into court in an attempt to clear their land title, but the case was dismissed under the premise that they had "no legal standing to sue" non-Indians.[25]

A third attempt to allot the Six Nations reservations (HR 18735) foundered in 1914, as did a New York state constitutional amendment, proposed in 1915, to effectively abolish the reservations. Even worse, from New York's viewpoint, in 1919 the U.S. Justice Department for the first time acted on behalf of the Iroquois, filing a suit which (re)established a 32 acre "reservation" in the state for the Oneidas.[26] The state legislature responded by creating yet another commission, this one headed by attorney Edward A. Everett, to conduct a comprehensive study of land title questions in New York and to make recommendations as to how they might be cleared up across-the-board, once and for all.[27] After more than two years of hearings and intensive research, Everett handed in a totally unanticipated conclusion: The Six Nations still possessed legal title to all six million acres of the Fort Stanwix treaty area.

> He cited international law to the effect that there are only two ways to take a country away from a people possessing it—purchase or conquest. The Europeans who came here did recognize that the Indians were in possession and so, in his opinion, thus recognized their status as nations...If then, the Indians did hold fee to the land, how did they lose it?... [T]he Indians were [again] recognized by George Washington as a nation at the Treaty of 1784. Hence, they were as of 1922 owners of all the land [reserved by] them in that treaty unless they had ceded it by a treaty equally valid and binding.[28]

Everett reinforced his basic finding with reference to the Treaties of Fort Harmar and Canandaigua, discounted both Buffalo Creek Treaties as fraudulent, and rejected both the leases of the state and those taken by entities such as the Holland and Ogden Companies as having no legal validity at all.[29] The Albany government quickly shelved the report rather than publishing it, but it couldn't prevent the implications from being discussed throughout the Six Nations. On August 21, 1922, a council meeting was held at Onondaga for purposes of retaining Mrs. Lulu G. Stillman, Everett's secretary, to do research on the exact boundaries of the Fort Stanwix treaty area.[30] The Iroquois land claim struggle had shifted from dogged resistance to dispossession to the offensive strategy of land recovery. The first test case, *James Deere v. St. Lawrence River Power Company* (32 F.2d 550), was filed on June 26, 1925 in an attempt to regain a portion of the St. Regis Mohawk Reservation taken by New York. The federal government declined to intervene on the Mohawks' behalf—though it was its "trust responsibility" to do so—and the suit was dismissed by a district court judge on October 10, 1927. The dismissal was upheld on appeal in April 1929.[31]

Efforts at Land Recovery

Things remained quiet on the land claims front during the 1930s, as the Haudenosaunee were mainly preoccupied with preventing the supplanting of their traditional Longhouse form of government by "tribal councils" sponsored by the Bureau of Indian Affairs via the Indian Reorganization Act of 1934. Probably as a means of coaxing them into a more favorable view of federal intentions under the IRA, Indian Commissioner John Collier agreed towards the end of the decade that his agency would finally provide at least limited support to Iroquois claims litigation. This resulted, in 1941, in the Justice Department's filing of *U.S. v. Forness* (125 F.2d 928) on behalf of the Allegany Senecas. The suit—ostensibly aimed at eviction of an individual who had refused to pay his $4 per year rent to the Indians for eight years—actually sought to enforce a resolution of the Seneca Nation cancelling hundreds of low cost 99 year leases taken in the City of Salamanca, on the reservation, in

1892. Intervening for the defendants was the Salamanca Trust Corporation, a mortgage institution holding much of the paper at issue. Although the case was ultimately unsuccessful in its primary objective, it did clarify that New York law had no bearing on Indian leasing arrangements.[32]

This was partly "corrected," in the state view, on July 2, 1948 and September 13, 1950, when Congress passed bills placing the Six Nations under New York jurisdiction in first criminal and then civil matters.[33] Federal responsibility to assist Indians in pursuing treaty-based land claims was nonetheless explicitly preserved.[34] Washington, of course, elected to treat this obligation in its usual cavalier fashion, plunging ahead during the 1950s—while the Indians were mired in efforts to prevent termination of their federal recognition altogether—with the flooding of 130 acres of the St. Regis Reservation near Messena (and about 1,300 acres of the Caughnawaga Mohawk Reserve in Canada) as part of the St. Lawrence Seaway Project.[35] The government also proceeded with plans to flood more than 9,000 acres of the Allegany Reservation as a by-product of constructing the Kinzua Dam. Although studies revealed an alternative siting of the dam would not only spare the Seneca land from flooding but better serve "the greater public good" for which it was supposedly intended, Congress pushed ahead.[36] The Senecas protested the project as a clear violation of the Fort Stanwix guarantees, a position with which lower federal courts agreed, but the Supreme Court declined to review the question and Army Corps of Engineers completed the dam in 1967.[37]

Meanwhile, the New York State Power Authority was attempting to seize more than half (1,383 acres) of the Tuscarora Reservation, near Buffalo, as a reservoir for the Niagara Power Project. In April 1958, the Tuscaroras physically blocked access of construction workers to the site and several were arrested (charges were later dropped). A federal district judge entered a temporary restraining order against the state, but the appellate court ruled that congressional issuance of a license the Federal Power Commission constituted sufficient grounds for the state to "exercise eminent domain" over native property.[38] The Supreme Court again refused to hear the resulting Haudenosaunee appeal. A "compromise" was then implemented in which the state flooded "only" 560 acres, or about one-eighth of the remaining Tuscarora land.[39]

Ganiekeh

By the early '60s, it had become apparent that the Iroquois, because their territory fell "within the boundaries of one of the original thirteen states," would be disallowed from seeking redress through the Indian Claims Commission.[40] The decade was largely devoted to a protracted series of discussions between state officials and various sectors of the Iroquois leadership. Agreements were reached in areas related to education, housing and revenue sharing, but on the issues of land claims and jurisdiction, the position of Longhouse traditionals was unflinching. In their view, the state holds no rights over the Iroquois in either sphere.[41] Their point was punctuated on May 13, 1974, when Mohawks from St. Regis and Caughnawaga occupied an area at Ganiekeh (Moss Lake), in the Adirondack Mountains. They proclaimed the site to be sovereign Mohawk territory under the Fort Stanwix Treaty—"[We] represent a cloud of title not only to [this] 612.7 acres in Herkimer County but to all of northeastern N.Y."—and set out to defend it (and themselves) by force of arms.[42]

After a pair of local vigilantes engaged in harassing the Indians were wounded by return gunfire in October, the state filed for eviction in federal court. The matter was bounced back on the premise that it was not a federal issue, and the New York attorney general—undoubtedly discomfited at the publicity prospects entailed in an armed confrontation on the scale of the 1973 Wounded Knee siege—let the case die.[43] Alternatively, the state dispatched a negotiating team headed by future governor Mario Cuomo. In May 1977, the "Moss Lake Agreement" was reached, and the Mohawks assumed permanent possession of a land parcel at Miner Lake, in the town of Altona, and another in the McComb Reforestation Area.[44] Mohawk possession of the sites remains ongoing in 1992, a circumstance which has prompted others among the Six Nations to pursue land recovery through a broader range of tactics and, perhaps, with greater vigor than they might have otherwise (e.g., Mohawk actions taken in Canada, concerning a land dispute at the Oka Reserve, near Montreal, during 1990).

The Oneida Land Claims

As all this was going on, the Oneidas had, in 1970, filed the first of the really significant Iroquois land claims suits. The case, *Oneida Indian Nation of New York v. County of Oneida* (70-CV-35 (N.D.N.Y.)), charged that the transfer of 100,000 acres of Oneida land to New York via a 1795 lease engineered by Governor Clinton was fraudulent and invalid on both constitutional grounds and because it violated the 1790 Trade and Intercourse Act. The suit was dismissed because of the usual "Indians lack legal standing" argument, but reinstated by the Supreme Court in 1974.[45] Compelled to actually examine the merits of the case for the first time, the U.S. District Court agreed with the Indians (and the Everett Report) that title still rested with the Oneidas.

> The plaintiffs have established a claim for violation of the Nonintercourse Act. Unless the Act is to be considered nugatory, it must be concluded that the plaintiff's right of occupancy and possession of the land in question was not alienated. By the deed of 1795, the State acquired no

rights against the plaintiffs; consequently, its successors, the defendant counties, are in no better position.[46]

Terming the Oneidas a "legal fiction," and the lower courts' rulings "racist," attorney for the defendants Allan Van Gestel appealed to the Supreme Court.[47] On October 1, 1984, the high court ruled against Van Gestel and ordered his clients to work out an accommodation, indemnified by the state, including land restoration, compensation and rent on unrecovered areas.[48] Van Gestel continued to howl that "the common people" of Oneida and Madison Counties were being "held hostage," but as the Oneidas' attorney, Arlinda Locklear, put it in 1986:

> One final word about responsibility for the Oneida claims. It is true that the original sin here was committed by the United States and the state of New York. It is also no doubt true that there are a number of innocent landowners in the area, i.e., individuals who acquired their land with no knowledge of the Oneida claim to it. But those facts alone do not end the inquiry respecting ultimate responsibility. Whatever the knowledge of the claims before then, the landowners have certainly been aware of the Oneida claims since 1970 when the first suit was filed. Since that time, the landowners have done nothing to seek a speedy and just resolution of the claims. Instead, they have as a point of principle denied the validity of the claims and pursued the litigation, determined to prove the claims to be frivolous. Now that the landowners have failed in that effort, they loudly protest their innocence in the entire matter. The Oneidas, on the other hand, have since 1970 repeatedly expressed their preference for an out-of-court resolution of their claims. Had the landowners joined with the Oneidas sixteen years ago in seeking a just resolution, the claims would no doubt be resolved today. For that reason, the landowners share in the responsibility for the situation in which they find themselves today.[49]

Others would do well to heed these words because,

as Locklear pointed out, the Oneida case "paved the legal way for other Indian land claims."[50] Not least of these are other suits by the Oneidas themselves. In 1978, the New York Oneidas filed for adjudication of title to the entirety of their Fort Stanwix claim—about 4.5 million acres—a case effecting not only Oneida and Madison Counties, but Broome, Chenango, Cortland, Herkimer, Jefferson, Lewis, Onondaga, Oswego, St. Lawrence and Tiago Counties as well (this matter was shelved, pending final resolution of the first Oneida claims litigation).[51] In December 1979, the Oneida Nation of Wisconsin and the Thames Band of Southgold, Ontario, joined in an action pursuing rights in the same claim area, but naming the state rather than individual counties as defendant.[52] The Cayuga Nation, landless throughout the twentieth century, has also filed suit against Cayuga and Seneca Counties for recovery of 64,015 acres taken during Clinton's leasing foray of 1789 (the Cayuga claim may develop into an action overlapping with those of the Oneida; see map).[53]

The Cayuga Land Claims

The latter case, filed on November 19, 1980, resulted from attempts by the Cayugas to negotiate some sort of land base and compensation for themselves with federal, state and county officials from the mid-70s onward. By August 1979, they had worked out a tentative agreement that would have provided them with the 1,852 acre Sampson Park area in southern Seneca County, the 3,629 acre Hector Land Use Area in the same county, and an $8 million trust account established by the Secretary of Interior (up to $2.5 million of which would be used to buy additional land).[54] Although not one square inch of their holdings was threatened by the arrangement, the response of the local non-Indian population was rabid. To quote Paul D. Moonan, Sr., president of the local Monroe Title and Abstract Company: "The Cayugas have no moral

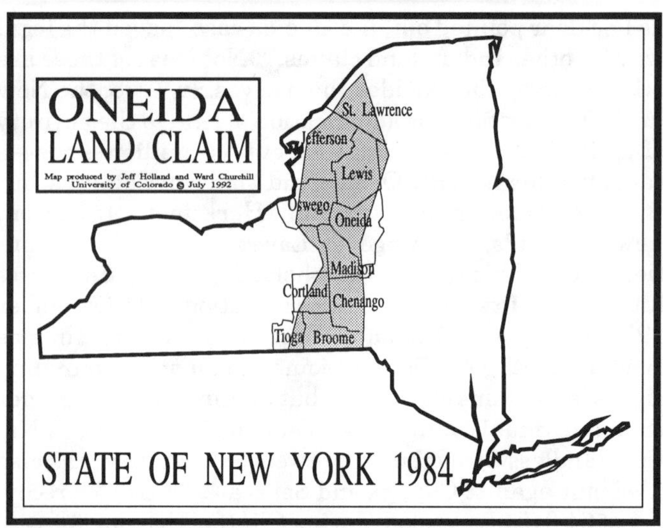

or legal justification for their claim." Wisner Kinne, a farmer near the town of Ovid, immediately founded the Seneca County Liberation Organization, premised on a virulent anti-Indianism. SCLO attracted several hundred highly vocal members from the sparsely populated county.

A bill to authorize the settlement subsequently failed due to this "white backlash," and so the Cayugas went to court to obtain a much larger area, eviction of 7,000 county residents and $350 million in trespass damages. Attempts by attorneys for SCLO to have the suit dismissed failed in 1982, as did a 1984 compromise offer initiated by Representative Frank Horton. The latter, which might have well been accepted by the Cayugas, would have provided them the 3,200 acre Howland Game Management Reserve along the Seneca River, a 2,850 acre parcel on Lake Ontario (owned by the Rochester Gas and Electric Company), and a 2,000 acre parcel adjoining Sampson State Park. Additionally, the Cayugas would have received "well in excess" of the $8 million they'd originally sought. While SCLO appears to have decided acquiescence was by this point the better part of valor, the proposal came under heavy attack from non-Indian environmentalists "concerned about the animals in the Howland Reserve." Ultimately, it was nixed by Ronald Reagan in 1987, not because he was concerned with area fauna, but because he was angry with Horton for voting against contra-aid. The suit is therefore ongoing.[55]

Salamanca

At the town of Salamanca, the leases to which expired at the end of 1991, the Allegany Senecas also undertook decisive action during the second half of the '80s. Beginning as early as 1986, they stipulated the intent not to renew, and to begin eviction proceedings against non-Indian lease and mortgage holders in the area, unless the terms of any new arrangement were considerably recast in their favor (i.e., clarification of Seneca title, shorter leasing period, fair rates for property rental, and "preeminent jurisdiction" over both the land and cash income derived from it).[56] A further precondition to lease renewal was that compensation be made for all non-payment and under-payment of fair rental values of Seneca property accruing from the last lease. Although these demands unleashed a storm of protest from local whites—who, as usual, argued vociferously that the Indian owners of the land held no rights to it—they were unsuccessful in both court and Congress.[57] At this juncture, all essential Seneca terms have been met, and Congress has passed the Seneca Nation Settlement Act of 1990, including a settlement award of $60 million (the cost of which is to be shared by federal, state and local non-Indian governments) for rental monies they should have received over the past 99 years, but didn't.[58]

Conclusion

The limited but real gains posted thus far, in both the Oneida land claims and with regard to renegotiation of the Salamanca lease, point to a viable strategy for a gradual recovery of Haudenosaunee land and jurisdictional rights in upstate New York during the years ahead. As of this writing, the second Oneida suit is in process, as is the Cayuga suit. Based against the sort of settlement achieved in the earlier Oneida win, these seem likely to generate, if not a truly fair resolution of the issues raised, a marked improvement in the circumstances of both nations. Within the next two years, a longterm lease with the Onondagas by which the State of New York has secured use of the land on which the City of Syracuse presently sits will expire. Following the pattern evidenced at Salamanca, it is likely that this too will work out favorably, providing a material basis from which the Onondagas can better pursue restoration of rural areas adjoining their presently tiny reservation.

Overall, it seems probable that such efforts at litigation and negotiation will continue over the next ten to twenty years, and may serve to enhance the relative positions of the Tuscarora and Mohawk nations as well as their four confederates. The increasing scope of native jurisdiction in New York which such a process would necessarily entail may accomplish a changed sensibility among the state's non-Indians as they discover firsthand that a genuine exercise of indigenous rights does not automatically lead to their disenfranchisement or dispossession of personal property. Indeed, it may be that at least some sectors of New York's non-Indian population may learn that coming under Indian jurisdiction can be preferable to remaining under the jurisdiction of the state (which has, among other things, one of the highest tax levies in the country). If so, it may be that the ongoing (re)assertion of Haudenosaunee sovereignty within the

1794 treaty territory may develop peacefully and with a reasonably high degree of Indian/white cooperation over the long run, reversing the unrelenting trajectory of Euroamerican avarice, duplicity and racism which has marked this relationship over the past two centuries.

However, the methods of litigation and negotiation will surely reach the limit of the state's willingness or ability to give ground, absent a profound alteration in the attitudes of the interloping white populace. Conflicts of the sort previewed at Ganiekeh and Oka will be the inevitable result. Something of a crossroads is thus at hand in northern New York state; things could go either way. And in the final analysis, the choice is one which resides with the state and its immigrant citizens. The Indians own the land by all conceivable legal, moral and ethical definitions. They always have, and will continue to until *they* decide otherwise. As a whole, they have demonstrated an amazing patience with those who have presumed to take what was and is not theirs. But such patience cannot last forever.

Notes

1. Jefferson and other "radicals" held U.S. sovereignty accrued from the country itself and did not "devolve" from the British Crown. Hence, U.S. land title could not devolve from the Crown. Put another way, Jefferson—in contrast to John Marshall—held that Britain's asserted discovery rights in North America had no bearing on U.S. rights to occupancy on the continent. See Wood, Gordon, *The Creation of the American Republic, 1776-1787,* University of North Carolina Press, Chapel Hill, 1969, pp. 162-96.
2. See generally, Graymont, Barbara, *The Iroquois In the American Revolution,* Syracuse University Press, Syracuse, NY, 1975. The concern felt by Congress with regard to the Iroquois as a military threat, and the consequent need to reach an accommodation with them, is expressed often in early official correspondence. See Ford, Washington C., *et al.* (eds. and comps.), *Journals of the Continental*

Congress, 1774-1789, (34 Vols.), U.S. Government Printing Office, Washington, D.C.,1904-1937.

3. Campisi, Jack, "From Fort Stanwix to Canandaigua: National Policy, States' Rights and Indian Land," in Christopher Vescey and William A. Starna (eds.), *Iroquois Land Claims,* Syracuse University Press, Syracuse, NY, 1988, pp. 49-65; quote from p. 55. Also see Manley, Henry M., *The Treaty of Fort Stanwix, 1784,* Rome Sentinel Publications, Rome, NY, 1932.
4. For an account of these meetings, conducted by New York's Governor Clinton during August and September 1784, see Hough, Franklin B. (ed.), *Proceedings of the Commissioners of Indian Affairs, Appointed by Law for Extinguishment of Indian Titles in the State of New York,* (2 Vols.), John Munsell Publishers, Albany, NY, 1861, pp. 41-63.
5. Campisi, *op. cit.,* p. 59. Clinton lied, bold faced. New York's references to the Genesee Company concerned a bid by that group of land speculators to lease Oneida land which the Indians had not only rejected, but which the state legislature had refused to approve. In effect, the Oneida's had lost no land, were unlikely to, and the governor knew it.
6. See Clinton, George, *Public Papers of George Clinton: First Governor of New York, Vol. 8,* Albany, NY, 1904.
7. The price paid by New York for the Onondaga lease was "1,000 French crowns, 200 pounds in clothing, plus a $500 annuity." See Upton, Helen M., *The Everett Report in Historical Perspective: The Indians of New York New York State Bicentennial Commission,* Albany, 1980, p. 35.
8. *Ibid,* p. 38.
9. The relevant portion of the statute's text reads: "[N]o sale of lands made by any Indians, or any nation or tribe of Indians within the United States, shall be valid to any person or persons, or to any state, whether having the right of pre-emption to such lands or not, unless the same shall be made and duly executed at some public treaty, held under the authority of the United States."
10. Upton, *op. cit,* p. 40.
11. For ratification discussion on the meaning of the Treaty of Canandaigua, see *American State Papers: Documents, Legislative and Executive of the Congress of the United*

States, from the First Session to the Third Session of the Thirteenth Congress, Inclusive, (Vol. 4), Gales and Seaton Publishers, Washington, D.C., 1832, pp. 545-70. On Tecumseh's alliance, see Edmunds, R. David, *Tecumseh and the Quest for Indian Leadership,* Little, Brown and Company, Publishers, Boston, 1984.

12. See Edwards, Paul D., *The Holland Company,* Buffalo Historical Society, Buffalo, NY, 1924.
13. See Nammack, Georgiana C., *Fraud, Politics, and the Dispossession of the Indians: The Iroquois Frontier and the Colonial Perlad,* University of Oklahoma Press, Norman, 1969. Also see Manley, Henry S., "Red Jacket's Last Campaign," *New York History,* No. 21, April 1950.
14. See Manley, Henry S., "Buying Buffalo from the Indians," *New York History,* No. 28, July 1947.
15. Kappler, Charles J., *Indian Treaties, 1778-1883,* Interland Publishing Co., New York, 1973, pp. 374-8. Also see Society of Friend (Hicksite), *The Case of the Seneca Indians in the State of New York,* Earl E. Coleman Publisher, Stanfordville, NY (reprint of 1840 edition), 1979.
16. Most principle leaders of the Six Nations never signed the Buffalo Creek Treaty. Each of the three consecutive votes taken in the Senate on ratification (requiring two-thirds affirmation to be lawful) resulted in a tie, broken only by the "aye" vote of Vice President Richard Johnson. See Manley, "Buying Buffalo from the Indians," *op. cit.*
17. U.S. House of Representatives, H. Doc. 66, 26th Cong., 2d Sess., January 6, 1841.
18. Kappler, *op. cit.*, p. 397.
19. The Tonawanda protest appears as U.S. Senate, S. Doc. 273, 29th Cong., 2d Sess., April 2, 1842.
20. On the award, made on November 5, 1857, see *Documents of the Assembly of the State of New York* 112th Sess., Doc. 51, Albany, 1889, pp. 167-70.
21. Upton, *op. cit.*, p. 53. The New York Supreme Court's invalidation of the leases is covered in *U.S. v. Forness,* 125 F.2d 928 (1942). On the court's deeming of the leases to be perpetual, see U.S. House of Representatives, Committee on Indian Affairs, *Hearings In Favor of House Bill No. 12270,* 57th Cong., 2d Sess., U.S. Government Printing Office, Washington, D.C., 1902.

22. Assembly Doc. 51, *op. cit.*, pp. 43, 408.
23. 28 Stat. *887*, March 2,1895.
24. *Hearings in Favor of House Bill No. 12270, op. cit.* p. 23.
25. *Ibid.*, p.66.
26. The original case is *Seneca Nation vs. Appleby*, 127 AD 770 (1905). It was appealed as *Seneca Nation vs. Appleby*, 196 NY 318 (1906).
27. The case, *United States v. Boylan*, 265 Fed. 165 (2d Cir. 1920), is important not because of the paltry quantity of land restored, but because it was the first time the federal judiciary formally acknowledged that New York had never acquired legal title to Iroquois land. It was also one of the very few times in American history when non-Indians were actually evicted in order that Indians might recover illegally-taken property.
28. New York State Indian Commission Act, Chapter 590, Laws of New York, May 12, 1919.
29. Upton, *op. cit.*, p. 99.
30. The document is Everett, Edward A., *Report of the New York State Indian Commission*, Albany, NY, March 17, 1922 (unpublished), pp. 308-9, 322-30.
31. Stenographic record of August 21, 1922 meeting, Stillman files.
32. Upton, *op. cit.*, pp. 124-9.
33. The total amount to be paid the Senecas for rental of their Salamanca property was $6,000 per year, much of which had gone unpaid since the mid-30s. The judges found the federal government to have defaulted on its obligation to regulate state and private leases of Seneca land, and instructed it to take an active role in the future. See Hauptman, Laurence M., "The Historical Background to the Present-Day Seneca Nation-Salamanca Lease Controversy," in *Iroquois Land Claims, op. cit.*, pp. 101-22. Also see Merrill, Arch, "The Salamanca Lease Settlement," *American Indian*, No. 1, 1944.
34. These laws, which were replicated in Kansas and Iowa during 1952, predate the more general application of state. Jurisdiction to Indians embodied in Public Law 280, passed in August 1953. U.S. Congress, Joint Legislative Committee, *Report* (Leg. Doc. 74), 83rd Cong., 1st Sess., U.S. Government Printing Office, Washington, D.C., 1953.

35. This was based on a finding in *United States v. Minnesota* (270 U.S. 181 (1926), s.c. 271 U.S. 648) that state statutes of limitations do not apply to federal action in Indian rights cases.
36. See Campisi, Jack, "National Policy, States' Rights, and Indian Sovereignty: The Case of the New York Iroquois," in Michael K. Foster, Jack Campisi and Marianne Mithun (eds.), *Extending the Rafters: Interdisciplinary Approaches to Iroquoian Studies,* State University of New York Press, Albany, 1984.
37. For the congressional position, and commentary on the independent study of alternative sites undertaken by Dr. Arthur Morgan, see U.S. Senate, Committee on Interior and Insular Affairs, *Hearings Before the Committee on Interior and Insular Affairs: Kinzua Dam Project, Pennsylvania,* 88th Cong., 1st Sess., U.S. Government Printing Office, Washington, D.C., May- December 1963.
38. For further detail on the struggle around Kinzua Dam, see Hauptman, Lawrence M., *The Iroquois Struggle for Survival: World War II 7o Red Power,* Syracuse University Press, Syracuse, NY, 1986.
39. *Tuscarora Indians v. New York State Power Authority,* 257 F.2d 885 (1958).
40. On the compromise acreage, see Hauptman, Laurence M., "Iroquois Land Claims Issues: At Odds with the 'Family of New York'," in *Iroquois Land Claims, op. cit.,* pp. 67-86.
41. It took another ten years for this to be spelled out definitively; *Oneida Indian Nation v. United States,* 37 Ind. Cl. Comm. 522 (1971).
42. For a detailed account of the discussions, agreements and various factions within the process, see Upton, *op. cit.,* pp. 139-61.
43. See Treur, Margaret, "Ganiekeh: An Alternative to the Reservation System and Public Trust," *American Indian Journal,* Vol. 5, No. 5, 1979, pp. 22-6.
44. *State of New York v. Danny White, et al.,* Civ. No. 74-CV-370 (N.D.N.Y.), April 1976; *State of New York v. Danny White, et al.,* Civ. No. 74-CV-370, Memorandum Decision and Order, 23 March 1977.
45. On the Moss Lake Agreement, see Kwartler, Richard, "'This Is Our Land': *Mohawk Indians v. The State of New*

York" in Robert B. Goldman (ed.), *Roundtable Justice: Case Studies in Conflict Resolution,* Westview Press, Boulder, CO, 1980.

46. *Oneida Indian Nation of New York v. County of Oneida,* 14 U.S. 661 (1974).
47. *Oneida Indian Nation of New York v. County of Oneida,* 434 F. Supp. 527, 548 (N.D.N.Y. 1979).
48. Van Gestel, Allan, "New York Indian Land Claims: The Modern Landowner as Hostage," in *Iroquois Land Claims, op. cit.,* pp. 123-39. Also see the revision published as "When Fictions Take Hostages," in James E. Clifton (ed.), *The Invented Indian: Cultural Fictions and Government Policies* (Transaction Books, New Brunswick, NJ, 1990, pp. 291-312), and "The New York Indian Land Claims: An Overview and a Warning," *(New York State Bar Journal,* April 1981).
49. *County of Oneida v. Oneida Indian Nation of New York,* 84 L.Ed.2d 169, 191 (1984).
50. Locklear, Arlinda, "The Oneida Land Claims: A Legal Overview," in *Iroquois Land Claims, op. cit,* pp. 141-53.
51. *Ibid,* p. 148.
52. This suit was later recast to name the state rather than the counties as primary defendant, and enlarged to encompass six million acres. It was challenged, but upheld on appeal; *Oneida Indian Nation of New York v. State of New York,* 691 F.2d 1070 (1982). Dismissed by a district judge four years later (Brennan, Claire, "Oneida Claim to 6 Million Acres Voided," *Syracuse Post-Standard,* November 22, 1986), it was reinstated in by the Second Circuit Court in 1988 *(Oneida Indian Nation of New York v. State of New York,* 860 F.2d 1145), and is ongoing as of this writing.
53. *Oneida Nation of Indians of Wisconsin v. State of New York* 85F.D.R. 701, 703 (N.Y.D.C. 1980).
54. New York has attempted various arguments to obtain dismissal of the Cayuga suit. In 1990, the state's contention that it had obtained bona fide land title to the disputed area in leases obtained in 1795 and 1801 was overruled at the district court level *(Cayuga Indian Nation of New York v. Cuomo,* 730 F. Supp. 485). In 1991, an "interpretation" by the state attorney general that reservation of land by

the Six Nations in the Fort Stanwix Treaty "did not really" invest recognizable title in them was similarly overruled (*Cayuga Indian Nation of New York v. Cuomo*, 758 F. Supp. 107). Finally, in 1991, a state contention that only a special railroad reorganization would have jurisdiction to litigate claims involving areas leased to railroads was overruled (*Cayuga Indian Nation of New York v. Cuomo*, 762 F. Supp. 30). The suit is ongoing.

55. The terms of the agreement were published in *Finger Lakes Times*, August 18, 1979.
56. For further details, see Lavin, Chris, "The Cayuga Land Claims," in *Iroquois Land Claims*, *op. cit.*, pp. 87-100.
57. The one jurisdictional exception is that the Second Circuit ruled in 1988 that a federal statute passed in 1875 empowers the City of Salamanca, rather than the Senecas, to regulate zoning within the leased area so long as the leases exist (*John v. City of Salamanca*, 845 F.2d 37).
58. The non-Indian city government of Salamanca, a sub-part of which is the Salamanca Lease Authority, filed suit in 1990 to block settlement of the Seneca claim as "unconstitutional," and to compel a new 99 year lease on its own terms (*Salamanca Indian Lease Authority v. Seneca Indian Nation*, Civ. No. 1300, Docket 91-7086). They lost and appealed. The lower court decision was affirmed by the Second Circuit Court on March 15, 1991, on the basis that the Senecas enjoy "sovereign immunity" from any further such suits.

The Black Hills Are Not For Sale

The Lakota Struggle for the 1868 Treaty Territory

The white man made us many promises, but he kept only one. He promised to take our land and he took it.

—Mahpiya Luta—
(Red Cloud)
1882

American Indians have suffered greatly and consistently in their efforts to hold onto their territory, not infrequently experiencing outright genocide in the process of confronting Euroamerican invaders. Nonetheless, the survivors have persistently sought to recover their homelands. The pattern has been replicated in hundreds of different settings across the face of North America. Perhaps the best known sustained struggle, is being waged by the Lakota Nation (otherwise known as the "Western Sioux" or "Teton Dakota," composed of the Oglala, Brûlé, Hunkpapa, Minneconjou, Sans Arc, Blackfoot and Two Kettles Bands) for the Black Hills Region. Its ultimate outcome will have a wide-ranging impact upon native rights to land and self-determination throughout the United States.

The Treaties of Fort Laramie and the "Great Sioux War"

In 1851, the United States entered into the first Fort

Laramie Treaty with the Lakota, Cheyenne, Arapaho, Crow and other indigenous nations of the northern and central plains regions. In large part, the treaty was an attempt by the federal government to come to grips with the matter of Indian territorality within the vast "Louisiana Purchase" area it had acquired from France earlier in the century. The Lakota were formally recognized in the 1851 treaty as being entitled to a huge tract centering upon their sacred lands, called Paha Sapa (Black Hills), including virtually all of what are now the states of South Dakota and Nebraska, as well as appreciable portions of Kansas, North Dakota, Montana and Wyoming, and a small portion of Colorado. In sum, the United States formally recognized Lakota sovereignty and national "ownership" of between 6 and 7 percent of the total territory now comprising the "lower 48" states.[1]

It was not long, however, before gold and silver were discovered in the Virginia City portion of Montana Territory, and a "short route" to these ore fields became essential to a U.S. economy beset by the demands of the Civil War (1861-65). Hence, at least as early as 1864, the government entered into open violation of the 1851 treaty, sending troops to construct a series of forts intended to secure what was called the "Bozeman Trail," directly through the western portion of the Lakota homeland. The Lakota, under the political leadership of Red Cloud, an Oglala, responded by forming an alliance with the Cheyenne and Arapaho, bringing their joint military forces to bear upon the trail during the winter of 1866-67. By early 1868, the United States, having suffered several defeats in the field, and finding its troops trapped within their forts, sued for peace.[2] This led, that same year, to a second Fort Laramie Treaty in which (in exchange for being allowed to withdraw its remaining soldiers in one piece) the federal government once again recognized Lakota sovereignty and national territorality, this time establishing a "Great Sioux Reservation" encompassing all of contemporary South Dakota west of the east bank of the Missouri River, and acknowledging that the "Greater Sioux Nation" was entitled to permanent use of "Unceded Indian Territory" involving large portions of Nebraska, Wyoming, Montana and North Dakota.[3] Further, the new treaty committed U.S. troops to prevent non-Indians from trespassing in Lakota territory, specified that it did nothing to "abrogate or annul" Lakota land rights acknowledged in the 1851 treaty,[4] and provided that:

> No [subsequent] treaty for cession of any portion of the reservation herein described which may be held in common shall be on any validity or force as against said Indians, unless executed and signed by at least three-fourths of all adult male Indians [the gender provision was a U.S., rather than Lakota, stipulation], occupying or interested in the same.[5]

Again, the United States was unwilling to honor the treaty for long. A Catholic priest, Jean de Smet, ventured illegally into the Black Hills and afterwards reported to the *Sioux Falls Times* (South Dakota) that he had discovered gold there.[6] In short order, this led to the government's reinforcing Lt. Colonel George Armstrong Custer's élite 7th Cavalry Regiment and violating both the 1851 and 1868 treaties by sending this heavy military force directly into the Hills on a "fact-finding" mission. Custer's 1874 report that he too had found gold in the Paha Sapa, much ballyhooed in the eastern press, led to another military foray into the Hills—the Jenny Expedition—during the summer of 1875.[7] The fact that there was gold in the heart of Lakota Territory, in their most holy of places, was thus confirmed to the satisfaction of Washington officials.

With that, the government sent yet another treaty commission to meet with the Lakota leadership, this time in an effort to negotiate purchase of the Black Hills.[8] When the Lakotas refused to sell (as was clearly their right,

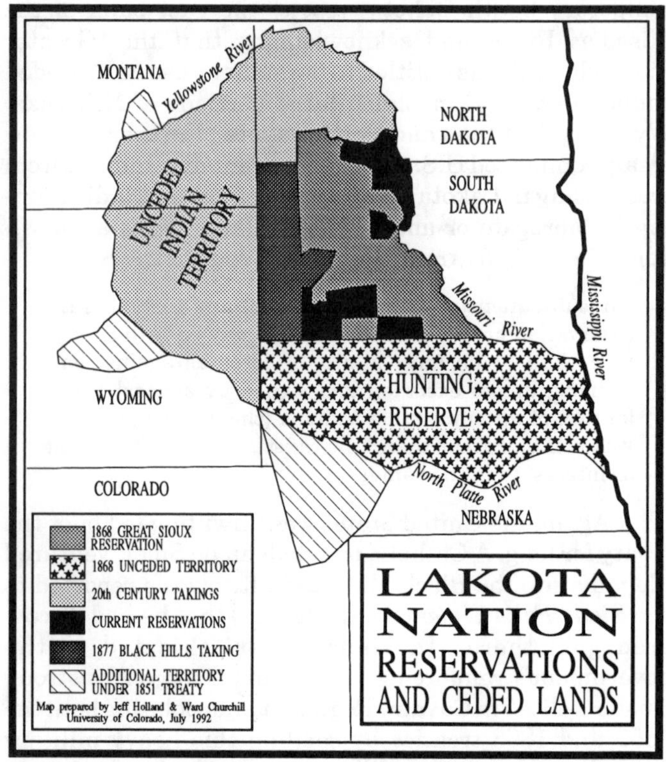

under both treaties), Washington responded by transferring its relations with them from the Bureau of Indian Affairs (BIA) to the Department of War. All Lakotas were ordered to gather at their "assigned agencies" within the Great Sioux Reservation by not later than the end of January 1876, although they plainly had every right to be anywhere they chose within their treaty territory. Those who failed to comply with this utterly unlawful federal directive were informed that they would be viewed as having "broken the peace" and consequently treated as "hostiles." Meanwhile, President Ulysses S. Grant completed the government's raft of treaty violations by secretly instructing his army commanders to disregard U.S. obligations to prevent the wholesale invasion of the Lakota heartland by non-Indian miners.[9]

Rather than submitting to federal dictates, the Lakotas gathered in the remote Powder River County of southeastern Montana, a part of their unceded territory, to discuss how they should respond. In turn, the army used this "gesture of hostility" as a pretext for launching a massive assault upon them, with the express intent of "crushing Sioux resistance completely, once and for all." The U.S. objective was to obliterate any Lakota ability to oppose federal expropriation of the Black Hills. The mechanism chosen to accomplish this task was a three-pronged campaign consisting of some 1,500 men each under Major Generals George Crook (coming into the Powder River Country from the south) and Alfred Terry (from the east). Another 1,000 men under Colonel John Gibbon were to approach from the west, and the Lakotas (as well as their Cheyenne and Arapaho allies) were to be caught between these powerful forces and destroyed.[10]

The army's plan failed completely. On June 17, 1876, Crook's entire column was met by an approximately equal number of Lakotas led by Crazy Horse, an Oglala. The soldiers were quickly defeated and sent into full retreat.[11] This was followed, on June 25, by the decimation of Custer's 7th Cavalry, attached to Terry's column, in the valley of the Little Big Horn River.[12] For the second time in a decade, the Lakota had successfully defended Paha Sapa, militarily defeating the U.S. Army in what has come to be known as the "Great Sioux War."

But the victory was bitter. Vengefully licking its wounds after having been unable to best the Indians in open combat, the army imported Colonel Ranald Mackenzie, a specialist who had perfected the craft of "total war" in earlier campaigns against the Kiowa and Comanche nations on the southern plains of present-day Texas and

Oklahoma. The new tactician spent the winter of 1876-77 tracking down individual Lakota and Cheyenne villages which had been rendered immobile by cold and snow. He then used sheer numbers to overpower each village as it was found, slaughtering women, children and old people as matter of course.[13] By the spring of 1877, in order to spare their non-combatants further butchery at the hands of the army, most Lakotas decided it was time to stop fighting. Two Hunkpapa leaders, Sitting Bull and Gall, took their followers to sanctuary in Canada, not returning until the 1880s. Having laid down his arms, Crazy Horse, preeminent among Oglala resistance leaders, was assassinated by the military on September 5, and the era of Lakota defensive warfare was brought to a close.[14]

The Theft of Paha Sapa

Undoubtedly as a result of the military advantage it ultimately gained over the Lakotas during the Great Sioux War, the U.S. Congress felt itself empowered to pass an act on February 28, 1877, taking a large portion of the Great Sioux Reservation containing the Black Hills (the unneeded Indian territory was taken at about the same time; see map).[15] There is strong evidence that Congress was well aware that this act was patently illegal, given that it had effected a slightly earlier measure suspending delivery of subsistence rations—to which the Lakota were entitled, both under their treaties and under the Laws of War—until such time as the Indians "gave up their claim over the Black Hills."[16] In other words, Congress set out deliberately to starve the captive Lakota population into going along with its plan. Even under these conditions, however, a commission headed up by George Manypenny and sent to obtain the Lakota consent, was unable to get the job done. While the 1868 treaty required that the agreement of 75 percent of all adult male Lakotas was required to legitimate any "Sioux Land Cession,"

Manypenny's commission came away with the signatures of only about 10 percent of the Lakota men. Nonetheless, Congress enacted its statute "lawfully" expropriating the Hills.[17]

Over the following two decades, erosion of Lakota sovereignty and land base were exacerbated by imposition of the Major Crimes and General Allotment Acts.[18] The Lakota economy was prostrated, and the political process by which the nation had traditionally governed itself was completely subverted. By 1890, despair at such circumstances had reached a level leading to the widespread adoption of the Ghost Dance religion, a belief that the rigorous performance of certain rituals would lead to a return of things as they had been before the Euroamerican invasion. This phenomenon, dubbed an "incipient uprising" by Indian agents, provided the government with an excuse to declare a state of military emergency during which Sitting Bull (last of the great "recalcitrant" leaders) was assassinated at his home near Standing Rock and some 350 of his followers massacred along Wounded Knee Creek, on what is now the Pine Ridge Reservation.[19] Lakota spiritual practices were then outlawed in general.[20] After that, Washington tended to view the Lakotas as being "thoroughly broken."

During the 1920s and '30s, Lakota sovereignty was diminished even further through imposition of the Indian Citizenship Act, followed by the Indian Reorganization Act (IRA).[21] The former did much to confuse Lakota national allegiances, engendering a distorted sort of loyalty to the United States among many younger Indians, especially men, desperate to overcome their sense of personal disempowerment. In practice, such "patriotism"—common to most colonial systems—has meant Indians being "allowed" to serve in the military of their oppressors, fighting and dying as mercenaries and in disproportionate numbers (usually against other peoples of color) during the Second World War, Korea and Vietnam. The IRA was in some ways even more insidious, putting in place a "more democratic and representative" form of "elected council" governance—owing its very existence to federal authority—as a replacement for the popular and consensus-oriented traditional Councils of Elders.[22] As a consequence, divisiveness within Lakota society increased sharply during the 1940s, with "progressives" in the tribal council orbit pitted by Washington directly against the much larger population of grassroots traditionals.[23]

By the mid-1950s, things had deteriorated to such an extent that Congress could seriously consider "termination" (i.e., externally and unilaterally imposed dissolution) of the Lakota Nation altogether.[24] Unlike the situation of the Menominees, Klamaths, and a number of other indigenous nations dissolved during the 1950s, the Lakota termination was not ultimately consummated. But by 1967, nearly half the "Sioux" population had been removed to city slums—Denver, Minneapolis, Chicago, San Francisco and Los Angeles were the preferred dumping grounds—through federal relocation programs designed to depopulate the land base of the reservations.[25] The degeneration of social cohesion resulting from this policy-generated diaspora has created staggering problems for the Lakota and other peoples which have never been resolved.

Other effects of advanced colonization were almost as devastating. The 1868 treaty territory has been reduced to a meager 10 percent of its original area and broken up into a "complex" of reservations geographically separating the bands from one another. Of the residual land base, assertion of BIA leasing prerogatives under a unilaterally assumed federal "trust responsibility" over Lakota property placed more than two-thirds of the most productive reservation acreage in the hands of non-Indian ranchers, farmers and corporate concerns.[26] Completely dispossessed of their land and traditional economy, modern Lakotas confront a circumstance on their reservations in which unemployment for Indians has hovered in the 90th percentile throughout the past half-century.[27] The implications of this situation are both predictable and readily apparent. The poorest county in the United States every year since World War II has been Shannon, on the Pine Ridge Reservation. Todd County, on the adjoining Rosebud Reservation, has kept pace, consistently placing among the ten poorest locales in the federal poverty index.[28]

The Legal Battle

Many Lakotas never accepted the circumstances of their colonization lying down. Realizing in the wake of the Wounded Knee Massacre that any direct military response to U.S. transgressions would be at best self-defeating, they opted instead to utilize the colonizers' own legal codes—and international pretensions as a "humanitarian power, bound by the laws of civilized conduct"—as a means of recovering what had been stolen from them.[29]

The First Court Case

In 1920, a federal law was passed which "authorized" the Lakotas to sue to government "under treaties, or agreements, or laws of Congress, on the misappropriation of any funds or lands of said tribe or band or bands thereof."[30] Despite appearances, the law was hardly altruistic on the part of the government. Realizing that there had been "difficulties" with the manner in which Lakota "consent" had been obtained for the 1877 Black Hills land cession, it saw the bill as a handy means to buy the now-impoverished Indians off and "quiet title" to the Hills once and for all. This scheme was revealed in 1923, when the Lakotas entered their suit with the federal Court of Claims, seeking return of their stolen land rather than the monetary compensation the U.S. had anticipated would be at issue. Not knowing what to do in the face of this unexpected turn of events, the court stalled for 19 years, endlessly entertaining motions and counter-motions while professing to "study" the matter. Finally, in 1942, when it became absolutely clear the Lakotas would not accept cash in lieu of land, the court dismissed the case, claiming the situation was a "moral issue" rather than a constitutional question over which it held jurisdiction.[31] In 1943, the U.S. Supreme Court refused to even review the claims court decision.[32]

The Claims Commission

The litigational route appeared to stalemated. But on August 13, 1946, the Indian Claims Commission Act was passed by a Congress anxious to put the best possible moral face on the government's past dealings with American Indians.[33] Motivation for the act accrued from the announced U.S. intention to sit in judgement of the nazi and imperial Japanese leadership for having engaged in "Crimes Against the Peace" (planning and engaging in "aggressive war"), War Crimes and other "Crimes Against Humanity." Among these crimes were mass forced relocations, slavery and genocide.[34] Under such circumstances, the federal government wished to present an impeccably moral face to the world. Section II of the new act defined the bases upon which Indians might sue for lands lost, including:

- Claims in law or equity arising under the constitution, laws, and treaties of the United States;

- Claims which would result if the treaties, contracts and agreements between the claimant and the United States were revised on the grounds of fraud, duress, unconscionable consideration, mutual or unilateral mistake, whether of law or of fact, or any other ground recognizable by the court of inquiry.[35]

Recognizing that such language might arguably cover the Black Hills taking, the Lakotas re-filed their original Court of Claims case with the Claims Commission in 1950. The commission, however, opted to view the case as having been "retired" by the 1942 Court of Claims dismissal and subsequent Supreme Court denial of *certiorari*. It likewise dismissed the matter in 1954.[36] The Court of Claims upheld the commission's decision on appeal from the Lakotas during the same year.[37] Undeterred by this failure of "due process," the Lakotas entered a second (very different) appeal, and in 1958:

> [T]he Indian Claims Commission [was] ordered by the Court of Claims to reopen the case on the grounds that the Sioux had previously been represented by inadequate counsel and as a consequence an inadequate record [had] been presented.[38]

In 1961, the U.S. Department of Justice attempted to have the Black Hills case simply set aside, entering a writ of mandamus seeking such "extraordinary relief" for the government; the Court of Claims rejected this tactic during the same year. The Claims Commission was thereby forced to actually consider the case. After a long hiatus, the commission announced that, having "studied the matter," it was reducing the scope of the issue to three elements:

- What land rights were acquired by the U.S. *vis-à-vis* the Black Hills in 1877?

- What consideration had been given by the U.S. in exchange for these lands?

- If no consideration had been given, had any payment been made by the United States?[39]

Proceeding from this basis, the commission entered a preliminary opinion in 1974 that Congress had been exercising its "power of eminent domain" in 1877, and that it had therefore been "justified" in taking the Hills from the Lakotas, although it was obligated to pay them "just compensation" for their loss, as provided under the fifth amendment to the U.S. Constitution.[40] The opinion denied any right of the Lakotas to recover the land taken from them and they therefore objected to it quite strongly. The federal government also took strong exception to the direction things were taking, based upon its reluctance to pay any large sum of money as compensation for territory it had always enjoyed free of charge. Hence, in 1975 the Justice Department appealed to the Court of Claims, securing a *res judicata* prohibition against the Claims Commission "reaching the merits" of any proposed Lakota compensation package.[41] Simply put, the commission was to be denied the prerogative of determining and awarding to the Lakotas anything beyond "the value of the land in question *at the time of taking.*" This stipulation resulted in the commission arriving at an award of $17.5 million for the entire Black Hills, against which the government sought to "offset" $3,484 in rations issued to the Lakotas in 1877.[42]

End Game Moves

The Lakotas attempted to appeal this to the Supreme Court, but the high court of the U.S. again refused to consider the matter.[43] Meanwhile, arguing that acceptance of compensation would constitute a bona fide land cession, and invoking the 1868 treaty consent clause, the Lakotas themselves conducted a referendum to determine whether three-fourths of the people were willing to relinquish title to Paha Sapa. The answer was a resounding "no."

The unexpected referendum results presented the

government with yet another dilemma in its continuing quest to legitimize its theft of Lakota territory. To make the best of an increasingly bad situation, Congress passed a bill in 1978 enabling the Court of Claims to "review" the nature and extent of Lakota compensation.[44] This the court did, "revising" the proposed award in 1979 to include 5 percent simple interest, accruing annually since 1877, adding up to a total of $105 million; lumped in with the original $17.5 million principal award, this made the federal offer $122.5 million.[45]

The Justice Department again attempted unsuccessfully to constrict the amount of compensation the government would be obliged to pay by filing an appeal with the Supreme Court. In 1980, the high court upheld the Claims Court's award of interest.[46] The Lakotas, however, remained entirely unsatisfied. Pointing to a second poll of the reservations, conducted in 1979, showing that the people were no more willing to accept $122.5 million than they had been $17.5 million in exchange for the Hills, and arguing that return of the land itself had always been the object of their suits, they went back to court. On July 18, 1980, the Oglalas entered a claim naming the U.S., the State of South Dakota, and a number of counties, towns and individuals in the U.S. District Court, seeking recovery of the land per se, as well as $11 *billion* in damages. The case was dismissed by the court on September 12, supposedly because "the issue at [had] already been resolved."[47]

In 1981, the U.S. Eighth Circuit Court of Appeals affirmed the district court's dismissal and, in 1982, the Supreme Court once again declined to hear the resultant Lakota appeal.[48] These decisions opened the way in 1985 for the Court of Claims to finalize its award of monetary compensation, as the "exclusive available remedy" for the Black Hills land claim.[49] In sum, further Lakota recourse in U.S. courts had been extinguished by those courts. The game had always been rigged, and the legal strategy had proven quite unsuccessful in terms of either achieving Lakota objectives or even holding the U.S. accountable to its own professed system of legality.

On the other hand, the legal route did mark solid achievements in other areas: pursuing it demonstrably kept alive a strong sense of hope, unity and fighting spirit among many Lakotas which might otherwise have diminished over time. Further, the more than 60 years of litigation had forced a range of admissions from the federal government concerning the real nature of the Black Hills expropriations; the Supreme Court, for example, had termed the whole affair a "ripe and rank case of dishonorable dealings" and "a national disgrace" in its 1975 opinion. Such admissions went much further toward fostering broad public understanding of Lakota issues than a "one-sided" Indian recounting of the facts could ever have. Cumulatively then, the Lakota legal strategy set the stage for both an ongoing struggle by Indians and for public acceptance of a meaningful solution to the Black Hills claim before the end of the twentieth century.

The Extralegal Battle

It is likely that the limited concessions obtained by the Lakota from U.S. courts during the 1970s were related to the emergence of strong support for the American Indian Movement (AIM) on the Pine Ridge and Rosebud Reservations during the early part of the decade. At the outset, AIM's involvement on Pine Ridge concerned the provision of assistance to local traditional Oglalas attempting to block the illegal transfer of approximately one-eighth of the reservation (the so-called Sheep Mountain Gunnery Range) to the U.S. Forest Service by a corrupt tribal administration headed by Richard Wilson.[50] AIM provided a marked stiffening of the Lakota resolve to pursue land rights by demonstrating a willingness to go toe-to-toe with federal forces on such matters, an attitude largely absent in Indian Country since 1890.

The virulence of the federal response to AIM's "criminal arrogance" in this regard led directly to the dramatic siege of the Wounded Knee hamlet in 1973, a spectacle which riveted international attention on the Black Hills land issue for the first time. In turn, this scrutiny resulted in analysis and an increasingly comprehensive understanding of the vast economic interests underlying federal policy in the Black Hills region (see map). This process steadily raised the level of progressive criticism of the government and garnered further non-Indian support to the Lakota position. Anxious to reassert its customary juridical control over questions of Indian land rights, the government engaged in what amounted to a counterinsurgency war against AIM and its traditional Pine Ridge supporters from 1973-76.[51]

By the latter year, however, it was a bit too late to effectively contain AIM's application of external pressure to the U.S. judicial system. In 1974, the Lakota elders had convened a treaty conference on the Standing Rock Reservation and charged Oglala Lakota AIM leader Russell Means with taking the 1868 Fort Laramie Treaty "before the family of nations."[52] Means therefore formed "AIM's diplomatic arm," the International Indian Treaty Council (IITC), and set about achieving a presence within the United Nations, not only for the Lakota, but for all the indigenous peoples of the Western Hemisphere. IITC accomplished this in 1977—largely on the basis of the work of its first director, a Cherokee named Jimmie Durham—when delegations from 98 American Indian nations were allowed to make presentations before a subcommission of the U.N. Commission on Human Rights at the Place of Nations in Geneva, Switzerland.[53]

In 1981, the U.N. reacted to what it had heard by establishing a Working Group on Indigenous Populations—an entity dedicated to the formulation of international law concerning the rights and status of indigenous nations *vis-à-vis* nation-states which had subsumed them—under the United Nations Economic and Social Council (ECOSOC).[54] The regularized series of hearings that were made integral to working group procedure provided an international forum within which American Indians and other indigenous peoples from Australia, New Zealand and Micronesia could formally articulate the basis of their national rights, and the effects of governmental abridgement of these rights.[55] By the late 1980s, the working group had completed a global study of the conditions under which indigenous peoples were forced to live, and had commissioned a comprehensive study of the treaty relationships existing between nation-state governments and various native nations.[56] The stated objective of the working group has become the eventual promulgation of a "Universal Declaration of Indigenous Rights," (due for draft submission to the U.N. General Assembly this year), holding the same legal and moral force as the Universal Declaration of Human Rights, 1948 Convention on Prevention and Punishment of the Crime of Genocide, assorted Geneva Conventions and other elements of international law.[57]

The result of this international approach was to deny the United States the veil of secrecy behind which it conducted its Indian affairs as a purely "internal matter." Exposed to the light of concentrated international attention, the federal government was repeatedly embarrassed by the realities of its own Indian policies and court decisions. As a consequence, federal courts became somewhat more accommodating in the Black Hills case than they might otherwise have been.

Still, when the Lakotas rejected monetary settlement of their land claim in 1979-80, AIM was instrumental in forging sentiment around the popular slogan "The Black Hills Are Not For Sale." This was again coupled to direct extralegal action when Russell Means initiated an occupation in 1981 of an 880 acre site near Rapid City in the Black Hills (see map). This was called "the first step in the physical reoccupation of Paha Sapa." The AIM action again caused broad public attention to be focused upon the Lakota land claim, and precipitated the potential of another major armed clash with federal forces; the latter possibility was averted at the last moment by a federal district judge who—reflecting the government's concern not to become engaged in another "Wounded Knee-type confrontation"—issued an order enjoining the FBI and U.S. Marshals Service from undertaking an assault upon the occupants of what was by then called Yellow Thunder Camp.[58]

Under these conditions, the government was actually placed in the position of having to sue the Indians in order to get them to leave what it claimed was federal property under control of the U.S. Forest Service.[59] AIM countersued on the basis that federal land-use policies in the Black Hills violated not only the 1868 treaty, but also Lakota spiritual freedom under the First Amendment to the U.S. Constitution and the American Indian Religious Freedom Act.[60] In 1986, the government was stunned when U.S. District Judge Robert O'Brien ruled in favor of AIM, finding that the Lakotas had every right to the Yellow Thunder site, and that the United States had clearly discriminated against them by suggesting otherwise. The Yellow Thunder ruling was a potential landmark, bearing broad potential for application in other Indian land claims in the United States. O'Brien's finding was severely undercut by the Supreme Court's recent "G-O Road Decision,"[61] however, and was consequently overturned by the Eighth Circuit Court.

Like the Lakota legal strategy, AIM's course of largely extralegal action has proven insufficient in itself to resolve the Black Hills land claim. Nonetheless, it had a positive bearing on the evolution of litigation in the matter, and help bring vital public attention to and understanding of the issues. In this sense, the legal and extralegal battles fought by Lakotas for Paha Sapa have been—perhaps inadvertently—mutually reinforcing. These two efforts may have finally created the context in which a genuine solution can finally be achieved.

The Bradley Bill

By the mid-1980s, the image of the United States regarding its treatment of the Lakotas had suffered so badly that a liberal New Jersey Senator, Bill Bradley, took an unprecedented step, introducing legislation to Congress which the Lakotas themselves had proposed.[62] With the goal of finally ending the Black Hills "controversy," the draft bill, S. 1453, proposed to "re-convey" title to 750,000 acres of the Hills currently held by the federal government, including subsurface (mineral) rights, to the Lakotas. Further, it provided that certain spiritual sites in the area would be similarly retitled. These sites, along with some of the 50,000 of the re-conveyed acres, would be designated a "Sioux Park"; the balance of the land returned would be designated a "Sioux Forest."

Additionally, considerable water rights within the South Dakota portion of the 1868 treaty territory would be reassigned to the Lakotas. A "Sioux National Council," drawn from all existing Lakota reservations, holding increased jurisdiction within the whole 8.5 million acres of the 1868 Great Sioux Reservation would also be established. Timbering and grazing permits, mineral leasing, etc., in the Black Hills would be transferred to Lakota control two years after passage of the bill (thus establishing a viable Lakota economic base for the first time in nearly a century). The $122.5 million awarded by the Court of Claims—plus interest accrued since 1980, a total of well over $200 million—would be disbursed as compensation for the Lakotas' historic loss of use of their land rather than as payment for the land itself. Finally, the draft bill posited that it would resolve the Black Hills claim *only,* and have had no wider effect on "subsisting treaties." In other words, with satisfactory settlement of the Hills issue in hand, the Lakotas would remain free to pursue resolution of their claims to the 1868 Unceded Indian Territory and the 1851 treaty territory.[63]

Although the Bradley Bill was obviously less than perfect—compensation remained very low, considering that the Hearst Corporation's Homestake Mine *alone* has extracted more than $18 *billion* in gold from the Black Hills since 1877,[64] and the U.S. and its citizens are left with considerable land and rights in the area to which they were never legally entitled—it represented a major potential breakthrough not only with regard to the Black Hills land claim, but to U.S.-Indian relations far more generally. Although the full Lakota agenda was not met by the bill, it probably came close enough that the bulk of the people would have endorsed it. That, more than anything, was a testament to their own perseverance in struggle, in the face of astronomical odds. The bill, however, foundered during the late 1980s in the wake of a campaign to "improve" upon it advanced by a rather mysterious individual named Phil Stevens.

Throughout his life, Stevens functioned as a non-Indian, fashioning for himself a highly-profitable defense contracting corporation in Los Angeles. Deciding to retire in 1984, he sold his company for an estimated $60 million. Thereupon, he claimed to have "discovered" he was a direct descendant from the noted Oglala leader, Standing Bear, and to have become consumed with a belated passion to "help" his people. In 1986, he began to approach certain disaffected elements within the reservation context, arguing that with his federal contacts and "negotiating expertise," he could better not only the monetary compensation portions of the Bradley Bill—increasing reparations to $3.1 billion—but improve upon its jurisdictional provisions as well.[65] He punctuated his points by spreading relatively small quantities of cash around destitute Lakota communities,[66] and stipulated that all that was needed was for him to be provided "proper authority"—that is, elevated into the nonexistent position of "Great Chief of All the Sioux"—in order to proceed with getting the job done.

Resistance to Stevens' posturing was intense in many quarters, especially among those who had worked most unstintingly to bring Bradley's initiative into being. Nonetheless, interest in the Steven's ideas had reached sufficient proportions by early 1988, that Gerald Clifford, chief negotiator and chair of the steering committee guiding the group working for its passage, was compelled to take Stevens to Washington, D.C., to broach his proposals to various key congresspeople.[67] The timing was most inopportune, given that Bradley had, since introducing his bill for a second time on March 10, 1987, been able to secure support for the legislation even from such notoriously anti-Indian senators as Lloyd Meeds (Washington). The chairs of both the House and Senate Interior Committees—Representative Morris Udall (Arizona) and Hawaii Senator Daniel Inouye had also agreed to serve as cosponsors.

> The baleful consequences of Stevens' Washington tour soon became evident. Bradley had no intention of amending his bill to include Stevens' $3.1 billion compensation package or getting caught in the crossfire between competing Sioux factions. With Clifford's reluctant concurrence, Bradley decided to hold his bill in abeyance until the Sioux settled their internal dispute.[68]

With the first truly significant congressional land return initiative in U.S. history thoroughly in tatters, Stevens quickly quit the field, withdrawing his flow of funds to the Lakota communities as well. Meanwhile, reactionary South Dakota Senator Tom Daschle capitalized on the situation, founding what he called the "Open Hills Committee," designed to "counter...the long-term campaign...by those who seek to replace the 1980 Supreme Court settlement with a massive land and even more massive money transfer."[69] The committee is chaired by Daschle's close friend David Miller, a neo-nazi "revisionist historian" at Black Hills State University in Spearfish, South Dakota.

> The Open Hills Committee [mainly] riled up what Miller himself described as South Dakota's considerable redneck population, people who would "just as soon load up shotguns" as return any portion of the Hills to the Sioux. In a part of the country where many people thought of Indians either as dirty drunks or crazed militants, the Open Hills Committee had no difficulty in recruiting.[70]

Within the context of mounting tension between Indians and whites in South Dakota in 1989, Daschle had no difficulty in teaming up with his fellow senator from the state, Larry Pressler, in securing an agreement from Inouye—by then chair of the Senate Select Committee on Indian Affairs—that there would be "no hearings, markups, or other action" taken on any Black Hills legislation without the express consent of the "South Dakota senatorial delegation."[71] In 1990, Pressler sought to follow up by introducing a resolution which would have required yet another reservation-by-reservation poll of the increasingly desperate Lakotas with regard to accepting the Supreme Court's 1980 cash award as "final resolution of the Black Hills question."[72]

Small wonder that "Clifford [and many others] view the mergence of Stevens' program as an unmitigated disaster, the work not of a savior but of a 'manipulator and salesman,' a gloryhound whose ties to the tribe were at best attenuated. (Clifford doubts Stevens' story about his relationship to Standing Bear.)"[73] Russell Means suspects that Stevens may have been a federal agent of some sort, or at least an individual aligned with the opponents of the Lakota land claims sent in to disrupt and discredit efforts to recover the Hills; "You don't have to be a cop," Means says, "to do a cop's work. And no provocateur could have done a better job than Phil Stevens in screwing up the Black Hills claim."[74] Uncharacteristically, even arch-conservative editor of the *Lakota Times*, Tim Giago, agrees with Means, describing Stevens as "a ringer, pure and simple."[75]

Conclusion

In the end, the question becomes whether some version of the Bradley Bill can ever really be passed in anything resembling its original form. If so, the Lakotas' long fight for their land, and for their integrity as a nation of people, will have been significantly advanced. Moreover, a legislative precedent will have been set which could allow other peoples indigenous to what is now known as the United States to begin the long process of reconstituting themselves. This, in turn, would allow the U.S. itself to begin a corresponding process of reversing some of the worst aspects to its ugly history of colonization and genocide against American Indians. The prospect remains, the bill's supporters have never abandoned hope, and Bradley himself has never completely discarded it. But it is now only a feeble glimmer of what it was five years ago. Likely, only a substantial upsurge of non-Indian support for the concept—unlikely, given the typical priorities manifested by even the most progressive sectors of Euroamerica—would now serve to salvage the legislative remedy.

In the alternative, if the bill is ultimately gutted, rejected, or simply discarded—and this fails to resolve what by any measure is the best known of all Indian land claims in North America—it will be a clear sign that the U.S. remains unswervingly committed to its long-standing policy of expropriating Indian assets by whatever means are available to it, and to destroying indigenous societies as an incidental cost of "doing business." In that event, the Lakota will have no real option but to continue their grim struggle for survival, an indication that the future may prove even worse than the past. The crossroads in this sense have already been reached.

Notes

1. The full text of the "Treaty of Fort Laramie with the Sioux, Etc., 1851" (11 Stat. 749), may be found in Kappler, Charles J., *Indian Treaties, 1778-1883,* Interland Publishing Co., New York, 1973, pp. 594-96. Context is well presented in Nadeau, Remi, *Fort Laramie and the Sioux,* University of Nebraska Press, Lincoln, 1967.
2. See Brown, Dee, *Fort Phil Kearny: An American Saga,* University of Nebraska Press, Lincoln, 1971, pp. 184-90. For further background, see Hafen, LeRoy R., and Francis Marion Young, *Fort Laramie and the Pageant of the West, 1834-1890,* University of Nebraska Press, Lincoln, 1938.
3. The full text of the 1868 Fort Laramie Treaty (15 Stat. 635) may be found in Kappler *op. cit.* Lakota territorality is spelled out under Articles 2 and 16. Additional background information may be obtained in Hyde, George E., *Red Cloud's Folk: A History of the Oglala Sioux Indians,* University of Oklahoma Press, Norman, 1937.
4. 1868 Treaty, Article 17.
5. *Ibid.,* Article 12.
6. See Ludlow, William, *Report of a Reconnaissance of the Black Hills of Dakota,* U.S. Government Printing Office, Washington, D.C., 1875. Also see Jackson, Donald, *Custer's Gold: The United States Cavalry Expedition of 1874,* University of Nebraska Press, Lincoln, 1966, p. 8.
7. *Ibid.* Also see Jenny, Walter P., *Report on the Mineral Wealth, Climate and Rainfall and Natural Resources of the Black Hills of Dakota,* 44th Congress, 1st Session, Exec. Doc. No. 51, Washington, D.C., 1876.
8. This was the "Allison Commission" of 1875. For the most comprehensive account of the commission's failed purchase attempt, see *Annual Report of the Commissioner of Indian Affairs, 1875,* U.S. Department of Interior, Washington, D.C., 1875.

9. See Pommershein, Frank, "The Black Hills Case: On the Cusp of History," *Wicazo Sa Review,* Vol IV, No. 1, Spring 1988, p. 19. The government's secret maneuvering is spelled out in a summary report prepared by E.T. Watkins, 44th Congress, 1st Session, Exec. Doc. No. 184, Washington, D.C., 1876, pp. 8-9.
10. See Andrist, Ralph, *The Long Death: The Last Days of the Plains Indians,* Collier Books, New York, 1964, pp. 276-292.
11. See Trebbel, John, *Compact History of the Indian Wars,* Tower Books, New York, 1966, p. 277. Also see Connell, Evan S., *Son of the Morning Star: Custer and the Little Big Horn,* North Point Press, San Francisco, 1984.
12. See Brown, Dee, *Bury My Heart At Wounded Knee: An Indian History of the American West,* Holt, Rinehart and Winston Publishers, New York, 1970, pp. 301-10. Also see Sandoz, Mari, *The Battle of the Little Big Horn,* Curtis Books, New York, 1966.
13. On the "total war" policy and its prosecution, see Andrist, *op. cit.,* p. 297. Also see, for a detailed example of one engagement in this process, Greene, Jerome A., *Slim Buttes, 1876: An Episode of the Great Sioux War,* University of Oklahoma Press, Norman, 1982.
14. Brown (1970), *op. cit.,* p. 312. Also see Sandoz, Mari, *Crazy Horse: Strange Man of the Oglalas,* University of Nebraska Press, Lincoln, 1942.
15. 19 Stat. 254 (1877).
16. Act of August 15, 1876, Ch. 289, 19 Stat. 176, 192; the matter is well covered in "1986 Black Hills Hearings on S. 1453, Introduction," (prepared by the office of Senator Daniel Inouye), reproduced in *Wicazo Sa Review, op. cit.,* at p. 10.
17. *Ibid.*
18. 18 U.S.C.A.—1153 (1885) and 25 U.S.C.A.—331 (1887), respectively. The allotment act is often referred to as the "Dawes Act," after its sponsor, liberal Massachusetts senator Henry Dawes.
19. See Andrist, *op. cit.,* pp. 351-52.
20. See Erdoes, Richard, *The Sun Dance People: The Plains Indians, Their Past and Present,* Vintage Books, New York, 1972, p. 174.

21. 8 U.S.C.A.—140 (a) (2) (1924) and 25 U.S.C.A. 461 (1934), respectively. The IRA is often called the "Wheeler-Howard Act," after its Senate and House sponsors.
22. A detailed examination of the IRA and its passage is to be found in Deloria, Vine Jr., and Clifford M. Lytle (1983), *The Nations Within: The Past and Future of American Indian Sovereignty,* Pantheon Books, New York, 1984.
23. Analysis of such trends may be found in Committee on Native American Struggles, *Rethinking Indian Law, National Lawyers Guild,* New York, 1982.
24. This would have occurred under House Concurrent Resolution 108 (67 Stat. B132); see Deloria, Vine Jr., and Clifford M. Lytle, *American Indians, American Justice,* University of Texas Press, Austin, 1983, pp. 17-18.
25. On the Menominees, see Peroff, Nicholas C., *Menominee DRUMS: Tribal Termination and Restoration, 1954-1974,* University of Oklahoma Press, Norman, 1982. On the Klamath, see Stern, Theodore, *The Klamath Tribe: The People and Their Reservation,* University of Washington Press, Seattle, 1965. For a more general view of U.S. termination and relocation policies, and their place in the broader sweep of federal affairs, see Drinnon, Richard, *Keeper of Concentration Camps: Dillon S. Myer and American Racism,* University of California Press, Berkeley, 1987.
26. This occurred as a result of an 1891 amendment (26 Stat. 794) to the General Allotment Act (25 U.S.C.A. 331) providing that the U.S. Secretary of Interior ("or his delegate," meaning the BIA) might lease out the land of any Indian who, in his opinion, "by reason of age or other disability" could not "personally and with benefit to himself occupy or improve his allotment or any part thereof." As Deloria and Lytle, *op. cit.*, observe on p. 10: "In effect this amendment gave the secretary of interior almost dictatorial powers over the use of allotments since, if the local agent disagreed with the use to which [reservation] lands were being put, he could intervene and lease the lands to whomsoever he pleased." Thus, by the 1970s, the bulk of the useful land on many reservations in the U.S.—such as those of the Lakota—had been placed in the use of non-Indian individuals or business enterprises, and at very low rates.

27. Jones, R., *American Indian Policy: Selected Issues in the 98th Congress,* Issue Brief No. 1B83083, Library of Congress, Governmental Division, Washington, D.C., (updated version, 2/6/84), pp. 3-4.
28. Department of Interior, Indian Health Service, *American Indians: A Statistical Profile,* U.S. Government Printing Office, Washington, D.C., 1988.
29. The language accrues from one of President Woodrow Wilson's many speeches on the League of Nations in the immediate aftermath of World War I.
30. 41 Stat. 738 (1920)
31. *Sioux Tribe v. United States,* 97 Ct. Cl 613 (1943); this was a thoroughly spurious argument on the part of the court insofar as treaties are covered quite well under Articles I and VI of the U.S. Constitution.
32. *Sioux Tribe v. United States,* 318 U.S. 789 (1943).
33. Ch. 959, 60 Stat. 1049 (1946). An excellent elaboration of the convoluted nature of the Claims Commission's mandate is to be found in Sutton, Imre (ed.), *Irredeemable America: The Indians' Estate and Land Claims,* University of New Mexico Press, Albuquerque, 1985.
34. A fine exposition on U.S. governmental sensibilities during the period leading up to implementation of the post-World War II tribunals may be found in Smith, Bradley F., *The Road to Nuremberg,* Basic Books, New York, 1981.
35. 60 Stat. 1049, 23 U.S.C. 70 *et. seq.* (1983).
36. *Sioux Tribe v. United States,* 2 Ind. Cl. Comm. (1956).
37. *Sioux Tribe v. United States,* 146 F. Supp. 229 (1946).
38. Inouye, *op. cit.*, pp. 11-12.
39. *United States v. Sioux Nation,* 448 U.S. 371, 385 (1968).
40. *Sioux Nation v. United States,* 33 Ind. Cl. Comm. 151 (1974); the opinion was/is a legal absurdity insofar as congress holds no such "power of eminent domain" over the territorality of any other nation.
41. *United States v. Sioux Nation,* 207 Ct. Cl. 243, 518 F. 2d. 1293 (1975).
42. Inouye, *op. cit.*, p. 12.
43. 423 U.S. 1016 (1975).
44. P.L. 95-243, 92 Stat. 153 (1978).
45. *Sioux Nation v. United States,* 220 Ct. Cl. 442, 601 F. 2d. 1157 (1975).

46. 488 U.S. 371 (1980).
47. *Oglala Sioux v. United States* (Cir. No. 85-062) (W.D.N.D. 1980), September 22, 1980.
48. 455 U.S. 907 (1982).
49. *Sioux Tribe v. United States,* 7 Cl. Ct. 80 (1985).
50. See Matthiessen, Peter, *In the Spirit of Crazy Horse, Viking Press,* New York, 1984, pp. 425-28. Also see Johansen, Bruce, and Roberto Maestas, *Wasi'chu: The Continuing Indian Wars,* Monthly Review Press, New York, 1979.
51. See Churchill, Ward, and Jim Vander Wall, *Agents of Repression: The FBI's Secret Wars Against the Black Panther Party and American Indian Movement,* South End Press, Boston, 1988, and the chapter titled "COINTELPRO-AIM" in the authors' *The COINTELPRO Papers: Documents from the FBI's Secret Wars Against Dissent in the United States,* South End Press, Boston, 1990.
52. This is well-covered in Weyler, Rex, *Blood of the Land: The Government and Corporate War Against the American Indian Movement,* Vintage Books, New York, 1984.
53. Durham's work is covered in the updated version of Vine Deloria, Jr.'s *Behind the Trail of Broken Treaties,* Delta Books, New York, 1983.
54. United Nations Sub-Commission on Prevention of Discrimination and Protection of Minorities Resolution 2 (XXXIV) of 8 September 1981; endorsed by the Commission on Human Rights by Resolution 1982/19 of 10 March 1982; authorized by the Economic and Social Council, (ECOSOC) Resolution 1983/34 of 7 May 1982.
55. See Independent Commission on International Humanitarian Issues, *Indigenous Peoples: A Global Quest for Justice,* Zed Press, London, 1987.
56. As concerns the study of conditions, this is the so-called "Cobo Report," U.N. Doc. E/CN.4/Sub.2/AC.4/1985/WP.5. Much of the Cobo Report's content also appears in Burger, John, *Report From the Frontier: The State of the World's Indigenous Peoples,* Zed Press, London, 1987.
57. See the 1986 Draft Declaration of Principles proposed by the Indian Law Resource Center, Four Directions Council, National Aboriginal and Islander Legal Service, National

Indian Youth Council, Inuit Circumpolar Conference and the International Indian Treaty Council.

58. Perhaps the most comprehensive assessment of the meaning of the AIM action during this period may be found in Churchill, Ward, "The Extralegal Implications of Yellow Thunder Tiospaye: Misadventure or Watershed Action?" *Policy Perspectives,* Vol. 2, No. 2, Summer 1982. Also see Weyler, *op. cit.*
59. *United States v. Means, et. al.,* Docket No. Civ. 81-5131 (D.S.D., December 9, 1985).
60. P.L. 95-431, 92 Stat. 153 (1978).
61. *Lyng v. Northwest Indian Cemetery Protective Association,* 56 U.S. Law Week 4292. For analysis, see Deloria, Vine Jr., "Trouble in High Places: Erosion of American Indian Religious Freedom in the United States," in M. Annette Jaimes (ed.), *The State of Native America: Genocide, Colonization, and Resistance,* South End Press, Boston, 1992, pp. 267-87.
62. The bill was drafted by the Black Hills Sioux National Council, nominally headed by Gerald Clifford and Charlotte Black Elk at Cheyenne River.
63. The full text of S. 1453 may be found at p. 3 of *Wicazo Sa Review, op. cit.*
64. On Homestake, see Weyler, *op. cit.,* pp. 262-3.
65. The figure was apparently arrived at by computing rent on the Black Hills claim area at a rate of eleven cents per acre for 100 years, interest compounded annually, plus $310 million in accrued mineral royalties. Much of the appeal of Stevens' pitch, of course, is that it came alot closer to the actual amount owed the Lakota than that allowed in the Bradley Bill.
66. For instance, he made a cash donation of $34,000 to the Red Cloud School, on Pine Ridge, in 1987.
67. On Pine Ridge, for example, Stevens had attracted support from the influential elder Oliver Red Cloud and his Grey Eagle Society, as well as then tribal attorney Mario Gonzales. His "plan" was therefore endorsed by votes of the tribal councils on Pine Ridge, Rosebud and Cheyenne River.
68. Lazarus, Arthur, *Black Hills, White Justice: The Sioux Nation versus the United States, 1775 to the Present,*

HarperCollins Publishers, New York, 1991, p. 424.
69. Quoted in *ibid.*, p. 425.
70. *Ibid.* Miller articulates his outlandish view of Black Hills regional history in *Wicazo Sa Review, op. cit.*
71. Lazarus, *op. cit.*, p. 425.
72. *Ibid.* The resolution failed to pass the Senate by a narrow margin.
73. *Ibid.*, p. 424.
74. Russell Means, conversation with the author, April 1991.
75. Tim Giago, statement on National Public Radio, May 1988.

Genocide in Arizona?

The "Navajo-Hopi Land Dispute" in Perspective

Genocide is always and everywhere a political occurrence.

—Irving Louis Horowitz—
Genocide

There are an estimated twenty billion tons of high grade, low-sulfur coal underlying a stretch of Arizona desert known as Black Mesa. Rich veins of the mineral rest so near the surface that erosion has exposed them in many places. A veritable stripminer's delight, the situation presents a lucrative potential to the corporate interests profiting from America's spiraling energy consumption. The only fly in the ointment is that the land which would be destroyed in extracting the "black gold" is inhabited by a sizable number of people who will not—indeed, from their perspective, cannot—leave. This problem has caused the federal government to engage in one of the more cynical and convoluted processes of legalized expropriation in its long and sordid history of Indian affairs.

Historical Background

It all began in the 1860s when the army fought the "Kit Carson Campaign," a vicious war designed to eliminate the Diné (Navajo) people of the Southwest as a threat to ranching and mining concerns. The war featured a scorched earth policy directed against such targets as the Diné sheep herds and the peach orchards which had been carefully established over several generations at the bottom of Cañon de Chelly, in northeastern Arizona. The plan to starve the Indians into submission worked very well, and culminated in a forced march of virtually the entire Diné people to a desolate concentration camp at Bosque Redondo, adjoining Fort Sumner in eastern New Mexico. About a third of them died of disease and exposure in barely two years.[1] In 1868, the government faced a scandal, having tried and convicted officers of the Confederate Army for engaging in comparable atrocities against U.S. troops at such prison camps as Andersonville. To quell accusations of hypocrisy, the government entered into a treaty with the Diné, releasing them from internment and acknowledging, among other things, their right to a huge piece of barren land, mostly in western new Mexico.[2]

Over the next decade, however, it was discovered that much of the new reservation was usable as rangeland. Consequently, the government continually "adjusted" the boundaries westward, into Arizona, until the territory of the Diné completely engulfed that of another people, the Hopi. Still this posed little problem. The Diné, whose economy was based on sheep herding, lived dispersed upon the land, while the Hopi, agriculturalists, lived clustered in permanent villages. Conflict was minimal; the two peoples coexisted in a sort of natural balance, intermarrying frequently enough to create an interethnic entity called the Tobacco Clan.[3]

This began to change in 1882, when President Chester A. Arthur, in order to provide jurisdiction to J.H. Fleming, an Indian agent assisting Mormon missionaries in kidnapping Hopi children ("to educate them"), created a Hopi Reservation within the area already reserved for the Diné. Arbitrarily designated as being a rectangle of one degree longitude by one degree of latitude, the new reservation left Moenkopi, a major Hopi village, outside the boundary. Conversely, much Diné pasturage—and at least 300 Diné—were contained within the area, a matter supposedly accommodated by wording that it would be the territory of the Hopi and "such other Indians as the President may select."[4]

For nearly a generation, equilibrium was maintained. Then, in 1919, a group of mining companies attempted to negotiate mineral leases on Diné land. In 1920, the traditional Diné council of elders ("chiefs"), a mechanism of governance drawn in equal proportions from each of the clans comprising the nation, and which still held undisputed power in such matters, unanimously rejected the idea. The companies lobbied, and, in 1923, the federal government unilaterally replaced the traditional Diné government with a "Grand Council" composed of individuals of the government's choosing. Comprised of men compulsorily educated off-reservation rather than traditionals, and owing their status to Washington rather than the people they ostensibly represented, the new council promptly signed the leasing instruments. Thereafter, the council was the only entity recognized by the U.S. as "legitimately" representing Diné interests.[5]

This experiment was such a success that an idea was shortly hatched to replace all traditional Indian governments with modern "democratic" forms, based on models of corporate management. As discussed in greater length in another chapter, "American Indian Self-Governance," this concept became law with the Indian Reorganization Act of 1934 (IRA). Indian resistance to the IRA varied from place to place. Generally, the more "acculturated" the people, the greater the ease with which it was accepted.[6] At Hopi, where the traditional Kikmongwe form of government was and is still very much alive, 90 percent of all people eligible to vote for or against reorganization simply refused to participate, boycotting entirely a referendum required to garner at least the illusion they had accepted reorganization. As BIA employee Oliver LaFarge observed at the time:

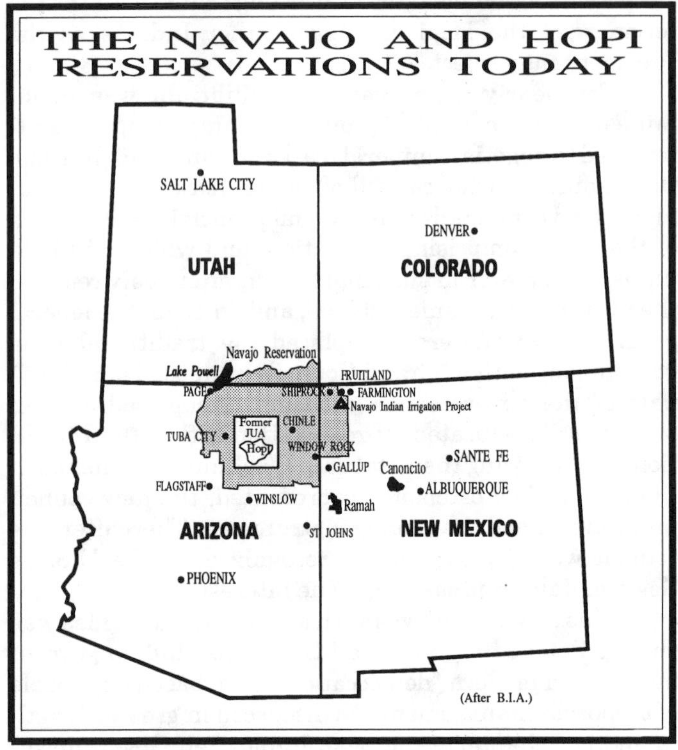

> [T]here were only 13 people in the [Hopi village of Hotevilla] willing to go to the polls out of a potential voting population of 250, [a spiritual leader] having announced he would have nothing to do with so un-Hopi a thing as a referendum. Here we also see the Hopi method of opposition...abstention of almost the whole village should be interpreted as a heavy opposition vote.[7]

The same situation prevailed in each of the Hopi villages. Indian Commissioner John Collier overcame this "difficulty" by declaring all abstentions to be "yes" votes, providing the appearance (to outsiders, such as the American public) that the Hopis had all but unanimously approved implementation of the IRA. Despite its clear rejection of Washington's governmental formula, Hopi was then quickly reorganized, opening a deep schism within that society which has not only never healed, but which is in some ways more acute today than it was fifty years ago.[8]

Effects of Reorganization

As is usually the case where patently imposed forms of governance are utilized by a colonial power to administer a subject people, the new Hopi tribal council rapidly learned to convert service to the oppressor into personal profit. Leadership of the 10-15 percent segment of Hopi society that had been assimilated into non-Hopi values via compulsory education and Mormon indoctrination—the sector which represented the total Hopi voter turnout during reorganization, and in all subsequent Hopi "elections"—had long been the station of the Sekaquaptewa family.[9] The men of the family—Abbott and Emory; later Emory Jr. and Wayne—rapidly captured political ascendancy within the council. Correspondingly, they garnered a virtual monopoly on incoming U.S. government contracts and concessions, business starts and the like. Their new wealth and position was duly invested in a system of patronage among the Mormon Hopis, and this most un-Hopi segment of Hopi society became far and away its richest and most powerful strata. In short order, what had remained a remarkably homogeneous and egalitarian culture was saddled with the ideological polarization, class structure and élitism marking Euroamerican "civilization."[10]

Meanwhile, Indian Commissioner Collier was quite concerned about the concept of reorganization—upon which he had staked his political future and personal credibility. His goal was to make IRA governments functional, "successful" reflections of mainstream corporate society. The Mormon Hopis were only too happy to oblige in moving Collier's grand scheme along, serving as a showpiece in exchange for a *quid pro quo* arrangement where they became the only Hopi entity the United States would deal with directly. The ability of the Kikmongwe to fulfill its traditional role of conducting Hopi affairs was drastically undermined. By 1940, the Sekaquaptewas and their followers had converted their alignment with the federal government into control of all Hopi political offices, appointed positions and controlled the budgets. In addition, they exerted control over the sole Hopi newspaper *(Qua Toqti),* grazing interests, and externally generated cash flow as well.

However, they had still bigger plans. These had emerged clearly by 1943, when the council, in collaboration with the Bureau of Indian Affairs (BIA) and over the strenuous objections of the Kikmongwe, successfully consummated a lobbying effort for the creation of "Grazing District 6," a 650,013 acre area surrounding the main Hopi villages and marked off for "exclusive Hopi use and occupancy." Insofar as nothing within the traditional Hopi lifeways had changed to cause them to disperse across the land, the only beneficiaries were the Sekaquaptewa clique. Their grazing activities and revenues were considerably expanded as a result of the establishment of the district. Meanwhile, some 100 Diné families who had lived on the newly defined District 6 land for generations were forced to relocate beyond its boundaries into the remainder of the 1882 Executive Order Area.[11]

The Mormons Come Marching In

By the early-1950s, with their gains of the 1940s consolidated and digested, the Sekaquaptewas were once again casting about for ways to expand their clout and income. Following the consolidation of Grazing District 6, they had allowed their council activities to lapse for several years while they pursued personal business enterprises. In 1951, however, they appear to have determined that reconstitution of the IRA government would be an expedient means through which to advance their interests. As devout Mormons, it was natural that they should retain the services of a well-connected Salt Lake City Mormon lawyer named John Boyden to pursue this end in the name of Hopi self-governance.[12] Undoubtedly sensing a potential for immense profitability both for himself and for his church, Boyden accepted the position of Hopi Tribal Attorney. His top priority, by agreement with the Sekaquaptewas, was to claim all of the 1882 Executive Order Area in the name of the Hopi IRA government. First, he wrote legislation allowing him to do so, and then pursued it through lawsuits such as the *Healing v. Jones* cases.[13]

Soon, the issues no longer focused primarily on the land, concomitant grazing rights and the like. By 1955, the mineral assets of the Four Corners region were being realized by the U.S. government and corporations.[14] Anaconda, Kerr-McGee, and other energy conglomerates were buying leases and opening mining/milling operations feeding the guaranteed market established by the ore buying program of the Atomic Energy Commission. Standard, Phillips, Gulf and Mobil (among others) were moving in on oil and natural gas properties.[15] The "worthless desert" into which the United States had shoved the Indians was suddenly being revealed as a resource mecca, and it was felt that the 1882 Executive Order Area might be a particularly rich locale.

Indications are that Boyden and the Sekaquaptewas originally hoped the courts would find that Hopi territory encompassed a portion of the Grants Uranium Belt. This did not pan out, however, and royalties (and contamination) from the uranium boom continued to accrue only to neighboring peoples such as Navajo and Laguna Pueblo. However, oil exploration proved a more lucrative proposition, and Boyden opened sealed bidding for leasing rights within District 6 during the fall of 1964. The proceeds came to $2.2 million, of which a flat $1 million in fees and bonuses was paid to Boyden's Salt Lake City law firm.[16]

With his own coffers brimming, the attorney turned to the service of his church as well as his Hopi and corporate clientele. Enlisting the assistance of a pair of regional politicos—Secretary of the Interior Stewart Udall (a fellow Mormon) and Colorado Representative Wayne Aspinall—both of whom professed that energy development would be "good for the West," he was able to negotiate a triangular coal leasing arrangement between the federally-approved Navajo and Hopi councils on the one hand, and the Peabody Coal Company (which he represented, along with the Hopi council) on the other. Not coincidentally, a controlling interest in Peabody was held at that time by the Mormon Church, for which Boyden was also serving as legal counsel during the lease negotiations. Kayenta, the location of the resulting Peabody mine on Black Mesa in the northern extreme of the 1882 Executive Order Area, sits astride what has turned out to be perhaps the richest low sulphur coal vein ever discovered in North America. Overall, the attorney's take on the deal is said to have again run into seven figures.[17] For him, things were moving right along.

The Nature of the "Land Dispute"

With a long-term money-maker functioning at Black Mesa, Boyden returned his attentions to his real agenda: securing the entirety of the Executive Order Area, and the fossil fuels underlying it, on behalf of the Sekaquaptewa faction. While opening moves in this gambit had been made during the 1950s, the serious campaign really got off the ground during the early 1970s. It was previously determined (in the second *Healing v. Jones* case), that since both the Hopi and Diné were entitled to "equal use and benefit" from the 1882 Executive Order Area outside of Grazing District 6, the Diné had no right to keep livestock in numbers exceeding "their half" of the federally established "carrying capacity" of the land. In a major suit in 1972, *Hamilton v. Nakai,* Boyden argued that the Diné could not exceed their half of the carrying capacity even if Hopis were not using the other half. Boyden was thereby able to obtain court orders requiring a 90 percent reduction in the number of Diné livestock within the Joint Use Area (JUA).[18] Any such reduction would be tantamount to starvation for a people like the traditional Diné, dependent for subsistence upon a sheep economy. Boyden and the Sekaquaptewas anticipated that this courtroom victory would literally drive their opponents out of the JUA, into the Navajo Nation proper. Afterwards, with virtually no Diné living in the contested territory, arguments concerning the exclusivity of Hopi interests and prerogatives therein would be much more plausible than had previously been the case.

On the judicial front, however, the Boyden/Sekaquaptewa side had apparently not calculated that the targeted Diné would have no place to go; the land base of the Navajo Nation was already saturated people and sheep. The Diné had no alternative but to refuse to comply, a situation which forced Boyden into a whole series of related suits, each of which generated additional judicial decrees against them. Among other things this included a freeze on building new homes, corrals or other structures within the JUA. But none of the decrees succeeded in forcing the Diné out of the 1882 area.[19] Federal authorities did not feel compelled to deploy the level of force necessary to implement their courts' various decisions.

The situation changed again with the arrival of the "energy crisis" of the 1970s. Overnight, "energy self-sufficiency" became a national obsession. Shale oil, coal gasification and other esoteric terminology became household matters of discussion. Congress sat down to do a quick inventory of its known energy assets, and, suddenly, the Black Mesa coal which had barely elicited a "ho-hum" response from legislators a few months before, became a focus of attention. Arizona superhawks such as Senator Barry Goldwater and Representative Sam Steiger saw a way to put their state on the energy map of "national interest" by consummating plans already laid by powerful economic entities such as Western Energy Supply and Transmission (WEST) Associates.[20]

There was only one hitch to the program: it was impossible to stripmine the land so long as Diné people were living on it. The solution, of course, for the federal government as well as the Hopi council and the energy corporations, was to remove the people. Hence, as early as 1971, Boyden offered his services in drafting a bill to be introduced in the U.S. House of Representatives calling for the formal division of the JUA into halves. The draft called for all Hopis living on the Diné side of the partition line to be compulsorily relocated into Hopi territory and vice versa. Given that virtually no Hopis actually lived in the JUA, the law would empty 50 percent of the desired acreage of population, opening it up for mining.[21] Several scientific studies already suggested that once stripmining and slurry operations commenced in so substantial a portion of Black Mesa, the adjoining areas would be rendered uninhabitable in short order, forcing the Diné off even their remaining portion of the 1882 area.[22] Under the guise of an "equitable resolution" to a property rights question, the Boyden/Steiger plan sought to dispossess the JUA Diné, accomplishing what the Mormon Hopis had been trying to do all along.

Steiger dutifully introduced his draft legislation in 1972, but it met with public relations problems. The forced mass relocation of indigenous people was something which had not been done in North America since the nineteenth century. While it squeaked through the House by a narrow margin, it stalled in the Senate.[23] The congressional fear seems to have been that, energy crisis notwithstanding, the American public might balk at such a policy. This seemed especially true in the immediate context of the civil rights, anti-war and Black Power movements. Democratic presidential nominee George McGovern came out against the idea of partition and relocation in the JUA, and even Goldwater, the arch-conservative, expressed doubts about the wisdom of the plan under such circumstances.[24] A plausible "humanitarian cover" was needed, under which to effect the legislation necessary to clear the population from much of the JUA.

Here, Boyden once again proved his mettle. Retaining David Evans & Associates—yet another Mormon-controlled Salt Lake City firm—to handle the "public image of the Hopi Tribe," he oversaw the creation of something called "the Navajo-Hopi range dispute." Within this scenario, which the Evans PR people packaged rather sensationally and then fed to the press in massive doses, the concnept that the Hopis and Diné occupying the JUA were at irreconcilable odds over ownership of the land. The result of this was a virtual "shooting war" between the two indigenous peoples fueled not only by the property rights dispute, but by "deep historical and intercultural animosities." No mention was made of mineral interests, or that Evans was simultaneously representing WEST Associates, eager as that consortium was to mine and burn JUA coal. As *Washington Post* reporter Mark Panitch recounted in 1974:

> The relationship between the Hopi council and the power companies became almost symbiotic. On the one hand, [Hopi Tribal Chairman Clarence] Hamilton's speeches written by Evans would be distributed through the public relations machinery of 23 major Western utilities [comprising the WEST group]. On the other hand, these utilities would tell their customers, often through local media contacts, that the Hopis were "good Indians" who

> wouldn't shut off the juice which ran their air conditioners...Because of the efforts by representatives of the Hopi to present the [IRA government's] viewpoint, the Hopi rapidly took on the aura of the underdog who just wanted to help his white brother. Some of the Navajo, on the other hand, were saying threatening things about closing down polluting power plants and requiring expensive reclamation of strip-mined land.[25]

The image of "range war type violence" was reinforced by Evans photographers' snapshots of out-buildings and junk vehicles abandoned at various locations in the JUA. These were used for target practice by teenaged "plinkers" (a common enough practice throughout rural America), and were often riddled with bullet holes. The Evans group presented their photos to the media as evidence of periodic "firefights" between Hopis and Diné. As Panitch put it:

> During 1971-72, few newspapers escaped a Sunday feature on the "range war" about to break out between two hostile tribes. Photos of burned corrals and shot up stock tanks and wells were printed...By calling Evans and Associates, a TV crew could arrange a roundup of trespassing Navajo stock. Occasionally, when a roundup was in progress, Southwestern newsmen would be telephoned and notified of the event.[26]

What real violence there was came mainly from a group of thugs, such as a non-Indian named Elmer Randolph, put on the payroll and designated as "Hopi Tribal Rangers" by the Mormon faction. Their specialty was beating to a pulp and arresting for trespass any Diné come to retrieve sheep which had strayed into Grazing District 6.[27] When a group of Diné attempted to erect a fence to keep their livestock off the Hopi land, the Sekaquaptewas first called a television crew to the spot and then personally tore the fence down, demanding before the cameras that the Arizona National Guard be dispatched to "restore order" within the JUA. This, too, was passed off by news commentators as a straight-faced indication of "the level of violence existing among the Indians."[28] The federal government was morally obligated, so the argument went, to physically separate the two "warring groups" before there were fatalities. Predictably, Representatvie Steiger gave this theme official voice:

> There is nothing funny about the violence which has already transpired—livestock mutilations, corral burnings, fence destruction, water tank burnings, and at least one shooting incident. If we permit ourselves to be seduced into some kind of legal procrastination and someone is killed, I am sure we would assume the responsibility that is patently ours. Let us not wait for that kind of catalyst.[29]

At this juncture, the powerful Goldwater decided the time was ripe to weigh in along the Boyden/Sekaquaptewa/Steiger axis. "I have not supported the Steiger approach mostly because it involved money [to relocate the impacted Diné]," Goldwater announced, "[but now] I do not think we have to pay money to relocate Indians, when in the case of the Navajo they have 16 million acres [outside the JUA]." He went on to assert with bold-faced falsity that the Diné had "literally tens of thousands of acres that are not being used" and which were therefore available to absorb those displaced by the partition and relocation proposal, ostensibly without significantly altering their way of life.[30] John Boyden seized this opportunity to draft a new bill, this one to be introduced by Goldwater and Arizona's other senator, Pat Fannin. It called for partition and the rapid, uncompensated, and compulsory relocation of all Diné residing within the Hopi portion of the JUA. By comparison, the Steiger draft bill, which had called for the federal government to underwrite all costs associated with relocation, including the acquisition of additional lands as needed to resettle those effected, seemed benign.[31] This, of course, did much to attract support to the latter.

Relocation Becomes Law

The Goldwater/Fannin initiative was a ruse designed to drive liberal Democrats into countering the draft bill's harsh proposals, with a "gentler" plan of their own. This assumed the form of House Resolution 10337, yet another draft instrument in which Boyden took a hand, this one introduced by liberal Utah Representative Wayne Owens. It called not only for compensation to the victims of the partition, as the Steiger draft had already done, but a decade-long time period during which the relocation was to be "phased in" so that those to be moved would not be overly traumatized. When Owens placed his proposition on the table, Steiger promptly abandoned his own draft and became an endorser of the Owens Bill, evidence that the scheme was indeed a ruse. This newly-hatched liberal/conservative coalition was destined to finally produce Boyden's desired result.

Despite a letter sent by Arizona Representative Manuel Lujan that passage of H.R. 10337 might result in "a bloodbath in northern Arizona that would make the My Lai Massacre look like a Sunday School picnic," and that it would in any event be "the most shameful act this government has perpetrated on its citizens since Colonial days," the Owens/Boyden concept was approved by the House Interior Committee by voice vote in February 1974.[32] It was then forwarded to the full house for passage, accomplished on May 29, 1974, by a vote of 290 to 38.[33] On the same day, U.S. District Judge James Walsh issued a contempt of court decree against Chairman Peter McDonald and the Navajo tribal government for having failed to comply with his order to reduce Diné livestock in the JUA.[34]

The bill was passed by the Senate shortly thereafter,

by a vote of 72-0 and in a somewhat different form than it had been approved by the House. Although this usually precipitates an ad hoc committee meeting involving representatives of both chambers in order to hammer out a mutually acceptable joint version of the legislation, in this instance the House took the extraordinary step of simply approving the Senate version without further discussion.[35] The statute was then routed on an urgent basis to President Gerald Ford, who signed it without reading it, while enjoying a ski vacation in Vail, Colorado.[36]

Enacted as Public Law 93-531, the bill required a 50-50 division of the JUA, with the actual partition boundary to be established by the federal district court in Arizona.[37] It established a three-member "Navajo-Hopi Relocation Commission," to be appointed by the Secretary of Interior. Within two years of the date the court's partition line was defined, the commission was charged with submitting a plan to Congress detailing how relocation was to be accomplished. Thirty days after Congress approved the relocation plan, a five year period would begin during which relocation would be carried out.

A total of $37 million was initially budgeted, both to underwrite the relocation commission's functioning, and to pay "incentive bonuses" of $5,000 to the head of each Diné family who "voluntarily" agreed to relocate during the first operational year of the program. Bonuses of $4,000 were slated to be paid to those who agreed to go during the second year, $3,000 during the third, and $2,000 during the fourth. In addition, each family of three or fewer individuals was deemed eligible to receive up to $17,000 with which to acquire "replacement housing." Families of four or more could receive up to $25,000 for this purpose.

P.L. 93-531 also contained several other important provisions. It directed the Secretary of Interior to implement Judge Walsh's order for Diné livestock reduction by impounding the animals outright. It authorized the sec-

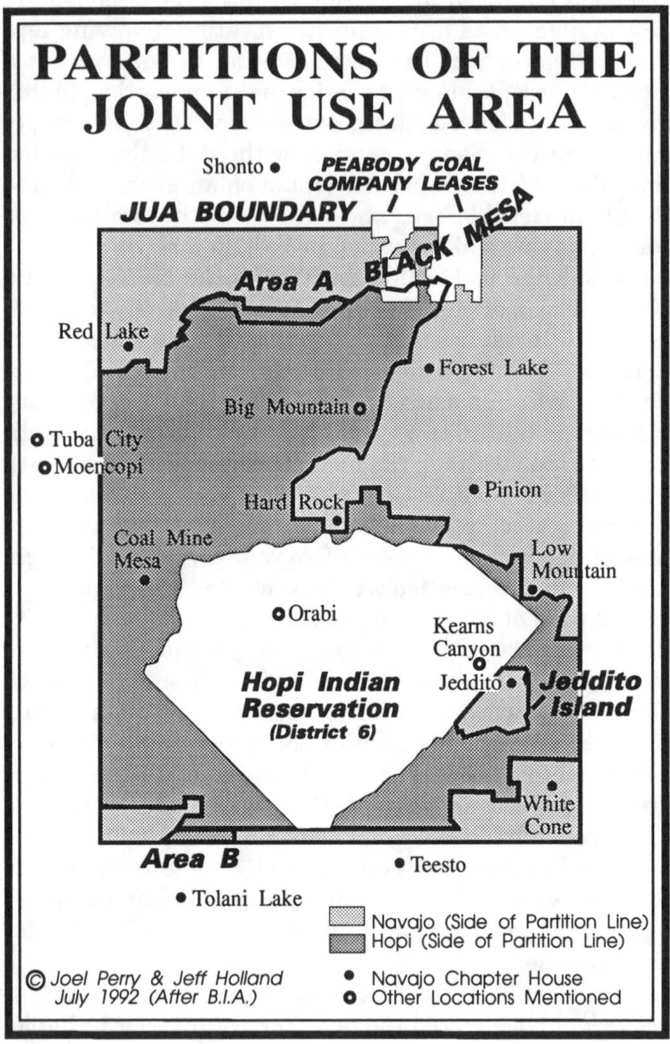
PARTITIONS OF THE JOINT USE AREA
Shonto
PEABODY COAL COMPANY LEASES
JUA BOUNDARY
BLACK MESA
Area A
Red Lake
Forest Lake
Big Mountain
Tuba City
Moencopi
Pinion
Hard Rock
Coal Mine Mesa
Low Mountain
Orabi
Kearns Canyon
Hopi Indian Reservation (District 6)
Jeddito
Jeddito Island
White Cone
Area B
Teesto
Tolani Lake
Navajo (Side of Partition Line)
Hopi (Side of Partition Line)
© Joel Perry & Jeff Holland July 1992 (After B.I.A.)
Navajo Chapter House
Other Locations Mentioned

retary to sell to the Navajo Nation up to 250,000 acres of land under jurisdiction of the Bureau of Land Management at "fair market value," and provided Navajo authority to acquire up to 150,000 additional acres of privately held land. (This is as opposed to 911,000 acres from which Diné were ordered removed in the JUA.)[38] The law also authorized litigation to resolve Hopi claims to land surrounding the village of Moenkopi, left out of the original Executive Order Area.[39]

Problems with P.L. 95-531

The first grit in P.L. 95-931's gears appeared almost immediately. Virtually none of the targeted people were likely to relocate on anything resembling a voluntary basis. The second followed shortly thereafter, when it was found that the size of the Diné population affected had been dramatically underestimated. This was due to language in the act which stipulated the partition would "include the higher density population areas of each tribe within the portion of the lands partitioned to each tribe to minimize and avoid undue social, economic, and cultural disruption insofar as possible." Congress had apparently accepted without question an assertion made by John Boyden through Evans and Associates that if this principle were adhered to, the number of impacted Diné would be "about 3,500."[40] There is no reason to assume this information was accurate.

More to the point, when the court's partition line, called the "Simkin" line after the Department of Interior official who charted it, was ultimately finalized on February 10, 1977, it conformed much more closely to coal deposits than to demography.[41] Those areas Peabody preferred to mine first, including portions of the northern JUA furthest from the Hopi mesas but adjoining the Kayenta mining sites, were included within the Hopi territory (see map). Consequently, estimates of the number of Diné to be relocated were raised to 9,525 by 1980,[42] and have now reached 17,500 people overall.[43] Only 109 Hopis were effected, and their relocation was completed in 1976.[44]

As the numbers forced to relocate became clear, the costs associated with the relocation program escalated wildly. In 1974, Congress had estimated the entire effort could be underwritten through allocation of $28 million in direct costs and another $9 million in "administrative overhead." By 1985 the relocation alone was consuming $4 million per year (having by then expended nearly $21 million in all). With a Diné population vastly larger (and more resistant) than originally projected, direct costs were by 1985 being estimated at a level of "at least $500 million."[45] Inflation and other factors have, since then, driven even this enormous sum considerably higher. Similarly, the original time-span conceived for relocation to be fully implemented—placing culmination of the program in 1982—quickly proved impractical. Revised several times, the completion date was by 1985 being projected as 1993.[46]

Predictably, Goldwater's assertion that the Navajo Nation had "tens of thousands" of idle acres outside the JUA onto which relocatees could move and continue their traditional lifeways proved utterly inaccurate. Leaving aside the spiritual significance of specific JUA geography to its Diné residents, it was well known that the entirety of the reservation, consisting of arid and semi-arid terrain, had been saturated with sheep (and thus with traditional people) since at least as early as the mid-1930s.[47] Meanwhile, the 400,000 acres of "replacement lands" authorized under P.L. 93-531 for acquisition by the Navajo Nation as a means of absorbing "surplus" relocatees was blocked by a combination of conflicting congressional interests, a requirement in the law that such land be within eighteen miles of the reservation's boundaries, non-Indian lobbying, and avarice on the part of the Navajo tribal government itself.[48] The result was that the relocatees were left with no place to go other than urban areas, antithetical to their way of life.

Belatedly, Congress began to "discover" the falsity of the "range war" hoax, and that the Hopis were hardly unified in their desire to see the Diné pushed from half the JUA. There was no excuse for the tardiness of their discovery. As early as the beginning of 1972, Kikmongwe Mina Lansa had come before the House Interior Committee while the Steiger Bill was being considered, and made it clear that the traditional Hopi majority wished to see the Diné remain on the land, insofar as this represented a barrier to stripmining in the JUA. She further informed the legislators that:

> The [IRA] council of people, Clarence Hamilton and others, say all Hopis are supporting this bill through the newspapers and publicizing to the world that both Hopi and Navajo are going to fight each other. These things are not true, and it makes us very ashamed to see that some of our young people who claim to represent us created much publicity in this way while in this capital lately.[49]

In 1975, Lansa took the unprecedented step (for a Kikmongwe) of openly participating in a largely non-Indian coalition seeking to repeal P.L. 93-531. "We should all work together against Washington to revoke this bill," she said. "The Hopi council favors this bill. But as a Hopi chief, I say no. The Hopis and Navajos can live right where they are."[50] She withdrew her support to the non-Indian group when one of its leaders, Bill Morrall, called for the abolition of both the Hopi and Navajo reservations, per se.[51] However, her opposition to the Hopi IRA government and the relocation law, and her support of the JUA Diné, remained outspoken and unswerving. In 1975 and 1976, she and other Hopi spiritual leaders such as David Monongye and Thomas Banyacya supported suits intended to challenge federal authority to implement policy on the say-so of the Hopi IRA government.[52]

The double standard of determining "equity" inherent to U.S. legal treatment of indigenous peoples also became increasingly apparent within the rationalizations through which the relocation act had been passed. Where the federal government or its non-Indian citizenry has been shown to have illegally acquired Indian land, the victims have never been allowed to recover their property. U.S. judicial doctrine has instead held that they are entitled only to "just compensation," in the form of money, and in an amount determined to be "fair" by those who stole the property in the first place.[53] No white population in North America has ever been relocated in order to satisfy an indigenous land right. Attorney Richard Schifter framed the question plainly and succinctly before the Senate Interior Committee in September 1972:

> Could it be, may I ask, that where the settlers are white, we pay the original owners off in cash; but where the settlers are Indian, we find expulsion and removal an acceptable alternative? Can such a racially discriminatory approach be considered as meeting the constitutional requirement for due process?[54]

Representative Sam Steiger offered the official (and patently racist) response to Schifter: "I would simply tell the gentleman that the distinction between that situation and this one is that in those instances we were dealing with non-Indians occupying and believing they have a right in the lands. Here we are dealing with two Indian tribes. That is the distinction."[55]

Under the circumstances, it had become obvious by 1977 that the sort of negative but minimal social, economic and cultural impact upon relocatees so blithely called for under P.L. 93-531 was simply impossible. Again, there was no excuse for the tardy realization. Aside from an abundance of Diné testimony on the likely consequences of relocation which was entered during the congressional deliberation process, anthropologist David Aberle had reported on May 15, 1973 to House Subcommittee on Indian Affairs that the outcome would be the sociocultural disintegration of the target population:

> Remove the sheepherder to a place where he cannot raise stock, remove the herd, and you have removed the foundation on which the family is vested. Demoralization and social disorganization are the inevitable consequences, and the younger people, no longer beneficiaries of a stable home life, become just another addition to the problems of maladjustment and alienation in our society.[56]

Yet the relocation program moved forward.

Impact Upon the Diné

Aberle was hardly the only expert warning that the consequences of P.L. 93-531 would be dire. As early as 1963, sociologists such as Marc Fried had been articulating the high costs of imposed relocation upon various populations.[57] By 1973, anthropologists like Thayer Scudder had also published in-depth studies specifically focusing upon the consequences of forcibly relocating landbased indigenous peoples from rural to urban environments.[58] And, of course, there were the predictions of the Diné themselves. Such information was coming, not only from the traditionals out on the land, but from younger, college-educated Navajos.[59] As for the traditionals, they were never less than unequivocal in their assessment. For instance, Katherine Smith, an elder from the Big Mountain area of the northern JUA, told senate investigators in 1972 that:

> I will never leave the land, this sacred place. The land is part of me, and I will one day be part of the land. I could never leave. My people are here, and have been here forever. My sheep are here. All that has meaning is here.

> I live here and I will die here. That is the way it is, and the way it must be. Otherwise, the people will die, the sheep will die, the land will die. There would be no meaning to life if this happened.[60]

As the relocation program came alive, such warnings began to be borne out. The impact was exacerbated by the tactics used to convince the Diné to "voluntarily" sign up for relocation. High on the list of these was the impoundment of sheep. The day after Judge Walsh signed the order declaring the Simkin partition line official, Hopi Tribal Chairman Abbott Sekaquaptewa (who replaced Clarence Hamilton in that position during 1976) ordered a group of his rangers into the Hopi portion of the JUA to begin seizing every head of Diné livestock they could lay their hands on. Sekaquaptewa had no legal authority to undertake such action,[61] but a special force of 40 SWAT-trained and equipped BIA police were immediately sent in to back him up.[62] This precipitated a crisis in which Walsh formally enjoined the Hopis from going ahead with their stock impoundment program.[63] Sekaquaptewa, seeming "almost eager for a shootout," defied the order, and demanded the government "get the army and some machine guns out here, because that's all the Navajos understand."[64]

Rather than arresting Sekaquaptewa for inciting violence and blatant contempt of court, the BIA's operational director in the JUA, Bill Benjamin (a Chippewa), attempted to placate him with a plan whereby the Bureau would buy up Diné sheep within the Hopi partition area at 150 percent of market rate. This, he argued, would remove many of the offending animals peacefully, while—in theory at least—provide the Diné with funds to underwrite their move to "their own side of the line." Under provisions of the law, Benjamin had five years in which to complete his stock reduction program. Using the buy-out scheme, he was able to secure 67,000 of the estimated

120,000 sheep being herded by Diné on Hopi-partitioned land. At the end of the year, however, the BIA refused to allocate the monies promised to make good on Benjamin's "purchases." The people whose stock was at issue were, of course, left destitute, while Benjamin was made to appear a liar, destroying the element of trust which the Diné had extended to him. As he himself put it at the time:

> Those people [the Diné] are under tremendous strain. They are facing the unknown of relocation, and as their stock is taken away they are losing a bank account and a way of life. Traditionally, their day was planned around the needs of the flock, and if they needed money they could sell a sheep or two. But as things are now, we can expect a lot of personal and family problems...All I know is that I can't deliver on a promise I made to people in a very difficult situation.[65]

The stock impoundment effort slowed after this, but has been continued at a steady, deliberate and—for the Diné—socially, economically and psychologically debilitating pace ever since. It has not, however, been the only coercive measure used. Judge Walsh's order making the Simkin line official also included an instruction renewing his earlier freeze on Diné construction within the Hopi partition area, other than with "a permit from the Hopi Tribe."[66] The Hopis, of course, have issued no such permits and have used their rangers to destroy any new structures which have appeared (as well as more than a few older ones). Even repair of existing structures has been attacked as a violation of the building freeze. This has caused a steady deterioration in the living conditions of the targeted Diné, as well as a chronic anxiety about whether the very roofs of their hogans might not be simply ripped off from over their heads.[67] The situation has now lasted eighteen years.

At the same time, those who bowed to the unrelenting pressure and accepted relocation were meeting a fate at least equally as harsh as that being visited upon those who refused. As of March 1984, not a single acre of rural land had been prepared to receive relocatees. For the approximately 30 percent of all targeted families who had allowed themselves to be moved into cities or towns, "even the Relocation Commission's statistics revealed a problem of tremendous proportions:"

> Almost 40 percent of those relocated to off-reservation communities no longer owned their government-provided house. In Flagstaff, Arizona, the community which received the largest number of relocatees, nearly half the 120 families who had moved there no longer owned their homes. When county and tribal legal services offices discovered that a disproportionate [number] of the houses had ended up in the hands of a few realtors, allegations of fraud began to surface. Lawsuits were filed by local attorneys; investigations were begun by the United States Attorney's Office, the Federal Bureau of Investigation, the Arizona Department of Real Estate, and the Relocation Commission; and the most in-depth review of the Relocation program which has ever been undertaken by a body of Congress was prepared.[68]

A classic case of what was and is happening is that of Hosteen Nez.

> In 1978, Nez, an 82-year-old relocatee, moved to Flagstaff from Sand Springs. Within a year, Nez suffered a heart attack, could not pay his property taxes or utility bills, lost his $60,000 ranch-style home, and moved back to the reservation [where he also had no home, having relocated from his old one].[69]

By the mid-1980s, relocatee reports of increased physical illness, stress and alcoholism, and family breakup were endemic.[70] At least one member of the relocation commission itself publicly denounced the program as being "as bad as...the concentration camps in World War II," and then resigned his position.[71] Local editorial writers had also begun to denounce the human consequences of P.L. 93-531 in the most severe terms imaginable:

> [I]f the federal government proceeds with its genocidal relocation of traditional Navajos to alien societies, [the problem] will grow a thousandfold and more...The fact that it is a problem manufactured in Washington does not ease the pain and suffering—nor does it still the anger that fills too many hearts.[72]

Use of the term "genocide" in this connection was by then not uncommon and was neither rhetorical nor inaccurate. Thayer Scudder and others had already scientifically documented the reality of what was being called "the deliberate, systematic, willful destruction of a people."[73] At least two careful studies had concluded unequivocally that U.S. policy *vis-à-vis* the JUA Diné violated a broad range of international laws, including the United Nations' 1948 Convention on Punishment and Prevention of the Crime of Genocide.[74] But still the government moved forward.

Diné Resistance

Resistance to extermination—whether physical or cultural—is a natural and predictable human response. In the case of the JUA Diné, it was foreshadowed in a statement to Indian Commissioner Philleo Nash by Navajo tribal council member Carl Todacheenie. The statement was made in 1953, shortly after the *Healing v. Jones* (II) decision:

> The only way the Navajo people are going to move, we know, is they have to have another Bataan Death March. The United States government will have to do that...We're settled out there [in the JUA], and we're not going to advise our people to move, no matter who says. They probably got to chop off our heads. That's the only

way we're going to move out of there.[75]

More than two decades later, on March 3, 1977, when Arizona Representative Dennis DeConcini (who had replaced Sam Steiger in 1976) attended a meeting of Diné at White Cone, in the southeastern Diné partition area, he heard exactly the same thing. "Livestock reduction means starvation to us," DeConcini was told by 84-year-old Emma Nelson. "Washington has taken our livestock without replacing it with any other way of making a living." Another area Diné, Chester Morris, was more graphic: "The enforcement of P.L. 93-531 means starvation, homelessness, mentally disturbed *[sic]*, alcoholism, family dislocation, crime and even death for many." "This is very emotional," Miller Nez, a local resident, went on, "and at some point I think we're going to resist any further attempt by Washington to take away our only source of support. I think sooner or later there will be killing of individuals."[76]

The Diné were, to be sure, already resisting, and had been for 23 years, simply by their refusal to comply with the terms of *Healing v. Jones.* It was escalated on October 2, 1977, when an elder named Pauline Whitesinger faced down a crew hired by the BIA to erect a barbed wire fence. When the crew began to construct a section bisecting Whitesinger's sheep graze, she told them to stop. When they didn't, she drove her pickup truck straight at them. They left, but returned the next day and resumed work. This time, she chased them away by throwing handfuls of dirt into their faces. Whitesinger was shortly arrested on assorted charges, but later acquitted.[77]

Often during the following year and a half, fencing crews showed up for work in the morning only to find that the wire and posts they'd laboriously installed the day before had been torn down during the night. During mid-summer 1979, a crew appeared on the land of elder Katherine Smith, only to find themselves staring into the muzzle of her .22 caliber rifle. She fired over their heads and, when they scattered, she began dismantling the fence before their eyes. Smith was arrested on serious charges, only to receive a directed verdict of acquittal from a judge responsive to her argument that she had been beside herself with rage in confronting a law she knew to be not only wrong, but immoral.[78]

At about the same time Smith was firing her rifle, the American Indian Movement (AIM) was conducting its Fifth International Indian Treaty Council (IITC) at the sacred site of Big Mountain in the Hopi partitioned portion of the northern JUA. Convened in that location at the request of the Diné elders, the council was intended as a means of garnering outside support for what the targeted population expected to be a bitter battle for survival. During the council, the elders prepared a statement which read in part:

> We do hereby declare total resistance to any effort or influence to be removed from our homes and ancestral lands. We further declare our right to live in peace with our Hopi neighbors.[79]

Traditional Hopi leaders David Monongye and Thomas Banyacya attended the council, extending unity and support from the Kikmongwe to the Big Mountain resistance. IITC pledged itself to take the situation of the JUA Diné before the United Nations.[80] Diné AIM leader Larry Anderson then announced his organization was establishing a permanent survival camp at the council site, located on the property of AIM member Bahe Kadenahe. Anderson also promised to establish a legal defense apparatus to support the Big Mountain effort as rapidly as possible. This was accomplished by securing the services of Boston attorney Lew Gurwitz to head up what became known as the Big Mountain Legal Defense/Offense Committee (BMLDOC). By 1982, BMLDOC, utilizing funds provided by the National Lawyers Guild (NLG), had opened a headquarters in Flagstaff, the most proximate town of any size to the JUA.[81]

Over the next two years, Gurwitz entered several suits on behalf of individual Diné people suffering under the impact of stock reduction, and began to assemble a legal staff composed primarily of student interns underwritten by the NLG.[82] He also began to organize an external support network for the Big Mountain resistance which at its peak had active chapters in 26 states and several foreign countries.[83] On a related front, BMLDOC put together an independent commission to study the international legal implications of federal relocation policy in the JUA, and collaborated with organizations such as the Washington, D.C.-based Indian Law Resource Center in making presentations to the United Nations Working Group on Indigenous Populations.[84]

As this was going on, more direct forms of physical resistance were also continuing. For instance, in 1980, Kadenahe was arrested along with 20 others (dubbed the "Window Rock 21") during a confrontation with BIA police. Charged with several offenses, he was later acquitted on all counts. At about the same time, elder Alice Benally and three of her daughters confronted a fencing crew, were maced, arrested and each charged with eight federal crimes. They too were eventually acquitted on all counts.

The spring of 1981 saw a large demonstration at the Keams Canyon BIA facility which caused Acting Commissioner of Indian Affairs Kenneth Payton to temporarily suspend livestock impoundment operations. In 1983, after livestock reduction had been resumed, Big Mountain elder Mae Tso was severely beaten while physically resisting impoundment of her horses. Arrested and jailed, she suffered two heart attacks while incarcerated. She was ultimately acquitted of having engaged in any criminal offense.[85]

Matters reached their peak in this regard during June 1986, in preparation for a federally-established date

(July 7 of that year) when outright forced relocation was to be implemented. The scenario called for large units of heavily armed BIA police and U.S. marshals to move into the Hopi partition area, physically removing all Diné who had refused to relocate in response to less drastic and immediate forms of coercion. In the event, BMLDOC managed to bring some 2,000 outside supporters into the contested zone, AIM made it known that its contribution to defense of the area would likely be "other than pacifistic," and the government backed down from the specter of what Gurwitz described as "70-year-old Diné grandmothers publicly engaged in armed combat with the forces of the United States of America."[86]

Rather than suffer the international public relations debacle which would undoubtedly have accompanied a resort to open warfare against the Diné resistance, federal authorities opted to engage in a waiting game, utilizing the relentless pressure of stock reduction, fencing and the like to simply wear down the opposition. Their strategy also seems to have encompassed the likelihood that, absent the sort of head-on government/Indian collision implicit to the imposition of an absolute deadline, the attention of non-Indian supporters would be difficult or impossible to hold. The defense coalition BMLDOC had so carefully nurtured was thus virtually guaranteed to atrophy over a relatively short term of apparent government inactivity, affording authorities a much greater latitude of operational secrecy in which to proceed.[87]

In 1988, BMLDOC attorney Lee Brooke Phillips, in collaboration with attorneys Roger Finzel and Bruce Ellison, filed a lawsuit, *Manybeads v. United States.* The action was an attempt to take pressure off the Diné by blocking relocation on the basis of the policy's abridgement of first amendment guarantees of religious freedom.[88] Although it initially seemed promising, the suit was dismissed by U.S. District Judge Earl Carroll on October 20, 1989 because of the Supreme Court's adverse ruling in the so-called "G-O Road Case" concerning the rights of indigenous people in northern California to specific geographic areas for spiritual reasons. At present, Phillips is engaged in appeals to have the *Manybeads* suit reinstated, but the outlook is not favorable.[89]

Resistance under these conditions adds up primarily to a continuing refusal to leave the land. By the summer of 1992, approximately 75 percent of the Diné originally targeted for relocation remain where they were at the outset, stubbornly replenishing their flocks despite ongoing impoundments, repairing hogans and corrals in defiance of the building freeze, and conducting periodic forays to dismantle sections of the hated partition line fence.[90] Although suffering the full range of predictable effects stemming from the government's longterm effort to push them quietly off their land, there is currently no indication they will alter their position or course of action.

Liberal Obfuscation

Almost from the moment it became evident Diné resistance would be a serious reality, the government began a campaign to mask the implications of P.L. 93-531 behind a more liberal and "humanitarian" façade. The first overt attempt along this line occurred in July 1978 when Barry Goldwater responded to a challenge presented by Diné elders Roberta Blackgoat and Violet Ashke during the culmination of AIM's "Longest Walk" in Washington, DC the same month. At their invitation, he traveled to Big Mountain to meet with the resisters. Goldwater used the occasion to try and confuse the issue, asserting that the relocation act entailed no governmental policy "that says that [the Diné] have to move or what [they] have to do."[91] Even the establishment press responded negatively to such a clumsy distortion.[92]

Finding such methods ineffectual, Goldwater quietly made it known that he would not oppose token gestures proposed by congressional liberals to create a public appearance that relocation was less harsh in its implications than was actually the case. The main weight of this effort fell upon Dennis DeConcini, who had replaced Wayne Owens as an Arizona senator in 1976, and Representative Morris Udall, who had already publicly sided with the Sekaquaptewas.[93] Both lawmakers tendered proposals to amend P.L. 93-531 to provide for "life estates" allowing limited numbers of Diné elders to remain on 90 acre parcels within the Hopi partition area until they died. No provisions were made to allow these selected elders to retain the familial/community context which lent meaning to their lives, have access to sufficient grazing land to maintain their flocks, or to pass along their holdings to their heirs. In effect, they were simply granted the "right" to live out their lives in impoverished isolation. Not unreasonably, the Diné began in short order to refer to the scheme as an offering of "death estates."

Nonetheless, a combination of the DeConcini and Udall initiatives were passed as Public Law 96-305 in 1980.[94] Touted as having "corrected the worst of the problems inherent to P.L. 93-531," the new law immediately became a focus of resistance in its own right. It was generally viewed, as Diné activist Danny Blackgoat put it in 1985, as "a way to divide the unity of the people, setting up struggles between relatives and neighbors over who should receive an 'estate,' and causing those who were offered estates to abandon those who weren't. That way, the resistance would fall apart, and the government would be able to do whatever it wanted." But, as Blackgoat went on to observe, "It didn't work. The people rejected the whole idea, and our struggle actually increased after the 1980 law was passed."[95]

As Diné resistance and outside support mounted, the liberals adopted a different strategy. Udall first engineered a February 25, 1986, memorandum of understanding whereby the relocation commission—which was by that point openly admitting it could not meet its goals—would essentially dissolve itself and pass over its responsibilities to the BIA. He then secured an agreement from both Ivan Sidney (who had replaced Abbott Sekaquaptewa as Hopi tribal chairman) and Indian Commissioner Ross Swimmer to forego forcible relocation, pending "further legislative remedy" of the situation. Next, he teamed up with Arizona congressman (now senator) John McCain to introduce "compromise legislation," House Resolution 4281, which would have allowed an exchange of land between Diné and Hopi within the partitioned areas without disturbing the basic premises of P.L. 93-531 in any way at all.[96]

The Udall-McCain Bill was already in the process of being rejected by the resistance—on the grounds that it accomplished nothing of substance—when Goldwater began entering his own objections to the effect that it was time to stop "coddling" the resisters. H.R. 4281 thus died without being put to a vote. This provoked New Mexico Representative Bill Richardson to propose a bill (H.R. 4872) requiring a formal moratorium on forced relocation until the matter could be sorted out. Udall killed this initiative in his capacity as chair of the House Interior and Insular Affairs Committee.[97] An informal stasis was maintained until 1987, when California Senator Alan Cranston introduced an initiative (S. 2452) calling for an 18 month moratorium on relocation, pending "further study" and the devising of a new resolution, "to which all parties might agree." This effort continues in altered form as of mid-1992—officially designated as S. 481—and is now cosponsored by Illinois Senator Paul Simon and Colorado Senator Tim Wirth. A lower chamber version of the bill, H.R. 1235, is presently cosponsored by 20 members of Congress.[98]

Meanwhile, with the help of Udall, McCain was able to push through a draft bill (S. 1236) which became P.L. 100-666 in 1989. The statute contains elements of the earlier, ineffectual, Udall-McCain draft land exchange legislation while requiring that the relocation commission be reactivated and that relocation go forward, to be completed by the end of 1993. At present, no new relocation commissioner has been named, although the search seems to have centered upon a former executive of the Peabody Coal Company.[99]

Sugar-Coated Genocide

As this manuscript goes to press, the government of the United States has done absolutely nothing to end the process of Diné cultural destruction it began with the passage of P.L. 93-531 in 1974. There has been no serious discussion of repealing the offending statute. To the contrary, Washington has steadfastly maintained the basic legitimacy of its policy, offering mere variations on the theme of relocation as "alternatives." As Colorado AIM leader Glenn T. Morris has observed, the options offered amount to "sugar coated genocide."[100] The fact that the actual physical eviction of the Diné resistance has not been attempted seems to have been little more than a tactical decision, pursuit of a war of attrition rather than a blitzkrieg.

In early 1989, the Peabody Coal Company requested that the federal Office of Surface Mining (OSM) approve expansion of its mining activities on Black Mesa. Although Peabody had never obtained permits, required by law since 1985, to operate at its already existing mine sites, the OSM raised no issue with this new application. Instead, it referred the matter for "review" within the framework of an officially commissioned and supposedly objective environmental impact study released on June 2, 1989. The study is suspect on a number of grounds, not least of which is an assertion that post-extraction reclamation of the area to be stripmined can be "100 percent effective." Such a claim is not supported scientifically, however, it is customarily advanced by representatives of Peabody Coal. Other defects in the study include apparently inadequate assessments of the effects of water drawdown for purposes of increased slurry operations, selenium accumulation, atmospheric pollution, and local social and cultural impacts. "Lack of available information" is typically cited as a reason for these deficiencies, despite the facts that the missing data are known to exist, and that a number of regional experts were never contacted for their opinions.[101] Although the study reputedly took four years to complete, public response time was limited by the OSM to 60 days, thus severely limiting the type and quantity of countervailing information which might be submitted.[102] While it is true that expanded mining operations in the northern JUA have not yet commenced, all indications are that an official sanction for such activity has already been orchestrated. This in turn establishes the prospect that the question of Diné resistance in the contested area may ultimately be "resolved" through the expedient of simply digging the very ground from beneath the resisters' feet.

The Diné position remains unchanged, as summed up by the impassioned statement of Roberta Blackgoat, a 75-year-old Diné resistance leader: "If they come and drag us all away from the land, it will destroy our way of life. That is genocide. If they leave me here, but take away my community, it is still genocide. If they wait until I die and then mine the land, the land will still be destroyed. If there is no land and no community, I have nothing to leave my grandchildren. If I accept this, there will be no Diné, there will be no land. That is why I will never accept it...I can never accept it. I will die fighting this law."[103]

Notes

1. See Kelly, Lawrence, *Navajo Roundup,* Pruett Publishing Co., Boulder, CO, 1970. Also see Thompson, Gerald, *The Army and the Navajo: The Bosque Redondo Reservation*

Experiment, 1863-1868, University of Arizona Press, Tucson, 1982. Also see Roessel, Ruth (ed.), *Navajo Stories of the Long Walk,* Navajo Community College Press, Tsaile, AZ, 1973.

2. Treaty of 1868, United States-Navajo Nation, 15 Stat. 667. For background on the "negotiations" going into this international agreement, see U.S. House of Representatives, Executive Document 263, 49th Congress, 1st Session, Washington, D.C., 1868. For further context on the treaty, see Iverson, Peter, *The Navajo,* University of New Mexico Press, Albuquerque, 1981.
3. For context, see Kluckhohn, Clyde, and Dorothea Leighton, *The Navajo,* Harvard University Press, Cambridge, MA, 1948. Also see Downs, James F., *The Navajo,* Holt, Rinehart and Winston Publishers, New York, 1972, and Waters, Frank, *Book of the Hopi,* Viking Press, New York, 1963. Concerning Diné-Hopi intermarriage, see *The Tobacco Clan,* a pamphlet circulated by the Big Mountain Legal Defense/Offense Committee, Flagstaff, AZ, *circa* 1984.
4. The Executive Order was signed on December 16, 1882, demarcating an area 70 miles long by 55 miles wide, enclosing some 2,472,095 acres. It is estimated that approximately 600 Diné and 1,800 Hopis lived within the demarcated zone at the time the order went into effect. For general history, see Kammer, Jerry, *The Second Long Walk: The Navajo-Hopi Land Dispute,* University of New Mexico Press, Albuquerque, 1980. For legal history, see *Healing v. Jones* (II), 210 F. Supp. 125 (D. Ariz 1962). Also see *Hopi Tribe v. United States,* 31 Ind. Cl. Comm. 16 (1973) (Docket 196).
5. U.S. Commission on Civil Rights, *The Navajo Nation: An American Colony,* Washington, D.C., September 1975. Also see Allan, R., "The Navajo Tribal Council: A Study of the American Indian Assimilation Process," unpublished 1983 report available from the *Arizona Law Review.*
6. The Indian Reorganization Act (IRA), 25 U.S.C.A. 461, is also known as the "Wheeler-Howard Act," after its Senate and House sponsors, Senator Burton K. Wheeler and Representative Edgar Howard. An in-depth analysis of the act may be found in Deloria, Vine Jr., and Clifford M. Lytle,

The Nations Within: The Past and Future of American Indian Sovereignty, Pantheon Books, New York, 1984. Also see Haas, Theodore H., "The Indian Reorganization Act in Historical Perspective," in Lawrence H. Kelly (ed.), *Indian Affairs and the Indian Reorganization Act: The Twenty Year Record,* University of Arizona Press, Tucson, 1954.

7. LaFarge, Oliver, *Notes for Hopi Administrators,* U.S. Department of Interior, Bureau of Indian Affairs, Washington, D.C., 1936; quoted in Indian Law Resource Center, *Report to the Kikmongwe and Other Traditional Hopi Leaders on Docket 196 and Other Threats to Hopi Land and Sovereignty,* Washington, D.C., 1979, p. 49.
8. La Farge, Oliver, *Running Narrative of the Organization of the Hopi Tribe of Indians,* an unpublished study in the Oliver La Farge Collection, University of Texas at Austin. Also see Lummis, Charles, *Bullying the Hopi* (Prescott College Press, Prescott, AZ, 1968), and Nash, Jay B., Oliver La Farge and W. Carson Ryan, *New Day for the Indians: A Survey of the Workings of the Indian Reorganization Act,* Academy Press, New York, 1938.
9. Thompson, Laura, *A Culture in Crisis: A Study of the Hopi Indians,* Harper and Brothers Publishers, New York, 1950. Also see the relevant chapters in Matthiessen, Peter, *Indian Country,* Viking Press, New York, 1984.
10. Kammer, *op. cit.,* p. 78. Further context may be obtained from Sekaquaptewa, Helen, and Louise Udall, *Me and Mine* (University of Arizona Press, Tucson, 1969), and Clemmer, Richard O., *Continuities of Hopi Culture Change* (Acoma Books, Ramona, CA, 1978).
11. Grazing District 6 has an interesting history. It was initially established in 1936 as at the request of the Mormon segment of Hopi society in exchange for their participation in the federally-desired reorganization of Hopi governance. At the time, it was provisionally constituted at 499,248 acres, pending the results of a U.S. Forest Service study which would fix its "permanent" acreage, based on actual Hopi "need" (210 F. Supp. 125 (1962)). In November 1939, the "exclusive Hopi use and occupancy area" was expanded to 520,727 acres, upon the recommendation of Forest Service official C.E. Rachford. This was

followed, in 1941, with a plan proposed by Indian Commissioner John Collier, responding to Mormon Hopi demands, to expand the grazing district to 528,823 acres. The Sekaquaptewas rejected the Collier proposal in council, arguing that their continued participation in IRA governance entitled them to more. A second Forest Service study was then commissioned, leading to a recommendation by Forester Willard Centerwall that "final boundaries" be drawn which encompassed what he computed as being 631,194 acres. This was accepted by the Sekaquaptewa faction. A 1965 BIA survey disclosed, however, that Centerwall had noticeably miscalculated; the real acreage encumbered within the final version of Grazing District 6 is actually 650,013. See Kammer, *op. cit.*, pp. 40-1.

12. Boyden was first retained by the Hopi IRA government in 1951, to file a claim for preeminence of Hopi mineral rights over the entirety of the 1882 Executive Order Area. This was done over the direct objections of the traditional Kikmongwe, who had delivered a formal proclamation in 1948 opposing any and all mineral development by their nation. The precipitating factor underlying the traditional position was the earlier issuance of a report by BIA Solicitor General Felix S. Cohen *(Ownership of Mineral Estate in Hopi Executive Order Reservation,* U.S. Department of Interior, Bureau of Indian Affairs, Washington, D.C., 1946). Of interest is Boyden's appearance before the Navajo Tribal Council almost as soon as the Cohen report was released, marketing his services in securing its interests *against the Hopis.* In late 1951, the Kikmongwe attempted to enter a suit with the Indian Claims Commission which would have blocked Boyden's actions "on their behalf" on the minerals front. The ICC dismissed this suit out of hand in 1955, arguing that the Kikmongwe were not the "federally recognized government" representing the Hopi Nation. See Parlow, Anita, *Cry, Sacred Land: Big Mountain, U.S.A.,* Christic Institute, Washington, D.C., 1988, pp. 198-9.

13. The primary initiative towards this end was Boyden's authoring of P.L. 85-547, passed by the U.S. Congress in 1958. The statute authorized litigation to resolve conflict-

ing land claims within the 1882 Executive Order Area, once and for all. This allowed Boyden to file what is called the *Healing v. Jones* (I) suit (174 F. Supp. 211 (D. Ariz. 1959)), by which he sought to obtain clear title to the entire 1882 parcel for his Mormon Hopi clients. The results of this foray were inconclusive. Hence, Boyden launched the earlier-cited *Healing v. Jones* (II) suit. This gambit failed in 1962, when a special three-judge panel from the U.S. District Court ruled that equal rights applied to both Hopis and Navajos outside of Grazing District 6; this mutually-held territory was proclaimed a "Navajo-Hopi Joint Use Area" (JUA). On appeal, Circuit Judge Frederick Hamley upheld the lower court, observing that—absent a treaty—Hopi held "no special interest" in the disputed area, and that any land rights it might actually possess were subject entirely to the federal "plenary power authority" accruing from the 1903 *Lonewolf v. Hitchcock* decision (187 U.S. 553). Hamley clarified his position as being that both Navajos and Hopis were "no more than tenants" in the Executive Order Area (174 F. Supp. 216). In 1963, the U.S. Supremé Court upheld Hamley's interpretation of the case. For further information, see Schifter, Richard, and Rick West, "*Healing v. Jones:* Mandate for Another Trail of Tears?" *North Dakota Law Review,* No. 73, 1974. Also see Whitson, Hollis, "A Policy Review of the Federal Government's Relocation of Navajo Indians Under P.L. 95-531 and P.L. 96-305," *Arizona Law Review,* Vol. 27, No. 2, 1985.

14. For example, in 1955, the BIA and University of Arizona College of Mines completed a $500,000 joint study of mineral resources on both Diné and Hopi lands, suggesting that extensive coal stripping and concomitant electrical power generation were likely in "the foreseeable future." The three-volume report specifically highlighted Black Mesa, in the northern portion of the JUA, as holding up to 21 billion tons of low sulphur coal beneath an almost nonexistent overlay of soil. In 1956, an independent study undertaken by geologist G. Kiersch for the Arizona Bureau of Mines (*Metalliferous Minerals and Mineral Fuels, Navajo-Hopi Indian Reservations*) estimated the Black Mesa deposits at 19 billion tons. By either assessment, the area

was seen to hold a rich potential for strip mining.

15. There were actually a total of sixteen energy corporations involved at this stage; see *Petroleum Today,* Winter 1965.
16. Oil exploration leases for Grazing District 6 were let by sealed bid during September and October of 1964, generating $984,256 for the top 56 parcels, $2.2 million overall. John Boyden's bill for setting up the leasing procedure was $780,000. The Sekaquaptewas saw to it that he received even more: a total of $1 million in "fees and bonuses" for "services rendered." Ironically, it turned out there was no oil at all under Grazing District 6. See Kammer, *op. cit.,* pp. 77-8.
17. As a matter of record, Boyden was a legal representative of Peabody Coal's attempted merger with Kennecott Copper during the very period he was negotiating Peabody's Black Mesa lease on behalf of the Hopi IRA government. The 35-year lease was signed in 1966, giving Peabody access to 58,000 acres sitting atop what the Arizona Bureau of Mines estimated in 1970 was 21 billion tons of readily accessible low sulphur coal. Peabody then opened the Kayenta Mine on the northern edge of the JUA, a location directly impacting only Diné, no Hopis. The agreement allowed the corporation to draw off desert ground water in order to slurry coal 273 miles, to Southern California Edison's Mohave Generating Station, near Bullhead, Nevada. The Navajo Nation was persuaded by Representative Aspinall, chair of the House Interior Committee and a personal friend of Boyden, to give up rights to some 31,400 acre feet per year in upper Colorado River water—as "compensation" for water used in the Peabody slurry operation—while simultaneously providing right of way for Arizona's Salt River Project to construct a 78 mile rail line from the mine site to its Navajo Power Plant, near the town of Page. Udall, whose job as Interior Secretary it was to protect all Indian interests in the affair, saw to it instead that the complex of agreements were quickly and quietly approved; his motivation may be found in the fact that the Interior Department's Bureau of Reclamation owned a 25 percent interest in the Navajo Power Plant, a matter which figured into Interior's plan to divert some 178,000 acre feet of the Diné share of Colorado River water

to its Central Arizona Project, meeting the needs of the state's non-Indian population. All in all, as an editorial writer in the *Gallup Independent* (New Mexico) was to observe on May 14, 1974, the whole thing was "a miserable deal for the Navajo Tribe." The Sekaquaptewas were, of course, delighted with the transaction and reputedly paid Boyden some $3.5 million from the Hopi share of the Peabody royalties over the years, for his skill in "finessing" the situation to their advantage. Meanwhile, the Mormon Church, of which both they and their attorney were members, and for which Boyden was also acting as an attorney, owned an estimated 8 percent of Peabody's stock (and a substantial block of Kennecott stock, as well) in 1965. The value of and revenue from the church's Peabody holding nearly doubled during the three years following Boyden's successful participation in the Black Mesa lease initiative. For further information, see Wiley, Peter, and Robert Gottlieb, *Empires in the Sun: The Rise of the New American West,* G.P. Putnam's Sons, New York, 1982. Also see Josephy, Alvin, "Murder of the Southwest," *Audubon Magazine,* July 1971.

18. The suit was *Hamilton v. Nakai* (453 F.2d 152 (9th Cir. 1972), *cert.* denied, 406 U.S. 945), in which Boyden introduced a 1964 BIA range use study indicating that the maximum carrying capacity of the JUA was 22,036 "sheep units." Under provision of the "equal entitlement" stipulations of *Healing v. Jones* (II), he argued, the Diné were entitled to graze the maximal equivalent of 11,018 sheep units in the JUA. He then introduced a BIA stock enumeration showing that some 1,150 traditional Diné families were grazing approximately 63,000 head of sheep and goats, 8,000 cattle, and 5,000 horses—the equivalent of 120,000 sheep units—a number the court was "compelled" to order reduced by about 90 percent. U.S. District Judge James Walsh concurred and, for reasons which are unclear, established a "cap" on Diné grazing rights even lower than 50 percent of carrying capacity: a maximum of 8,139 sheep units.
19. These suits include *Hamilton v. McDonald* (503 F.2d 1138 (9th Cir. 1974)), *Sekaquaptewa v. McDonald* (544 F. 2d. 396 (9th Cir. 1976)) and *Sidney v. Zah* (718 F.2d 1453 (9th

Cir. 1983)). For further information, see Lapham, Neil, "Hopi Tribal Council: Stewardship or Fraud?" *Clear Creek Journal*, n.d.; available as a pamphlet from the Big Mountain Legal Office, Flagstaff, AZ.

20. WEST Associates is a consortium of 23 regional utility companies which banded together with the federal Bureau of Reclamation in 1964 to advance a unified strategy for energy development and profit-making in the Southwest. Members include Arizona Public Service Company, Central Arizona Project, El Paso (TX) Electric, El Paso Natural Gas, Public Service of New Mexico, Southern California Edison, Tucson (AZ) Gas and Electric, the Salt River (AZ) Project, Texas Eastern Transmission Company, Los Angeles (CA) Water and Power, San Diego (CA) Gas and Electric, Nevada Power Company, Utah Power and Light, Public Service Company of Colorado, Pacific Gas & Electric. The WEST group is closely interlocked with the so-called "Six Companies" which have, since the 1930s, dominated dam construction, mining and other major development undertakings in the western U.S.; these include Bechtel, Kaiser, Utah International, Utah Construction and Mining, MacDonald-Kahn, and Morrison-Knudson. And, of course, the ripples go much further. In 1977, for example, Bechtel was a key player in a corporate consortium—including Newmont Mining, Williams Company, Boeing, Fluor, and the Equitable Life Insurance Company—which bought Peabody Coal after John Boyden's 1966 attempt to effect a merger between Peabody and Kennecott Copper was blocked by Congress on anti-trust grounds. In any event, by the late 1960s, WEST had developed what it called "The Grand Plan" for rearranging the entirety of the Southwest into a "power grid" involving wholesale coal stripping, dozens of huge slurry-fed coal-fired generating plants, a complex of new dams (including those such as Glen Canyon and Echo Canyon, which have in fact been built) for hydroelectric generation purposes, several nuclear reactors adjoining uranium mining/milling sites, and a fabric of high-voltage transmission lines girdling the entire region. Given that infrastructural development costs were designed to be largely underwritten by tax dollars, the potential profitability of the plan for

WEST members and affiliated corporations are absolutely astronomical over the long term. See Wiley and Gottlieb, *op. cit.*

21. For further information on the initial draft bill, see Tehan, Kevin, "Of Indians, Land and the Federal Government," *Arizona State Law Journal*, No. 176, 1976.
22. Several such studies are alluded to in Ralph Nader Congress Project, *The Environmental Committees*, Grossman Publishers, New York, 1975. These should be understood in the context of the 1970 *Arizona Bureau of Mines Bulletin*, No. 182 ("Coal, Oil, Natural Gas, Helium and Uranium in Arizona"), which articulated the range of incentives available for massive "energy development" programs in the area. For contextual information, see Churchill, Ward, "Letter From Big Mountain," *Dollars and Sense*, December 1985.
23. The Senate did not vote the idea down. Rather, it set out to stall any decision it might make until after the 1972 elections. This was accomplished by the House scheduling hearings on the relocation issue in Winslow, Arizona. See U.S. Congress, Senate, Subcommittee on Indian Affairs of the Committee on Interior and Insular Affairs, *Authorizing Partition of Surface Rights of Navajo-Hopi Land: Hearings on H.R. 11128* (hereinafter referred to as *Authorization Hearings*), 92d Cong., 2d Sess., Washington, D.C., September 14-15, 1972.
24. McGovern wrote in a letter to Navajo Tribal Chairman Peter McDonald that if "there has been no satisfactory agreement reached [between the Hopis and Diné] before next January [1973], I will propose comprehensive new legislation to resolve the problem in such a way that no family is needlessly removed from its home land" (quoted in the *Gallup Independent*, August 3, 1972). On Goldwater, see Kammer, *op. cit.*, pp. 97-8.
25. Panitch, Mark, "Whose Home on the Range? Coal Fuels Indian Dispute," *Washington Post*, July 21, 1974. It is worth noting that, before going freelance, Panitch had worked as a reporter for the *Arizona Star* in Tucson, covering the land dispute. In this capacity, he had been repeatedly conned into reporting false or distorted information by the Evans PR effort. His analysis of what

happened thus offers a significant degree of first-hand authenticity and credibility.

26. *Ibid.* For additional information, see Conason, Joe, "Homeless on the Range: Greed, Religion and the Hopi-Navajo Land Dispute," *Village Voice,* July 29, 1986.
27. As Kammer *(op. cit.)* observes on p. 92: "A particularly nasty incident began when Randolph ordered a ninety-seven-year-old Navajo named Tsinijinnie Yazzie to get off his horse and submit to arrest for trespassing with his sheep. Yazzie did not understand English and remained mounted, so Randolph jerked him off his horse, injuring him seriously. Randolph [then] jailed Yazzie on charges of trespassing and resisting arrest."
28. See Panitch's article on the incident in the *Arizona Star,* March 26, 1972.
29. *Authorizing Partition of Surface Rights of Navajo-Hopi Land, op. cit.,* p. 23. Perhaps ironically, Navajo Tribal Chairman Peter McDonald played directly into his opponents' script by announcing that unless federal authorities acted to curb the Sekaquaptewas" tactics, the Diné would "get their fill of this and take things into their own hands" (*Arizona Sun,* March 1, 1972.)
30. Quoted in Kammer, *op. cit.,* p. 105.
31. Fannin went on record as having cosponsored the draconian idea, not only to "avoid violence," but because Diné overgrazing was "killing" the JUA *(Navajo Times,* September 27, 1973). That this was a rather interesting concern for a lawmaker whose professed objective was to see the entire area stripmined and depleted of ground water went unremarked at the time.
32. The Lujan language accrues from a "dear colleagues" letter he disseminated to Congress on March 16, 1974. In the alternative, Lujan had cosponsored, with Arizona Representative John Conlan, a 1973 proposal that the Diné should be allowed to purchase JUA land from the Hopi, or that congress might appropriate monies for this purpose. These funds might then be used for whatever purpose the Hopis chose, including acquisition of land south of Grazing District 6, upon which no Diné lived, but under which there was no coal. Mineral rights within the JUA would continue to be shared by both peoples. The idea was that such

compensation would serve to satisfy both the "equal interest" provisions of the *Healing v. Jones* (II) decision and elementary justice for the Hopis without committing the U.S. to engage in human rights violations against the Diné. New Mexico Senator Joseph Montoya carried a version of the Lujan/Conlan initiative into the Senate. It is a testament to the extent to which the "land dispute" was and is really about mining that the enlightened approach offered by the Lujan/Conlan initiative met with vociferous resistance from the entirety of the Boyden/Sekaquaptewa/Goldwater/Steiger group, as well as WEST Associate lobbyists. The only responsive party to the proposition turns out to have been the McDonald administration at Navajo, which had been formally offering to buy out Hopi surface interests in the JUA since 1970.

33. The lopsidedness of the House vote is partially accounted for by the fact that influential Arizona Representative Morris "Moe" Udall, brother of former Interior Secretary Stuart Udall, withdrew his opposition to H.R. 10337. He did so, by his own account, at the specific request of Helen Sekaquaptewa, a family friend and fellow Mormon. Udall's articulated position had previously been quite similar to that of Lujan, Conlan, and Montoya *(Congressional Record,* May 29, 1974, p. H4517).
34. *Sekaquaptewa v. McDonald, op. cit.;* it is noted that McDonald was assessed a penalty of $250 per day for each day "excess" stock remained within the JUA.
35. A good portion of the credit for this atypical situation seems due to the effective and sustained lobbying of the Interior Department's Assistant Secretary for Land Management Harrison Loesch, an ardent advocate of mineral development on "public lands" and early supporter of the Steiger draft legislation. It is instructive that less than a year and a half after P.L. 93-531 was passed, Loesch was named vice president of Peabody Coal.
36. Kammer, *op. cit.*, pp. 128-9.
37. 88 Stat. 1714 (1974), otherwise known as the "Navajo-Hopi Settlement Act."
38. On this point, see Whitson, *op. cit.*, pp. 379-80.
39. The litigation provision accrued from an effort by Goldwater, *et al.* to simply assign ownership of 250,000 acres

surrounding Moenkopi to the Hopis. An amendment introduced jointly by South Dakota Senator Abourezk and New Mexico Senator Montoya narrowly averted this outcome, by a vote of 37-35, authorizing a court determination instead.

40. This Boyden/Evans myth was still being repeated as late as the beginning of 1977 by federal mediator William Simkin, charged with establishing the exact placement of the partition line by Judge Walsh. Simkin fixed the number of Diné to be relocated under his plan at 3,495. See *Navajo Times,* January 24, 1977.
41. The 1977 Simkin partition line is virtually identical to that originally proposed by Sam Steiger in 1971. The Steiger line had been drawn by John Boyden, in consultation with Peabody Coal. See Kammer, *op. cit.,* p. 134.
42. Navajo-Hopi Indian Relocation Commission (NHIRC), *1981 Report and Plan,* Flagstaff, AZ, April 1981.
43. This figure is advanced by Whitson *(op. cit.,* p. 372), using the *NHIRC Statistical Program Report* for April 1985 (Flagstaff, AZ, May 3, 1985): The commission found that 774 Diné families had been certified and relocated from the Hopi partition zone by that point, while 1,555 families had been certified but not yet relocated. Another 1,707 Diné families had refused both certification and relocation. Using the conventional commission multiplier of 4.5 persons per "family unit," Whitson projected a "conservative estimate of between 10,480 and 17,478 persons, 3,483 of whom had been relocated by May 1985."
44. NHIRC, *1981 Report and Plan, op. cit.*
45. U.S. Department of Interior Surveys and Investigations Staff, *A Report to the Committee on Appropriations, U.S. House of Representatives, on the Navajo and Hopi Relocation Commission* (hereinafter referred to as *Surveys and Investigations Report),* Washington, D.C., January 22, 1985, p. 12.
46. *Ibid.;* testimony of Relocation Commission Chairman Ralph Watkins, p. 6.
47. See U.S. Congress, Senate, *Relocation of Certain Hopi and Navajo Indians,* 96th Cong., 1st Sess., Washington, D.C., May 15, 1979.
48. The problem began in July 1975, when Navajo Chairman

McDonald announced his government's intent to purchase the full 250,000 acres in BLM replacement lands in House Rock Valley, an area known as the "Arizona Strip" north of the Colorado River. The idea was met first with furious resistance by non-Indian "environmentalist" and "sporting" organizations such as the Arizona Wildlife Federation and the Save the Arizona Strip Committee (which advocated abolishing Indian reservations altogether). Next, it was discovered that a dozen Mormon families held ranching interests in the valley, and that brought Arizona's Mormon Representative Moe Udall into the fray. In 1979, Udall introduced legislation, ultimately incorporated into P.L. 96-305, the 1980 amendment to P.L. 93-531, which placed Hard Rock Valley out-of-bounds for purposes of Diné acquisition. The next selection was the 35,000 acre Paragon Ranch in New Mexico, apparently chosen by the administration of Navajo Chairman Peterson Zah, who succeeded McDonald, for its energy development potential rather than as a viable relocation site. In 1982, Interior Secretary James Watt blocked this initiative by withdrawing the ranch from public domain, thereby making it unavailable for acquisition (47 Fed. Reg. 9290); Zah filed what was to prove to be an unsuccessful suit, seeking to compel the land transfer *(Zah v. Clark,* Civ. No. 83-1753 BB (D. N.M., filed Nov, 27, 1983)). Meanwhile, in early 1983, the Navajo government indicated it had selected 317,000 acres of public and private lands in western New Mexico, contiguous with the eastern border of the Navajo Nation. The plan met with such fierce reaction from local ranchers that it was soon abandoned *(Surveys and Investigations Report, op. cit.,* p. 24). On June 24, 1983, Zah announced the selection had been switched to five parcels in Arizona *(Navajo Times,* June 29, 1983). By May of 1985, only the Walker Ranch, a 50,000 acre tract, had actually been acquired. There were and are serious problems with water availability, and the ability of the land to sustain grazing was and still is subject to serious question ("Water Rights become Issue in Acquiring Land for Tribe," *Arizona Daily Sun,* April 7, 1985). Such surface water as is available comes mainly from the Río Puerco, heavily contaminated by the massive July 1979 United Nuclear

Corporation Church Rock uranium spill 51 miles upstream at Sanders, AZ (Mann, L.J., and E.A. Nemecek, "Geohydrology and Water Use in Southern Apache County," *Arizona Department of Water Resources Bulletin* I, January 1983). Nonetheless, the first relocatees were moved onto this land in 1987 (Parlow, *op. cit.*, p. 202). As of 1992, there has been no improvement to the situation.

49. Quoted in the *Arizona Republic*, February 17, 1977.
50. Quoted in the *Arizona Star*, August 13, 1975.
51. Morrall was quoted in the *Arizona Daily Sun* (July 9, 1975) as saying, "[The Indians'] future lies in forgetting their 'Separate Nation' status and become *[sic]* dues paying Americans like the rest of us."
52. *Lomayatewa v. Hathaway,* 52 F.2d 1324, 1327 (9th Cir. 1975), *cert.* denied, and *Suskena v. Kleppe,* 425 U.S. 903 (1976).
53. Examples of this principle are legion. As illustration, see the U.S. Supreme Court's "resolution" of the Black Hills Land Claim, 448 U.S. 907 (1982).
54. Schifter's query appears in *Authorization Hearings, op. cit.*, p. 208. It is possible the committee might have been swayed by the question. Such logic was, however, more than offset by the efficient and persistent lobbying of the committee's staff director, Jerry Verkler, who appears to have been, among other things, feeding inside information on the committee deliberations directly to Evans and Associates. Shortly after P.L. 93-531 was safely passed in 1974, Verkler left government service. In January 1975, he was named manager of the Washington, D.C. office of Texas Eastern Transmission Company, one of the WEST Associates consortium. By 1980, he had been promoted to fill a position as the corporation's Vice President for Government Affairs. See Kammer, *op. cit.*, pp. 135-6.
55. Steiger's statement appears in the transcript of a meeting of the House Subcommittee on Indian Affairs, November 2, 1973, lodged in the committee files of the National Archives, Washington, D.C., at p. 127.
56. U.S. Congress, House, Subcommittee on Indian Affairs, Committee on Interior and Insular Affairs, *Relocation of Certain Hopi and Navajo Indians,* 92d Cong., 2d Sess., Washington, D.C., April 17-18, 1972, p. 35.

57. See, for example, Fried, Marc, "Grieving for a Lost Home," in L.J. Dunn (ed.), *The Urban Condition*, Basic Books, New York, 1963, pp. 151-71.
58. Scudder, Thayer, "The Human Ecology of Big Projects: Impact of River Basin Development on Local Populations," *Annual Review of Anthropology*, No. 2, 1973, pp. 45-61.
59, For example, see Gilbert, Betty Beetso, "Navajo-Hopi Land Dispute: Impact of Forced Relocation on Navajo Families," unpublished Master of Social Work thesis, Arizona State University, Tempe, 1977.
60. Smith's statement was made to Wendy Moskop, an aide to Massachusetts Senator Ted Kennedy, during a fact-finding trip to the JUA in 1974. Quoted in a flyer distributed by the Big Mountain Legal Defense/Offense Committee, Flagstaff, AZ, *circa* 1982.
61. Walsh's February 10, 1977 order did provide for both Hopi and Navajo jurisdiction on their respective sides of the partition line. However, it also specifically stated that livestock impoundment might proceed only under supervision of the secretary of the interior, who was charged with assuring "the civil rights of persons within the area are not obstructed" in the process. Sekaquaptewa's approach simply discarded Diné civil rights as an irrelevancy.
62. According to Kammer *(op. cit.*, p. 157), "[BIA Phoenix Area Office Director John] Artichoker had the police supplied with enough arms to repulse a tank assault. Weapons flow in from a special BIA arsenal in Utah included grenade launchers and automatic rifles."
63. Sekaquaptewa is quoted in the *Gallup Independent* (March 9, 1977) as saying, regardless of the judge's view, his rangers "couldn't have an ordinance around without enforcing it."
64. The "eager for a shootout" description comes from *ibid.* Abbot Sekaquaptewa is quoted from the *Gallup Independent*, March 18, 1977.
65. The details of Benjamin's plan, and quotation of his remarks, are taken from Kammer, *op. cit.*, p. 158. For analysis of the impact of the compulsory stock reduction program upon the targeted Diné, see Wood, John J., *Sheep is Life: An Assessment of Livestock Reduction in the Former*

Navajo-Hopi Joint Use Area, Department of Anthropology Monographs, Northern Arizona University, Flagstaff, 1982.

66. The actual order is unpublished. It is quoted in part, however, in *Sekaquaptewa v. McDonald* (II), *op. cit.,* and *Sidney v. Zah, op. cit.*
67. See Whitson, *op. cit.,* pp. 404-6, for details on the effects of the building freeze.
68. *Ibid.,* p. 389. Whitson draws upon several sources in advancing her claims: Memorandum, "Relocatees Sale and Nonownership of Their Replacement Homes," David Shaw (NHIRC staff) to Steve Goodrich (NHIRC executive director); NHIRC Report and Plan, June 1983; *Surveys and Investigations Report;* Schroeder, James, "U.S. Probing Fraud Claims in Relocation of Navajos," *Arizona Republic,* March 7, 1984; *Monroe v. High Country Homes,* Civ. No. 84-189 PCT CLH (D. Ariz, filed Feb. 9, 1984).
69. *Ibid.,* p. 388.
70. See Scudder, Thayer, "Expected Impacts of Compulsory Relocation of Navajos with Special Emphasis on Relocation from the Former Joint Use Area Required by P.L. 93-531," unpublished report, March 1979.
71. "Federal Commissioner says Relocation is like Nazi concentration camps," *Navajo Times,* May 12, 1982.
72. See Scudder, Thayer, with the assistance of David F. Aberle, Kenneth Begishe, Elizabeth Colson, Clark Etsitty, Jennie Joe, Jerry Kammer, Mary E.D. Scudder, Jeffrey Serena, Betty Beetso Gilbert Tippeconnic, Roy Walters, and John Williamson, *No Place To Go: Effects of Compulsory Relocation on Navajos,* Institute for the Study of Human Issues, Philadelphia, 1982.
74. See Churchill, Ward, "JUA/Big Mountain: Examination and Analysis of U.S. Policy Within the Navajo-Hopi Joint Use Area Under Provisions of International Law," *Akwesasne Notes,* Vol. 17, Nos. 3-4, May-August 1985.
75. Todacheenie is quoted in Kammer, *op. cit.,* p. 79.
76. All quotes appear in the *Gallup Independent,* May 5, 1977.
77. See Kammer, *op. cit.,* pp. 1-2; Parlow, *op. cit.,* p. 200.
78. See Kammer, *op. cit.,* pp. 209-10; Parlow, *op. cit.,* p. 201.
79. Quoted in Parlow, *op. cit.,* p. 201. For further information, see Lee, Pelican, *Navajos Resist Forced Relocation: Big*

Mountain and Joint Use Area Communities Fight Removal, self-published pamphlet, 1985.

80. This effort was maintained until 1984, at which point AIM fragmented and IITC virtually collapsed due to the insistence of some elements of the leadership of each organization on supporting Sandinistas rather than Indians in Nicaragua. Strange as this may seem, IITC mounted what might be called a "flying tribunal," sending it around the country to purge "unreliable individuals" guilty of expressing an "impure political line" by demanding rights of genuine self-determination for the Miskito, Sumu and Rama peoples of Nicaragua's Atlantic Coast region. Among those discarded was Gurwitz (in late 1986), who had served as the hub of the BMLDOC operation. The national and international support networks he had built up eroded very quickly, leaving the Big Mountain resistance with only a small—and relatively ineffectual—portion of the organized external support base it had once enjoyed. As for IITC, at last count, it was down to a staff of three operating from an office in San Francisco. While no longer a functional entity, it is, to be sure, "ideologically pure."
81. Anderson contacted Gurwitz during a National Lawyers Guild conference in Santa Fe, New Mexico during the spring of 1982. Gurwitz responded immediately, opening the Flagstaff office during the fall of the same year.
82. Perhaps most notable among the interns was Lee Brooke Phillips, who ultimately succeeded Gurwitz as head of the legal defense effort. BMLDOC was redesignated as the "Big Mountain Legal Office" (BMLO) in 1987.
83. Parlow, *op. cit.*, p. 117. The foreign countries at issue included Switzerland, West Germany, Austria, Italy, Canada, Great Britain and Japan.
84. The Indian Law Resource Center intervention was presented to the Working Group by staff attorney Joe Ryan on August 31, 1981. The independent commission, composed of Joan Price, Loughrienne Nightgoose, Omali Yeshitela and Ward Churchill, was first convened during the annual Big Mountain Survival Gathering, April 19-22, 1984. Its collective findings were presented to the elders over the following year.

85. For further information on these and other aspects of the physical resistance, see Parlow, *op. cit.*, esp. pp. 115-151 and 201-2. Also see Matthiessen, Peter, "Forced Relocation at Big Mountain," *Cultural Survival Quarterly,* Vol. 12, No. 3, 1988.
86. The quote is taken from a speech made by Gurwitz at the University of Colorado/Colorado Springs, February 17, 1986.
87. The federal judgement seems to have been quite sound in this regard, as should be apparent from the events described in note 80, above. At present, organized support for the Big Mountain resistance has fallen to less than 10 percent of 1986 levels, and continues to decline. As of late 1989, the BMLO facility in Flagstaff, established by Gurwitz in 1982, had to be closed for lack of financial support.
88. The *Manybeads* suit was based in large part upon initially successful litigation of the Yellow Thunder case *(United States v. Means, et al.,* Docket No. Civ. 81-5131, Dist. S.D., Dec. 9, 1985), in which attorneys Ellison, Finzel and Larry Leventhal argued that the entire Black Hills region is of spiritual significance to the Lakota. The same principle was advanced on behalf of the Diné resistance with regard to the Big Mountain area. However, the favorable decision reached by the U.S. District Court in Yellowthunder was overturned by the 8th Circuit Court of Appeals in the wake of the Supreme Court's G-O Road Decision. This in turn led to the dismissal of *Manybeads.*
89. Shortly after the *Manybeads* suit was entered, a second suit, *Attakai v. United States,* was filed, contending that specific sites within the Hopi partition area of the JUA are of particular spiritual significance to the Diné. This case remains active, although the only positive effect it has generated as of the summer of 1992 has been a ruling by Judge Carroll that the federal government and/or Hopi tribal council are required to provide seven days prior notification to both the Big Mountain Legal Office and Navajo tribal council of the "development" of such designated sites. In principle, this is to allow the Diné an opportunity to present information as to why targeted sites should not be physically altered. Rather obviously,

however, the time-period involved is too short to allow for effective response. For further information, see Diamond, Phil, "Big Mountain Update," *Akwesasne Notes,* Vol. 21, No. 6, Midwinter 1989-90. Concerning the G-O Road decision, see Deloria, Vine Jr., "Trouble in High Places: Erosion of American Indian Rights to Religious Freedom in the United States," in M. Annette Jaimes (ed.), *The State of Native America: Genocide, Colonization, and Resistance,* South End Press, Boston, 1992, pp. 267-87.

90. During the spring of 1990, the Big Mountain Legal Office estimated that as many as 9,000 of the "at least 12,000" Diné subject to relocation under P.L. 93-531 remained on the land. Official government estimates were unavailable. For further information, see Lacerenza, Deborah, "An Historical Overview of the Navajo Relocation," *Cultural Survival Quarterly,* Vol. 12, No. 3, 1988.

91. Quoted from *Navajo Times,* August 31, 1978. At the time Goldwater made this statement, Judge Walsh's order approving the Simkin partition line and requiring relocation of all Dinés within the Hopi partition area had been in effect for more than a year and a half.

92. For example, on August 31, 1978, the *Arizona Star* editorialized, under the title "Goldwater's Confusion," that the senator, "who either has uniformed or inaccurate sources on Arizona Indian affairs, has not spent enough time gathering firsthand information or he has simply lost interest in the subject. If the latter is true, [he] should refrain from public comment."

93. It is instructive to note that Representative Wayne Owens, who sponsored Boyden's successful draft legislation, went to work for Boyden's Salt Lake City law firm after being voted out of office in Arizona. He now serves as a congressman from Utah. Such apparent conflict of interest situations are normal within the context of U.S. Indian Affairs.

94.Stat. 932; 25 U.S.C. 640d-28 (1983). Perhaps one reason this superficial deviation from the P.L. 93-531 hard line was passed with relatively little furor was that John Boyden died in mid-1980. He was replaced as attorney for the Hopi IRA government by John Kennedy, a senior partner in Boyden's law firm. By all accounts, the stance and attitudes adopted by Boyden over nearly 30 years of involvement in the "land dispute" have been continued unchanged.

95. Danny Blackgoat, interview on radio station WKOA, Denver, March 13, 1985. For further development of this theme, see Redhouse, John, *Geopolitics of the Navajo-Hopi Land Dispute,* self-published, 1985.
96. Parlow, *op. cit.*, p. 202.
97. *Ibid.* The author quotes Indian Commissioner Ross Swimmer as applauding Udall's action in at least momentarily opening the door for the BIA to begin forced relocation operations. Although Swimmer himself has been replaced as head of the BIA, the sentiments he represented within the Bureau have not changed appreciably.
98. Diamond, *op. cit.*
99. *Ibid.*
100. The term is taken from a speech by Morris delivered at the Federal Building, Denver, May 19, 1989.
101. Diamond, *op. cit.*
102. *Ibid.*
103. The quote is taken from a talk given by Roberta Blackgoat during International Women's Week at the University of Colorado/Boulder, during March 1984. Mrs. Blackgoat is one of several elder women who emerged as primary spokespersons for the Big Mountain resistance during the 1980s. Her son, Danny, served for a period as head of the BMLDOC office in Flagstaff (see note 95, above).

The Struggle for Newe Segobia

The Western Shoshone Battle for Their Homeland

> Of course our whole national history has been one of expansion...That the barbarians recede or are conquered, with the attendant fact that peace follows their retrogression or conquest, is due solely to the power of the mighty civilized races which have not lost their fighting instinct, and which by their expansion are gradually bring peace into the red wastes where the barbarian peoples of the world hold sway.
>
> —Theodore Roosevelt—
> *The Strenuous Life*
> 1901

In 1863, the U.S. entered into the Treaty of Ruby Valley (13 Stat. 663) with the Newe (Western Shoshone) Nation, agreeing—in exchange for Indian commitments of peace and friendship, willingness to provide right-of-way through their lands, and the granting of assorted trade licenses—to recognize the boundaries encompassing the approximately 24.5 million acres of the traditional Western Shoshone homeland, known in their language as Newe Segobia (see map).[1] The U.S. also agreed to pay the Newes $100,000 in restitution for environmental disruptions anticipated as a result of Euroamerican "commerce" in the area. Researcher Rudolph C. Ryser has observed that:

> Nothing in the Treaty of Ruby Valley ever sold, traded or gave away any part of the New Country to the United States of America. Nothing in this treaty said that the

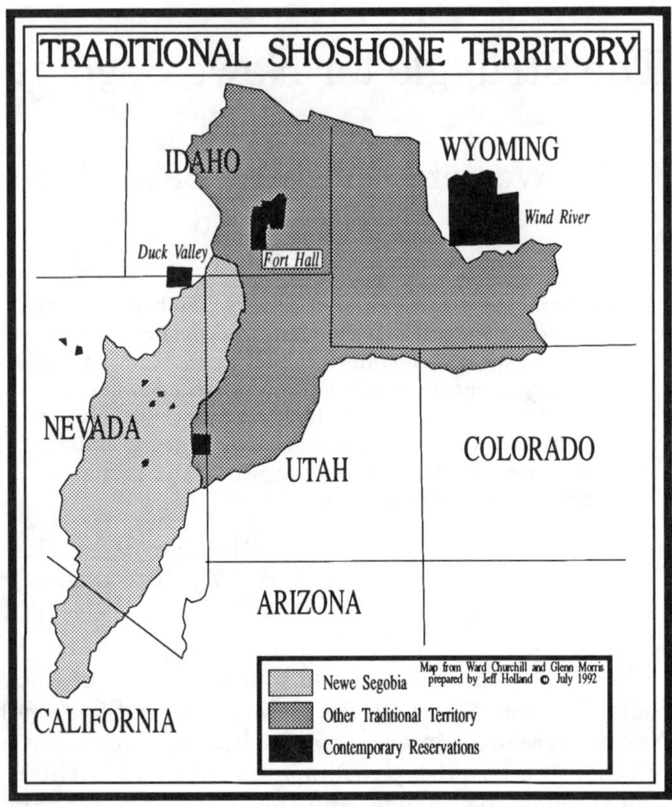

United States could establish counties or smaller states within New country. Nothing in this treaty said the United States could establish settlements of U.S. citizens who would be engaged in any activity other than mining, agriculture, milling and ranching.[2]

From the signing of the treaty until the mid-twentieth century, no action was taken by either Congress or federal courts to extinguish native title to Newe Segobia.[3] Essentially, the land was an area in which the U.S. was not much interested. Still, relatively small but steadily growing numbers of non-Indians did move into Newe territory, a situation which was generally accommodated by the Indians so long as the newcomers did not become overly presumptuous. By the late 1920s, however, conflicts over land use had begun to sharpen. Things worsened after 1934, when the federal govemment installed a tribal council form of government—desired by Washington but rejected by traditional Newes—under provision of the Indian Reorganization Act (IRA).[4] It was to the IRA council heading one of the Western Shoshone bands, the Temoak, that attorney Ernest Wilkinson went with a proposal in early 1946.

Anatomy of a "Land Dispute Resolution"

Wilkinson was a senior partner in the Washington-based law firm Wilkinson, Cragen and Barker, commissioned by Congress toward the end of World War II to draft legislation creating the Indian Claims Commission (ICC; see "Perversions of Justice" in this volume). The idea he presented to the Temoak council was that his firm be retained to "represent their interests" before the Claims Commission.[5] Ostensibly, his objective was to secure the band's title to its portion of the 1863 treaty area. Much more likely, given subsequent events, his purpose was to secure title for *non*-Indian interests in Nevada, and to collect the 10 percent attorney's fee he and his colleagues had written into the Claims Commission Act as pertaining to any compensation awarded to native clients.[6] In any event, the Temoaks agreed, and a contract between Wilkinson and the council was approved by the Bureau of Indian Affairs in 1947.[7] Wilkinson followed up, in 1951, with a petition to the claims commission that his representation of the Temoaks be construed as encompassing the interests of the entire Newe Nation. The commission concurred, despite protests from the bulk of the people involved.[8] As Dan Bomberry, head of the Seventh Generation Fund, has observed:

> When the U.S. succeeded in forcing the Indian Reorganization Act upon tribes, installing puppet governments, the ultimate U.S. aim was to make Indians a resource colony, like Africa was for Europe. Sometimes the issue is coal or uranium and sometimes its just open land ...The role of the Indian Claims commission is to get the land of tribes who do not have puppet governments, or where the traditional people are leading a fight to keep land and refuse money.[9]

From the outset, Wilkinson's pleadings, advanced in court by his partner, Robert W. Barker, led directly away from Newe rights over the Ruby Valley Treaty Territory. The Shoshone objectives in agreeing to go to court have been explained by tribal elder Saggie Williams, a resident of Battle Mountain.

> All we wanted was for the white men to honor the treaty. [We] believed the lawyers we hired were to work for the Indians and to do what the Indians asked. But they didn't. They did as they pleased and told us we didn't have any land. At the time, we didn't talk about selling our land with the lawyer because we had the treaty, which settled the land question; it protected [our] lands."[10]

Glenn Holly, a Temoak leader of the contemporary land claims struggle, explains that, "Most of our people never understood that by filing with the Claims Commission, we'd be agreeing we lost our land. They thought we were just clarifying the title question."[11] However:

> Barker filed the claim in 1951, asserting that the Western Shoshones had lost not only their treaty lands, but also their aboriginal land extending into Death Valley, California. He put the date of loss at 1872 (only nine years after the Treaty of Ruby Valley), and he included in the twenty-four million acre claim some sixteen million acres that the Shoshones insist were not occupied by anyone but Indian bands, and that were never in question. But

the U.S. Justice Department agreed with Barker's contention. Since opposing attorneys agreed, the Claims Commission did not investigate or seek other viewpoints.[12]

Clarence Blossom, one of the Newe elders who signed the original contract with Wilkinson, and who supported Barker for a time, points out that, "The land claim was never explained to the people. The old people do not even understand English. It was years later that I read that once you accept money, you lose your land. The government pulled the wool over our eyes. If I had known what was going on, I never would have accepted the attorney contract."[13] As Raymond Yowell, a member of the Temoak Band Council and another original signatory, laid it out in a 1978 issue of *Native Nevadan:*

> A majority of the people present [at a 1965 mass meeting called to confront the attorneys] objected to the way Barker was giving up the remaining rights to our lands and walked out...Soon after, at [another such] meeting, about 80 percent of the people showed their opposition by walking out. It is important that at these meetings *Barker insisted we had no choice* as to whether to keep title to some lands or to give them up for claims money. The only choice was whether to approve or disapprove the [compensation package]. And if we disapproved we would get nothing (emphasis added).[14]

Ultimately, the Wilkinson, Cragen and Barker firm received a $2.5 million federal subsidy for "services rendered" through its "resolution of the matter" in a fashion which was plainly detrimental to the express interests of its ostensible clients.[15] Shawnee scholar/activist Glenn T. Morris has summarized the matter in what is probably the best article on the Western Shoshone land struggle to date:

> In 1962, the commission conceded that it "was unable to discover any formal extinguishment" of Western

> Shoshone to lands in Nevada, and could not establish a date of taking, but nonetheless ruled that the lands were taken at some point in the past. It did rule that approximately two million acres of Newe land in California was taken on March 3, 1853 [contrary to the Treaty of Ruby Valley, which would have supplanted any such taking], but without documenting what specific Act of Congress extinguished the title. Without the consent of the Western Shoshone Nation, on February 11, 1966, Wilkinson and the U.S. Iawyers arbitrarily stipulated that the date of valuation for government extinguishment of Western Shoshone title to over 22 million acres of land in Nevada occurred on July 1, 1872. This lawyers' agreement, entered without the knowledge or consent of the Shoshone people, served as the ultimate loophole through which the U.S. would allege that the Newe had lost their land.[16]

By 1872 prices, the award of compensation to the Newe for the "historic loss" of their territory was calculated, in 1972, at $21,350,000, an amount revised upwards to $26,154,600 (against which the government levied an offset of $9,410.11 for "goods" delivered in the 1870s). These calculations were certified on December 19, 1979.[17] In the interim, by 1976, even the Temoaks had joined the other Newe bands in maintaining that Wilkinson and Barker did not represent their interests; they fired them, but the BIA continued to renew the firm's contract "on the Indians' behalf" until the Claims Commission itself was concluded in 1980.[18] Meanwhile, the Newes retained other counsel and filed a motion to suspend commission proceedings with regard to their case. This was denied on August 15, 1977, appealed, but upheld by the U.S. Court of Claims on the basis that if the Newe desired "to avert extinguishment of their land claims, they should go to Congress" rather than the courts for redress. $26,145,189.89 was then placed in a trust account with the U.S. Treasury Department in order to absolve the U.S. of further responsibility in the matter.[19]

> One analyst of the case suggests that if the United States were honest in its valuation date of the taking of Newe land, the date would be December 19, 1979—the date of the ICC award—since the [commission] could point to no other extinguishment date. The U.S. should thus compensate the Shoshone in 1979 land values and not those of 1872. Consequently, the value of the land "that would be more realistic, assuming the Western Shoshone were prepared to ignore violations of the Ruby Valley Treaty, would be in the neighborhood of $40 billion. On a per capita basis of distribution, the United States would be paying each Shoshone roughly $20 million...The [U.S.] has already received billions of dollars in resources and use from Newe territory in the past 125 years. Despite this obvious benefit, the U.S. government is only prepared to pay the Shoshone less than a penny of actual value for each acre of Newe territory.[20]

The Newes as a whole have refused to accept payment for their land, under the premise articulated by Yowell, now Chair of the Western Shoshone Sacred Lands Association: "We entered into the Treaty of Ruby Valley as co-equal sovereign nations...The land to the traditional Shoshone is sacred. It is the basis of our lives. To take away the land is to take away the lives of the people."[21] Glenn Holly concurs: "Nothing happened in 1872. No land was 'taken' by the government. We never lost that land, we never left that land, and we're not selling it. In our religion, it's forbidden to take money for land. What's really happening is that the U.S. government, through this Claims Commission, is stealing the land from us right now."[22] "We should have listened to our old people," Yowell sums up, "They told us Barker was selling out our lands. It took me years to realize it."[23]

The Dann Case

Giving form to this sentiment, two sisters—Mary and Carrie Dann—refused eviction from their homes by the U.S. Bureau of Land Management (BLM), which claimed by that point to own property that had been in their family for generations. The two women then challenged all U.S. title contentions within the Newe treaty area when the Bureau attempted to enforce its position in court.

In 1974, the Dann sisters were herding cattle near their home [a ranch outside Crescent Valley, Utah] when a BLM ranger stopped them and demanded to see their grazing permit. The Danns replied that they didn't need a permit since this wasn't U.S. land, but the land of the Western Shoshone Nation. They were charged with trespassing. "I have grazed my cattle and horses on that land all my life," Carrie Dann asserted, "and my mother did before me and her mother before her. Our people have been on this land for thousands of years. We don't need a permit to graze here."[24]

The trespassing case was filed in the U.S. District Court for Reno, where the sisters invoked aboriginal land rights as a defense. The ensuing litigation has caused federal courts to flounder about in disarray ever since. As John O'Connell, an attorney retained by the Newes to replace Barker, and who has served as lead counsel in defending the Danns, has put it:

> We have asked the government over and over again in court to show evidence of how it obtained title to Shoshone land. They start groping around and can't find a damn thing. In fact, the relevant documents show the United states never wanted the Nevada desert until recently. There's no doubt in my mind that the Western Shoshones still hold legal title to most of their aboriginal territory. The great majority of them still live there and they don't want money for it. They love that desert. But if the Claims Commission has its way, the United States may succeed in finally stealing the land "legally."[25]

In 1977, the district court ruled that the Danns were indeed "trespassers"—fining them $500 each, an amount they have steadfastly refused to pay—because the Claims Commission had allegedly resolved all title questions. This decision was reversed on appeal to the Ninth Circuit Court in 1978 because, in the higher court's view, the question of land title "had not been litigated, and has not been decided."[26] On remand, the district court engaged in a conspicuous pattern of stalling, repeatedly delaying its hearing of the case for frivolous reasons. "The judge never wanted [the second] trial," O'Connell recalls. "At one point I accused the government of deliberately delaying the Dann case long enough to get the Indian claims check written, under the theory that once payment was received Indian title would have been extinguished and the Danns would have been prevented from asserting it. The judge admitted on record that he was 'sympathetic with the government's strategy'" in this regard.[27] In the end, this is exactly what was done.

> In other words, a $26 million payment to Indians who never sought it, tried to stop it, and refused to accept it—payment for lands that were alleged by the payer to have been "taken" in 1872, but which the courts have finally affirmed were never "taken" at all—is now being used as the instrument to extinguish Indian title.[28]

The district court, however, in attempting to reconcile its mutually contradictory determinations on the same topic, observed that, "Western Shoshone Indians retained unextinguished title to their aboriginal lands *until December of 1979,* when the Indian Claims Commission judgement became final (emphasis added).[29] This, of course, demolished the articulated basis—that a title transfer had been effected more than a century earlier—for the commission's award amount. It also pointed to the fact that the commission had comported itself illegally in the Western Shoshone case insofar as the Indian Claims Commission Act explicitly disallowed the commissioners (never mind attorneys representing the Indians) from extinguishing previously unextinguished land titles. Thus armed, the Danns went back to the Ninth Circuit and obtained another reversal of the lower court's decision.[30]

The government appealed the circuit court's ruling to the Supreme Court. Entering yet another official (and exceedingly ambiguous) estimation of when the Newe title was supposed to have been extinguished, the justices reversed the circuit court's reversal of the district court's last ruling. Having thus served the government's interest on appeal, the high court declined in 1990 to hear an appeal from the Danns concerning the question of whether they might retain individual aboriginal property rights based on continuous occupancy even if the collective rights of the Newe were denied.[31] Tom Luebben, another of the non-Indian attorneys involved in defending Newe rights, has assessed the U.S. litigational methods employed.

> It is clear that one of the main strategies the government uses in these cases is simply to wear out the Indians over decades of struggle. The government has unlimited resources to litigate. If the Indians win one victory in court, the government just loads up its legal guns, adds a new, bigger crew of fresh lawyers, and comes back harder. It's the legal equivalent of what the cavalry did a hundred years ago. There's simply no interest in justice. It's hardball all the way. The government has all the time in the world to achieve its goals. The Indians run out of money, they get tired of fighting, they get old, and finally, after ten to twenty years, somebody says, "The hell with it; let's take what we can. It's really understandable that it worked out that way, but it's disgusting and it's wrong."[32]

Thus far, such tactics have proven unsuccessful against the Newe: "A new [resistance] strategy was hatched [in 1990] to sue the government for mineral and trespass fees from 1872 to 1979. The logic of the argument was that since the courts now recognize that the Shoshones did have legal title until the Claims Commission took it away in 1979, they are entitled to mineral and trespass fees for 109 years. This would amount to billions of dollars due the Shoshones; it was hoped that this amount [would be] sufficient to cause the government to negotiate. But the [district] court rejected this new intervention on the technical grounds that the specific interveners were not parties to the original claim. This suit may yet re-emerge.[33] For their part, the Dann sisters have announced the intent to go back into court with a new suit of their own, contending that the continuous use and occupancy evidenced by Newes on the contested land "prior to the authority of the Bureau of Land Management" (which began in 1935) affords them tangible rights to pursue their traditional livelihood. "They hope," says analyst Jerry Mander, "to carve a hole in the earlier [judicial] decisions...which might open a doorway for the rest of the Western Shoshones" to do much the same thing.[34]

Perhaps most importantly, as of this writing the Dann sisters remain on their land in defiance of federal authority. Their physical resistance, directly supported by most Newes and an increasing number of non-Indians, forms the core of whatever will come next. Carrie Dann is unequivocal: "We have to be completely clear. We must not allow them to destroy Mother Earth. We've all been assimilated into white society but now we know it's destroying us. We have to get back to our own ways."[35] Corbin Harney, a resistance leader from the Duckwater Shoshone Community in northern Nevada, reinforces her position: "We don't need their money. We need to keep these lands and protect them."[36]

The Most Bombed Nation on Earth

Federal officials tend to be equally straightforward, at least in what they take to be private conversation. Mander quotes one Interior Department bureaucrat, a reputed "Jimmy Carter liberal" responsible for seeing to it that Indians get a "fair shake," as saying in an interview: "[L]et me tell you one goddamn thing. There's no way we're ever letting any of the Indians have title to their lands. If they don't take the money, they'll get nothing."[37] The accuracy of this anonymous assertion of federal policy is amply borne out. An offer of compromise extended by a portion of the Shoshone opposition in 1977—that the Newes would drop their major land claim in exchange for establishment of a three million acre reservation, guarantee of perpetual access to specified sacred sites outside the reservation, and payment of cash compensation against the remaining twenty-one million acres—was peremptorily rejected by then Secretary of the Interior Cecil Andrus. No explanation of this decision was ever offered by the government other than that the secretary considered their being relegated to a landless condition to be in the Newes' "best interests."[38]

Leo Kurlitz, an assistant to Andrus and the Interior Department's chief attorney at the time the compromise offer was rejected, admits that he "didn't give the legal issues much thought."[39] Admitting that he was "uncomfortable" with the very idea that the Shoshones "still seem to possess title" to their land, he acknowledges that "under no circumstances was I going to recommend that we create a reservation...I saw my job as assessing the resource needs of the Shoshones, but I couldn't recommend that we establish a reservation."[40] Mander's unnamed source says much the same thing, observing that, "These Indian cases make me so damned uncomfortable, I wish I didn't have to work on them at all."[41] He professes a certain bewilderment that at least some indigenous nations refuse to be bought off: "I really can't understand what these people want. Their lawyers get them great settlements—the Shoshones were awarded $26 million, and the Sioux may get [more than $200 million] for the Black Hills—and damn if they don't turn around and start talking about land."[42]

Such uniform and undeviating adamance on the part of Interior Department personnel that not so much as a square inch of the Nevada desert, other than the minor reservations already designated as such, will be committed for Newe use and occupancy may seem somewhat baffling. Their collective willingness to lay out considerable quantities of tax dollars—with interest, the Western Shoshone settlement award now exceeds $60 million[43]—in order to retain absolute control over this barren and lightly populated territory raises further questions as to their motivations. So far as is presently known, there are no mineral deposits or other resources in the disputed area sufficient to warrant such a posture. A hallowed U.S. psuedo-philosophy, extended from the nineteenth century "Manifest Destiny" which holds that Indians are by definition "disentitled" from retaining substantial quantities of real property, may account for some of the unwillingness to allow American Indians what is rightfully theirs.[44] Also, concern that a significant Newe land recovery might serve to establish a legal precedent upon which other indigenous nations could accomplish similar feats undoubtedly plays a role.[45]

But more to the point, federal usurpation of Newe land rights since 1945 has converted much of their "remote" and "uninhabited" territory into a sprawling complex of nuclear weapons testing facilities. In addition to the more than 100 experimental detonations conducted in the Marshall Islands, mostly in the 1950s and '60s, more than 650 U.S. atomic test blasts have thus far occurred at the Energy Resource and Development Administration's Nevada Test Site, located within the military's huge Nellis Gunnery Range in southern Nevada.[46] This has made Newe Segobia an area of vital strategic interest to the United States and, although the Shoshones have never understood themselves to be at war with the United States, it has afforded their homeland the dubious distinction of becoming by a decisive margin "the most bombed country in the world."[47] This devastation and radioactive contamination of an appreciable portion of Newe property is presently coupled to a plan to locate what will perhaps be *the* primary permanent storage facility for high level nuclear waste at Yucca Mountain, a site well within the affected area.[48] Moreover, the Pentagon has long since demonstrated a clear desire, evidenced in a series of plans to locate its MX missile system there, to possess most of the remaining Newe treaty territory, a vast and "vacant" geography lying north of the present testing grounds.

The plans for the MX missile system, which involved bringing approximately 20,000 additional non-Indians onto Newe land, creating another 10,000 miles of paved roads, and drawing down 3.15 billion gallons of water from an already overtaxed water table in order to install a mobile missile system accommodating some 200 nuclear warheads, provoked what may have been the first concerted Shoshone response to military appropriation of their rights.49 As Corbin Harney put it at a mass meeting on the matter convened in October 1979, after the Carter administration had made its version of the MX program public, "Now we are witnessing the real reason why we are being forced to accept money for lands."50 Glenn Holley articulated the implications of the MX project to the Newes:

> Water is life [and the MX system will consume our water resources altogether]. Another thing the MX will destroy is the natural vegetation: the herbs like the badeba, doza, sagebrush, chaparral, Indian tea...Not only the herbs but other medicines like the lizard in the south, which we use to heal the mentally sick and arthritis. There will also be electric fences, nerve gas, and security people all over our lands. It will effect the eagles and the hawks, the rock chuck, ground squirrel, rabbit, deer, sage grouse, and rattlesnake. If this MX goes through, it will mean the total destruction of the Shoshone people, our spiritual beliefs and our ways of life.[51]

From there, overt Newe opposition to nuclear militarism became both pronounced and integral to assertion of their land claims. This was spelled out in a resolution first published by the Sacred Lands Association during the early 1980s: "The Western Shoshone Nation is calling upon citizens of the United States, as well as the world community of nations, to demand that the United States terminate its invasion of our lands for the evil purpose of testing nuclear bombs and other weapons of war."[52]

This stance, in turn, attracted attention and increasing support from various sectors of the non-Indian environmental, freeze and anti-war movements, all of which are prone to engaging in large-scale demonstrations against U.S. nuclear testing and related activities. Organizations such as SANE, Clergy and Laity Concerned, Earth First!, and the Sierra Club were represented at the 1979 mass meeting. Their loose relationship to the Shoshone land claim struggle has been steadily reinforced by groups like Friends of the Earth, the Environmental Defense Fund, and the Hundredth Monkey Project during the years since.[53] As Mander puts it:

> [In this regard], there have been some positive developments. Many of the peace groups have belatedly recognized the Indian issue and now request permission from the Western Shoshone Nation to demonstrate on their land. The Indians, in turn, have been issuing the demonstrators "safe passage" permits and have agreed to speak at rallies. The Western Shoshone National Council has called the nuclear testing facility "an absolute violation of the Treaty of Ruby Valley and the laws of the United States"...Peace activists are instructed that if they are confronted or arrested by U.S. government officials while on Shoshone land, they should show their Shoshone permits and demand to continue their activities. Furthermore, in case of trial, the defendants should include in their defense that they had legal rights to be on the land, as granted by the landowners."[54]

Looking Forward

It is in this last connection that the greatest current potential may be found, not only for the Newes in their struggle to retain (or regain) their homeland, but for (re)assertion of indigenous land rights more generally, and for the struggles of non-Indians who seek genuinely positive alternatives to the North American status quo. In the combination of forces presently coalescing in the Nevada desert lie the seeds of a new sort of communication, understanding, respect, and the growing promise of mutually beneficial joint action between native and non-native peoples in this hemisphere.

For the Shoshones, the attraction of a broad—and broadening—base of popular support for their rights offers far and away the best possibility for bringing to bear the kind and degree of pressure necessary to compel the federal government to restore all, or at least some sizable portion, of their territory. For the non-Indian individuals and organizations involved, the incipient unity they have achieved with the Newes represents a conceptual breakthrough. Further, it is a practical demonstration that active support of native land rights can tangibly further their own interests and agendas. For many American Indians, particularly those of traditionalist persuasion, the emerging collaboration of non-Indian groups in the defense of Western Shoshone lands has come to symbolize the possibility that there are elements of the dominant population that have finally arrived at a position in which native rights are not automatically discounted as irrelevancies or presumed to be subordinate to their own. On such bases, bona fide alliances can be built.

These efforts reveal a most important lesson for those attempting to forge a truly American radical vision, and who seek to translate it into reality. Namely, Native Americans cannot hope to achieve restoration of the lands and liberty which are legitimately ours without the support and assistance of non-Indians. Further, non-Indian activists struggling toward a new social order will fail to free it from the fundamentally imperialistic nature of today's system—thus dooming it to replicate some of its most negative aspects—unless they also work to liberate indigenous land and lives as well. Both sides of the equation are bound together in a symbiotic fashion by virtue of a shared continental habitant, a common oppressor, and an increasingly interactive history. There is no viable option but to go forward together, joining hands to insure our collective well-being, and that of our children, and our children's children.

It is perhaps ironic, but undoubtedly appropriate, that Newe Segobia, long thought by the invading culture to have been one of the most useless regions in all of North America, and therefore one of the last areas to be functionally incorporated into its domain, should be the locale in which this lesson is first realized in meaningful terms. Yet, in its way, because it so plainly exemplifies some of the worst in Indian/white relations, the Western Shoshone resistance and the outside support it has come to attract offers us a map to the road we must all traverse if we are to attain a future which separates itself finally and irrevocably from the colonialism, genocide and ecocide which have come before.

Notes

1. The full treaty text may be found in Kappler, Charles J., *Indian Treaties, 1778-1883,* Interland Publishers, New York, (2nd edition) 1972.
2. Ryser, Rudolph C., *Newe Segobia and the United States of America,* Occasional Paper, Center for World Indigenous Studies, Kenmore, WA, 1985. Also see Matthiessen, Peter, *Indian Country,* Viking Press, New York, 1984, pp. 261-89.
3. Actually, under U.S. law, a specific Act of Congress is required to extinguish aboriginal title; *United States ex rel. Hualapi Indians v. Santa Fe Railroad,* 314, U.S. 339, 354 (1941). On Newe use of the land during thls period, see

Clemmer, Richard O., "Land Use Patterns and Aboriginal Rights: Northern and Eastern Nevada, 1858-1971," *The Indian Historian,* Vol. 7, No. 1, 1974, pp. 24-41, 47- 9.

4. Ryser, *op. cit.*, pp. 15-6.
5. Wilkinson had already entered into negotiations to represent the Temoak before the Claims Commission Act was passed; *ibid.*, p. 13, n. 1.
6. The Temoaks have said consistently that Wilkinson always represented the claim to them as being for land rather than money. The firm is known to have run the same scam on other Indian clients; *ibid.*, pp. 16-7.
7. *Ibid.*, p. 16. Also see Coulter, Robert T., "The Denial of Legal Remedies to Indian Nations Under U.S. Law" (*American Indian Law Journal* Vol. 9, No. 3, 1977, pp. 5-9), and Coulter, Robert T., and Steven M. Tullberg, "Indian Land Rights" (in Cadwalader, Sandra L., and Vine Deloria, Jr. [eds.], *The Aggressions of Civilization: Federal Indian Policy Since the 1880s,* Temple University Press, Philadelphia, 1984, pp. 185-213, quote at pp. 190-1).
8. See Morris, Glenn T., "The Battle for Newe Segobia: The Western Shoshone Land Rights Struggle," in *Critical Issues in Native North America, Vol. II,* International Work Group for Indigenous Affairs (IWGIA), Copenhagen, 1990, pp. 86-98.
9. Quoted in Mander, Jerry, *In the Absence of the Sacred: The Failure of Technology and the Survival of the Indian Nations,* Sierra Club Books, San Francisco, 1991, pp. 307-8.
10. *Ibid* p. 309.
11. Quoted in *ibid.*, p. 310.
12. *Ibid.*, p. 308.
13. Quoted in *ibid.*, p. 310.
14. Quoted in *ibid.*, p. 309.
15. *Ibid.*, p. 308.
16. Morris, *op. cit.*, p. 90. The case is *Western Shoshone Identifiable Group v. United States,* 11 Ind. Cl. Comm. 387, 416 (1962). The whole issue is well covered in Forbes, Jack D., "The 'Public Domain' in Nevada and Its Relationship to Indian Property Rights," *Nevada State Bar Journal,* No. 30, 1965, pp. 16-47.
17. The first award amount appears in *Western Shoshone Identifiable Group v. United States,* 29 Ind. Cl. Comm. 5

(1972), p. 124. The second award appears in *Western Shoshone Identfiable Group v. United States,* 40 Ind. Cl. Comm. 305 (1977).

18. The final Court of Claims order for Wilkinson's retention in *Western Shoshone Identifiable Group v. United States,* 593 F.2d 994 (1979). Also see "Excerpts from a Memorandum from the Duckwater Shoshone Tribe, Battle Mountaln Indian Community, and the Western Shoshone Sacred Lands Assoclation in Opposition to the Motion and Petition for Attorney Fees and Expenses, July 15, 1980," in Committee on Native American Struggles, *Rethinking Indian Law,* pp. 68-9.
19. *Western Shoshone Identifiable Group v. United States,* 40 Ind. Cl. Comm. 311 (1977). The final award valued the Shoshone land at $1.05 per acre. The land in question brings about $250 per acre on the open market at present.
20. Morris, quoting Ryser, *op. cit,* p. 8, n. 4.
21. Quoted in Ryser, *op. cit.,* p. 20.
22. Quoted In Mander, *op. cit.,* p. 301.
23. Quoted in *ibid.,* pp. 308-9.
24. *Ibid.,* p. 311.
25. Quoted in *ibid.,* p. 302.
26. *United States v. Dann.* 572 F.2d 222 (1978). For background, see Foot, Kristine L., "*United States v. Dann* What It Portends for Ownership of Millions of Acres in the Western United States," *Public Land Law Review,* No. 5, 1984, pp. 183-91.
27. Quoted in Mander, *op. cit.,* p. 312.
28. *Ibid.*
29. *United States v. Dann,* Civ. No. R-74-60, April 25, 1980.
30. *United States v. Dann,* 706 F.2d 919, 926 (1983).
31. Morris, *op. cit,* p. 94.
32. Quoted in Mander, *op. cit,* p. 318.
33. *Ibid.,* pp. 316-7.
34. *Ibid.,* p. 317.
35. Quoted in *ibid.,* p. 313.
36. Quoted in *ibid.*
37. Quoted in *ibid.,* p. 316.
38. Conversation with Raymond Yowell, Reno Nevada, April 1991.
39. Quoted in Mander, *op. cit.,* p. 314.

40. Quoted in *ibid.*
41. Quoted in Mander, *op. cit.*, p. 315.
42. Quoted in *ibid.*
43. Estimate provided by Raymond Yowell, *op. cit.*
44. For detailed examination of this doctrine, see Horseman, Reginald, *Race and Manifest Destiny: The Origins of Racial Anglo-Saxonism,* Harvard University Press, Cambridge, MA, 1981.
45. This, of course, was precisely the situation the entire Indian Claims Commission process of paying compensation rather than effecting land restoratlons was designed to avert. See Carlson, Leonard A., "What Was It Worth," Economic and Historical Aspects of Determining Awards in Indian Land Claims Cases," in Imre Sutton (ed.), Irredeemable America: The Indians' Estate and Land Claims, University of New Mexico Press, Albuquerque, 1985, pp. 87-110.
46. On testing in Micronesia, see Clay, Jason, "Militarization and Indigenous Peoples, Part 1: The Americas and the Pacific," *Cultural Survival Quarterly,* Report No. 3, 1987. On testing in Nevada, see Thorpe, Dagmar, *Newe Segobia: The Western Shoshone People and Land,* Western Shoshone Sacred Lands Association, Lee, NV, 1982.
47. Nietschmann, Bernard, and William Le Bon, "Nuclear States and Fourth World Nations," *Cultural Survival Quarterly,* Vol. 11, No. 4, 1988, p. 4-7.
48. The Yucca Mountain plan is probably covered best in *To Protect Mother Earth,* a documentary film directed by Joel Freedman (Cinnamon Productions, 1990).
49. See Knack, Martha C., "MX Issues for Native American Communities," in Francis Hartigan (ed.), *MX in Nevada: A Humanistic Perspective,* Nevada Humanities Press, Reno, 1980, pp. 59-66.
50. Quoted in Mander, *op. cit.*, p. 313.
51. Quoted in *ibid.*, pp. 312-3.
52. Quoted in Nietschmann and Le Bon, *op. cit.*, p. 7.
53. The latter is probably the least known of these groups. For informatlon on its outlook, see Keyes, Ken Jr., *The Hundredth Monkey,* Vision Books, Coos Bay, OR, 1982.
54. Mander, *op. cit.*, p. 316.

Last Stand at Lubicon Lake

An Assertion of Indigenous Sovereignty in North America

We've been pushed as far as we can go. This is where we make our stand.

—Chief Bernard Ominayak—
1989

At times the situation facing a small indigenous group can illuminate the fate of larger groups. Specific circumstances become indicative of more general problems. The ongoing struggle of the Lubicon Lake Band of Cree in northern Alberta to preserve their ancestral land base, way of life, and identity as a people is a case in point. The methods and motivations of Canadian governmental and corporate entities to deny such things to the people of Lubicon Lake add up to a prospectus for all the indigenous peoples in the Anglo-dominated portion of this hemisphere. The matter has become a model of present-day genocide, and thus a critical issue for all Native North America.

The Legal Limbo

In 1899 a delegation from the Canadian government traveled through northern Alberta to secure the signatures of representatives from various American Indian groups to an international document titled Treaty Eight.[1] The purpose of this instrument, as had been the case of each of the other Canadian-Indian treaties (a legal process begun in 1781), was to gain "clear title" to as much Indian land as possible for the British Crown. In exchange, under provisions of Treaty Eight, each Indian band was to receive a formally acknowledged ("reserved") area within its traditional domain for its own exclusive use and occupancy, as well as hunting, fishing and trapping rights within much larger contiguous territories. Additionally, each band was to receive a small monetary settlement for lands lost, and each individual band member was to receive—in perpetuity—an annual cash stipend.[2]

It was well understood in Ottawa at the time that the treaty commissioners had failed to contact, or secure agreement to the terms and conditions of Treaty Eight, from many of the small bands scattered across the vast area encompassed by the document. The Canadian government nonetheless chose to view these bands as being equally bound by the treaty, and relied upon the Indians' "moccasin telegraph" to spread the word. An improvised arrangement was established wherein members of previously unnotified bands could show up at agencies serving the signatory groups in order to receive annual per capita payments. Little or no thought appears to have been devoted by the government to deciding how to keep such intermingling sorted out for record-keeping purposes, or how Canada might go about meeting its obligation to demarcate acceptable reserved areas for each late-notice band as it became identified.[3]

It took a decade for members of the Lubicon Lake Band to receive word of Treaty Eight, around 1910. At that point, band members gradually began to make an annual trek to Whitefish Lake, location of the agency serving another Cree group, in order to receive their annuities. The local Indian agent, following government guidelines, recorded their names on his pay-list. For the next twenty-five years, the Lubicons continued to live as they always had, unconcerned with what went on in Ottawa, or even at Whitefish Lake.[4]

In 1935, however, the residents of Lubicon Lake

were informed that, given the appearance of their names on the list of Whitefish Lake payees, they were considered by Canada to be part of that more southerly band. Therefore, the government argued, they were living in a location outside "their" reserved land and should relocate nearer the Whitefish Lake agency. Lubicon Lake inhabitants protested this misidentification and requested the establishment of an official reserve of their own.[5] This led, in 1939, to a visit from C.P. Schmidt, Alberta Inspector of Indian Agents, for purposes of investigating their claim. The visit, in turn, resulted in a report by Schmidt to Ottawa stipulating that he had concluded the people at Lubicon Lake were in fact a band distinct from those at Whitefish Lake, and were thus entitled to their own reserve.[6]

The Canadian government initially accepted Schmidt's recommendation, as well as his census fixing the Lubicon population as being 127 persons. By multiplying this number by the 128 acres per person the government felt was a sufficient land base for Indians, the Lubicon Lake Reserve was deemed to cover some 25 square miles. An aerial survey was conducted and, in 1940, the lines of the new reserve were preliminarily drawn on the map.[7] All that remained was the formality of a ground survey to set the reserve boundaries definitively. But this task was preempted by a shortage of qualified surveyors caused by Canada's involvement in World War II, and the finalization of the reserve was postponed.[8]

During the summer of 1942 a man named Malcolm McCrimmon was sent to Alberta to see that the province's annuity pay-lists were in order. McCrimmon's stated concern, as part of a broader desire to "put all of Canada's resources behind the war effort," was to insure that "these Indians are not getting something for nothing." To this end, he arbitrarily rewrote the rules pertaining to eligibility for per capita payments so that all who had been added to the Treaty Eight pay-lists after 1912 were eliminated out-of-hand, and then went on to require that "an individual must furnish acceptable proof that his male ancestors were of pure Indian blood."[9] Given that only written birth records were posited as constituting such proof, and that Indians traditionally maintained no such records, it is clear the latter clause was an attempt not only to limit the number of recognized Indians who could receive annuities, but also to eliminate them altogether. McCrimmon removed the names of more than 700 northern Alberta Indians—including 90 of the 154 then belonging to the Lubicon Lake Band—from the pay-lists. He also recommended specifically against establishment of the Lubicon Lake Reserve because there were no longer "enough eligible Indians to warrant" such action. The reserve's lawful existence was prevented from recognition by the permanent "postponement" of the land survey.[10]

The Disappearing Act

On April 17, 1952, the director of the Technical Division of (Alberta's) Provincial Lands and Forests wrote to the Federal Department of the Interior in Ottawa that:

> Due to the fact that there are considerable inquiries regarding the minerals in the [Lubicon Lake] area, and also the fact that there is a request to establish a mission at this point, we are naturally anxious to clear our records of this provisional reserve if the land is not required by this Band of Indians.

Alberta then informed Ottawa that the Lubicon Lake site seemed "too isolated" to be effectively administered as a permanent reserve, and that:

> It is recommended that the twenty-four sections of land set aside for a reserve at Lubicon lake be exchanged for [a more convenient site]...[The Deputy Minister for Provincial Lands and Forests had no] objections to the trans-

> fer *though there is no assurance that the mineral rights could be included [with the "more convenient" site]...If the reserve at Lubicon is retained, the Band would have the mineral rights...[We] recommend the exchange be made even if mineral rights cannot be guaranteed...* (emphasis added).[11]

This flurry of correspondence from Alberta was capped off by an ultimatum handed to the federal government on October 22, 1953:

> It is some years now since [the Lubicon Lake site was provisionally reserved]...[and] it would be appreciated if you would confirm that the proposal to establish this reservation has been abandoned. *If no reply has been received within 30 days, it will be assumed that the reservation has been struck from the records* (emphasis added).[12]

At the federal end, the Department of Interior allowed inaction to take the place of its acknowledged obligations to the Lubicon Lake Cree. Thus the province of Alberta was allowed to play the heavy in the emerging national policy of energy development in the Canadian north.[13] This was clearly admitted in a letter of February 25, 1954, from the Alberta regional Supervisor for Indian Affairs to the Indian agent within whose area of responsibility the Lubicons fell:

> As you are no doubt aware, the Deputy Minister [for Provincial Lands and Forests] had from time to time asked when our Department [of Interior was likely to make a decision as to whether or not to take up [the Lubicon Lake] Reserve. *There were so many inquiries from oil companies to explore the area that it was becoming embarrassing to state that it could not be entered.* That situation existed when our Branch [Indian Affairs] was advised that unless the Department gave a definite answer before the end of 1953 the *Provincial Authorities were disposed to cancel the reservation and return it to Crown Lands which then could be explored...*This was

discussed when I was in Ottawa last October. I was of the opinion that our Branch had taken no action and that *the block [of land at Lubicon Lake] would automatically return to Provincial Crown Lands...* (emphasis added).

The supervisor then explained that the federal government was very well aware of the implications of this line of action and instructed his agent to collaborate directly in effecting the expropriation of Lubicon resources:

In approaching the subject [of "a more accessible" reserve site] with the Indians, *I think it would be well to keep in mind that the mineral rights [at Lubicon Lake] may be very much more valuable than anything else...If this Block [of land at Lubicon] was given up, then it is very unlikely that mineral rights would be made available with the surface rights of any other reserve that might be picked up...* (emphasis added).[14]

The minerals with which government correspondence was primarily concerned at the time mostly consisted of oil and natural gas, rich deposits of which had earlier been determined by Petro-Canada, Ottawa's own energy corporation, to underlie the entire Peace River region. Petro-Canada had already enlisted a preliminary consortium of ten transnational energy giants—including Royal Dutch Shell, Shell Canada, Exxon, Gulf, and Standard Oil of California—to become involved in "exploration and development" of the area. Both the federal and provincial governments stood to reap a considerable profit on the bargain, with only the rights of a few small groups of Indians standing in the way of "progress." The obvious "solution" was to deny Indian rights within the intended development zone, and completely remove them from the area.[15]

As if outright robbery of land and mineral rights weren't enough, there appears to have been substantial official resistance (especially within the Alberta government) to providing *any* acreage with which to establish substitute or "replacement" reserves for Indians targeted for coerced relocation. As for the Lubicons in particular, governmental discourse included outright liquidation by early 1955, made clear in an instruction issued by the federal [Interior] Departmental Superintendent of Reserves and Trusts to his staff:

> Consult the appropriate files and advise whether action was taken by the Department to officially establish [the Lubicons] as a Band, for at the time any such action appears rather short-sighted, and if this group was established as an official Band, *it will serve our purposes very well at the present time...* (emphasis added).[16]

In another memo, the Alberta Regional Supervisor for Indian Affairs clarified the government's intent in denying the Lubicons' existence:

> [T]he Whitefish Lake Band have no objection to [the Lubicon Lake people] being transferred...to their Band and I am suggesting [the local Indian agent] contact those members [of the Lubicon Lake Band] who are at present residing at Whitefish Lake and Grouard and ascertain if they wish to file applications for transfer. If they all wish to transfer it would reduce the Lubicon Lake Band membership to approximately thirty...[17]

Elsewhere, the supervisor observed that, "It is quite possible that the seven families [who had been approached and said they'd accept enfranchisement in another band if they could not have a reserve at Lubicon Lake itself] will make application for enfranchisement in the near future...Should they do so I would recommend that enfranchisement be granted...The few remaining members of the [Lubicon Lake] Band could no doubt be absorbed into some other band."[18] In the interests of oil, then, the Lubicons finished the decade of the 1950s with the gains of the 1930s and early '40s largely erased. The specter of administrative elimination as an identifiable human group confronted them, in internationally defined legal terms, with genocide.[19]

Development Begins

The abundant availability and low cost of oil through the 1960s stalled the hopes for quick development by Canada and Alberta. But the OPEC-induced "energy crisis" of the early '70s changed the assessment of the cost effectiveness of development. In 1973, investments were secured with which to finally begin the building of an all weather road from Edmonton through the Lubicon Lake area.[20]

During the interim, however, the Lubicons had had ample opportunity to overcome their initial confusion concerning the government's various ploys, and had all but unanimously rejected the notion that they should be merged with the rolls of other bands. At about the same time road construction commenced to the south, the traditional governing council at Lubicon Lake met to reaffirm the existence (and right to continuing existence) of the band. It was also decided that, since Ottawa had done nothing positive to solve the "question" of who in fact belonged to the band, the band would exercise its sovereign right to determine this itself, independent of federal concerns and criteria. Those who had allowed themselves to be placed upon the rolls of other bands had largely returned and resumed their indemnification as Lubicons by the end of the year.[21]

For approximately five years a rough stasis was again maintained, as road work dragged on and on. The Lubicons continued to live and conduct their affairs very much as they had throughout the twentieth century, despite the persistent federal and provincial policy controversies their existence had sparked. Then, in 1978, as road completion reached the Lubicon Lake region, there was a sudden upsurge in seismic and other forms of oil and gas exploration. As outsiders poured into the area, setting dynamite charges, bulldozing access roads and marking cut-lines, the true dimension of what was happening was finally revealed. With their entire way of life in jeopardy, the Indians could no longer ignore the government. They were forced to mount a formal response.[22] As they themselves explained it in 1983:

> Until about 10 years ago the questions of land, band membership, mineral rights and rights generally were essentially academic. Our area was relatively isolated and inaccessible by road. We had little contact with outsiders, including Government officials. We were left pretty much alone. We were allowed to live our lives, raise our families, and pursue our traditional way of life without much interference. [But] about 10 years ago the provincial government started construction of an all-weather road into our area. The purpose of the road is clearly to facilitate development of our area. The road was completed about five years ago...Faced with the prospect of an influx of outsiders into our traditional area, we tried to file a caveat with the Provincial Government, the effect of which would have been to formally serve notice on all outsiders of our unextinguished, aboriginal claim to the area.[23]

Alberta refused to file the caveat, and the Lubicons attempted to force the matter in federal court:

> The Provincial Government asked the court to postpone hearing the case until another case being tried in the Northwest Territories was decided. The case in the Territories went against the Indians; however, the decision read that the court would have found for the Indians, had the law been written as it was in Alberta and Saskatchewan...The Province then went back to court and asked for another postponement, during which they rewrote the relevant Provincial legislation, making the changes retroactive to before the time we tried to file our caveat...In light of the rewritten, retroactive Provincial legislation, the [federal] judge dismissed our case as no longer having

> any basis in law...It is noteworthy that the Federal Government chose to exercise its trust responsibility [to the Indians] during the caveat case by filing a brief *on behalf of the Provincial Government...* (emphasis added).[24]

Under conventional Canadian trust provisions, the Lubicons then petitioned Ottawa to provide them with the financial support to seek injunctive relief through the courts, and to appoint a special land claims commissioner to attempt to resolve land title issues in the Peace River region. In 1980, these requests were rejected. During the summer of 1981, "the Provincial Government declared our community to be a Provincial hamlet, surveyed it, divided it up into little 2-acre plots, and tried to force our people to either lease these plots, or accept them as 'gifts' from the Province. People who supported the Provincial Government's Hamlet and Land Tenure Program were promised services and security. People who opposed the program faced all kinds of consequences..."[24]

> Fearing that acceptance of the Provincial Hamlet and Land Tenure Program would jeopardize our land rights, we asked the Province to delay implementation of their program until its effect on our land rights could be determined. They refused, stating that they had checked the legal implications of the program and had been assured that there was "no relationship between land claims and land tenure"...When we continued to question the effect implementation of their program would have on our land rights, they resorted to a legalistic form of deception. One old woman, who can neither read nor write, signed a program application form after being told that she was signing for free firewood. Another was told that she was signing for an Alberta Housing trailer. A third was told she was signing a census form.[26]

The real relationship between Alberta's Hamlet and Land Tenure Program on the one hand, and land right/land claims on the other, was amply revealed the following year: "When it became absolutely and unavoidably clear that we would not get anywhere with the Provincial Government, we appealed to the Federal Minister [for Indian Affairs]. He responded by sending the Province a telex requesting a six-month delay in the implementation of the Provincial land tenure program, during which time, he said, he hoped to resolve the question of our land rights...The Provincial Minister of Municipal Affairs responded to the Federal Minister's telex with a letter, questioning the very existence of our Band, and *stating that our community could not be part of a land claim anyway, since it was now a Provincial Hamlet, and was no longer classed as unoccupied Crown land...* (emphasis added)."[21]

Legal Stalemate

The federal minister involved, E. Davie Fulton, appears to have been something of a maverick in governmental circles, and was unconvinced by Alberta's argument. Further, he actually sat down and talked with the Lubicon leadership, reaching the conclusion that the band's position was not unreasonable and could be accommodated in some fashion by both Ottawa and the province. He convened a meeting between representatives of his own federal Indian ministry and the provincial government of Alberta during January of 1982, intending to negotiate a resolution to the Lubicon land issue "agreeable to all parties concerned." (Typically, the Indians themselves were entirely excluded when it came to such high-level deliberations over their rights and fate.) Negotiations broke down almost immediately, however, when:

> During the meeting between Federal and Provincial officials, the Province rejected out-of-hand most if not all of the points discussed between Federal officials and officials of the Band. Provincial officials refused to consider

> the question of land entitlement until they were satisfied as to the "merits" of that entitlement. They refused to agree to a timetable for determining the merits of that entitlement. They refused to consider the land which had been originally selected or which included our traditional community of Little Buffalo Lake. They refused to include mineral rights. They refused to consider any compensation whatsoever. They even refused to meet with any representatives of the Band.[28]

In the wake of the January meeting, the Lubicons once again requested financial assistance from the Indian ministry with which to litigate their land claims. Fulton denied the request on the ostensible basis that, "The negotiating route has not been exhausted" despite the clarity of Alberta's intransigence.[29] At a council meeting, the Lubicons then resolved, in view of this inflexibility and the bad faith evident in the Alberta government's continuing pursuit of the Hamlet and Land Tenure Program, to suspend all further dealings with the provincial government. It was also decided to pursue legal remedies despite Fulton's default on federal trust obligations, on the basis of the limited band resources and whatever external support might be mustered. Consequently, a second legal action was entered by the Lubicon Lake Cree before the Alberta Court of the Queen's Bench in February, 1982.[30]

> In the second legal action we asked the court for a declaration that we retain aboriginal rights over our traditional lands, that these rights include mineral rights, that these rights are under exclusive Federal jurisdiction, and that the oil and gas leases granted by the Province [on Lubicon land] are null, void and unconstitutional, or at least subject to Indian rights. We also asked the court to grant an immediate injunction preventing the oil companies from undertaking further development activities in our area.[31]

Attorneys for Alberta and for the various corporations involved argued that the province enjoyed immunity

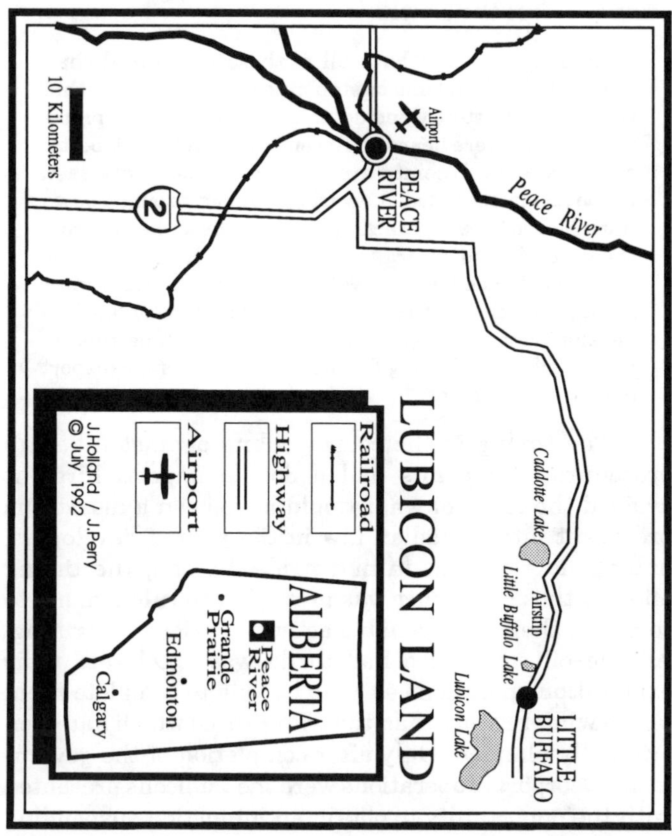

from the desired injunctive relief, and that the corporations (including Petro-Canada, a purely federal entity) were sheltered under the same mantle of immunity because they were contractual agents of the province. To its credit, the court ruled in favor of the Lubicons on this outrageous thesis. But it then closeted itself to consider a range of procedural arguments raised by the province and corporations concerning why the injunctive matter should not be heard, even though the Indians were entitled to bring it before the bench.

> Ultimately, we beat back all of these procedural challenges, but not in time to stop much of the damage that we'd hoped to stop. Concluding arguments on the procedural points were heard on December 2, 1982. In Alberta, such procedural points are usually decided very fast. However, in this case, a decision was not brought down until March 2, 1983, exactly three months to the day from the time concluding arguments were heard. These three months coincided exactly with the oil companies' winter season, which is of course the period of most intense development activity, since the ground at this time of year is frozen, allowing for the relatively easy transport of heavy equipment.[32]

The timing of the court's ruling against Alberta's procedural arguments had a double impact. First, it avoided the entry of what would have been a disastrous precedent into Canadian law in the eyes of developers, halting development in mid-stride. Second, the timing allowed those the court was preparing to rule against to complete their objectionable activities prior to its ruling. All the oil companies had to do was accelerate their exploration operations so as to be able to complete them in one winter rather than the two or three which had been originally planned. Only after completion of the governmental/corporate operations were the Lubicons presented with the opportunity to obtain an injunction suspending them.

This injunction was the limit of the Lubicons' legal "success." With the most environmentally damaging aspects of the oil extraction process largely completed, the court was free to rule that pumping operations could proceed insofar as they—in themselves—presented "no real threat" to the Cree way of life. No attempt was made to determine whether the sheer infusion of outsiders into the formerly isolated Lubicon territory might not have precisely this effect. As a result of the court's de facto non-intervention in oil exploitation, the value of the petroleum being pumped from the immediate area of the Lubicon claim had exceeded $1 million (U.S.) per day by mid-1987, and was rising rapidly.[33]

Concerning the broader issues of land rights and jurisdiction, the court held that it could not resolve the issues because, as federal Indian minister Bill McKnight (who had replaced Fulton, relieved as being "too sympathetic" to his charges) later put it: "The band...attempted to follow two mutually exclusive processes—a settlement under Treaty [Eight] and a settlement in aboriginal title."[34] The court made no comment at all on the fact that it had been the government itself which had barred exercise of Lubicon rights under the treaty while simultaneously holding that they were covered by the document, at least for purposes of extinguishing aboriginal title. Further, the court offered no hint as to what, in its view, would be the correct course for the band to pursue in order to effect a settlement under Crown Law.

The Lubicons took the matter to the Alberta Court of Appeal, which upheld the lower court's decision in January, 1985. In March, and again in May of the same year, the Supreme Court of Canada refused to hear the case.[35] Although the Lubicons have continued to pursue legal remedies in the Canadian courts since then, the weight of their efforts to achieve a real solution has shifted to other strategies.

Assertion of Lubicon Sovereignty

In 1982, under the leadership of Chief Bernard Ominayak, the people of Lubicon Lake (defining themselves at this point as being some 250 individuals) began to express an ever sharper articulation of their traditional rights as a wholly sovereign people.[36] Following this logic, they increasingly deemphasized their right—under provision of Treaty Eight—to the 25.4 square mile reserve provisionally demarcated in 1940. Instead, they reasoned that since they themselves had not signed a treaty of cession they had ceded no land at all. Therefore, they began to articulate their land claim in terms of the territory historically used by their ancestors for purposes of hunting, fishing, trapping, occupancy and trading purposes. In total, this amounts to approximately 1,000 times the area involved in the 1940 reserve Alberta had so resolutely attempted to cheat them out of. This 25,000 square mile tract of land claimed by aboriginal right comprises about 25 percent of the entire province of Alberta. In addition, the Indians stipulated that they were due some $900 million (U.S.) for damages done their territory during the period of illegal Canadian occupancy.[37]

The initial government response scoffed at such "presumptuousness." During 1983 and '84, the Lubicons, rather than continue to argue their case in governmentally sanctioned (and controlled) courts, launched a public outreach and education campaign designed to secure widespread popular support. To the government's surprise and consternation, the response to this effort was so favorable that it was forced to take steps to contain the situation. An "independent investigation" was launched in 1984 by the Reverend Dr. Randall Ivany, Ombudsman of Alberta. He dutifully went through the motions of examining the Lubicon claims before releasing a report, titled *Complaints of the Lubicon Lake Band of Indians.*[38] He reached the predictable conclusions that there was "no substance" to the Indians' allegations, and "no factual basis" to their charge that various layers of the Canadian government were engaged in the practice of cultural genocide.[39] This official outcome, designed to undercut the rising tide of public sentiment supporting the Lubicons, actually heightened support because of its blatant transparency.

At about this time, Ominayak and other Lubicon

leaders began to issue statements to the effect that they were considering conducting a boycott, large-scale demonstrations, and other disruptions of the 1988 Winter Olympics, to be held in Calgary, Alberta. In something of a panic, the government began to adopt what it must have felt were extraordinary measures in an effort to avert an international embarrassment and scrutiny of its policies against indigenous peoples. Ivany's sham investigation was quickly replaced by another, functioning under auspices of the Department of Indian and Northern affairs.[40]

The first tangible result of this change in government attitude was the offer, made on December 10, 1985 and recommended by Fulton, of the original 1940 reserve area, complete with mineral rights, which had appeared so "problematic" to Canadian policy-makers only a year before.[41] The overture was rejected on the same day by the Lubicons, with Chief Ominayak pointing out that it was the government's own greed and deviousness which had blocked establishment of the reserve for nearly half a century, forcing the Indians to pursue the full extent of their aboriginal rights. The Lubicons, he said, would be prepared to enter into any serious negotiations concerning Canadian recognition of their sovereignty and the real scope of their land claim.[42]

After a quick huddle in the national capital, the federal government returned in January 1986 with an *ex gratia* award—which it had previously refused to do on two separate occasions—of $1.5 million (Canadian) to cover the cost of Lubicon litigation for reserved land rights, to date. The Indians accepted the payment, and then filed suit in April for that amount plus an additional $750,000 (Canadian) to cover future costs of litigation; in November of 1986, the April suit was amended in federal court to encompass $1.4 million in past litigation costs and $2 million in projected legal fees.[43] In the latter month, the Lubicons also stepped up their campaign to organize actions attendant to the XV Winter Olympics, undertaking their first truly mass mailing on the subject and sending a delegation to Europe to engage in a speaking tour mustering support.[44]

Meanwhile, in June, Fulton had been replaced by Roger Tassé, a former federal Minister of Justice, in an attempt to arrive at a "negotiated settlement" in which the band would drop its plans for the Olympics and its broad land claims in exchange for clear title to a tract approximately the size of the 1940 reserve. Following a consensus of the group, Ominayak agreed to meet with federal officials, but only on condition that the government of Alberta would be completely excluded from participation in the proceedings. In July, after only preliminary discussions, the Lubicons broke off negotiations when it became clear that Ottawa was not yet prepared to take up the matter of the aboriginal land claim in any meaningful way.[45]

In January 1987, the Lubicons announced they had determined in council that the band was now comprised of 458 individuals, some 250 of whom did not appear on federal Indian registration lists, and that they were prepared to accept a 90 square mile reserve centering upon the community of Little Buffalo, over which they would exercise full governmental control. They also claimed undisturbed hunting, fishing and trapping rights over an area of approximately 4,000 square miles. In order for these rights to have meaning, the Lubicon band stipulated that they have a voice equal to those of other governments in determining corporate licensing and the development policy in their region. Ominayak also stated that the Lubicons would henceforth begin, by force if necessary, to evict crews within the reserve proper, and elsewhere as need be. In March, the 90 square mile reserve claim was amended to read "92 square miles/236 square kilometers" in a motion filed with the Court of Queen's Bench in Alberta.[46]

In May 1987 a Lubicon delegation again toured

Europe, explaining the band's position, rallying support to the proposed Olympic boycott. They also prepared an intervention on their case to be submitted to the United Nations Working Group on Indigenous Populations the same summer.[47] Another delegation project was a partially successful effort to convince various European museums to withdraw participation in the Olympics by refusing to lend objects to "The Spirit Sings," a Canadian government-sponsored exhibition of American Indian artifacts scheduled for display in conjunction with the Calgary Olympics.[48] Other Lubicon spokespeople were traveling and speaking in the United States at the same time, and public response to the Lubicons' outreach efforts in both Europe and North America continued to be quite positive.[49]

In the face of mounting international pressure, both Ottawa and Alberta appointed formal negotiators—Brian Malone for the federal government and Jim Horsman for the province—in October 1987. The federal government simultaneously released *The Fulton Report,* a plan prepared by the former Indian minister calling for tripartite meetings between Ottawa, Alberta and the Lubicons designed to resolve the land claim and sovereignty issues "equitably" and "permanently."[50]

The Lubicon leadership rejected the idea, pointing to the outcome of a similar tripartite negotiating arrangement signed on December 23, 1986, between Ottawa, Alberta and the 1,000 member Fort Chippewyan Band of Cree, in which the Indians' aboriginal land claims had been compressed into a mere 20 square mile reserve, divided into nine separate locations. Ominayak stated that his people hardly considered this to be the "productive result of negotiations" touted by Alberta, at least not from the indigenous perspective.[51] He followed up on January 23, 1988, by releasing through the *Calgary Herald* the information that the Lubicons had entered into a formal alliance with other bands and many whites in the north country, and that these "Indians and non-Indians in Alberta, Saskatchewan and Quebec have agreed to set up a resident army on Lubicon territory...[and] provincial fish and wildlife officials will be subject to arrest and trial" in the event they attempted to interfere with the exercise of Lubicon sovereignty anywhere within the 4,000 square mile area to which the band had direct and immediate claims.[52]

With the Olympic games started, and the Lubicons and their supporters mounting highly visible demonstrations outside "The Spirit Sings" exhibition,[53] neither Alberta nor Ottawa had a ready response to this development. The last thing either government wanted at that particular juncture was the outbreak of an actual "shooting war" between Canada and a small group of Indians only a few hundred miles to the north of Calgary. On February 4, Minister for Aboriginal Affairs McKnight—citing as cause the fact that the Lubicons were still adamant in their refusal to even talk to representatives of the Alberta government, or allow the release of genealogical data on the band to provincial authorities—officially requested that the province agree to transfer title over the contested area back to the federal government for purposes of effecting some resolution.[54] The provincial government refused and on February 10 released a thoroughly whiny press release complaining that it was impossible for it to negotiate a settlement with the Lubicons because the Indians refused to allow Alberta's representatives to attend meetings concerning the disposition of land and resources the province considered to be its own. The statement failed to mention that this was precisely the same sort of insulting and demeaning treatment Alberta had dealt Indians all along.[55]

Finally, on March 17, 1988, in a speech before the House of Commons Standing Committee on Aboriginal Affairs and Northern Development, McKnight publicly admitted that the Lubicon Lake Cree have every right to pursue aboriginal title to all lands within which they could demonstrate they had once conducted their traditional way of life. The government would no longer raise procedural issues as a means to block litigation of the matter. Further, he suggested—probably as a result of the international attention the Lubicons had garnered through their extralegal activities—"further delay [in bringing the matter to an acceptable resolution] serves no one."[56] He also made it clear that the federal government was now prepared to enter a suit against Alberta Premier Don Getty unless the "Lubicon Lake matter" was "settled soon."[57]

The Daishowa Connection

Even before McKnight made his speech in the House of Commons signifying that the Lubicons had managed to split the two layers of government opposing them, Getty had offered Alberta's response. On February 8, 1988, the premier and Alberta Forestry Minister LeRoy Fjordbotten announced that the provincial government had entered into an agreement with the Japanese forestry corporation, Daishowa, to construct a pulp mill and launch a timbering operation approximately 65 miles south of Little Buffalo.[58]

> The new pulp mill will be the largest hardwood pulp mill in Canada. It will employ about 600 people, 300 to take down and transport trees to the new mill, 300 to turn the trees into pulp. It will "produce" 1,000 metric tons of pulp per day, 340,000 metric tons per year. It will consume trees at the rate of about...4 million per year. The trees will come from a timber lease which covers an area of over 29,000 sq. kilometers, more than 11,000 square miles. *The timber lease to supply the new pulp mill completely covers the entire Lubicon traditional area* (emphasis in original).[59]

This astute move forced a reconciliation of the Ot-

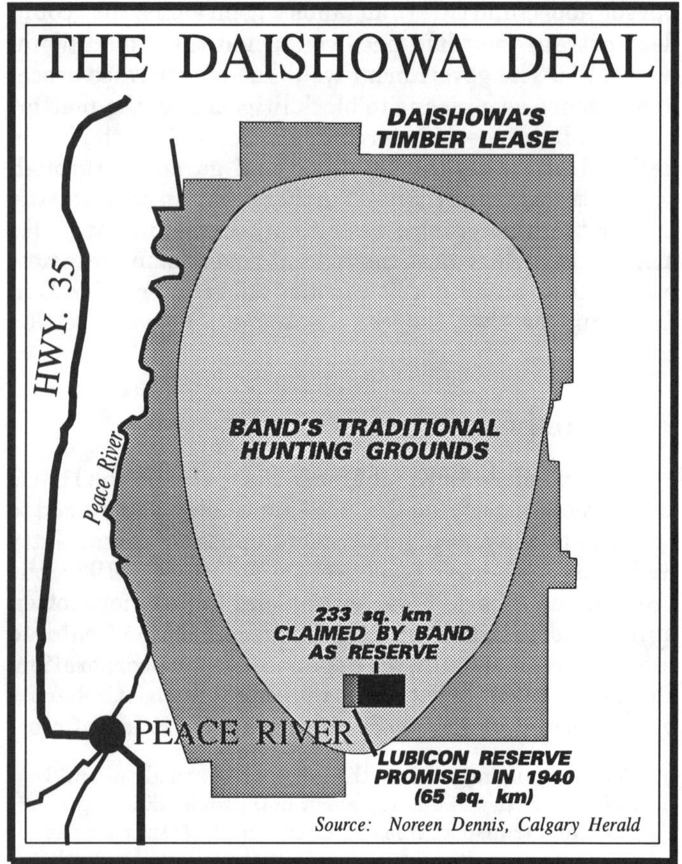

Source: Noreen Dennis, Calgary Herald

tawa and Alberta positions:

> The new pulp mill will...cost more than 500 million dollars, including $75 million in Federal and Provincial Government grants. $9.5 million of the Government subsidy is being provided by Federal Indian Affairs Minister Bill McKnight, in his capacity as Minister responsible for the so-called Western Diversification Program. The Western Diversification Program is a political slush fund

> set by the Federal Government to try and prop up faltering political fortunes in western Canada. In his capacity as Indian Affairs Minister, Mr. McKnight is of course also supposedly responsible for insuring that the constitutionally recognized rights of aboriginal people in Canada are respected.[60]

In addition, as Fjordbotten put it, "The Alberta government will be building rail and road access and other infrastructure to cost $65.2 million over the next five years, a necessary requirement to proceed in this relatively remote location. Lack of such access has long been an impediment to development of the forest industry in Northern Alberta."[61] In other words, the province intended to go for the Lubicon jugular. The announcements led Assembly of First Nations National Chief Georges Erasmus to demand that Canadian Prime Minister Brian Mulroney fire McKnight for conflict of interest.[62] For his part, Ominayak went on the Canadian Broadcasting Corporation radio station in Edmonton on February 9 to warn that, "we're not going to allow anybody to come in and cut down our trees within our traditional lands." When asked by talk show hostess Ruth Anderson "how far [he] would go" to prevent the logging, he replied:

> It just depends on how hard the other side is going to push. We basically decided that we're going to start asserting our own jurisdiction. Now they announce this pulp mill and also that they're going to be leasing all the timber rights or trees that are going to be needed for the pulp mill that we have on our traditional lands.[63]

The exchange continued, with Anderson asking whether the Lubicons would "resort to violence to stop this latest assault on what you claim is your land?" Ominayak replied that, "our preference would be to not get into violence. But again, it all depends on how forceful the other side wants to be. But whatever it takes, that's what we're going to do." Elsewhere, he observed that the

Lubicons are preparing to make a "last stand" on their land, and on their right: "We're not threatening, we're not bluffing...and we would like to keep it as peaceful as possible. I just don't know how much longer we can go on like this."[64]

Such warnings carried a tangible ring of authority. As analyst John Goddard has observed, "It is hard to imagine an Indian band better prepared" to pursue its national rights "than the Lubicon Lake band of early 1988."

> By the time the Olympic Games opened in Calgary, the Lubicon people...commanded international support and the means to convert that support into political power. They had prevailed in disputes with Union Oil and all the other dozens of other oil companies that had gone from posting "No Trespassing" signs to asking the band's permission to work in Lubicon territory...Band members controlled the ninety square miles they had identified as [their] reserve. Plans for a new community were ready for tender...Essentially, the Lubicon Lake Cree remained a cohesive Indian society led by purposeful elders and a gifted chief.[65]

Faced with the prospect of armed confrontation, Premier Getty at last began to give bits of ground, offering in March to immediately place the 1940 acre reserve area claimed by Alberta into Lubicon control, and to align with the Indians in negotiating for additional acreage from Ottawa. Ominayak declined the transfer, but accepted the latter proposal, joining with Getty in calling for establishment of a three-member tribunal to hear and effect a binding resolution upon the Lubicon claims against both the province and the central government.[66] McKnight, however, stonewalled the idea, countering that if "Alberta wishes to be bound by a tribunal in providing Alberta land to the Lubicons, that is Alberta's right," and that he expected the province to provide a 45 square mile parcel "in full satisfaction of *all* Lubicon claims," thus exempting

Ottawa from any responsibility in the situation whatsoever.[67] On May 17, he filed suit to compel Getty to accede to his demands.

Confrontation

There followed several months of legal maneuvering in which McKnight thwarted all efforts to achieve a reasonable compromise. Finally, on October 6, 1988, James O'Reilly, the Lubicons' head litigator, appeared before the Alberta Court of Appeal at Calgary to read a statement prepared by his clients suspending further involvement in the Canadian judicial process. "This effort has been in vain," it stated. "From this day, we will no longer participate in any court proceedings in which the Lubicons are presently a party, whether in this court, the Court of Queen's Bench in Alberta, the Federal Court of Appeal or the Federal Court of Canada." Instead, it continued, by October 15, "the Lubicon Nation intends to assert and enforce its aboriginal rights and its sovereign jurisdiction as an independent Nation, with its own law enforcement and court systems."[68]

> The plan was to erect checkpoints on the four main roads into Lubicon territory. As of October 15, 1988, band members would stop all vehicles. Anybody wishing to work in the area would have to buy permits from the band office at the same rates as those paid to the Alberta government. All payments would be due in advance. Companies would have to submit copies of existing provincial authorizations to the band and post copies of approved Lubicon permits at all work sites...Oil-company employees refusing to acknowledge the band's authority would be turned back at the checkpoints. Officially, band members would be unarmed. But they had prepared spiked boards to throw across the road in an emergency, and some members hinted broadly that guns would also be at hand.[69]

"We don't have any choice," Ominayak informed reporters shortly after O'Reilly had read the Lubicon statement. "It's time we protect what is ours. As of 1:00 p.m. on October 15, anybody who wants to come on our land will have to deal with us and recognize this land is ours."[70] "After fifty years of trying to get their own home recognized as their home, and their own land, and a fair deal," O'Reilly observed as the roadblocks went up, "and of being thrown from federal broken promise to federal broken promise and nothing happening, and nothing on the horizon, and their way of life being destroyed, and the United Nations having reproached Canada to do something about it and Canada saying basically, 'We don't care what you say,' and flouting international law—enough is enough! The Lubicons intend to make this literally their last stand."[71]

By the afternoon of the 15th, all oil company activity on Lubicon land had ceased—a matter which was variously estimated to cost the corporations from $260,000 to $430,000 (Canadian) per day—and Vice President Koichi Kitagawa of the Daishowa Corporation had expressed concern with the future of his company's planned enterprise in the area.[72] By then, Premier Getty had upped the provincial settlement offer from 25.4 to 79 square miles.[73] The Lubicons responded that recent births had expanded their population to a total of 478 people; using the standard multiplier of 128 acres per Indian which pertained across Canada, they therefore computed their minimum entitlement as being 95.6 square miles. They also asserted a claim to a ten percent royalty applicable to all resources illegally extracted from their territory during the previous half-century (a sum Getty admitted would be "in excess of $100 million," meaning that total oil and gas revenues derived from Lubicon land had been over $5 billion up to that point).[74]

On October 21, the Royal Canadian Mounted Police staged a "raid" to dismantle the Lubicon checkpoints.

They were met with no resistance, given that Getty was already promising that such provincial "law enforcement" would be mostly symbolic, that the 27 Lubicons arrested would be immediately released, and that the gesture would inaugurate a new round of negotiations designed to resolve the Alberta/Lubicon conflict once and for all.[75] Ominayak stipulated that, should the province deviate from this script, the roadblocks would be instantly reinstated and maintained indefinitely. In this, he received pledges of physical support from the Treaty Eight chiefs who vowed to replace, on a "body for body" basis, anyone hauled away by the RCMP.[76]

> Eugene Steinhauer of Saddle Lake, a former president of the Indian Association and one of Alberta's best-known Indian leaders, left a hospital bed to be there. Chiefs from other bands around Alberta could be seen, including Lawrence Courtoreille, vice-president for Alberta of the Assembly of First Nations, and leaders such as Mohawk Chief Billy Two Rivers of Kahnewake near Montreal. Members of the Committee Against Racism from Calgary held placards saying "Support the Lubicon." News reporters and photographers were out in force, representing the national television networks, the radio networks, the Southam and Canadian Press news services, an Italian wire service and dozens of Alberta print and broadcast outlets...A group of clergy led by Peter Hamel of the Anglican Church of Canada joined the ranks. A Dutch member of the European parliament, Herman Verbeek, arrived separately, telling reporters, "It is important that Canadians be aware that people in Europe and all over the world know what is happening here"...Radio talk shows focussed on the issue. "Do you recognize the Lubicon nation as sovereign?" asked the moderator of CBC Edmonton's "Phone Forum." Responses ran 80 percent in the band's favor.[77]

In terms of more direct actions:

> The protest spread to other parts of the country. In

> Montreal, the Mohawks of Kahnewake slowed traffic on the Mercier Bridge [for two days] to distribute 10,000 Lubicon support flyers. In Brantford, Ontario, fifteen members of the Six Nations Mohawk reserve blocked highway traffic briefly in a similar show of solidarity. In Labrador, partly emboldened by the Lubicon move, a community of Innu Indians camped at the end of a military runway at Goose Bay to protest low-level military flights over their caribou lands. More than 150 people were arrested, then released.[78]

Under these conditions, Getty flew to the town of Grimshaw, near the Lubicon land, to meet with Ominayak on October 22. By nightfall, an agreement had been hammered out wherein 95 square miles of land would be transferred to the Lubicons. Of this, Alberta committed to providing 79 square miles outright, with full subsurface rights. The remaining sixteen square miles were to be purchased from the province for the Indians by Ottawa, with Alberta retaining subsurface rights subject to Lubicon veto power over any provincial development scheme(s).[79] Both sides agreed to begin negotiations concerning cooperative administration of entities devoted to environmental oversight and wildlife management, and to jointly propose a more complete resolution package—including financial compensation and economic development support for the Lubicons—to the central government.[80]

> What an enormous victory the Grimshaw Agreement was. More had been accomplished in a week of confrontation than in a decade of official meetings and court appearances. Getty had [been forced to] develop an appreciation of how badly the Lubicon people had been treated over the years, telling Ominayak privately that he felt "ashamed" to have been part of the earlier government...For band members, the agreement vindicated a long-term strategy to build power and use it. The victory seemed to show that even the smallest and most remote of Canadian native societies, by holding together and

working hard, could develop enough muscle to prevail over legal and political inequities.[81]

As Ominayak put it the same evening: "We've done something today that could have been done years ago in a very short time compared with the forty-eight years we've been waiting...I hope we have shown today that if we put up a united front, there is not too much they can do to stop us...And with that, I thank all the community members, and say, 'Federal government—the Lubicons are coming at you.'"[82]

Federal Subversion

For its part, Ottawa reacted to the changed situation with a certain initial confusion when negotiations began on November 29, 1988. The immediate response of McKnight and his aides was to retreat, conceding that the Lubicon band membership should total 506 people, and that the land agreement worked out at Grimshaw was therefore quite reasonable. By the end of the second week of talks, the government had committed itself to providing $34 million to construct housing, roads, sewers, electrification, and public buildings on the reserve. A $5 million trust from which the Lubicons could draw annual interest to use as a lever to engage in economic development was also offered. This left only the issue of compensation for prior resource exploitation hanging when the talks were recessed for the Christmas/New Year holidays. Things appeared to be going very well.[83]

When negotiations resumed, however, it seemed the federal team had utilized the break to regroup itself in order to adopt an entirely different posture. The change was capped on January 24, 1989, when Ottawa spokesperson Brian Malone tabled what he called "a final, take-it-or-leave-it settlement offer." The terms of the proposal included only $30 million in "infrastructural development funding." It accepted the Lubicon membership rolls as a "working figure only," leaving actual band membership subject to approval of low-level functionaries (acting registrar Jim Allen had already gone behind the December agreement and was demanding "documentation" of the genealogy of scores of band members); this obviously held implications as to the quantity of land which would ultimately end up in Lubicon possession. Finally, it sought to void both the Lubicons' rights to compensation and their international efforts to secure support.

> Nothing in the written offer suggests that the band [would be] free to sue the federal government for compensation. The current wording obliges the band to "cede, release and surrender" all aboriginal claims and rights to current and future legal actions related to aboriginal rights. Under the provisions, the band must also agree to withdraw its complaints from the United Nations Human Rights Committee, "to acknowledge settlement of its grievance against Canada," before the compensation issue is settled...[Worse], nothing in the offer is binding, unlike the original treaties, which are guaranteed in the Canadian constitution. "Any agreement arising out of this offer...will be subject to parliamentary appropriations during eh applicable fiscal year," the text of the Lubicon offer states. If parliament failed for any reason to advance enough money to fulfill the agreement from year to year, implementation would be suspended.[84]

The reason for Ottawa's reassertion of a hard line, rejected categorically by the Lubicons the day it was tabled, quickly became apparent. In February 1989, Pierre Cadieux—bearing with him a whole new strategy with which to undermine and destroy the Lubicons—replaced William McKnight as head of Aboriginal Affairs.[85] Cadieux's concept was drawn from the classic vernacular of divide and conquer.

> First, the federal unit tried to identify a dissident faction within the Lubicon ranks that might be used to overthrow

> Ominayak. When such a faction proved nonexistent, federal players tried to create one, aiming to overthrow Ominayak or, alternatively, split the band. when that attempt also failed, federal players recruited native people from all over northern Alberta to create a new band designed to lay claim to Lubicon territory and accept the federal offer. The idea was cynical and brutal, but it provided the mechanism by which federal authorities could impose a settlement, ward off the United Nations Human Rights Committee, scotch the Grimshaw Agreement, and divide native people in the interior against each other so that the Lubicon people could never again mount an effective aboriginal-rights challenge.[86]

A part of the maneuver was to convince individual Indians who were not Lubicons, or who had no desire to live in Lubicon territory, to enroll in the band and then accept "land in severalty" elsewhere.[87] In this fashion, both the sense of unity evidenced by the band, and the basis of its assertion of collectivity in its land claims might be severely undercut. The tactic, of course, places the government, which had been actively seeking to diminish or eliminate Lubicon membership altogether for nearly a century, in the position of suddenly and completely reversing itself, expanding the rolls will-nilly over the protests of the Indians. Within weeks, Cadieux claimed to have received a petition submitted by "182 people who are unhappy with the leadership of Bernard Ominayak...and who wish to receive their own 160 acre parcels of land in severalty."[88] Cadieux's representatives, while adamantly refusing to provide copies of the document, contended that "60 or 70" of the people signing the petition were "names familiar to those who are familiar with the [Lubicon] band list."[89] Cadieux promptly offered federal resources for the signatories—whom he dubbed "the disenfranchised Lubicons"—to retain an attorney, Bob Young, while pursuing registration as status Indians and attending land claims, each award of which was to be deducted from the

95 square mile Lubicon settlement offer.[90]

In the end, the petition turned out to be forged, and to have contained the names of no enrolled Lubicons at all. By then, however, the effort to depose Ominayak—who had himself called for an election when rumors of "factionalism" had first surfaced—had failed when he was *unanimously* continued in office by a band poll conducted in late May. The government, meanwhile, had shifted gears:

> On August 28, 1989—eight months after the Ottawa talks—Pierre Cadieux constituted the newly registered Indians as an official band. The Woodland Cree band, he called it, using a generic term of the Cree of the northern woodlands. Not since the early treaty days had a band been formalized so quickly—within twelve weeks of Young's application, and ahead of about seventy aboriginal societies across the country who had been waiting up to fifty years for band status...Woodland members registering as status Indians had also jumped queue on thousands of native people waiting to regain status lost through marriage. Registration can often take years; some of Young's clients were processed in a week.[91]

On July 5, 1990, the ersatz band—of "300," "350," or "700" members; federal officials contradicted one another on the number, and kept the actual membership list secret—voted to fulfill its end of the bargain by signing an "accord" in which they received a reserve of 71 square miles to the west of Lubicon Lake, all of it without subsurface rights. It was arranged that sixteen square miles of this would be "sold back" to the government for $512,000 ($50 per acre) even before transfer occurred. Infrastructural development monies of $29 million were allocated. Another $19 million in "economic development funds" were also allotted to underwrite a series of unspecified projects. Each Woodland band member was paid $50 in federal funds to cast an "aye" vote in the referendum conducted to approve the "settlement." Each voter was also promised a check in the amount of $1,000 as "compensation for past losses" once the measure was passed.[92]

Later, they were informed that both the $50 and $1,000 payments were to be deducted from future welfare payments. In addition, the total amount of "compensation" paid—$713,400—would be charged against the monies due as payment for the sixteen square mile parcel acquired by Ottawa, as well as infrastructural and economic development funds.[93] Hence, the Woodland Band "owed" the federal government approximately $153,000 before its first member ever set foot on the new reserve. Before this travesty became public knowledge, the government let its other shoe drop. On July 7, Brian Malone announced during a speech at Cambridge, England, that Cadieux's office was organizing yet another instant band, this one at Loon Lake, about forty miles northeast of Lubicon. The group was said to be composed of 172 people represented by an assistant to Young. They wanted, Malone stated smugly, a "good deal," one "comparable to that extended to the people of the Woodland Cree Reserve."[94]

> With the Woodland agreement to the west and an impending Loon Lake agreement to the northeast, Lubicon society was slowly being pulled apart. Exactly how many Lubicon members had defected was not certain. Malone told his Cambridge audience that 180 had gone to Woodland and 80 to Loon Lake, although representatives for the two groups put the numbers at "about 100" and "fewer than 25" respectively. Whatever the figures, the damage was enormous. People signing their names to the new band lists were following a course logical to anybody living in a world where the law is arbitrary, and where rewards and punishments are distributed at random; but almost everybody seemed to be paying a price. In some Lubicon families, one spouse had joined the Woodland group, the other had not. [In others], several children had joined...the others had not.[95]

Like the Lubicons' legal offensive of the early '80s,

their diplomatic initiatives had clearly foundered by 1991. This has left Ominayak and others in the Lubicon leadership—badly worn by more than a decade of continuous and intensive struggle—in the position of having to start anew with yet a different approach, meanwhile reorganizing and revitalizing the morale of their destitute and emotionally battered people. Unfortunately, his options have been steadily constricted by unrelenting official intransigence and duplicity, to the point where genuine armed resistance may become the sole card remaining available to them. Certainly, the threat of such a course is the only thing which ever garnered appreciable results, however transiently, in terms of altering the government's posture. Similarly, in early 1992, it was the only means by which Daishowa—which had by then completed construction of a $500 million pulp plant to the north of the Lubicon land—was averted from commencing the wholesale cutting of trees in the area.[96] As Ominayak has said all along, violence is something to be avoided, but "we'll do whatever it is that's necessary to assert our rights."[97]

The Lubicon Future—and Ours

The bets, as they say, are hardly in on the outcome at Lubicon Lake. At one level, it is certainly not realistic to expect that a small Indian band, even with a considerable number of allies, could militarily defeat the combined forces of several transnational corporations and an advanced nation-state such as Canada. Being forced to pursue the military option in literal terms would undoubtedly prove utterly catastrophic for the Lubicons and their "on-line" supporters. Of this, there can be little doubt. Yet, failing to resist the imposition of governmental policy, or offering resistance only through channels approved by Canadian officials, is a course of action which has long since demonstrated that it will yield similarly catastrophic results for the Indians, both in terms of their administrative liquidation as peoples, and by way of insuring the destruction of the environment upon which all of us depend for our very survival. When the issues are framed in this way, it becomes as Ominayak has said, "a good day to die."

What the Lubicon Lake Cree have going for them, beyond the sheer righteousness and correctitude of their position, is the fact that they have been able to attract widespread international attention and support to their cause. Whatever happens next in northern Alberta will happen in the full glare of world scrutiny, and under the full weight of world opinion. "Liberal democratic" nation-states such as Canada depend heavily upon their ability to clamp a lid of secrecy over their internal applications of lethal force for political purposes, thereby maintaining their ability to posture as "humanitarian" entitles within the geopolitical arena. The Lubicons have proven themselves singularly successful in stripping away the necessary blanket of state secrecy in their own case, and have thus placed themselves in an ideal position to call the bluff of Canada's domestic saber rattlers. Canadian pursuit of a military or paramilitary option as a means of "resolving" the Lubicon claims to land and sovereignty thus carries with it undeniable and extremely negative consequences for the Canadian state itself. It is this political rather than military dimension to the Indian strategy which gives the Lubicon assertion that Canada will either have to "kill us or acknowledge our rights" its ring of truth.

It is possible that Canadian officialdom, or at least some elements of it, will prove so narrowly racist and obtuse as to undertake an outright war against the Indians along Peace River. In that case, the unremittingly ugly history of the Anglo domination in North America will be marked by yet another in its long series of genocidal occurrences. On the other hand it is entirely possible, under the circumstances created by the Lubicons, that wiser heads will prevail and that some settlement acceptable to the Indians will at last be negotiated by the Canadian government. If this occurs—given that the Lubicons are overtly demanding a resumption of control over their own government, legal system, identification of citizenry, and resources, as well as traditional lands—it will be a major breakthrough in the reassertion of indigenous sovereignty on this continent.

The stakes are very high at Lubicon Lake. Whatever else may be said with regard to the struggle there, the tactics and positions developed by this tiny band of Cree are deserving of study and emulation in many places. And all of us owe them an incalculable debt for having had the courage and vision to both frame things in their proper terms and bring matters to a head. In a very real sense, as go the Lubicons, so go we all.

Notes

1. See George Brown and Ron Mcguire, *Indian Treaties in Historical Perspective* (Ottawa: Research Branch, Indian and Northern Affairs Ministry of Canada, 1979). Additional background may be found in John L. Tobias, "Canada's Subjugation of the Plains Cree, 1879-1885," in J.R. Miller, ed., *Sweet Promises* (Toronto: University of Toronto Press, 1991).
2. These are essentially boilerplate terms, covered in David Laird, *Our Indian Treaties* (Winnipeg: Manitoba Free Press, 1905). Also see Richard Price, ed., *The Spirit of the Alberta Indian Treaties* (Montreal: Institute for Research on Public Policy, 1980).
3. See Dennis F.K. Madill, *Treaty Research Report: Treaty Eight* (Ottawa: Treaties and Historical Research Centre, Indian and Northern Affairs Ministry of Canada, 1986.) Also see George F.G. Stanley, *The Birth of Western Canada* (Toronto: University of Toronto Press, 1975).
4. E. Davie Fulton, *Lubicon Lake Indian Band Inquiry: Discussion Paper* (Ottawa: Office of the Minister for Indian

Affairs, 1986). Also see Brown and Mcguire, *op. cit.*

5. See Richard Daniel, *Land Rights of Isolated Communities in Northern Alberta* (Edmonton: Isolated Communities Advisory Board, 1975).
6. Alberta Municipal Affairs Department, *Report on the Land Tenure Project, 1975-1983* (Edmonton: Provincial Government of Alberta, 1983). Also see Human Resources Development Authority, *An Analysis of the People and Resources of the Little Buffalo Lake Area* (Edmonton: Provincial Government of Alberta, 1969).
7. Indian Affairs Canada, *Indian Acts and Amendments, 1868-1950* (Ottawa: Research Branch: Indian and Northern Affairs Ministry of Canada, 1981).
8. See Davie, *op. cit.* Also see John Goddard, "Last Stand of the Lubicon," *Equinox,* November 1987.
9. The process is covered in Harold Cardinal, *The Unjust Society: The Tragedy of Canada's Indians* (Edmonton: M.G. Hurtig Ltd., Publisher, 1969).
10. For details on McCrimmon's maneuvering during this period, see John Goddard, *Last Stand of the Lubicon Cree* (Vancouver/Toronto: Douglas and McIntire Publishers, 1991, pp. 21-7). For formal analysis, see James O'Reilly, *Whither the Indian?* (Montreal: Canadian Bar Association, 1969).
11. Letter, Alberta Regional Supervisor of Aboriginal Affairs to the Minister of Aboriginal Affairs, May 19, 1953.
12. Letter, Director of the Technical Division of (Alberta) Lands and Forests to the Minister of Aboriginal Affairs, October 22, 1953.
13. Cardinal, *op. cit.*
14. Letter, Alberta Regional Supervisor of Aboriginal Affairs to the Minister of Aboriginal Affairs, February 25, 1954.
15. *Last Stand of the Lubicon Cree, op. cit.*, pp. 74-85.
16. Directive, Superintendent of Reserves and Trusts to Lubicon Lake Indian Agent, February 9, 1955.
17. Letter, Alberta Supervisor of Aboriginal Affairs to Lubicon Lake Indian Agent, January 23, 1955.
18. Letter, Alberta Supervisor of Aboriginal Affairs to Lubicon Lake Indian Agent, January 21, 1955.
19. For detailed elaboration of the intent in utilizing the term "genocide" in this context, see Ward Churchill, "Genocide:

Toward a Functional Definition," *Alternatives*, Vol. XI, No. 3, July 1986, pp. 401-30.

20. Lubicon Lake Band Council, *Lubicon Lake Band Presentation to the Standing Committee on Aboriginal Affairs and Northern Development: General History* (Ottawa: House of Commons, 1953, p. 15); hereinafter referred to as *Lubicon Presentation.*
21. "Last Stand of the Lubicon," *op. cit.* Also see Sally M. Weaver, *Making Canadian Indian Policy, 1968-1970* (Toronto: University of Toronto Press, 1981).
22. "Last Stand of the Lubicon," *op. cit.*
23. *Lubicon Presentation, op. cit.*, pp. 14-5. For background, see Indian Affairs Canada, *Contemporary Indian Legislation, 1951-1978* (Ottawa: Research Branch, Indian and Northern Affairs Canada, 1981).
24. *Lubicon Presentation, op. cit.*, pp. 15-6.
25. *Ibid.*, pp. 17-8. For a multifaceted elaboration of the legal basis for the Lubicon position, see Bradford W. Morse, ed., *Aboriginal Peoples and the Law: Indian, Métis and Inuit Rights in Canada* (Ottawa: Carlton University Press, 1985).
26. *Lubicon Presentation, op. cit.*, p. 18.
27. *Ibid.*, pp. 19-20.
28. *Ibid.*, pp. 20-21.
29. *Ibid.*, p. 21.
30. *Ibid.*
31. *Ibid.*, p. 22.
32. *Ibid.*, p. 23. Also see *Facts About the Lubicon Lake Indian Band Land Claims* (Edmonton: Office of the Supervisor of Aboriginal Affairs, February 10, 1988, p. 2); hereinafter referred to as *Lubicon Land Claims.*)
33. Canadian Broadcasting Corporation report, February 2, 1988; the CBC contends "about 100" oil companies now have an interest in the Lubicon land. Also see Human Resources Authority, *op. cit.*
34. For good descriptions of McKnight's positions and operational style, see *Last Stand of the Lubicon Cree, op. cit.*, pp. 159-62, 165-70.
35. *Lubicon Land Claims, op. cit.*, p. 3.
36. *Ibid.*
37. *Ibid.*, p. 2.

38. Randall Ivany, *Special Report of the Ombudsman for Alberta Regarding Complaints of the Lubicon Lake Cree Band* (Edmonton: Government of Alberta, 1984).
39. *Lubicon Land Claims, op. cit.*, p. 4.
40. *Ibid.*
41. *Ibid.*, p. 3.
42. Statement of Chief Bernard Ominayak, Edmonton, Alberta, December 11, 1985.
43. *Lubicon Land Claims, op. cit.*, p. 3.
44. "Indians vow to boycott Olympics, *Calgary Herald,* November 19, 1986.
45. *Lubicon Land Claims, op. cit.*, p. 2.
46. *Ibid.*
47. *Ibid.*, p. 3.
48. *Ibid.*
49. The Lubicons also connected with resident stateside supporters/organizers such as Ms. Dorothy Still Smoking during this period.
50. Fulton, *op. cit.*
51. Statement of Chief Bernard Ominayak, Edmonton, Alberta, January 14, 1988.
52. *Lubicon Land Claims, op. cit.*, p. 5.
53. See, as examples of the mainstream press coverage the Lubicons obtained, Allen Connery, "Why Lubicons are protesting," *Calgary Herald,* January 27, 1988; Paul Ogresko, "Sharing the Blame: Boycott Hits Olympic Museum," *Calgary Sunday Sun,* January 31, 1988; and Steve Hume, "The Spirit Weeps: Power, Genius and Hypocrisy at the Glenbow Exhibit," *The Edmonton Journal,* February 14, 1988.
54. *Lubicon Land Claims, op. cit.*, p. 3.
55. *Ibid.*
56. McKnight's exact quote: "The band has now rejected all recent initiatives under the Treaty 8 process and apparently intends to pursue its case against Alberta for Aboriginal title. That is their right."
57. "Indian Affairs may sue Alta over Lubicons," *Ottawa Citizen,* February 2, 1988. Also see Graham Fraser, "McKnight condemns Alberta move on land claimed by Lubicons," *Toronto Globe and Mail,* February 11, 1988.
58. Press Release, "Daishowa" (New Buffalo, Alberta: Lubicon

Lake Band of Cree, February 18, 1988, p. 1).

59. *Ibid.*
60. *Ibid.*, p. 2.
61. Government of Alberta, Press Release N.R. 055, February 8, 1988. Also see Karen Booth and David Holehouse, "Horsman to bypass band," *The Edmonton Journal*, February 16, 1988.
62. Letter, National Chief George Erasmus, Council of First Nations, to the Right Honorable Brian Mulroney, Prime Minister of Canada, February 16, 1988.
63. Quoted in Karen Booth, "Lubicon prepare for 'last stand' on land claim," *The Edmonton Journal*, January 25, 1988.
64. Quoted in Mark Lowey and Kathy Kerr, "Lubicon support on the rise," *Calgary Herald*, February 25, 1988.
65. *Last Stand of the Lubicon Cree, op. cit.*, p. 159.
66. "Getty emerging from the shadows," *Calgary Herald*, March 17, 1988. Also see "Getty calls play," *The Edmonton Journal*, March 17, 1988.
67. Quoted in *Last Stand of the Lubicon Cree, op. cit.*, p. 167.
68. *Ibid.*, p. 170.
69. *Ibid.*, p. 171.
70. Quoted in *ibid.*, p. 170.
71. Quoted in *ibid.*, p. 172-3.
72. See *ibid.*: lost oil revenues, p. 185; Daishowa, p. 166.
73. *Ibid.*, p. 179.
74. See *ibid.*: on population and land, p. 185; on royalties, p. 181.
75. *Ibid.*, pp. 188-91.
76. Press Release, Council of Treaty Eight Chiefs, Calgary, October 21, 1988.
77. *Last Stand of the Lubicon Cree, op. cit.*, pp. 173, 180-1.
78. *Ibid.*, p. 186.
79. Ominayak specified that one square mile would be located at a Bison Lake burial ground, one square mile at Haig Lake, and the balance at Lubicon Lake; *ibid.*, p. 193.
80. The basic terms and provisions of the "Grimshaw Agreement" are covered in *ibid.*, pp. 192-3.
81. *Ibid.*, p. 195.
82. Quoted in *ibid.*, p. 194.
83. The negotiations are covered in *ibid.*, pp. 196-8.
84. *Ibid.*, p. 200. Among other things, the "offer" also rejects

outright a $16 million agricultural development project proposed by the Lubicons, and a $2.6 million vocational education center and maintenance shop. Instead, $100,000 would be provided to afford "training opportunities."

85. "Cadieux to head Indian Affairs," *Toronto Globe and Mail*, February 14, 1989.
86. *Last Stand of the Lubicon Cree, op. cit.*, p. 203.
87. For analysis of the implications of this move, see Indian Association of Alberta, *Statement on the Indian Title to Lands Surveyed "In Severalty" Under Treaty Number Eight* (Ottawa: Treaty and Aboriginal Rights and Research Center, 1981).
88. Quoted in *Last Stand of the Lubicon Cree, op. cit.*, p. 206.
89. *Ibid.*
90. Discussion with Sharon Venne, Alfred, NY, November 1990 (tape on file). As Goddard puts it, "After years of accusing Ominayak of 'jacking up' membership figures to get more land, federal authorities were now accusing him of cutting members out."
91. *Last Stand of the Lubicon Cree, op. cit.*, p. 209. On the generic nature of the term employed, see James G.E. Smith, "Wester Woods Cree," in *Handbook of North American Indians, Volume Six: Subarctic* (Washington, D.C.: Smithsonian Institution, 1981). Cadieux claimed authority to do what he did under provision of Article 17 of the Indian Act: "The Minister may, whenever he considers it desirable, constitute new Bands and establish new Band Lists with respect thereto from existing Band Lists, or from the Indian Register, if requested to do so by persons proposing to form new Bands." "No protest can be made," the article concludes. See *Indian Acts and Amendments, op. cit.*
92. Discussed in *Last Stand of the Lubicon Cree, op. cit.*, p. 211. The numerical discrepancies are apparently accounted for in the fact that the government wished to portray the Woodland Cree as a larger and more substantial group than the Lubicons for public relations purposes while simultaneously minimizing their numbers for purposes of computing their land entitlement. Hence, a number of Metis and non-status Indians were lumped into the band

roll, inflating the number to "700" for public consumption. Meanwhile, the land apportionment was based against only the 355 status Indians who were enrolled. In the end, 713 persons—the government claimed this was 87 percent of eligible voters—were paid to endorse the federally proposed settlement package. Ninety-eight point five percent complied by voting "aye."

93. *Ibid.*, p. 212.
94. Quoted in *ibid.*, p. 213.
95. *Ibid.*
96. Telephone conversation with Sharon Venne, February 16, 1992.
97. CBC Edmonton broadcast, February 19, 1992.

Part III
Other Battles

Industrial Slave
capitalist and communist
    imperialists
smiling with false faces
beckoning us
with their lies about progress
wanting us to enjoy
    the rape of Earth
    and our minds

Industrial Slave
forked tongue legalistic contract
chains
turning our visions into tech no logical
dreams
national security war makers
desecrating the natural world
and god still trying to get over
what you done to his boy

Industrial Slave
material bound
law and ORDER
religious salvation
individually alone
Industrial Slave.

—John Trudell—
from *Living in Reality*

Radioactive Colonization

A Hidden Holocaust in Native North America

> Our defeat was always implicit in the history of others; our wealth has always generated our poverty by nourishing the prosperity of others, the empires and their native overseers...In the colonial and neocolonial alchemy, gold changes to scrap metal and food into poison...[We] have become painfully aware of the mortality of wealth which nature bestows and imperialism appropriates.
>
> —Eduardo Galeano—
> *Open Veins of Latin America*

The unstated rationales guiding the federal governments of both the United States and Canada in their contemporary handling of native peoples and territories are straightforward. It is not considered geopolitically expedient to allow a scattering of small, mostly landlocked nations to exercise anything resembling real sovereignty within their own borders. Moreover, it has been discovered that, perhaps ironically, the barren residual landbase left to Indians in the twentieth century is extremely resource-rich: about two-thirds of all known U.S. "domestic" uranium reserves and one-third of its low-sulfur coal lie under Indian land. In addition, as much as a quarter of the oil and natural gas are in reservation areas. Substantial assets of commercial and strategic minerals such as gold, silver, copper, bauxite, molybdenum and zeolites are at issue, as are water in the arid West, and other "renewable resources" like timber.[1] The pattern of resource distribution in Canada is comparable.[2]

With such holdings, it would seem logical that the two million indigenous people of North America—1.6 million in the U.S. and another half million in Canada—would be among the continent's wealthiest residents.[3] As even the governments' own figures reveal, however, they receive the lowest per capita income of any population group and evidence every standard indicator of dire poverty: highest rates of malnutrition, plague disease, death by exposure, infant mortality, teen suicide, and so on.[4] The U.S. government in particular has found that by keeping native assets pooled in reservation areas under its "trust" authority, it is able to channel them at very low rates to preferred corporations, using a "tribal" administrative apparatus it established during the late 1930s as a medium for leasing purposes.[5] Thus, as of 1984, stateside Indians were receiving only an average of 3.4 percent of the market value of uranium extracted from their land, 1.6 percent of the value of their oil, 1.3 percent for natural gas, and a little under two percent for coal. For the same items, royalty rates paid to non-Indians are often six times higher.[6]

This boon to the U.S. economy has been enhanced by the government's utilization of its self-proclaimed "plenary" power over Indians and Indian land to relax or dispense with environmental protection standards and job safety regulations, further lowering extraction and production costs while allowing certain of the more odious forms of production and waste disposal associated with advanced industrial technologies to be conveniently located—out of sight and mind of the mainstream public—in Indian area.[7] In substance, native people have been consigned to a status of "expendability" by federal, state, and corporate economic planners. Again, the pattern is little different in Canada.[8]

From the perspective of North America's social, political and economic elites, the advantages of maintaining discrete Indian territories under trust control thus greatly

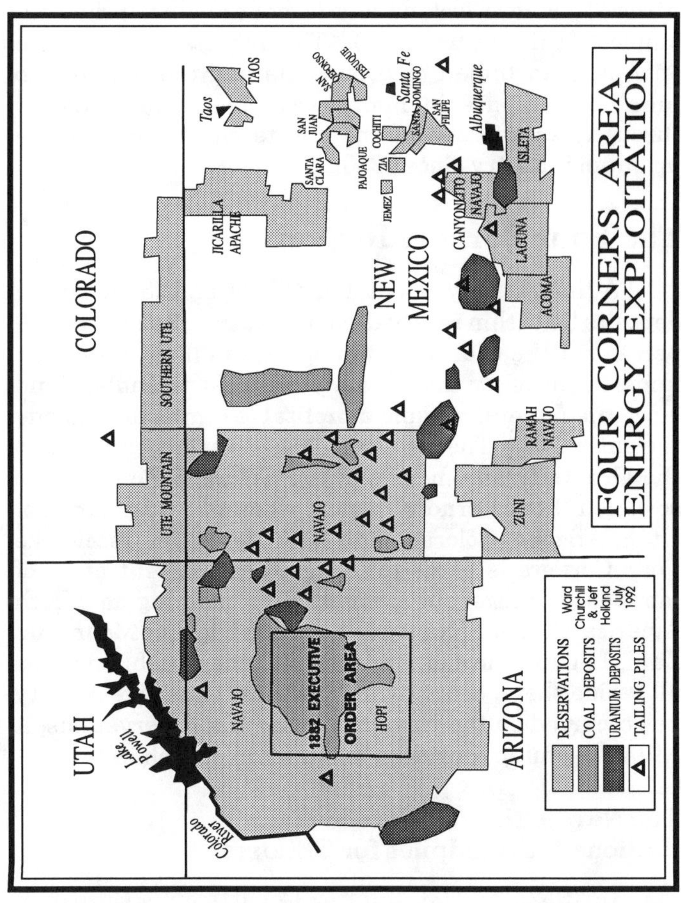

outweigh any potential benefit accruing from final absorption of these residual areas.[9] The history of conquest, military or otherwise, which has always marked the U.S. and Canadian relationship to Native North America has correspondingly transformed itself into a process of colonization, albeit of an "internal" variety peculiar to highly-evolved settler states (Australia, New Zealand, South

Africa, Northern Ireland and Israel are other prime examples of this phenomenon).[10] The impacts of this system on American Indian environments and the people who inhabit them are in many ways best demonstrated through examination of the effects engendered by the uranium industry since 1950.

The Four Corners Region

Although only about two-thirds of U.S. uranium deposits lie within reservation boundaries, as much as 90 percent of the country's mining and milling have been undertaken on or immediately adjacent to Indian land since the mineral became a profitable commodity during the early '50s.[11] The bulk of this activity has occurred in the Grants Uranium Belt of the Colorado Plateau, the so-called "Four Corners" region, where the boundaries of Utah, Arizona, Colorado and New Mexico intersect. The Four Corners is home to the greatest concentration of landbased indigenous population remaining in North America: the Diné (Navajo), Southern Ute, Ute Mountain, Zuni, Laguna, Acoma, and several other Pueblo nations all reside there. Since by far the most extensive activity has occurred on the Navajo and Laguna Reservations, it will be useful to consider the situation of each in turn.

The Navajo Nation: Radioactive Sandpiles for Children

In 1952, the U.S. Interior Department's Bureau of Indian Affairs (BIA) awarded the Kerr-McGee Corporation the first contract—duly rubberstamped by the federally-created and supported Navajo Tribal Council—to mine uranium on Diné land, employing about 100 Indian miners at two-thirds the off-reservation pay scale.[12] In the same year, a federal inspector at the corporation's mine near the reservation town of Shiprock, New Mexico, found the ventilation fans in the facility's main shaft were not functioning.[13] When the same inspector returned in 1955, the fans ran out of fuel during his visit. By 1959, radiation levels in the Shiprock mine were estimated as being 90 to 100 times the maximums permissible for worker safety.[14] Nothing was done about the situation before the uranium deposit played out and the Shiprock operation was closed in 1970.[15]

At that point, Kerr-McGee simply abandoned the site, leaving the local community to contend with 70 acres of uranium tailings containing about 85 percent of the original radioactivity found in raw uranium ore, much of it continuously emitted in clouds of radon and thoron gas. The huge mounds of waste, which remain virulently mutogenic and carcinogenic for thousands of years, begin less than 60 feet from the only significant surface water in the Shiprock area, the San Juan River.[16] It was shortly discovered that the BIA had "overlooked" inclusion of a clause requiring the corporation to engage in any sort of post-operational cleanup.[17] As Richard O. Clemmer has explained the problem:

> [R]adon and gases, while themselves inert, readily combine with the molecular structure of human cells and decay into radioactive thorium and [polonium]. Radon and thoron gases, if inhaled, irradiate cells in the lining of the respiratory tract, causing cancer. The millions of gallons of radioactive water [released by the uranium industry also] carry deadly selenium, cadmium, and lead that are easily absorbed into the local food chain, as well as emitting alpha and beta particles and gamma rays. Human ingestion of radioactive water can result in alpha particles recurrently bombarding human tissue and eventually tearing apart the cells comprising that tissue. Uranium-bearing tailings are constantly decaying into more stable elements and therefore emit radiation, as do particles of dust that blow with the wind and truck travel on dirt roads.[18]

The Bureau had also neglected to include much in the way of follow-up health care. Of the 150-odd Navajo miners who worked underground at the Shiprock facility over the years, eighteen had died of radiation-induced lung cancer by 1975.[19] By 1980, an additional twenty were dead of the same disease, while 95 more had contracted serious respiratory ailments and cancers.[20] The incidence of cleft palate and other birth defects linked to radiation exposure had also risen dramatically, both at Shiprock and at downstream communities that had drinking water contaminated by the uranium tailings.[21] The same could be said for Downes Syndrome, previously unknown among Diné.[22] Around the Kerr-McGee mine at Red Rock, where the most basic safety standards had also gone unenforced by federal inspectors, a similar pattern prevailed.

> The AEC [Atomic Energy Commission] claimed that it did not possess information about the health problems of uranium miners [or communities adjacent to uranium mines]. Unions and the Public Health Service physicians disagreed. Dr. Victor Archer at NIOSH [National Institute for Occupational Safety and Health] claimed that European physicians had noted a high incidence of lung cancer in uranium miners prior to 1940; the National Commission on Radiation Protection and the International Commission on Radiation Protection were aware of the potential hazards from radon gas by the early 1940s...Given that it had known that some cancers develop only after 10 to 20 years after initial exposure, it is inexcusable that the AEC had not analyzed the literature on radiation-related deaths in the mining industry. As far back as the 1950s, it was widely known that 70 percent of German and Czech pitchblende and uranium miners who worked in the industries from the 1920s and earlier had died of lung cancer.[23]

Dr. Joseph Wagoner, director of epidemiological research at NIOSH, stated that both the cancer deaths and apparent mutogenic effects of Kerr-McGee's operations at Shiprock and Red Rock "present serious medical and ethical questions about the responsibility of [the corporation and] the federal government, which was the sole purchaser of uranium during the early uranium period."[24] In 1979, eleven Red Rock miners suffering from lung cancer and/or fibrosis of the lungs, their families, and the families of fifteen miners who had already died of the respiratory maladies, filed what was to be an unsuccessful damage suit against the U.S. Department of Energy, Atomic Energy Commission and Kerr-McGee.[25]

> Several Navajos who worked in the uranium mills in the 1950s and 1960s [and who were] also afflicted with lung cancer or pulmonary diseases...joined the uranium miners in suing the federal government and uranium companies for compensation. Conditions in the mills were deplorable. An abandoned Shiprock mill was found to have $100,000 worth of yellowcake [pure, milled uranium] between two layers of roofing, while workers tell of stirring yellowcake in open, steam-heated floor pans.[26]

The evidence continued to mount. Yet, by 1982—amidst ongoing federal assurances that there was really "no particular health hazard," and that resulting revenues would lead eventually to "economic self-sufficiency" and "jobs galore" for the impoverished Diné—42 more major mines and seven new mills were operating on Navajo land, while another fifteen major uranium projects were on the drawing board.[27] A substantial part of the Diné economy, both existing and projected, was being quite deliberately distorted to conform to the demands of the uranium industry, regardless of the effects on the Indians. The degree of confluence between governmental and corporate interests, as well as the intensity with which uranium development at Navajo was being pursued during this period, is indicated in a 1977 article in *Business Week*:

> Currently, 3,200 miners work underground and 900 more are in open pit operations. By 1990, the industry will need 18,400 underground miners and 4,000 above ground...Once on the job, Kerr-McGee estimates that it costs $80,000 per miner in training, salary and benefits, as well as the costs for the trainees who quit. Kerr-McGee is now operating a training program at the Church Rock mine on the Navajo Reservation. The $2 million program is financed by the U.S. Labor Department. Labor Department sponsors hope the program will help alleviate the tribe's chronic unemployment.[28]

Kerr-McGee remained the major corporate player, but had been joined by United Nuclear Corporation and Exxon. The rate of exploitation had grown frenzied.

> Kerr-McGee's Church Rock No. 1 mine went into production early in 1976, and it estimated that production of uranium ore will reach...nearly 1 million tons per year by 1978. If Church Rock No. 2 and No. 3 mines come on stream in 1980 and 1983 respectively, annual production would approach 3 million tons per year.[29]

As the pace of such activities accelerated, so too did the environmental and human costs. On July 16, 1979, the United Nuclear uranium mill at Church Rock, New Mexico was the site of the largest radioactive spill in U.S. history. A mill pond dam broke under pressure and released more than 100 million gallons of highly contaminated water into the Río Puerco. As has been observed elsewhere, despite "the greater publicity surrounding the Three Mile Island nuclear plant accident in March 1979, Church Rock resulted in the nation's worst release of radioactivity [until federal dumping at the government's Hanford weapons plant was revealed in 1990; see below]."[30]

About 1,700 Navajo people were immediately affected, their single source of water irradiated beyond any conceivable limit. Sheep and other livestock were also found to be heavily contaminated from drinking river water in the aftermath, yet United Nuclear refused to supply adequate emergency water and food supplies; a corporate official was quoted as saying, in response to local Diné requests for assistance, "This is not a free lunch."[32] Rather than trying to minimize the damage, the corporation stonewalled for nearly five years before agreeing to pay a minimal—$525,000—out-of-court settlement to its victims.[33] The corporation was greatly aided in achieving this favorable outcome by an official finding that downstream Diné had suffered "little or no damage" as a result of the spill.[34]

Government officials at both the federal and state levels were later shown to have actively colluded with the corporation, both before and after the disaster. According to the Southwest Research and Information Center, an Albuquerque-based environmental organization, the whole thing was readily avoidable. United Nuclear, the group demonstrated, had known about cracks in the dam structure at least two months before the break. No costly repairs were made, however, because "political pressure was brought to bear."[35] Even more striking, given the magnitude of what had so recently occurred, "New Mexico Governor Bruce King in 1981 told the New Mexico Environmental Improvement Agency to allow [United Nuclear] to *continue* an illegal water discharge [from its Church Rock mine], which the staff had been attempting to control for over a year (emphasis added)."[36] Similarly, the Kerr-McGee mine at Church Rock was allowed, quite illegally, to continue discharging upwards of 80,000 gallons of contaminated fluid per day—"dewatering" its primary shaft—into the local supply of surface water.[37] In actuality, this steady emission of effluents by the United Nuclear and Kerr-McGee mines has caused far more serious contamination of the Church Rock area than the spill in 1979.[38]

Such circumstances are hardly unique. When the

Navajo Ranchers Association around Crownpoint, seeking to prevent what had occurred at Church Rock from happening to them, filed suit in federal court in 1978 to block Mobil Oil from launching a pilot uranium project in the Dalton Pass area, the judge ruled that the corporation's activities would have "insufficient impact" to necessitate so much as an environmental impact study.[39] In 1979, he refused to allow the plaintiffs to cancel Mobil's leases to their land, which the BIA had approved over their objections.[40] When the Diné plaintiffs argued in 1980 that their pastoral way of life would be destroyed by the plans of Mobil, Gulf, Kerr-McGee, Exxon and a dozen other energy corporations which had by then queued up to mine uranium near Dalton Pass, the judge responded that he couldn't understand why they'd want to continue it anyway, given the "opportunity" for them to become miners and millers.[41] Such thinking was upheld by the Ninth U.S. Circuit Court of Appeals, and this matter, too, was eventually "settled" on terms entirely acceptable to the corporations.[42]

Things are no better with regard to cleanup. Despite passage of the much-touted Uranium Mine Tailings Radiation Control Act in 1978,[43] the first attempt to address the question of radioactive wastes on Navajo land—tailings abandoned around the Foote Mineral Company mill near Shiprock in 1968—was not completed until 1986. This project was finished in such "timely" fashion only because Harold Tso, head of the Navajo Environmental Protection Administration, had himself convinced the tribal government to begin expending royalty monies on the effort as early as 1973.[44] The next three such operations at Navajo—clearing tailings piles at long-abandoned mill sites in Monument Valley and Tuba City, Arizona (Rare Metals Corporation), and Mexican Hat, Utah (Texas Zink Corporation)—are all under exclusive federal control. Scheduled for completion in late 1991, none were finished by the summer of 1992.[45] Virtually nothing has been done with mill tailings around Church Rock, or at several other comparable locations on the reservation.[46]

Nor is this the end of it. A 1983 study by the federal Environmental Protection Agency (EPA) concluded there were nearly 1,000 additional "significant" nuclear waste sites surrounding the proliferation of abandoned mines, large and small, scattered about Diné territory. Cleanup of these locations was/is not required by any law, and they were designated by the EPA as "too remote" to be of "sufficient national concern" to warrant the expense of attempting their rehabilitation.[47] And so they remain, from White Mesa in the east to Tuba City in the west, hundreds upon hundreds of radioactive "sandpiles," still played on by Diné youngsters and swept by the wind across the land.[48] Such is the fate of the largest indigenous nation—in terms of both landbase and population—in the United States.

Laguna Pueblo: An Energy Policy that Brings Genocide to Light

At the neighboring Laguna Pueblo in New Mexico, the situation is perhaps worse. In 1952, the Anaconda Copper Company, a subsidiary of the Atlantic-richfield Corporation, was issued a lease by the BIA to 7,500 acres of Laguna land on which to undertake open pit uranium mining and an adjoining milling operation. By 1980, the resulting Jackpile-Paguate Mine was the largest in the world, encompassing some 2,800 acres. It has been estimated that it would take 400 million tons of earth—enough to cover the entire District of Columbia 45 feet deep—to fill it in.[49] Of the earth removed, approximately 80 million tons was good grade uranium ore.[50] By the time the facility closed in 1982, Anaconda had realized about $600 million from its operation at Laguna.[51]

In the process, the corporation, in collaboration with federal "development officers," virtually wrecked the traditional Laguna economy, recruiting hundreds of the small community's young people into wage jobs even as their environment was being gobbled up and contaminated.[52] As the latter issue was framed with regard to mining by an investigator in the early '80s:

> [Anaconda's] mining techniques require "dewatering," i.e., the pumping of water contaminated by radioactive materials to facilitate ore extraction. Since 1972, the Jackpile Mine has wasted more than 119 gallons per minute through this dewatering procedure. Altogether more than 500 million gallons of radioactive water have been discharged. This water, already radioactive from contact with uranium ore underground, is pumped over the 260-acre tailings pile comprised of overburden and processed ore sitting on soft, porous rock. From the tailings pond, this radioactive water either sinks back into the aquifer, evaporates, or seeps out of the tailings pond into the arroyos and drainage channels of the tiny Río Mequino stream that is fed by a natural spring near the tailings dam.[53]

Concerning milling:

> At the Bluewater Mill, eighteen miles west of the Laguna Reservation [on the western boundary of the adjoining Acoma Pueblo, a 30 mile trip by rail, with raw ore hauled in open gondolas] near the bed of the San Jose River, Anaconda has added a 107-acre pond and a 159-acre pile comprising 13,500,000 tons of "active" tailings and 765,033 tons of "inactive" residues.[54]

The effects of the Anaconda undertakings combined with those of other corporations are devastatiung. Among them is the operation of a Sohio-Reserve mill at Cebolleta, about a mile from the Laguna boundary, processing 1,500 tons of uranium ore per day. The Cebolleta mill's tailings pond covered 50 acres, its tailing pile had reached a height of 350 feet. Near Marquez, about fifteen miles northeast of Laguna, the Bokum Minerals Corporation had opened a shaft mine, and Kerr-McGee announced plans in 1979 to open a second.[55] Other projects were also in the works.

> Near Mount Taylor and San Mateo, 20 miles north of the Laguna and Acoma Reservations, six different companies have drilled exploration holes in eight different areas. Gulf is sinking a deep underground shaft into the Navajos' and Acomas' sacred Mount Taylor, and mining has already changed the configuration of life in the area. Although Gulf acknowledges no responsibility, water supplies became so contaminated with Bentonite from drilling mud that the National Guard trucked water into San Mateo for residents' home use, and Gulf has drilled a new community well. Radon gas vents from Gulf's mine were located so close to the school that the New Mexico EID forced the school to close.[56]

Not surprisingly, given all this, the Environmental Protection Agency informed the Lagunas in 1973, and again in 1977, that their only substantial source of surface water, the Río Paguate, was seriously contaminated with Radium-226 and other heavy metals.[57] In 1979, it was revealed by the federal General Accounting Office that the groundwater underlying the whole of the Grants Uranium Belt, into which Laguna's wells are tapped, was also highly irradiated.[58] By then, it had become known that Anaconda had used low-grade uranium ore, well pulverized, as the gravel with which it had "improved" and expanded the Laguna road network. Soon, it was discovered that comparable material had been used in the building of the tribal council building, community center, and newly-constructed Jackpile Housing complex, all supposed "benefits" of the uranium boom.[59]

In 1977, the Tribal Council belatedly began efforts to negotiate an arrangement by which Anaconda might be required to correct the situation. As at Navajo, however, it was quickly discovered that the BIA had failed to make post-operational cleanup a part of the contract it had signed on the Indians' "behalf."[60] When the Jackpile-Paguate Mine was closed in 1982, the corporation provided only a $175,000 public relations grant designated to help with "retraining" of the suddenly unemployed Laguna work force.[61] The EPA explained that the Indians had "nothing to worry about" because of the irradiation of their homes and other buildings, because radiation levels therein—"while higher than normal"—were still at a "reasonably low level." No mention was made of the fact that a "U.S. Public Health Service physician [had already] suggested that small doses of radiation exposure may actually promote more disease than larger doses because cells are damaged, rather than destroyed outright. Irradiated sex cells in parents can result in birth defects."[62]

Negotiations continued, nonetheless. From the Laguna side this was obviously because of the environmental devastation with which they had been left. After 1983, the federal government began to actually encourage this, as the extent of the damage began to attract public attention, and generate pressure, in nearby Albuquerque and among non-Indian environmental organizations. The Indian position was simple enough:

> The Lagunas [asked] only to be able to graze their livestock, use the water safely, and breath the air without worrying about lung cancer. Unlike [some] uranium mines, which lie in remote, unpopulated areas, one pit lay just 1,000 feet away from the Pueblo community of Paguate. Without proper protection of the groundwater, the mine pit area would remain covered with toxic, saline wastelands, according to the Interior Department. DOI predicted that without reclamation, 95 to 243 additional radiation-induced cancer deaths could be expected within 50 miles of the mine.[63]

Anaconda was recalcitrant, rejecting the Laguna position as "unrealistic," and denouncing the government's data as "inaccurate" by as much as a factor of 100.[64] In 1985, the corporation threatened to sue both its native victims and the Department of Interior as a means of "clarifying" that neither held a "legitimate right" to compel cleanup of the Jackpile site.[65] During the second half of the '80s, however, the corporation's posture began to soften. This was apparently due in part to general public relations concerns and in part because it had become interested in the long-range prospect of returning to its operations on the reservation. In 1986, Anaconda stipulated that it believed reclamation of its wastes would cost a total of $17 million, and that it might—given options on renewing its mineral leases—be prepared to underwrite this expense. The Lagunas countered that the figure was far too low, with the result that the corporation agreed to fund an Indian-staffed "environmental rehabilitation program" in the amount of $43.6 million over a ten year period.[66]

The program won't necessarily make a lot of difference in any event. After an extensive study of the difficulties and expense inherent in rehabilitation of land and water contaminated by uranium mining and milling, the Los Alamos Scientific Laboratory, the premier U.S. nuclear research center, figuratively threw up its hands. "Perhaps the solution to the radon problem," its team of scientists concluded in the laboratory's 1978 *Mini-Report,* "is to zone uranium mining and milling districts so as to forbid human habitation."[67] This recommendation dovetailed quite nicely with a suggestion made somewhat earlier by the National Academy of Science that was incorporated into the Federal Energy Department's "Project Independence" in 1974. The idea was that locales such as the Four Corners region be designated "National Sacrifice Areas" in the interests of U.S. economic stability and energy consumption.[68]

Given that both Anaconda and the government facilitators involved in hatching the Laguna "reclamation" deal were surely aware of this prospectus, it seems probable that the whole thing will turn out to be just one more charade, an elaborate ruse worked out to defuse popular resistance to far greater levels of uranium production in the area during the second half of the '90s. If so, the ploy has worked to a frightening extent. Certainly, the emergent public concern with what was happening at Laguna, on the Navajo Reservation, and elsewhere in the Four Corners, so evident during the early 1980s, has largely dissipated over the past ten years. The way to wholesale geographical sacrifice looks wide open, given only the appropriate economic climate in which to foster it. Such a prospectus conforms very well with the government's 1989 refusal to adopt any sort of uniform standards for rehabilitation of uranium mining and milling zones.[69]

Of course, as American Indian Movement (AIM) leader Russell Means has pointed out, given the land-linked nature of indigenous societies, the sacrifice of any geographic region means the sacrifice of all native peoples residing within it.[70] Unlike the transient, extractive corporations doing business on their land, and the broader consumer society of which they are a part, land-linked peoples cannot simply pick up and leave whenever a given piece of real estate is "used up." To do so would be to engage in an act of utter self-destruction in terms of their identity and sociocultural integrity; in effect, of their cultural survival itself.[71] On the other hand, staying put in the face of the sort of "development" previewed at Laguna and Navajo points clearly to their rapid physical eradication. Hence, the obvious correspondence of the density of native population around the Grants Uranium Belt and the concept of National Sacrifice Areas led Means to conclude that U.S. energy policy, especially as regards uranium mining and milling, amounts to "genocide...no more, no less."[72]

The Black Hills Region

A second region designated for potential national sacrifice is the area around the Black Hills, including

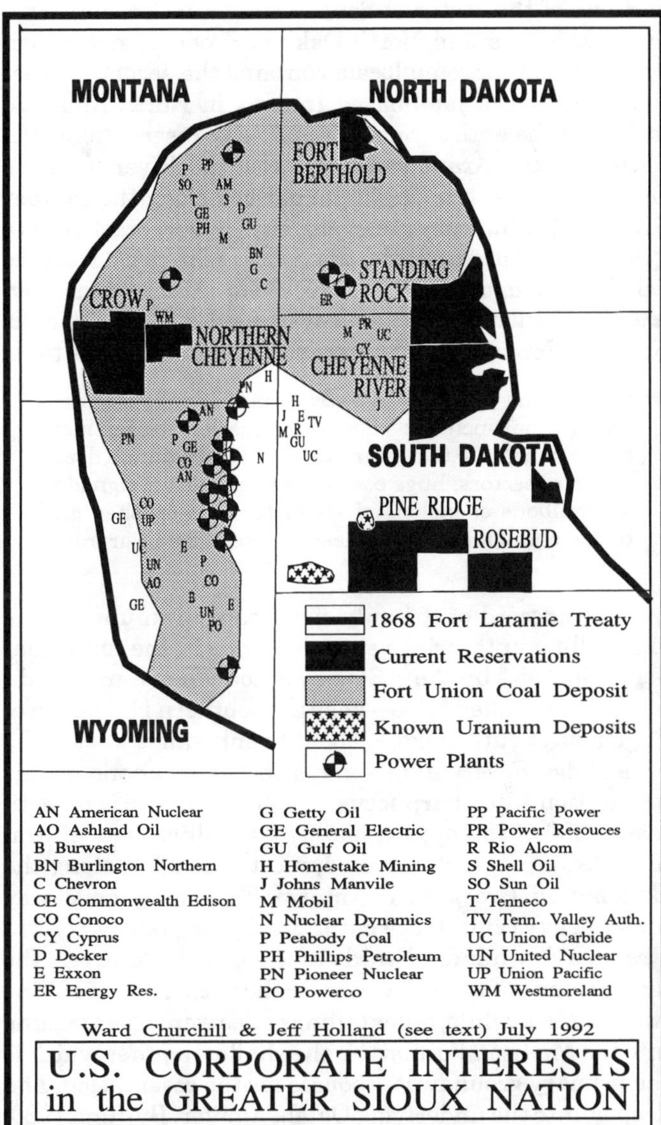

Ward Churchill & Jeff Holland (see text) July 1992

U.S. CORPORATE INTERESTS in the GREATER SIOUX NATION

portions of the states of South Dakota, Nebraska, Wyoming, Montana and North Dakota. Probably not coincidentally, the targeted locale contains the second largest concentration of land-based Indians in North America, including the entire "Sioux Complex" of reservations, the Shoshone and Arapaho peoples of Wind River, and the Crow and Northern Cheyenne nations along the Powder River. All told, more than 40 energy corporations are vying for position within this extremely rich "resource belt." As of August 1979, some 5,163 uranium claims—averaging twenty acres apiece—were held in the Black Hills National Forest alone.[73] As one observer put it at the time:

> Overall, the plans for industrializing the hills are staggering. They include a giant energy park featuring more than a score of 10,000 megawatt coal-fired plants, a dozen nuclear reactors, huge coal slurry pipelines designed to use millions of gallons of water to move crushed coal thousands of miles, and at least fourteen major uranium mines.[74]

The record of the only significant uranium mining and milling enterprise yet undertaken in the area, that begun in 1954 by the AEC at an abandoned army ordinance depot called Igloo—near the southern Hills town of Edgemont, South Dakota, about twenty miles west of the Pine Ridge Reservation—snaps the implications of this proposition into sharp focus. On June 11, 1962, an estimated 200 of the approximately 3.5 million tons of uranium tailings which resulted, most of it piled along the Cottonwood Creek in downtown Edgemont, gave way under heavy rains. Once in the creek, they washed downstream a few hundred yards to the Cheyenne River, the major source of surface water for the western half of Pine Ridge.[75] Meanwhile, other tailings piles were also leaching into the Madison Formation, the shallow aquifer which is the primary groundwater source for the reservation, and deeper, into the underlying Oglala Aquifer. By June 1980, the Indian Health Service announced that well water in the village of Slim Buttes, in the affected Red Shirt Table portion of the reservation, was testing at radiation levels three times the national safety standard; a new well tested at fourteen times the "safe" level.[76] The U.S. Department of Interior summed up the situation in a 1979 report:

> Contamination is well beyond the safe limit for animals. Escape by infiltration into the water table or by breakout to stream drainages could cause contamination by dangerous levels of radioactivity. Stock or humans using water from wells down gradient from tailing ponds would be exposed. Plants and animals encountering contaminated flows or contaminated sediments deposited in drainage channels would be exposed. Increasing the danger is the nondegradable and accumulative nature of this type of contamination.[77]

Tribal President Stanley Looking Elk then requested that $175,000 of a $200,000 federal allocation for reservation water management be devoted to obtaining uncontaminated water supplies for the inhabitants of Slim Buttes and surrounding areas. The request was approved, but in a manner entirely reminiscent of the United Nuclear posture at Church Rock, the BIA stipulated that it could be used *only for cattle.*[78] At the same time, studies indicated a Shiprock-like pattern in which stillbirths, infant deformities such as cleft palate, and cancer deaths had all increased markedly in the affected area since 1970.[79] Government spokespersons adamantly insisted, as they had when the Igloo operation was established, that there was "no public health hazard" in its uranium operations, which by then had been closed down.[80]

Officials were still saying this in 1982, when they also began to admit that the Igloo/Edgemont locale was so contaminated it would make an ideal spot for a national nuclear waste dump.[81] Their unsuccessful drive to win public endorsement of this idea—which they claimed involved only "minimal health risk"—included a "concession" to the sensibilities of the nearby Oglala Lakotas of Pine Ridge: during the period 1985-87, the government finally "fixed" the problem of surface water pollution.[82] By this, it is meant that federal contractors removed the mass of tailings from the banks of Cottonwood Creek, moved it a few miles *closer* to the reservation and dumped it on a barren plateau. There, it is now "secured" by a chain-link and barbed wire fence, posted with small metal signs emblazoned with nuclear symbols and bearing the caption, "Hazardous Wastes." As of this writing, the contaminants are still blowing freely in the wind.[83]

Such fences had, by this point, also made their appearance on Pine Ridge itself, demarcating a section of what was called the "Gunnery Range." A bleak 382,000 acre area located on the Red Shirt Table around Sheep Mountain and encompassing the northwestern eighth of the reservation, the land had been "borrowed" by the U.S. War Department in 1942 as a practice range for the training of aerial gunners. It was, by agreement, to be returned to the Oglalas at the conclusion of World War II, but never was. Instead, it was retained by the government in a vague "trust" status for the next quarter-century.[84] During the early 1970s, as part of a broader agenda to recover land in the region, the people of Pine Ridge ended the long limbo which had prevailed in the matter by mounting an effort to regain control over their property. (See "The Black Hills Are Not for Sale," in this volume.)

All things being equal, they might well have been successful. Unbeknownst to them, however, a secret experiment in satellite mapping undertaken jointly by the National Aeronautics and Space Administration (NASA) and the National Uranium Research and Evaluation Institute (NURE, a component of the U.S. Geological Survey) in 1970 had revealed a rich deposit of intermixed uranium and molybdenum underlying the Sheep Mountain locale.[85] Far from exhibiting a willingness to restore the land to the Oglalas, the government had therefore quietly made plans to effect a permanent transfer of the Gunnery Range to itself. When the Indians physically resisted this idea, bringing in the American Indian Movement to support them, an outright low-intensity war was launched by the government in 1973. Three years later, with at least 69 "insurgents" dead on Pine Ridge and another 340 having suffered serious physical assaults, federal authorities felt it was safe to proceed.[86]

On January 2, 1976, outgoing Tribal President Dick Wilson, who had actively collaborated in the counterinsurgency campaign conducted against his own ostensible constituents, signed an illegal agreement with the Interior Department wherein title to the disputed area was formally passed from the Oglalas to the National Park Service, which, in turn, added it to the existing Badlands National Monument.[87] Congress consummated the arrangement in 1977 by passing Public Law 90-468, an act stipulating that the Indians might recover surface use of the Gunnery Range at any time they expressed a desire to do so (by referendum), but that all mineral rights would forever belong to the United States.[88] By 1979, it was also noted that within this supposed addition to the "public domain":

> The Air Force retained an area [and fenced it off in much the same fashion as the DOE site outside Edgemont] near which residents have sighted large containers being flown by helicopter. These reports have raised strong suspicions that the Gunnery Range was being used as a dump for high-level military nuclear waste, which may be leaking radioactivity into the Aquifer. In the same area, the rate of stillborn or deformed calves has skyrocketed.[89]

Even as all this was going on, it was discovered that tailings at the Susquehanna-Western mill site—on the

Wind River Reservation, near Riverton, Wyoming—was causing serious ground water contamination on the west side of the Hills. Following the usual procedure, the corporation had simply walked away when it was finished with the facility in 1967.[90] "Because it was located on non-Indian land within reservation boundaries, the [Department of Energy] did not consider it an Indian site" and therefore ranked it as a high priority for cleanup.[91] The government's idea, vociferously rejected by Wind River's Arapahos and Shoshones, was to move the wastes a few miles, onto reservation land proper. Only when the State of Wyoming sided with the Indians in 1986, insisting that it wanted the material dumped nowhere within its borders, did DOE alter its position.[92] As in the Edgemont example, however, most of the tailings remain on or near their original location at present.[93]

In the end, all that appears so far to have averted uranium development in the Black Hills of the scope evident along the Grants Belt was the same set of factors which interrupted its continuation in the Four Corners. Declining U.S. energy consumption rates and reaction to the Three Mile Island nuclear plant accident of March 1979, in combination with the Atomic Energy Commission's having met the ore-buying quotas established for it in the 1950s (and revised upward during the early '70s) by 1981, brought about a precipitous decline in uranium prices.[94] A pound of yellowcake, which had once brought $43, garnered only $15 by '81.[95] By mid-1982, virtually all U.S. uranium production had been suspended in favor of importing cheaper material from abroad. The spectacular "boom" cycle in the U.S. domestic uranium market therefore entered a "bust" phase which has lasted a decade to date.

Other U.S. Locations

Although the Four Corners and Black Hills regions

were the scenes of by far the most intensive uranium development activities during the boom period, they were not alone. At the Spokane Reservation in Washington state, the BIA engineered a mining and milling lease on behalf of the Dawn Mining Company, partly owned by the much larger Newmont Mining Corporation, in 1964. The Bureau's post-operational land reclamation clause to the contract specifically exempted the company from responsibility for any environmental damage resulting from "ordinary wear and tear and unavoidable accidents in their normal use." Dawn was required to post only a $15,000 bond to insure cleanup whenever it completed its business on Spokane land. This occurred in 1981 and 1982, for the mining and milling operations respectively.[96] By then, the contours of disaster were already emerging.

> In 1977 BIA geologist Jim LeBret, a Spokane tribal member, discovered dangerous toxic wastes trickling from the mine at Blue Creek, a favorite camping and picnic spot for tribal members before uranium mining had begun. He was accompanied by his father and uncle, who had discovered uranium on the reservation and previously owned interests in Dawn Mining. They left in tears after seeing the canary-yellow trickle of waste water and the destruction it had caused.[97]

The BIA's only response was to order Dawn to build a dam, which contained the toxic wastes for several years, until after the company had pulled out.[98] This stop-gap was obviously inadequate to address the problem.

> Even more serious contamination occurred late after mining had stopped and the trickle had grown to a 75 to 400 gallons per minute stream of wastes. The Indian Health Service said in 1983 that the heavy metal and acid contamination was "appalling" and recommended the BIA "prevent livestock and humans from consuming the water in question by whatever means necessary" (emphasis in original). When the EPA tested the "seepage" [in 1984], the radiological chemist in Las Vegas said he had

> never seen such radioactive mine waste water before [Uranium 238 levels were *4,000 times* the area's natural level, 40 times the EPA's maximum "safe" limit].[99]

What Anaconda had threatened to do with regard to the Jackpile-Paguate mine, Dawn actually did at Spokane, filing suit against the Department of Interior in 1982 as a defense against being compelled to underwrite any part of restoring the Blue Creek environment, an effort estimated to require a minimum of $10 million. Despite Dawn's having gleaned up to $45 million in profits from the Spokane operation over the years, the company's president, Marcel DeGuire, pled poverty, claiming his firm's only assets were the abandoned mill and mine. He also asserted—but could not substantiate—that Dawn had already spent $4 million "restoring" the environment.[100]

> It was not until 1987 that the EPA [finally] forced the company to stop the discharge—six years after the mining stopped and ten years after the LeBrets noticed the discharge. By then it was too late for the reservation stream, Blue Creek, which previously had provided habitat for about thirteen thousand rainbow trout. In the spring of 1988 only five or six adults returned to spawn. [The] EPA admitted that if the mine had not been on Indian land, it would probably have come to someone's attention sooner.[101]

As of mid-1992, virtually nothing has been done to repair the damage to Blue Creek, and cleanup of the tailings piles surrounding Dawn's mill site have not even been scheduled for federal action.[102] A somewhat better result has been obtained with regard to the Western Nuclear Corporation's Sherwood mine and mill, also on the Spokane Reservation. Not built until 1978, neither facility had time to cause great environmental impact before being closed in 1982. In 1989, largely for public relations and tax reasons, the corporation transferred ownership of both facilities to the Spokane people, and provided $4.4 million in reclamation funds.[103] Cleanup at these sites is nearly complete.[104]

> Between 1944 and 1952, the University of California's Los Alamos Scientific Laboratory (LASL), now operated on contract by the [Department of Energy], dumped liquid and solid wastes from its bomb-manufacturing projects into three nearby canyons. Since 1952, solid and liquid radioactive wastes have been treated at one of two ion-exchange plants. Solid, radioactive waste is buried in 60-foot-deep, asphalt-lined shafts or in 55-gallon drums at several sites. Within the 56 acres encompassed by LASL's boundaries, there are about 300,000 tons of solid wastes, including 20 pounds of plutonium...About 25,000 gallons of liquid radioactive wastes are pumped daily into nearby canyons. The canyon streams feed into the Río Grande six miles southeast at Otowi Bridge on [land belonging to the San Ildefonso Pueblo]. A 1978 report assured the public that "no migration of radioactive contaminants away from disposal sites has been observed by the continuing monitoring program." But officials now admit the inaccuracy of the report...Sediments on San Ildefonso sacred lands have revealed plutonium levels ten times higher than concentration attributed to fallout, although LASL maintains that these concentrations are "well below...guides established to protect human health."[105]

In addition to plutonium, tritium—"a radioactive gas or water vapor that is virtually impossible to control because it combines readily with oxygen and can be incorporated into the organic molecules in the human body and in nature"—has been found in concentrations two to five times normal levels in area mule deer, ravens and other birds. Cesium-137 has been found in mule deer at levels up to 35 times the norm.[106] Public opposition to such contamination has been constrained by the fact that north-central New Mexico is part of one of the country's more chronically depressed areas and LASL provides some 8,650 jobs, more than $150 million in income to area residents (including Indians not only from San Ildefonso, but from the nearby San Juan and Santa Clara pueblos as well).[107] Although the San Ildefonso governing council has passed several resolutions of concern about pollution from LASL, it has, under the circumstances, often professed an abiding sense of helplessness to attempt anything more. "What can we do?" one council member has been quoted as asking. "We have no say up there."[108]

A similar, though more extravagant example is that of the Hanford nuclear weapons manufacturing facility, located in Washington state, about 30 miles upstream from the Yakima Reservation, and operated by the AEC on behalf of the military from 1944 until its closure in 1989. Officials at the plant consistently utilized a "Top Secret" classification covering their procedures—much about what was really done at Hanford is still classified, and may remain so for decades—as a shield behind which to pretend that "nothing adverse to the public welfare" was occurring. It was not until well after the fact, in mid-1990, that citizens began to learn that the government had "cut costs" by ignoring even the most rudimentary public safety precautions. By 1991, it was known that, since 1945, plant managers had ordered that more than 440 *billion* gallons of water heavily laced with everything from plutonium to ruthenium be poured into shafts drilled into the earth for "disposal" purposes.[109] In addition, anywhere from 700,000 to 900,000 gallons of extraordinarily contaminated fluids are known to have leaked from a 177-unit underground "tank farm" in which wastes were stored.[110] The local aquifer has long since been reached by these virulent contaminants, as has the nearby Columbia River.[111]

> Not only has the Hanford plant been discharging and leaking radiation into the river for forty-five years, but serious accidents have occurred at the reactors. One

> could perhaps excuse the accidental release of radiation, but on several occasions huge clouds of isotopes were created knowingly and willfully. In December [1952], about 7,800 curies of radioactive Iodine 131 were deliberately released in an experiment designed to detect military reactors in the Soviet Union (only 15 to 24 curies of Iodine 131 escaped at Three Mile Island in 1979).[112]

The true extent of environmental degradation around Hanford, while unknown—and steadfastly denied by "responsible officials"—is likely to be considerable and quite widespread.[113] One strong evidence of this came as early as 1962, with a Hanford worker who had eaten oysters caught hundreds of miles downstream at the mouth of the Columbia River. When he went to work the next day, he set off the radiation alarm at the Hanford plant.[114] More generally:

> Abnormally high incidence of thyroid tumors and cancers have been observed in populations living downwind from Hanford. Strontium 90, Cesium 137, and Plutonium 239 have been [atmospherically] released in large quantities, as was, between 1952 and 1967, Ruthenium 106. People in adjacent neighborhoods were kept uninformed about these releases—before, during and after—and none were warned that they were at risk for subsequent development of cancer. (Some experts have estimated that downwind farms and families received radiation doses ten times higher than those that reached Soviet people living near Chernobyl in 1986).[115]

Another indicator is to be found in the fact that, following the pattern it established at Edgemont, the government began in 1984 to pursue a vigorous initiative to site a major nuclear waste dump on or very close to Yakima land (alternatively, officials selected the Umatilla Reservation, also in Washington state, and the Nez Percé Reservation, in northern Idaho, as preferred waste dump locations).[116] The plan was narrowly averted in 1988, mainly because of a sustained inter-tribal/intercultural opposition organized and spearheaded by Yakima leader Russell Jim.[117] Under provision of the 1982 Nuclear Waste Policy Act, the Yakimas have also been able to secure $12.8 million in federal funding—the State of Washington has received another $11.2 million—to study the degree and effects of nuclear contamination already present in their environment.[118]

Northern Saskatchewan: Radioactive "Super-Waste"

Although Australian, Namibian and Canadian ores all contributed to undermining the viability of U.S. uranium production in the early 80s, those of Canada were probably most decisive.[119] This is mainly due to the existence of several deposits of uranium in the northern portion of the province of Saskatchewan, first mapped during the 1960s, which are unrivalled in their richness.

> Uranium ore normally contains only a few tenths of a percent uranium. In contrast, several large deposits in northern Saskatchewan contain ore grading in the tens of percent. Further, most of the rich deposits are close to the surface, which lowers the cost of getting the ore out of the ground. Many of these deposits are more than 100 times richer than the competing mines in the rest of the world. For example, the average grade of the Eliot Lake, Ontario uranium deposits is .1 percent, while the Cigar Lake deposit in Saskatchewan has an average grade of 15 percent...In 1979 when pockets of 45 percent ore were being mined at Cluff Lake, the owners bragged that in one day they took out over $9 million [Canadian] worth of uranium. It is so profitable to mine uranium in Saskatchewan that the province is known in industry circles as "the Saudi Arabia of the uranium industry."[120]

While the proportion of uranium to tailings material contained in these ores has made it possible to realize a markedly greater margin of profit in northern Saskatchewan production than elsewhere, even while noticeably undercutting the price of competitors, it also means that the waste by-products of mining and milling in the province are much "hotter" than anywhere else in the world. Specifically, since the residual radioactivity contained in tailings is directly proportionate to the percentage of uranium contained in the original ore, wastes in northern Saskatchewan are up to 100 times more potent than those found in, say, the Four Corners region of the U.S.[121] Put another way, only one one-hundredth the quantity of mining and milling would be necessary in northern Saskatchewan to produce the same qualitative impact on people and environment evident at Laguna or Navajo. In actuality, much more than this has already been done.

> The large volume of...solid radioactive wastes produced by a uranium mill is hard to comprehend. The 4 million [metric] tonnes of radioactive mill wastes produced by the Rabbit Lake mine alone is enough to cover almost knee deep a two-lane highway 800 kilometers long...In January 1987 production of solid uranium wastes reached at least 130 million [metric] tonnes—about 110 million in Ontario and 20 in Saskatchewan. This amount represents a volume easily capable of covering a two lane highway a metre deep all the way from Vancouver to Halifax, coast to coast.[122]

Analyst Brian Goldstick has produced the accompanying chart, indicating the anticipated quantity of tailings from each northern Saskatchewan mill through the end of the century. Further, the aggregate discharge of liquid wastes, which have a greater and more immediate environmental impact than solid wastes, have been approximately twice as large by volume. The Rabbit Lake mill alone pumped about 7.7 million liters of radioactive effluent into the habitat each day from 1975 until it closed down in 1985.[123] In addition to its radioactive toxicity, the waste water emitted by this and other mills contain high concentrations of lead, arsenic, zinc, manganese, cad-

Solid Radioactive Uranium Mill Wastes In Northern Saskatchewan – Present and Prospective

Mine	Quantity (metric tonnes)	Years Of Operation
Uranium City Area:		
Beaverlodge	6,000,000	1952-82
Gunnar	5,500,000	1955-64
Lorado	360,000	1957-60
Rabbit Lake	4,000,000	1975-85
Collin's Bay	1,930,000	1985-91
Cluff Lake		
Phase I	84,000	1981-84
Phase II	2,700,000	1984-95
Key Lake	4,500,000	1982-2000
Total	25,074,000	

Brian Goldstick, *Wollaston*

mium, and other deadly pollutants.[124] Small wonder that, as in the United States, the affected locales have come to be referred to as "sacrifice areas."[125]

Another parallel to the U.S. experience is that creation of the situation has been marked by extensive governmental/corporate collusion. In fact, both the federal government in Ottawa and the provincial government of Saskatchewan established their own profit-making firms in order to benefit from the anticipated uranium bonanza; Ottawa dubbed its corporation Eldorado Nuclear Ltd., while the provincial administration selected Saskatchewan Mining Development Corporation. Similar to the

U.S. scenario, the Canadian government created a mechanism through which to coopt or confuse the resistance of the indigenous people on whose land the mining would be done. This assumed the form of what is called the "Saskatchewan Indian Nations Corporation" (SINCO), which insures that "native preference" will be exercised when hiring is done for such menial occupations as driving trucks and guarding mining and milling facilities.[126]

Throughout the 1970s, the provincial government busily utilized tax revenues to create an infrastructure necessary only to the uranium industry, including thousands of kilometers of roadways connecting projected mining sites in the north to the planned distribution center in Saskatoon, located far to the south.[127] The private beneficiaries of this massive expenditure of public funds were, of course, always intended to be such private concerns as the U.S.-owned Gulf Minerals Corporation, and the Japanese utility, Kyushu Ltd., to which Saskatchewan Mining and Eldorado Nuclear jointly pledged delivery of 12.7 million kilograms of low-cost uranium concentrate over a thirteen-year period beginning in 1987.[128] The "constellation of transnational resource corporations now active in northern Saskatchewan include French, German, American and Japanese interests."[129]

Development

In truth, governmental mining and milling of good-to-high grade uranium has been going on in northern Saskatchewan at a relatively moderate pace since 1952, beginning with the first of what were eventually to be 25 open pit and underground mines around an ersatz town called "Uranium City." Before the greater profitability of higher-grade mines elsewhere caused it to be phased out in 1982, Eldorado Nuclear had spent fully 30 years "keeping overhead down" at the Uranium City complex by dumping both liquid and solid wastes directly into Lake

Athabasca, from whence considerable contamination continues to flow down the Slave River to the Mackenzie, and then into the Arctic Ocean.[130] The "town" itself existed solely to serve the uranium industry. Before the mines, no one lived there; after the mines, the population sank from its high of more than 4,000 in 1979 to fewer than 200 in 1983. A good thing, too, because, as at Anaconda/Laguna, it was found that the corporation had again cut costs, this time by building everything from the street to the hospital using uranium tailings. In 1977, for instance, it was discovered that classrooms in the local CANDU High School—governmentally-named to commemorate Canada's first on-line nuclear reactor—showed radon levels 60 times higher than the allowable limit; the school was nonetheless used for another five years.[131]

By the mid-70s, what became a government-sponsored boom was beginning to materialize. In 1975, Eldorado opened the Rabbit Lake Mine, in the northeastern portion of Saskatchewan, digging into an ore deposit ranging from .3 to 3 percent in purity. An open pit about 550 yards wide and 150 deep was created before the most profitable ore played out and the mine was closed in 1984. Eldorado, in collaboration with the Gulf Minerals Corporation, had built the largest uranium mill in northern Canada—producing some $100 million (Canadian) per year in yellowcake—to service its Rabbit Lake endeavor, but it was not closed when the mine shut down.[132] Instead, beginning in 1982, the mill was expanded to accommodate the even greater volume of ore—of much higher grade—expected from a new mine the corporation was opening at nearby Collin's Bay, on Wollaston Lake.[133]

> The Collin's Bay open pit mine is especially dangerous because the uranium is actually under the bottom of Wollaston Lake. In order to get at the uranium, part of the lake was diked off and drained in 1984. Mining below the bottom of the lake began in the spring of 1985. The

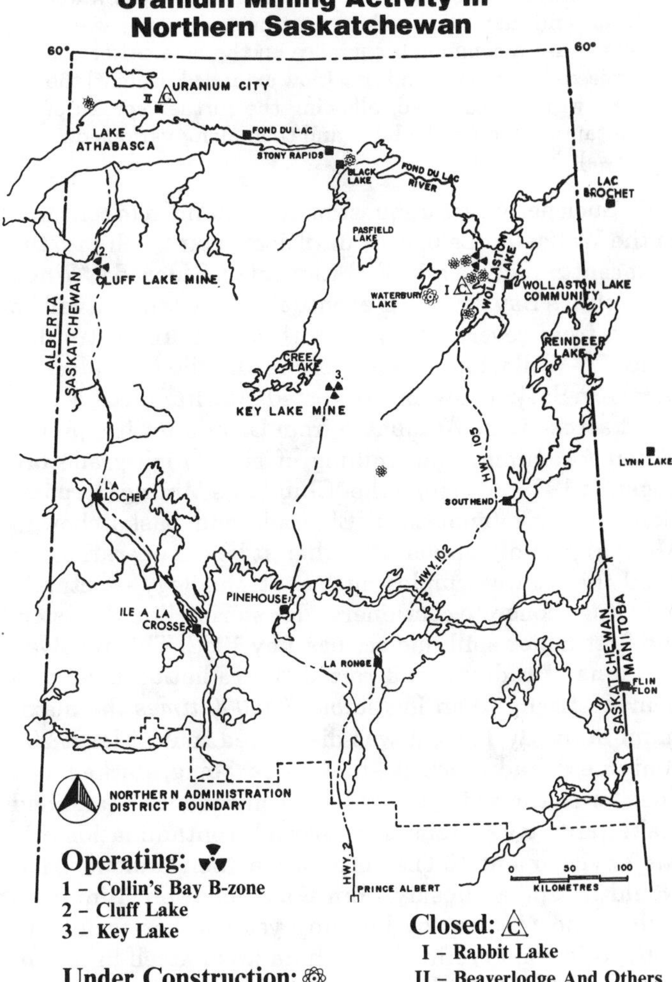

Brian Goldstick, *Wollaston.*

> pit is separated from the rest of the lake by a thin dike of steel that extends only about one metre above the water level, and may not be able to withstand strong waves which are a common occurrence on the lake. After the projected six years of mining [now extended to eight] the dike will be destroyed, allowing the further spread of contamination [in the lake, and then along various outflows].[134]

Such activity is unquestionably intended to continue in the Wollaston Lake area until some point well into the next century, given a 1985 statement by Eldorado: "When the Collin's Bay deposit is eventually depleted, ore will be mined from several deposits within a 12 kilometre distance."[135] Wollaston is, however, hardly the only place in northern Saskatchewan so afflicted. At Cluff Lake, southward across Lake Athabasca from Uranium City, preparation for mining and milling of super-high-grade ore began in 1978. Although the "Cluff Lake Mining Corporation" (and combination of Eldorado and Saskatchewan Mining) proudly announced when it began operations in 1980 that it was employing "new technology"—actually only huge concrete containers—for storing liquid wastes, the first major spill had occurred by 1982. This involved two tons of radium, and raised the radiation level of a nearby stream to an incredible *600,000 times* the maximum limit. By 1986, it was discovered that at least 200 containers had cracked—they were being stacked two deep for reasons of "economy and convenience"—and had leaked another 2.5 tons of comparable contamination into the environment.[136] The corporation then announced it would accept a subsidy from Saskatchewan Mining to "solve" the problem by building yet another facility in 1987, this one to refine the radium waste itself in collaboration with a French consortium, AMOK.[137]

The Key Lake Mine, opened in 1983 by an international consortium including Saskatchewan Mining, Eldorado Nuclear, and Uranez (a German firm) calling itself the "Key Lake Mining Corporation," in central Saskatchewan is the most southerly of all such operations in the province. It is now the largest open pit in the world. The mine is estimated to contain more than 84 million kilograms of uranium in an average ore grade of 2.5 percent; the corresponding mill capacity of 5.5 million kilos per year makes up about 12 percent of "free world" yellowcake output.[138]

> Much to the embarrassment of [Key Lake Mining], within the first three months of operation at least 12 major spills of radioactive wastes occurred. The largest was in January, 1984 when over 100 million litres of radioactive liquid with radiation levels 20 times the regulation level spilled over the retaining walls of a holding pond.[139]

In many ways, all of this was simply a prelude to what will undoubtedly be the most dangerous operation of all, the mining of an ore pocket at Cigar Lake, discovered in 1981 but kept secret from the Canadian public until 1984, after "business details" had been worked out among governments and corporations in several countries.

> The most significant uranium deposit ever discovered is at Cigar Lake adjacent to Waterbury Lake. It is located 115 kilometres northeast of the Key Lake mine and 55 kilometres west-southwest of the Rabbit Lake mine. The Cigar Lake ore body is the world's largest [super]-high-grade deposit. It contains over 100 million kilos of uranium at an average grade of 15 percent, with pockets as high as 60 percent. This is twice as big and six times as rich as the Key Lake "monster deposit." In addition, potential reserves at Cigar Lake are estimated to contain a further 50 million kilos at a grade of 4.7 percent.[140]

The international consortium quietly assembled to comprise the "Cigar Lake Mining Corporation" include not only Saskatchewan Mining and Eldorado Nuclear, but Cogema Canada Ltd. (a Montreal-based subsidiary of the

French Commissariat de l'Energie Atomique), Idemitsu Uranium Exploration Corporation, Ltd. (a Japanese firm based in Calgary), and the Corona Grande Corporation. Mining start-up at Cigar Lake has been delayed for several years because of certain "technical difficulties." Although the huge deposit is well concentrated in a 2,000 by 100 meter area, it is located more than 400 meters below ground, a factor which virtually necessitates shaft mining. Given the richness of the ore and the depth of the shafts required, it is considered impossible, or at least cost-prohibitive, to ventilate the mine sufficiently to create anything resembling "safe" conditions for miners. Hence, to date, at least $50 million (Canadian) has been spent to develop appropriate robotics to extract the ore. As is standard practice, the government has not bothered to conduct public hearings on the matter of what will happen to resulting "super-waste" once mining operations begin sometime in 1993 or early 1994.[141]

Impacts

There are some 30,000 people resident to the mining region of northern Saskatchewan, more than 20,000 of them native Dene (Chipewyan) and Métis. As in the U.S., these indigenous people are among the very poorest in North America. Also like their U.S. counterparts in the uranium mining zones, the province's northern "Treaty Indians are hospitalized 61 percent more often than the average Saskatchewan resident. Since 1975, hospitalization for cancer, birth defects and circulatory illnesses have increased dramatically (between 123 and 600 percent in the northern population aged 15 to 64—the entire labor force). At the same time, there is a large increase in hospitalizations among young children for digestive disorders and birth anomalies."[142]

Unlike their southern cousins, however, the native people of Saskatchewan have never been concentrated on reservations. To the contrary, they are scattered across the entire northerly expanse of the province in 35 towns and villages, availing themselves of hunting, fishing and trapping rights over broad areas. Concomitantly, they subsist to a much higher degree on traditional diet, taken from the land, than do Indians in the lower 48 U.S. states.[143] That they are suffering much the same signs of generalized health deterioration as U.S. Indians forced to live in constant close proximity to uranium production sites is indicative of the extent to which the entire northern Saskatchewan ecology has already been contaminated by the uranium industry.

The environment downstream from Eldorado Nuclear's Beaverlodge mine and mill at Uranium City, for example, has been extensively studies over the past twenty years. As early as 1977, a survey found that about a quarter of the lake chub in waters contaminated by tailings run-off suffered eye mutations, including pupil deformities and lens cataracts:

> There was no evidence of infection or parasitic encystment within the eye. Cataracts may result from genetic makeup, nutritional deficiency, environmental effects, or a combination of the three. Certain factors such as high radiation, parasitic infection, or the presence of specific chemicals can contribute to cataract formation.[144]

The incidence of such deformities among suckers and other fish which feed along the bottom, where radioactive sediments quickly settle, was even higher. While native people in the area do not usually consume bottom-feeders, they do consume lake whitefish and other species which eat them, and which thereby acquire an appreciable portion of the bottom-feeders' contamination. Fish collected from lakes downstream from the Beaverlodge facility in a 1979 study demonstrated as much as 100 times more radioactivity in their tissue as fish collected from uncontaminated lakes.[145] Another study, conducted downstream from the Dubyna Mine at Uranium City, revealed northern pike with radiation counts averaging 6,500 times normal in the flesh, up to 11,000 times normal in the bone; lake trout were also found to have much greater than normal concentrations of uranium, thorium and Lead-210, while northern pike showed the greatest concentration of radium.[146]

In the area known as "Effluent Creek" downstream from the Rabbit Lake complex, which runs into Wollaston Lake's Hidden Bay, a 1978 study found ammonia concentrations so extreme that there was "a complete absence of benthic invertebrates in bottom samples along the entire length of the creek...[and] there was at least localized impact in Hidden Bay in the vicinity of the Effluent Creek mouth."[147] In proximate areas of the lake itself:

> In terms of impact on fish, the study documents that toxicity tests of the Rabbit Lake waste discharge "on several occasions found the tailings effluent acutely lethal to rainbow trout." Laboratory tests from March 1977 to January 1979 putting rainbow trout in precipitation pond effluent, found that all fish died in 96 hours, even when the effluent concentration was only 10 percent. In July 1978 tests were conducted putting sucker fry collected from Collin's Bay into plastic containers submerged for 56 hours in Effluent Creek, the inlet to Horseshoe Lake, and precipitation pond effluent. The water was found to be acutely lethal in all but the Effluent Creek sample.[148]

Downstream from the Dubyna mine, three aquatic plants—water lily, milfoil and sedge—were studied. Water lily consistently revealed concentrations of radium 11,000 times greater than normal; milfoil showed an average 14,000 times the normal level of uranium; sedge collected 13,000 times the normal level of Lead-210.[149]

> Vegetation...has also been analyzed. In 1983 a researcher from the Department of Biology at the Univer-

sity of Saskatchewan determined quantities of [Lead-210 and Polonium-210] in vegetation at two sites in the Rabbit Lake area, Collin's Creek and Hidden Bay, and for comparison purposes, two sites near the Churchill River, Birch Hill and Otter Rapids. The Rabbit Lake sites showed significantly greater accumulation in four of the ten species analyzed: blueberry, labrador tea, green alder,and black spruce. Collin's Creek was found to be a "hot spot" for all species except dry-land cranberry. A different study in another area looking at uranium levels in trees found the greatest amount in the growing tips of twigs, followed by the bark, leaves and wood.[150]

The study, conducted by Dr. Stella M. Swanson, concluded that radionuclides are collected by plant-life in the following descending order: lichen, moss, shrubs and trees. Lichens and moss accumulate radioactivity at a rate five to ten times greater than shrubs and trees, respectively. Moss and lichens absorb contamination from the atmosphere while "higher" plant-forms tend to take it in through the roots, making their contamination a somewhat more localized phenomenon than with "lower" forms.[151]

Humans, of course, directly consume some of these plants and thereby ingest contaminants. Blueberry, for instance, is the greatest radionuclide collector among shrubs, and is an integral part of the northern native diet at certain times of the year. Moreover, vegetation composes the *whole* diet of virtually every bird and mammal which, along with fish, comprise more than two-thirds of the traditional Indian larder in the upper reaches of Saskatchewan. Caribou, to name one example, subsist primarily on moss and lichens. Moose and deer consider the young tips of shrubs and trees to be a high delicacy. Water fowl consume shoots from each of the three plants studied.[152]

In the Canadian context, only a few studies examine accumulation of radioactivity by mammals. This area

> warrants more attention as there have been two reports of a cow moose carrying a two-headed fetus being shot near Wollaston Lake. Further Wollaston residents have often shot moose from the Rabbit Creek area, and people have seen moose drinking from the tailings ponds.[153]

Even fewer investigations have been conducted with regard to contamination of the indigenous people affected. Probably the closest was a study conducted from 1965 to 1969 with regard to the effects of mining and milling much lower grade ore in Ontario upon 25 relatively proximate Inuit communities in the Northwest Territories. The results showed levels of soft tissue and bone irradiation as much as 100 times normal, at times exceeding even the maximum limits established by the notoriously lax International Commission on Radiation Protection.[154] A comparable study of the Sami population of northern Finland revealed average concentrations of Polonium-210 in the blood at eight times the normal level.[155]

To date, neither the government of Canada nor of Saskatchewan has offered any sort of realistic plan to dispose of the rapidly proliferating wastes they are generating, nor have the array of transnational corporations which are involved. Rather, they have combined to offer what are, at best, utterly cosmetic "remedies" such as "revegetating" tailings piles. While prettying up thousands of acres of lethal waste—turning it all into "nice moose pastures," as one Eldorado official has put it—cannot be said to accomplish anything at all to combat the pollution, it might possibly make the effects even *worse*:[156]

> It is important to realize that plant growth on top of a tailings area does not mean the spread of contamination is stopped. Limited plant growth has been achieved with massive fertilizer application and natural plants have regrown along the edges. But plant growth can actually increase the quantity of radon gas escaping from wastes. This is because radium travels up through the roots and is distributed in the leaves. Thus the surface area avail-

able for radon release is greatly increased...In addition, root penetration allows water to seep through [any] protective soil cover and into tailings, allowing ground water to be polluted. As well, the plants themselves become contaminated through uptake of toxic materials, which pose a danger to animals eating them.[157]

None of this can be new or especially mysterious information to the governments and corporations pursuing such "rehabilitation" schemes. The Los Alamos Scientific Laboratory reached precisely the same conclusions concerning the "disutility" of revegetation nearly fifteen years ago, in the 1978 study in which it contended that human populations should be forbidden in uranium mining and milling zones.[158] Overall, then, "paranoid" assessments by Indians and allied non-Indian "radicals" that northern Saskatchewan is being quietly but steadily written off as a gigantic National Sacrifice Area takes on considerable substance.[159] And, as with similar plans in the United States, the people of the land necessarily will be sacrificed along with the land itself.

Back in the U.S.A.

During the 1970s, it was a standard slogan among environmental activists, a truth apparently now forgotten, that "radioactive contamination is forever." Today, it has become something of a commonplace among North American progressives, including important sectors of the environmental movement, to consider nuclear issues "passé," as if they had—or could have—gone away. Some, like Barry Commoner, have gone so far as to adopt a smug and self-congratulatory tone, pointing to an imagined "collapse of the nuclear industry" as evidence of a "grassroots victory over big business and big government."

In one major area of production—nuclear power—public intervention has already had a powerful effect: in the

> United States it has brought the industry to an ignominious halt. The nuclear power industry is paralyzed because intense public opposition has made the industry pay its environmental bill, most dramatically by forcing the abandonment of the $5.3 billion plant at Shoreham, Long Island.[160]

While much of the "credit" for temporarily consolidating public sentiment against the nuclear industry must go to the spectacular nature of the 1986 Chernobyl disaster rather than to organizing, it *is* true that the anti-nuke movement posted some impressive tactical wins.[161] Popular opposition *did* have much to do with what happened at Shoreham, as well as the cancelling of reactor construction at other locations such as Seabrook, New Hampshire, and Point Conception and Diablo Canyon in California, well before Chernobyl.[162] Similarly, well-focused activism played a significant role in bringing about the closure of existing reactors like that at Fort St. Vrain, Colorado, and several military-use facilities.[163]

> As of [May 1992], reactors at Hanford, WA, and at Savannah River, SC, are out of commission (the K-Reactor at Savannah River was restarted in December 1991, but shut down within days because it leaked radioactive tritium into streams); the uranium production plant at Fernald, OH, is closed permanently; uranium enrichment facilities at Portsmouth, OH, and Paducah, KY, are halted temporarily; and [plutonium] production at Rocky Flats [Colorado] has ended.[164]

Hopeful as these achievements are, however, what is occurring in northern Saskatchewan should be enough to disabuse *anyone* of the notion that the nuclear industry is somehow "dead." Even Commoner admits that, in 1982, there were only 72 operational nuclear reactors in the United States, whereas there are now 110.[165] These figures undoubtedly represent a slowing in the pace of reactor construction—95 facilities were under construction in the

U.S. in 1980, only a dozen today—but hardly a "stoppage."[166] Careful observers will also have noticed a marked upsurge in the propaganda (a.k.a. "advertising") of the U.S. nuclear industry's "Big Four"—the Westinghouse, Babcock & Wilcox, Bechtel, and Combustion Engineering corporations—and their subsidiaries, reintroducing the alleged benefits of the "peaceful atom" over the past two years.[167] Perhaps even more to the point, the energy policy announced by George Bush in 1991 is about as diametrically opposed to Commoner's pleasant script as it is possible to be: the president's plan calls for the building of *several hundred more* reactors within the next twenty years, at a cost of between $390 billion and $1.3 *trillion.*[168]

Other signs of an impending resurgence in the U.S. nuclear industry also exist. Anaconda, for example, has indicated an interest in reopening its Jackpile-Paguate Mine at Laguna by 1995.[169] Marjane Ambler, a leading apologist for this sort of activity on Indian land, has predicted that mining and milling will not only resume at Navajo, Spokane and Wind River, but on the Ute Mountain Reservation in Colorado; the Cañoncito Reservation and Zuni, Acoma, Zia, and Jemez pueblos in New Mexico, and the Hualapai Reservation in Arizona.[170] Unmentioned in her scenario are significant uranium deposits under the Crow and Northern Cheyenne Reservations in Montana, and the Gunnery Range deposit at Pine Ridge.[171] Such wholesale development would, of course, dwarf the degree of radioactive colonization evident in Indian Country between 1950 and 1980.

The mechanism through which this can be accomplished is also present in a much more coherent form than was the case fifteen years ago. Beginning in 1977, at the very height of the last U.S. uranium boom, the Federal Energy Administration provided $250,000 in "seed money"—an amount increased to $24 million annually in 1979 by the DOE—to create an entity capable of both coordinating and creating a more plausible façade of "Indian consent" to such exploitation.[172] Dubbed the "Council of Energy Resource Tribes" (CERT), the new organization was composed of the chairs of the federally-created tribal councils on what were already known to be the 25 most mineral-rich reservations in the country (the number of "participating tribes" has now grown to 43).[173] The first task assigned CERT was to assemble a comprehensive inventory of energy assets in U.S. Indian Country as a whole, dubbed the "Sears and Roebuck catalog of reservation resources" by critics.[174] Its second task was to assist in conceiving and implementing a plan by which more efficient corporate penetration might be accomplished.[175] This last placed CERT—over strong objections by a majority of those whose interests it supposedly represented—in a position of serving as central broker and liaison in virtually all Indian Energy resource transactions, a matter which quickly attracted millions in ongoing corporate funding.[176]

Although the uranium bust of the 1980s affected CERT as it did sponsoring companies, the organization simply devoted more attention to fossil fuel extraction, and to smoothing the way for the placement of nuclear waste dumps on Indian land, such as that scheduled for location at the Mescalero Apache Reservation in New Mexico sometime in 1993.[177] It has also moved itself into a position to reconcile environmental conflicts in Indian Country more generally:

> By 1984 the number of tribal requests for CERT's environmental technical assistance had mushroomed...In that year the EPA awarded CERT $125,000 to study wastes on 25 pilot reservations. Later, the EPA provided $90,000 to establish an environmental information base and provided other, relatively small contracts for regional meetings...To increase tribal support the CERT board created the CERT Technical Services Corporation, which was designed to market [such] technical assistance.[178]

In sum, CERT is now *ideally* situated to facilitate a full-scale resumption of uranium mining and milling in Indian Country. Further, it is well-placed to bring about construction of many, perhaps all, of the reactors called for in the 1991 Bush plan in the same locale. Not only would such a strategy represent a genuine consummation of the National Sacrifice Area concept of the 1970s—with all the implied advantages of subsequent unrestricted use of sacrificed areas this entails—it would carry the added attraction of going virtually unnoticed by the general public until well after the fact. When questioned on the matter, governmental and corporate spokespersons could simply deny that the facilities themselves were being constructed. After all, they had no particular difficulty in masking the reality of what was going on in Indian Country the first time around, at least until the process was almost completed.

Even in a non-Indian setting like Cincinnati, the DOE, in collaboration with the Department of Defense, was able to pass off its Fernald, Ohio uranium mill as a "pet food factory" for 37 years, during which time it quietly dumped at least 167,000 pounds of radionuclides into the Great Miami River, another 298,000 pounds into the atmosphere, and still another 12.7 million pounds into leaking earthen pits.179 The same combination of players was able to hide the release of more than two million pounds of radioactive mercury from its Oak Ridge, Kentucky plant until 1988.180 Until the same year, they were able to deny that the Rockwell International's operation of the Rocky Flats weapons facility—just west of Denver, Colorado—had resulted in extensive plutonium contamination of both water and landscape in a broad arc extending from Broomfield in the north to Golden in the south.181 How much more easily and effectively might the government, business, and a "cooperating agency" like CERT be able to disguise what was underway in the "Great American Outback" where only a relative handful of Indians reside?

The Tools for Fighting Back: Choosing Between an Indigenous Agenda and "Electric Facism"

There is a long-standing crucial defect in the U.S. anti-nuclear movement—and the broader environmental movement of which it was/is mostly a part. From the Clamshell and Abalone Alliances of the 1970s to the Freeze Movement of the 1980s, non-Indian activists have focused all but exclusively on the very final stages of the nuclear cycle.[182] In other words, they have inevitably concentrated on the reactors and weapons composed of by-products eventually refined from the yellowcake uranium mined and milled at the front end of the cycle, on Indian land. Hence, their victories, however satisfying in an immediate sense, have always been tactical, never strategic. Put another way, whenever they've been successful in closing or preventing a reactor in one place, their opponents have simply built another (or two) somewhere else; whenever they've caused weaponry to be removed from one location, it's merely been shifted to another.[183]

If the specter of rampant nuclearism is ever to be truly abolished, such approaches must be changed, and drastically so. The key to a strategic vision for anti-nuclear activism is and has always been in finding ways to sever nuclear weapons and reactors from their roots. This means, first and foremost, that non-Indians cast off the blinders which have led them to the sort of narrow "not in my back yard" sensibility voiced by Barry Commoner and his erstwhile vice presidential running mate, LaDonna Harris (a Comanche and founding member of CERT).[184] Rather than endlessly combatting the end-products of the nuclear industry, the movement as a whole must shift its emphasis to preventing uranium from being taken out of the ground in the first place. This, in turn, means focusing everyone's primary energy and attention, not on places like Seabrook and Diablo Canyon, inhabited though they may be by "important" population sectors (i.e., Euroamericans), but upon places peopled by "mere Indians": Key Lake and Cigar Lake in Canada, for example, or Navajo, Laguna, and a number of other reservations in the United States.[185]

Ultimately, stopping the processes of uranium extraction in Indian Country, and consequent nuclear proliferation elsewhere, will be impossible so long as the structure of colonial domination on the reservations is maintained. This means that coordinative and brokering organizations like CERT, and the prevailing system of "tribal governance," must be opposed right along with the non-Indian governments and corporations which invented and sustain them. A first priority—probably the first priority—for the anti-nuclear movement, the broader environmental movement, and for North American progressivism in general, *must* be the decolonization of Native North America. To accomplish this, indigenous liberation groups like the American Indian Movement must be accorded a central role in setting the agenda for and defining the priorities of radical social change on this continent.[186]

In the alternative (if it may be called that), there is at best only the prospect of what the French commentator André Gorz, in examining his own country's nuclear industry, once termed "electric fascism."[187] More likely, in North America, the radioactive colonization of Indian Country will go on and on, until—like some proverbial miner's canary sent first into shafts to detect with their lungs the presence of lethal gas—Indians die of the contaminants to which their "betters" have forcibly subjected them.[188] Unlike the canary, however, Indians by their deaths provide no early warning of the fate about to befall those who sacrifice them in this fashion. This is true because, unlike miners who rely upon canaries, those who sacrifice Indians have no place to turn for safe haven once their victims have died.

The ecological effects of radioactive colonization know no boundaries. Radon gas and windblown radioactive particulates do not know they are intended to stop when they reach non-Indian territory. Contaminated water does not know it is supposed to pool itself only under Indian wells. Irradiated flora and fauna are unaware they are meant only for consumption by indigenous "expendables." The effects of such contaminants are just as fatal to non-Indians as they are to Indians; the longevity of radionuclides is still just as "forever" now as it was twenty years ago; nothing has really changed in these respects since John Gofman and Arthur Tamplin first published *Poisoned Power* in 1971.[189] Neither genocide nor ecocide can be "contained" when accomplished by nuclear means. The radioactive colonization of Native North America therefore threatens not only Indians, but the survival of the human species itself.

The tools for fighting back against any threat begin, it is said, with a precise understanding of the danger and, from there, the best means by which to counter it. In this instance, the situation is simple enough: we are all—Indian and non-Indian alike—finally in the same boat. At last there is no more room for non-Indians to maneuver, to evade, to find more "significant" issues with which to preoccupy themselves. Either the saving of indigenous lives becomes a matter of preeminent concern, or *no* lives will be saved. Either Native North America will be liberated, or liberation will be foreclosed for *everyone*, once and for all. The fight will either be waged on Indian land, for Indian lives, or it will be lost before it really begins. We must take our stand, together. And we are *all* running out of time in which to finally come to grips with this fact.

Notes

1. U.S. Department of Interior, *Indian Lands Map: Oil, Gas, and Minerals on Indian Reservations* (Washington, DC:

U.S. Government Printing Office, 1978).

2. See Robert Page, *Northern Development: The Canadian Dilemma* (Toronto: McClelland and Stewart Publishers, 1986).
3. On the size of U.S. Indian population, see Lenore A. Stiffarm and Phil Lane, Jr., "The Demography of Native North America: A Question of American Indian Survival," in M. Annette Jaimes, ed., *The State of Native America: Genocide, Colonization, and Resistance* (Boston: South End Press, 1992, pp. 23-53). On the numbers in Canada, see Olive Patricia Dickenson, *Canada's First Nations: A History of Founding Peoples from Earliest Times* (Norman: University of Oklahoma Press, 1992, p. 418).
4. U.S. Bureau of the Census, Population Division, Racial Statistics Branch, *A Statistical Portrait of the American Indian Population* (Washington, DC: U.S. Government Printing Office, 1984); U.S. Department of Health and Human Services, *Chart Series Book* (Washington, DC: Public Health Service HE20.9409.988, 1988).
5. This refers to the so-called Indian Reorganization Act (48 Stat. 948), passed in 1934 and implemented throughout the remainder of the decade. For further information, see Vine Deloria, Jr., and Clifford M. Lytle, *The Nations Within: The Past and Future of American Indian Sovereignty* (New York: Pantheon Press, 1984). Also see Richard Nafziger, "Transnational Energy Corporations and American Indian Development," in Roxanne Dunbar Ortiz, ed., *American Indian Energy Resources and Development* (Albuquerque: University of New Mexico Institute for Native American Development, 1980, pp. 9-38).
6. Joseph G. Jorgenson, "The Political Economy of the Native American Energy Business," in Joseph G. Jorgenson, ed., *Native Americans and Energy Development, II* (Boston: Anthropology Resource Center/Seventh Generation Fund, 1984, pp. 9-20). It is noteworthy that Congress supposedly "fixed" the problem legislatively during the early 1980s, but without actually changing anything; see "Congress Approves Royalty Management Bill without Royalty Increase," *Federal Lands*, December 27, 1982.
7. Lorraine Turner Ruffing, "The Role of Federal Policy in American Indian Mineral Development," in Dunbar Ortiz,

op. cit. Also see Klara B. Kelly, "Federal Indian Land Policy and Economic Development in the United States," in Roxanne Dunbar Ortiz and Larry Emerson, eds., *Economic Development in American Indian Reservations* (Albuquerque: University of Mexico Institute for Native American Development, 1979, pp. 129-35).

8. Kenneth Coates and Judith Powell, *The Modern North: People, Politics, and the Rejection of Colonialism* (Toronto: James Lorimer Publishers, 1989).
9. The underlying ideas are articulated quite well in Michael Garrity, "The U.S. Colonial Empire is as Close as the Nearest Reservation," in Holly Sklar, ed., *Trilateralism: Elite Planning for World Management* (Boston: South End Press, 1980, pp. 238-68).
10. For the original application of this concept to the Native North American context, see Robert K. Thomas, "Colonialism: Classic and Internal," *New University Thought,* Vol. 4, No. 4, Winter 1966-67. Interestingly, the basic premise at issue here has been officially admitted by the U.S. government; see U.S. Commission on Civil Rights, *The Navajo Nation: An American Colony* (Washington, DC: U.S. Government Printing Office, 1975). On Canada, see Menno Boldt, "Social Correlates of Nationalism: A Study of Native Indian Leaders in a Canadian Internal Colony," *Comparative Political Studies,* Vol. 14, No. 2, Summer 1981, pp. 205-31.
11. This is true despite the racist and utterly misleading emphasis placed by some analysts on the handful of mines and mills north of the Navajo Reservation, on the Colorado Plateau. A prime example is Raye C. Ringholz's *Uranium Frenzy: Boom and Bust on the Colorado Plateau* (Albuquerque: University of New Mexico Press, 1989), which manages to miss the matter of uranium mining in Indian Country altogether. For a much more accurate view, see Richard Hoppe, "A Stretch of Desert along Route 66—The Grants Belt—Is Chief Locale for U.S. Uranium," *Engineering and Mining Journal,* Vol. 79, No. 11 (1978), pp. 79-93. Also see Winona LaDuke, "A History of Uranium Mining," *Black Hills/Paha Sapa Report,* Vol. 1, No. 1, 1979.
12. In addition to the Navajos employed as underground miners by Kerr-McGee during this period, somewhere

between 300 and 500 were involved in "independent" Small Business Administration-supported operations mining shallow (50 feet or less) deposits of uranium ore. The proceeds were sold in small lots to the Atomic Energy Commission's ore-buying station, located at the Kerr-McGee milling plant near Shiprock. These miners left behind between one and two hundred open shafts, all emitting radon gas into the atmosphere. See Harold Tso and Lora Mangum Shields, "Navajo Mining Operations: Early Hazards and Recent Interventions," *New Mexico Journal of Science,* Vol. 12, No. 1, Spring 1980.

13. J.B. Sorenson, *Radiation Issues: Government Decision Making and Uranium Expansion in Northern New Mexico* (Albuquerque: San Juan Regional Uranium Study Working Paper 14, 1978, p. 2).
14. *Ibid.* Also see Jessica S. Pearson, *A Sociological Analysis of the Reduction of Hazardous Radiation in Uranium Mines* (Washington, DC: National Institute for Occupational Safety and Health, National Health Service, 1975).
15. At that point, it is estimated that the corporation had extracted well over 2.5 million tons of uranium ore. See Phil Reno, *Navajo Resources and Economic Development* (Albuquerque: University of New Mexico Press, 1981, p. 138).
16. Author's measurement. As Tso and Shields note in their article ("Navajo Mining Operations," *op. cit.*): "This tailings pile is also within one mile of a day care center, the public schools...the Shiprock business district and cultivated farm lands."
17. This was standard Bureau practice. See Justas Bavarskis, "Uranium: The West Mines, Mills and Worships Radioactive Fuel," *High Country News,* March 10, 1978. He is relying in part on U.S. Environmental Protection Agency, *Radiological Quality of the Environment in the United States, 1977* (Washington, DC: U.S. Government Printing Office, 1977, pp. 58-67). Also see Tom Barry, "The BIA and Mineral Leases," *Navajo Times,* November 2, 1978.
18. Richard O. Clemmer, "The Energy Economy and Pueblo Peoples," in *Native Americans and Energy Development, II, op. cit.,* pp. 101-2.
19. M.J. Samet, *et al.,* "Uranium Mining and Lung Cancer

Among Navajo Men," *New England Journal of Medicine,* No. 310, 1984, pp. 1481-4. Also see Anthony S. Schwagin and Thomas Hollbacher, "Lung Cancer Among Uranium Miners," in *The Nuclear Fuel Cycle* (Cambridge, MA: Union of Concerned Scientists, 1973).

20.Richard Nafziger, "Uranium Profits and Perils," in *Red Paper* (Albuquerque: Americans for Indian Opportunity, 1976). Also see Christopher McCleod, "Uranium Mines and Mills May Have Caused Birth Defects among Navajo Indians," *High Country News,* February 4, 1985.

21. Lora Mangum Shields and Alan B. Goodman, "Outcome of 13,300 Navajo Births from 1964-1981 in the Shiprock Uranium Mining Area" (unpublished paper delivered at the American Association of Atomic Scientists Symposium, New York, May 25, 1984).

22. *Radiological Quality of the Environment in the United States, 1977, op. cit.,* pp. 62-6.

23. Lynn A. Robbins, "Energy Development and the Navajo Nation: an Update," in *Native Americans and Energy Development, II, op. cit.,* p. 119.

24. Quoted in Tom Barry, "The Deaths Still Go On: How Agencies Ignored Uranium Danger," *Navajo Times,* August 31, 1978.

25. "Claims Filed for Red Rock Miners," *Navajo Times,* July 26, 1979. Also see Tom Barry, "Bury My Lungs at Red Rock," *The Progressive,* October 1976, pp. 25-7.

26. Robbins, *op. cit.,* p. 121; Marjane Ambler, "Uranium Millworkers Seek Compensation," *APF Reporter,* September 1980.

27. Winona LaDuke, "How Much Development?" *Akwesasne Notes,* Vol. 11, No. 1, Spring 1979.

28. "Manpower Gap in the Uranium Mines," *Business Week,* November 1, 1977. For context, see Nancy J. Owens, "Can Tribes Control Energy Development?" in Joseph G. Jorgenson, ed., *Native Americans and Energy Development* (Boston: Anthropology Resource Center, 1978).

29. W.D. Armstrong, *A Report on Mineral Revenues and Tribal Economy* (Window Rock, AZ: Navajo Office of Minerals Development, June 1976).

30. Marjane Ambler, *Breaking the Iron Bonds: Indian Control of Energy Development* (Lawrence: University of Kansas

Press, 1990, p. 175). Also see Janet Siskind, "A Beautiful River That Turned Sour," *Mine Talk*, Summer/Fall 1982, pp. 37-59.

31. *Breaking the Iron Bonds, op. cit.*, pp. 174-5. Also see Winona LaDuke, "A History of Uranium Mining," *Black Hills/Paha Sapa Report*, Vol. 1, No. 1, Summer 1980. In this article, LaDuke quotes a New Mexico Environmental Improvement Agency report, dated earlier the same year, which was leaked to the Southwest Research and Information Center. In this document, it is acknowledged that spill-area livestock exhibited "higher than normal levels of Lead 210, Polonium 210, Thorium 230, and Radium 236." The state recommended the Diné not eat mutton thus contaminated. Indian Health Service Area Director William Mohler nonetheless suggested they go ahead and eat their animals, cautioning only that they should "perhaps" avoid eating organ tissues, where radioactive toxins might be expected to concentrate most heavily. Mohler agreed, however, that the meat was probably "inappropriate" for commercial sale. In other words, he deemed the animals "safe enough" for consumption by mere Indians, but not by non-Indians in New York or London. See J.W. Schomisch, "EID Lifts Ban on Eating Church Rock Cattle," *Gallup Independent*, May 22, 1980.
32. Quoted in Dan Liefgree, "Church Rock Chapter Upset at UNC," *Navajo Times*, May 8, 1980.
33. Frank Pitman, "Navajos-UNC Settle Tailings Spill Lawsuits," *Nuclear Fuel*, April 22, 1985.
34. "EID Finds that Church Rock Dam Break had Little or No Effect on Residents," *Nuclear Fuel*, March 14, 1983.
35. Chris Shuey, "the Puerco River: Where Did the Water Go?" *The Workbook*, No. 11, 1988, pp. 1-10. Also see Steve Hinschman, "Rebottling the Nuclear Genie," *High Country News*, January 19, 1987.
36. *Breaking the Iron Bonds, op. cit.*, p. 175. The instruction was delivered by memo, from Governor King to Thomas E. Baca of the Environmental Improvement Agency on January 9, 1981 (copy on file). For context, see "Mine Dewatering Operation in New Mexico Seen Violating Arizona Water Standards," *Nuclear Fuel*, March 1, 1982.
37. The laws violated by the United Nuclear and Kerr-McGee

dewatering procedures are the Public Law 92-500 (the "Clean Water Act of 1972," 86 Stat. 816) and P.L. 93-523 (the "Safe Drinking Water Act of 1974," 88 Stat. 1660). Although they are federal statutes, enforcement is left to individual states. They are often suspended altogether on Indian reservations. See Christopher McCleod, "Kerr-McGee's Last Stand," *Mother Jones*, December 1980.

38. *Breaking the Iron Bonds, op. cit.*, p. 175.
39. *Walter H. Peshlakai, et al. v. James R. Schlesinger, et al.*, V.S.D.C. for the District of Columbia, Civ. No. 78-2416 (1978). For analysis, also see Tom Barry, "Navajo Legal Services and Friends of the Earth Sue Six Federal Agencies over Alleged Careless Mining Policies," *American Indian Journal*, February 1979, pp. 5-7.
40. "Judge Reviewing Request to Stop Mobil Project," *Navajo Times*, July 19, 1979.
41. Quoted in Hansley Hadley, "Between Sacred Mountains," *Navajo Times*, December 7, 1983.
42. *Peshlakai v. Duncan*, 476 F.Supp. 1247, 1261 (1978).
43. Public Law 95-604 (92 Stat. 3021). For analysis, see Bob Rankin, "Congress Debates Cleanup of Uranium Mill Wastes," *Congressional Quarterly*, August 19, 1978, p. 2180.
44. The role of Harold Tso and his agency in getting things rolling—at *Indian* expense—is mentioned in Ford, Bacon & Davis Utah, *A Summary of the Phase II-Title I Engineering Assessment of Inactive Uranium Mill Tailings, Shiprock Site, N.M.* (Salt Lake City: ford, Bacon & Davis Utah Engineering Consultants, 1977, p. 65).
45. Ambler, *op. cit.*, p. 179. Present state of incompletion verified through site inspection by the author.
46. Site inspections by the author.
47. U.S. Environmental Protection Agency, *Potential Health and Environmental Hazards of Uranium Mine Wastes* (Washington, DC: U.S. Government Printing Office, 1983, pp. 1-23). It should be noted that the Navajo Environmental Protection Administration has again tried to address the situation, this time by diverting federal funds designated for the reclamation of abandoned coal mines on their land for use in cleaning up some of the worst uranium mine sites. Such monies are, however, greatly insufficient to the

task. See "Congress Unlocks $30 Million Mine Land Funds," *Navajo Times*, July 10, 1987.

48. Haunting sequences of Diné children playing in the proliferation of abandoned tailings piles around Tuba City are contained in the film *Four Corners: A National Sacrifice Area?* (San Francisco: Earth Image Films, 1981).
49. The Jackpile-Paguate Mine was supplanted for the dubious distinction of the world's largest by Namibia's Rossing Mine only after the former's closure in 1982. See Dan Jackson, "Mine Development on U.S. Indian Lands," *Engineering and Mining Journal*, january 1980. Also see John Aloysius Farrel, "The New Indian Wars," *Denver Post*, November 20-27, 1983.
50. Clemmer, *op. cit.*, pp. 98-9.
51. *Breaking the Iron Bonds, op. cit.*, p. 181.
52. Clemmer (*op. cit.*) estimates at page 99 that this involved some 450 others, or about "roughly three-quarters of the Laguna work force." Another 160 Acomas were also employed, mainly at the Bluewater mill. Also see Employment Security Commission of New Mexico, *Major Employers in New Mexico by County, 1976* (Santa Fe: mimeo, 1976).
53. Clemmer, *op. cit.*, p. 99.
54. *Ibid.*, pp. 97-8. Also see Hope Aldrich, "Problems Pile Up at Uranium Mills," *Santa Fe Reporter*, November 13, 1980.
55. Clemmer, *op. cit.*, pp. 97-8. Also see Hope Aldrich, "The Politics of Uranium," *Santa Fe Reporter*, December 7, 1978.
56. Clemmer, *op. cit.*, p. 98. Also see Lynda Taylor and G. Theodore Davis, "Uranium Mining and Milling: The Human Costs," unpublished paper presented at the New Mexico Physicians for Social Responsibility Conference, Albuquerque, March 10, 1980.
57. Radium-226 levels were calculated as being 30 times "safe" levels. U.S. Environmental Protection Agency, unpublished report, number deleted (unauthorized copy filed with the Southwest Research and Information Center, Albuquerque, June 1973).
58. Comptroller General of the United States, "EPA Needs to Improve the Navajo Safe Water Drinking Program" (Washington, DC: General Accounting Office, September

10, 1980).

59. Report by Johnny Sanders (Chief, Environmental Health Services Branch), T.J. Harwood (Director, Albuquerque Area Indian Health Service), and Mala L. Beard (ACL Hospital District Sanitarian) to the Governor of the Laguna Pueblo, August 11, 1978; copy on file with the Southwest Research and Information Center, Albuquerque.
60. Gerald F. Seib, "Indians Awaken to Their Lands' Energy Riches and Seek to Wrest Control from Companies," *Wall Street Journal*, September 20, 1979.
61. *Breaking the Iron Bonds, op. cit.*, p. 181.
62. Taylor and Davis, *op. cit.*, quoting Dr. Joseph Wagoner.
63. *Breaking the Iron Bonds, op. cit.*, p. 182.
64. Marjane Ambler, "Lagunas Face Fifth Delay of Uranium Cleanup," *Navajo Times Today*, February 4, 1986.
65. The threatened litigation is mentioned in U.S. Department of Interior, Bureau of Land Management, *Jackpile-Paguate Uranium Mine Reclamation Project Environmental Impact Statement* (Albuquerque: Bureau of Land Management, October 1986, p. 1).
66. "Agreement Signed for Reclamation of Jackpile Mine in New Mexico" (Washington, DC: Department of Interior News Release, December 12, 1986).
67. D.R. Dreeson, "Uranium Mill Tailings: Environmental Implications," *Los Alamos Scientific Laboratory Mini-Report*, February 1978, pp. 1-4.
68. The term "National Sacrifice Area" accrues from Thadias Box, *et al.*, *Rehabilitation Potential for Western Coal Lands* (Cambridge, MA: Ballinger Publishing Co., 1974), the published version of a study commissioned by the National Academy of Sciences and submitted to the Nixon administration for potential implementation as federal policy in 1972. Policy incorporation occurs in U.S. Department of Energy, Federal Energy Administration, Office of Strategic Analysis, *Project Independence: A Summary* (Washington, DC: U.S. Government Printing Office, November 1, 1974).
69. *Breaking the Iron Bonds, op. cit.*, p. 183.
70. Russell Means, "The Same Old Song," in Ward Churchill, ed., *Marxism and Native Americans* (Boston: South End Press, 1983, p. 25).

71. The matter has been well-studied, and the conclusion is inescapable. See, for example, Thayer Scudder, *et al.*, *No Place To Go: Effects of Compulsory Relocation on Navajos* (Philadelphia: Institute for the Study of Human Issues, 1982).
72. Means, *op. cit.*
73. Amelia Irvin, "Energy Development and the Effects of Mining on the Lakota Nation," *Journal of Ethnic Studies,* Vol. 10, No. 2, Spring 1982.
74. Harvey Wasserman, "The Sioux's Last Fight for the Black Hills," *Rocky Mountain News,* August 24, 1980.
75. Peter Matthiessen, *Indian Country* (New York: Viking Press, 1984, pp. 203-18).
76. Madonna Gilbert (Thunderhawk), "Radioactive Water Contamination on the Red Shirt Table, Pine Ridge Reservation, South Dakota" (Porcupine, SD: Women of All Red Nations, unpublished report, March 1980).
77. Quoted in Women of All Red Nations, "Radiation: Dangerous to Pine Ridge Women," *Akwesasne Notes,* Vol. 12, No. 1, Spring 1980. Also see Patricia J. Linthrop and J. Rotblat, "Radiation Pollution in the Environment," *Bulletin of Atomic Scientists,* September 1981, especially p. 18.
78. "Radiation: Dangerous to Pine Ridge Women," *op. cit.*
79. *Ibid.* Such results are consistent with findings in broader, non-reservation, settings. See Earl E. Reynolds, "Irradiation and Human Evolution," in his *The Process of Ongoing Human Evolution* (Detroit: Wayne State University Press, 1960, esp. p. 92). Also see Arthur R. Tamplin and John W. Gofman, *Population Control Through Nuclear Pollution* (Chicago: Nelson-Hall Publishers, 1971).
80. The Igloo operation was suspended in 1972. Like Kerr-McGee at Navajo, and Anaconda at Laguna, the government made no effort to clean up the radioactive wastes it had generated; see Matthiessen, *op. cit.*
81. "Nuclear Waste Facility Proposed Near Edgemont," *Rapid City Journal,* November 19, 1982.
82. "Edgemont Waste Facility No Health Hazard Says Chem-Nuclear Corporation," *Rapid City Journal,* December 10, 1982. Author's site visits. Photos of the new tailings piles, fence and signs, taken by Cynthia Martinez, appear in Ward Churchill, ed., *Critical Issues in Native North Amer-*

ica, Vol. II (Copenhagen: International Work Group on Indigenous Affairs, 1991, pp. 39, 41).

83. Site visit by the author.
84. Jacqueline Huber, *et al., The Gunnery Range Report* (Pine Ridge, SD: Office of the President, Oglala Sioux Tribe, 1981).
85. On the NASA/NURE collaboration, see Peter Matthiessen, *In the Spirit of Crazy Horse* (New York: Viking Press, [second edition] 1991, p. 417). On disposition of minerals discovered thereby, see J.P. Gries, BIA Report 12: *Status of Mineral Resource Information on the Pine Ridge Reservation, South Dakota* (Washington, DC: U.S. Department of Interior, 1976).
86. A list of the dead, as well as the dates and causes of death, is contained in Ward Churchill and Jim Vander Wall, *The COINTELPRO Papers: Documents from the FBI's Secret Wars Against Dissent in the United States* (Boston: South End Press, 1990, pp. 393-5); for reproduction of an official document describing the Indian resistance as "insurgents"—rather than as "radicals" or "political extremists"—see page 271. For further details of the way in which the war was waged, see Ward Churchill and Jim Vander Wall, *Agents of Repression: The FBI's Secret Wars Against the Black Panther Party and the American Indian Movement* (Boston: South End Press, 1988).
87. U.S. National Park Service, "Memorandum of Agreement Between the Oglala Sioux Tribe of South Dakota and the National Park Service of the Department of Interior to Facilitate Establishment, Development, Administration, and Public Use of the Oglala Sioux Tribal Lands, Badlands National Monument" (Washington, DC: U.S. Department of Interior, January 2, 1976). The transfer was illegal insofar as the still-binding 1868 Fort Laramie Treaty requires the express consent of three-quarters of *all* adult, male Lakotas before any Lakota land cession can be considered legally valid; the clause was designed specifically to *prevent* maneuvers such as those between Wilson and his federal sponsors. For more on Wilson and the treaty, see Rex Wyler, *Blood of the Land: The U.S. Government and Corporate War Against the American Indian Movement* (New York: Vintage Books, 1984).

88. U.S. National Park Service, *Master Plan: Badlands National Monument* (Denver: Rocky Mountain Regional Office, February 1978). The clause allowing recovery of surface rights to the land by the Lakotas completely inverts the treaty requirement that such a referendum must be conducted before a land *cession* can be considered valid.
89. Irvin, *op. cit.*, p. 99.
90. Marjane Ambler, "Wyoming to Study Tailings Issue," *Denver Post*, February 5, 1984.
91. *Breaking the Iron Bonds, op. cit.*, p. 179.
92. U.S. Department of Energy, *Environmental Assessment on Remedial Action at the Riverton Uranium Mill Tailings Site, Riverton, Wyoming* (Albuquerque: Department of Energy, June 1987).
93. Site visit by the author.
94. "GRI Projects 1 percent Annual Growth Rate in U.S. Energy Use through 2010," *Inside Energy*, August 15, 1988.
95. John D. Smillie, "Whatever Happened to the Energy Crisis?" *The Plains Truth*, April 1986. Actually, the 1979 price of yellowcake was probably greatly and illegally inflated, having risen from $6 per pound in 1972 to $41 in 1977. In the latter year, Westinghouse Corporation, the largest commercial buyer in the U.S., filed a price fixing suit against nearly every uranium producing company in the world. The suit was rendered moot by the market bust before it could be decided; *Breaking the Iron Bonds, op. cit.*, p. 78.
96. The history is contained in *Dawn Mining Company v. Clark*, Civ. No. 82-974JLQ, District Court for Eastern Washington (1982).
97. *Breaking the Iron Bonds, op. cit.*, p. 176.
98. *Ibid.*
99. *Ibid.* Ambler is relying on a letter from Paul B. Hahn, Chief of the Evaluation Branch, EPA Office of Radiation Programs, Las Vegas Facility, to Richard Parkin, Chief of the Water Compliance Section, EPA Region 10, dated February 18, 1987.
100. *Dawn Mining Company v. Clark, op. cit.*
101. *Breaking the Iron Bonds, op. cit.*, pp. 176-7.
102. Site visit by the author.

103. On the start-up of the Sherwood facility, see Stan Dayton, "Washington's Sherwood Project: A Newcomer in an Orphan District," *Engineering and Mining Journal,* November 1978. On the extent of environmental degradation at Sherwood, see U.S. Department of Interior, Bureau of Indian Affairs, *Sherwood Uranium Project, Spokane Indian Reservation: Final Environmental Statement* (Portland, OR: Bureau of Indian Affairs Area Office, August 19, 1976). On Western Nuclear's transfer of both mine and mill to the Spokanes, see U.S. Department of Interior, Bureau of Indian Affairs, "Mineral Resource Facilities Maintenance Contract for the Sherwood Mine-Mill Complex" (Portland, OR: Bureau of Indian Affairs Area Office, December 1989).
104. Site visit by the author.
105. Clemmer, *op. cit.,* p. 103.
106. *Ibid.,* p. 104.
107. Employment Security Commission of New Mexico, *op. cit.*
108. Clemmer, *op. cit.,* p. 104.
109. Elouise Schumacher, "440 Billion Gallons: Hanford wastes would fill 900 King Domes," *Seattle Times,* April 13, 1991. No one need worry about this, however, given that the EPA has recently discovered that tobacco smoking (*rather than* such radioactive pollution by the government and major corporations) is the primary "environmental hazard" in the United States. Correspondingly, as the author discovered during a 1989 visit to Hanford, the many near-abandoned buildings at the plant—situated directly atop the greatest known release of carcinogenic waste in human history—have been designated by law as no smoking zones. One incurs a $2,500 fine—imposed by the very entity which is solely responsible for what has happened at Hanford—for lighting up one cigarette on a U.S. airliner, while those who dumped a near half-billion gallons of radioactive toxins into the public water supply waltz off merrily, without so much as a slap on the wrist. Such are the present priorities of environmental consciousness in the U.S., implicitly endorsed even by a wide spectrum of those describing themselves as "progressive" or "politically conscious."
110. Kenneth B. Noble, "The U.S. for Decades Let Uranium

Leak at Weapon Plant," *New York Times,* October 15, 1988. Also see Martha Odom, "Tanks That Leak, Tanks That Explode...Tanks Alot DOE," *Portland Free Press,* Vol. 1, No. 5, May 1989.

111. Matthew L. Wald, "Wider Peril Seen in Nuclear Waste from Bomb Making," *New York Times,* March 28, 1991.
112. Helen Caldicott, M.D., *If You Love this Planet: A Plan to Heal the Earth* (New York: W.W. Norton Publishers, 1992, p. 89).
113. At one point, plant officials even attempted to "lose" key documents concerning what it had done at Hanford. See Larry Lang, "Missing Hanford Documents Probed by Energy Department," *Seattle Post-Intelligencer,* September 20, 1991.
114. *Ibid.,* p. 89. Also see Susan Wyndham, "Death in the Air," *Australian Magazine,* September 29-30, 1990.
115. Caldicott, *op. cit.,* p. 90. Also see Keith Schneider, "Seeking Victims of Radiation Near Weapon Plant," *New York Times,* October 17, 1988.
116. Marjane Ambler, "Nuke Waste Sites Border Indian Lands," *Navajo Times,* October 8, 1984. Also see Warner Reeser, *Inventory of Hazardous Waste Generators and Sites on Selected Indian Reservations* (Denver: Council of Energy Resource Tribes, 1985).
117. Marjane Ambler, "Law Recognizes Tribal Concerns: DOE Ignores Them, Says 3 Tribes," *Navajo Times Today,* April 29, 1985. Also see Marjane Ambler, "Russell Jim is Pro-Safety, Not Anti-Nuclear," *High Country News,* July 7, 1988. The 1988 Congressional decision to build the waste facility at Yucca Mountain, Nevada, rather than in Washington or Idaho, is mentioned in *Breaking the Iron Bonds, op. cit.,* p. 234.
118. Public Law 97-425 (96 Stat. 2201).
119. A.D. Owen, "The World Uranium Industry," *Raw Materials Report,* Vol. 2, No. 1, Spring 1983.
120. Miles Goldstick, *Wollaston: People Resisting Genocide* (Toronto: Black Rose Books, 1987, pp. 74-5).
121. Actually, the problem may be even more severe, given that the greater proportion of non-radioactive material in the by-products of lower grade ore may serve to some extent in retarding radon and thoron emissions. If so, then the

effect is exponential; both the "quality" and quantity of radioactive contamination in northern Saskatchewan would be higher than at comparable U.S. sites. See John Moelaert, "This Dust Is Making Me Sick," *The Energy File,* April 1979.

122. Goldstick, *op. cit.*, p. 107.
123. *Annual Report, 1984* (Ottawa: Eldorado Nuclear, Ltd., March 7, 1985.
124. National Research Council of Canada, Associate Committee on Scientific Criteria for Environmental Quality, *Lead in the Canadian Environment* (Ottawa: NRCC Publications, December 1973). Also see Atomic Energy Control Board, Advisory Panel on Uranium Tailings, *The Management of Uranium Tailings: An Appraisal of Current Practices* (Ottawa: AECB Report 1196, September 1978, p. 13).
125. For use of the term, see Goldstick, *op. cit.*, p. 74.
126. *Ibid.*, pp. 75-7.
127. David McArthur, "Surface Leases and Socio-Economic Considerations of Uranium Mining" (Ottawa: Mining Law Institute Occasional Papers, June 1983).
128. Jim Harding, "Saskatchewan: The Eye of the Uranium Controversy," *Briarpatch,* April 1985.
129. Goldstick, *op. cit.*, p. 78. Also see Bud Jorgensen, "Easing of Uranium Export Rules Urged for Canada," *Toronto Globe and Mail,* May 4, 1986.
130. Atomic Energy Control Board, *op. cit.*, p. 3.
131. Goldstick, *op. cit.*, pp. 79-80; Moelaert, *op. cit.*
132. Although Eldorado Nuclear, as a wholly government-created entity, is ostensibly owned "by the people of Canada," it has been far less forthcoming with its financial information than many private concerns. Brian Goldstick has calculated the profitability of the Rabbit Lake operation based on Eldorado's 1984 report that its operation had produced more than 1.6 million kilograms of yellowcake during its lifetime, and then multiplying by the average $62.50 (Canadian) price per kilo which prevailed during the same period.
133. Milling at the Rabbit Lake facility did not stop while the building involved in its expansion was going on, of course. When construction workers sought to reveal the safety hazards which resulted, and to unionize in self-defense,

Eldorado summarily fired them and then cancelled its contract with their employer, Enerpet Construction Ltd. of Calgary. Scab labor—apparently willing to risk a high degree of irradiation in exchange for a government paycheck—was used to complete the project. See "Men Say Fired For Unionizing," *The Star Phoenix* (Saskatoon), January 24, 1984.

134. Goldstick, *op. cit.*, pp. 81-2.
135. Quoted in *ibid.*, p. 82.
136. A total of 2,916 such containers had stacked up by 1983, when mining of the first Cluff Lake ore pocket was completed. Three years later, the number was thought to have tripled, and by now there may be more than 20,000. Under the best of conditions, the containers are expected to last only 100 years, while the half-life of much of the material within them is as long as 80,000 years. Neither the corporation nor the government has explained what is supposed to happen to the wastes after the end of its first century of storage. See Terry Pugh, "Garbage Never Looked So Good," *Briarpatch*, September 1986.
137. The Saskatchewan investment was $2.3 million (Canadian). Cluff Lake Mining estimated that it could produce 56,700 kilograms of yellowcake and 283,000 grams of gold—at an aggregate value of $4.5 million—just from the radium wastes "on hand." AMOK, one-third of which is owned by the French government's Commissariat de l'Energie Atomique—which tests and builds France's nuclear weapons—committed to buy the bulk of the yellowcake. See "AMOK Solves Problem of Radioactive Waste," *Toronto Globe and Mail*, August 16, 1986.
138. Goldstick, *op. cit.*, p. 84; Jorgenson, *op. cit.*
139. Goldstick, *op. cit.*, p. 85.
140. *Ibid.*
141. *Ibid.*, pp. 85-6.
142. Diana Ralph, "Faulty Prescription for Northern Native People: Health-Damaging Development and Little Care" (unpublished paper completed in February 1984, quoted by Goldstick, *op. cit.*, p. 24).
143. Murray Dobbin, ed., *Economic Options for Northern Saskatchewan* (Saskatoon: Northern Saskatchewan Economic Options Conference, 1984, p. 11).

144. R.G. Ruggles and W.J. Rowley, *A Study of Water Pollution in the Vicinity of the Eldorado Nuclear Ltd., Beaverlodge Operation, 1976 and 1977* (Edmonton: Environmental Protection Service, 1978).
145. Stella M. Swanson, "Levels of Ra226, Pb210, and Utotal in Fish Near a Saskatchewan Uranium Mine and Mill," *Health Physics*, Vol. 45, No. 1, July 1983, pp. 67-80.
146. Saskatchewan Research Council, *Chemistry and Biology Division, Environmental Overview Assessment for the Dubyna 31-Zone Uranium Production Program for United Nuclear Ltd.* (Saskatoon: Saskatchewan Research Council, December 13, 1978, p. 71).
147. D.J. Robinson, F.G. Ruggles and A. Zaida, *A Study of Water Pollution in the Vicinity of Gulf Minerals Rabbit Lake Uranium Mine, 1978* (Regina: Environmental Canada Surveillance Report EPS-5-W and NR-83-1, 1978, pp. i, 11).
148. *Ibid.*, p. i, quoted and paraphrased in Goldstick, *op. cit.*, p. 116.
149. Saskatchewan Research Council, *op. cit.*, p. 44.
150. Goldstick, *op. cit.*, p. 116.
151. Swanson, *op. cit.*, p. 10.
152. *Ibid.*, p. 19.
153. Goldstick, *op. cit.*, p. 110.
154. R.B. Holtzman, "Ra266 and the Natural Airborne Nuclides Pb210 and Po210 in Arctic Biota," in William Snyder, ed., *Radiation Protection* (New York: Pergamon Press, 1968, pp. 1,087-96).
155. P. Kaarnen and J.K. Miettinen, "Po210 and Pb210 in Environmental Samples in Finland," in *Radiological Concentration Processes: Proceedings from the International Symposium Held in Stockholm, April 25-29, 1966* (New York: Pergamon Press, 1966, pp. 279-80).
156. Quoted in Goldstick, *op. cit.*, p. 121.
157. *Ibid.*
158. Dreeson, *op. cit.*
159. See, for example, the opening paragraph in the introduction to Goldstick (*op. cit.*, p. 12): "The uranium industry is more active in northern Saskatchewan than any other place in the western world. For the native people of the area it is the dominant force continuing the destructive

momentum built up over 300 years of colonialism. If the present trend continues, the result will be genocide."

160. Barry Commoner, *Making Peace with the Planet* (New York: The New Press, [5th edition] 1992, pp. 103-4).
161. On the context of Chernobyl and its effects, see World Commission on Environment and Development, *Our Common Future* (London/New York: Oxford University Press, 1987).
162. On Seabrook and Diablo Canyon, see Harvey Wasserman, *Energy War: Reports from the Front* (Westport, CT: Lawrence Hill and Co., 1979). On Point Conception, see *Indian Country, op. cit.*
163. Two reactors in the U.S.—those at Fort St. Vrain and Hanford—were based on the same defective gas-cooled design as the Soviet reactor at Chernobyl, using "hoppers of boronated steel balls which fall into holes in the graphite moderator block i the current to magnetic latches is interrupted." See Amory B. Lovins and L. Hunter Lovins, *Brittle Power: Energy Strategy for National Security* (Andover, MA: Brick House Publishing, 1982, p. 197).
164. Marcia Klotz, *et al.*, *Citizen's Guide to Rocky Flats: Colorado's Bomb Factory* (Boulder: Rocky Mountain Peace Center, 1992, p. 6).
165. Commoner, *op. cit.*, pp. 87-8.
166. *Ibid.*, p. 88.
167. Caldicott, *op. cit.*, pp. 36-7, 65, 152. Ironically but predictably, the nuclear industry has purported to adopt as its own the environmental movement's new top priorities: greenhouse gases and the global warming produced thereby. Only atomic energy, the story goes, can offer a "clean, safe and reliable alternative" to the huge level of gaseous emission produced by coal and oil-fired electrical generators.
168. U.S. Department of Energy, Nuclear Information and Resource Service, *Nuclear Power and National Energy Strategy* (Washington, DC: U.S. Government Printing Office, April 1991).
169. Preliminary work appears to have begun already; site visit by author, June 1992.
170. *Breaking the Iron Bonds, op. cit.*, p. 173.
171. See map of Crow resources, *ibid.*, p. 36.

172. On "seed money," see *ibid.*, p. 95; on 1979 DoE funding level, p. 100. Overall, see Winona LaDuke, "The Council of Energy Resource Tribes," in *Native Americans and Energy Development, II, op. cit.*, pp. 58-70.
173. *Breaking the Iron Bonds, op. cit.*, p. 95. The 1988 member councils were those at Ute Mountain and Southern Ute, Florida Seminole, Navajo, Nez Percé, Yakima, Oklahoma Cherokee, Jicarilla Apache, Pine Ridge Sioux, Standing Rock Sioux, Cheyenne River Sioux, Rosebud Sioux, Blackfeet, Spokane, Tulé River, Turtle Mountain Chippewa, Uintah and Ouray Ute, Chemeheuvi, Coeur d'Alene, Cheyenne-Arapaho, Northern Cheyenne, Walker River, Pawnee, Shoshone-Bannock, Umatilla, Penobscot, Kalispel, Muckleshoot, Saginaw Chippewa, Ponca, Rocky Boy Chippewa-Cree, Crow, Flathead, Fort Belknap, Fort Berthold, Fort Peck, Hopi, Hualapai, and the Acoma, Jemez, Santa Ana, Zia and Laguna pueblos.
174. Geoffrey O'Gara, "Canny CERT Gets Money, Respect, Problems," *High Country News*, December 14, 1979. Also see Winona LaDuke, "CERT: An Outsider's View In," *Akwesasne Notes*, Summer 1980.
175. *Breaking the Iron Bonds, op. cit.*, pp. 95-100. It should be noted that, although CERT deliberately fostered a bare-knuckled image of itself as an "Indian OPEC" during its early days, it was always explicitly accommodationist. Founding director Peter McDonald obtained federal funding by first pledging unequivocal support to the government and promising that the organization's members were "posed to make a massive contribution to the national effort [to achieve energy self-sufficiency]." See O'Gara, *op. cit.* It should also be mentioned that the individual hired by McDonald to head up CERT's resource development policy and its implementation, Ahmed Kooros, was former oil minister for the Shah of Iran. See Mike Meyers, "Ahmed Kooros: A Discussion," *Akwesasne Notes*, Late Spring 1980.
176. Probably the best overall Indian critique of CERT offered during this period was Philip "Sam" Deloria's "CERT: It's Time for an Evaluation," *American Indian Law Newsletter*, September/October 1982. Also see Ken Peres and Fran Swan, "The New Indian Elite: Bureaucratic Entrepre-

neurs," *Akwesasne Notes*, Late Spring 1980.

177. CERT was a prime mover in seeking to convince either the Yakimas, the Umatillas, or the Nez Percés to accept a high-level dump during the second half of the 1980s; see U.S. Environmental Protection Agency, *EPA Policy for the Administration of Environmental Programs on Indian Reservations* (Washington, DC: U.S. Government Printing Office, November 8, 1984). It assumed the same role with regard to possible siting of such a facility on the Rosebud Sioux Reservation in South Dakota during the late 1980s; discussion with Ed Valandra, former Rosebud council member, April 1992. Its role at Mescalero was equally prominent; discussion with Doug Dorame, Mescalero Apache, April 1992.

178. *Breaking the Iron Bonds, op. cit.*, p. 115. Ambler quotes DoE official Marie Monsen as describing EPA as being CERT's new "glamor girl" by 1990.

179. Caldicott, *op. cit.*, p. 90; Klotz, *op. cit.*, p. 6.

180. Oak Ridge Environmental Peace Alliance, *A Citizen's Guide to Oak Ridge* (Knoxville, TN: OREPA Publications, 1989).

181. On water contamination, see Joan Lowy and Janet Day, "Flats Water Threat Cited," *Rocky Mountain News*, December 7, 1988. On extent of ground contamination, see Nicholas Lenssen, *Nuclear Waste: The Problem that Won't Go Away* (Washington, DC: Worldwatch Institute Paper 106, December 1991, pp. 34-5).

182. On the Clamshell and Abalone Alliances, see *Energy War, op. cit.* On the Freeze Movement, see Michael Albert and David Dellinger, eds., *Beyond Survival: New Directions for the Disarmament Movement* (Boston: South End Press, 1983); despite the suggestion that "new directions" are involved, there is *no* discussion of possibly decolonizing the source(s) of uranium, thus severing the nuclear weapons structure from its root.

183. In fact, a good case can be made that the capacity for U.S. nuclear weaponry has actually gone up since George Bush announced "cuts" in such weapons in September 1991 and January 1992. See Klotz, *op. cit.*, p. 11.

184. On LaDonna Harris' role in founding CERT, as well as serving as Commoner's Citizen Party running mate in

1980, see *Breaking the Iron Bonds, op. cit.*, pp. 93-4, 101-2.

185. This is a variation of the "Mere Gook Rule" articulated by Noam Chomsky and others to explain the callousness with which U.S. policymakers view the suffering they inflict; upon non-white peoples at home and abroad ;while pursuing the "national interest"; see Edward S. Herman, *Beyond Hypocrisy: Decoding the News in an Age of Propaganda* (Boston: South End Press, 1992, pp. 54-6). That Euroamerican progressivism might be tinged with a touch of the same perspective tends to speak for itself.
186. Much can be learned from the Australian anti-nuclear movement, which made aboriginal rights a centerpiece of its strategy, and which therefore has been much more effective than its U.S. and Canadian counterparts in halting front-end nuclear activities in their country. See C. Tatz, *Aborigines & Uranium and Other Essays* (Victoria: Heineman Educational Publications, 1982).
187. André Gorz, *Ecology as Politics* (Boston: South End Press, 1980, pp. 102-14).
188. Felix Cohen, "Dean of American Indian Law," coined the Indian/miner's canary analogy to describe certain juridical and policy phenomena in the U.S. Winona LaDuke and other native rights activists have since applied it in the more physical manner used here. See Felix S. Cohen, "The Erosion of Indian Rights, 1950-53: A Case Study in Bureaucracy," *Yale Law Journal*, No. 62, 1953, p. 390.
189. John W. Gofman (Ph.D., M.D.) and Arthur R. Tamplin (Ph.D.), *Poisoned Power: The Case Before and After Three Mile Island* (Emmaus, PA: Rodale Press, [2nd edition] 1979).

The Water Plot

Hydrological Rape in Northern Canada

There are strange things
done in the midnight sun
By the men who toil for gold;
The Arctic Trails have
their secret tales
That would make your blood run cold...

—Robert Service—

In northern Canada, a water diversion scheme far larger than anything yet undertaken in the United States has been planned, piloted, and awaits only the right climate of public opinion to become a reality.[1] By diverting Canada's hydroelectricity and clean, fresh waters to support the growing demand of the lower 48 U.S. states, the plan's proponents argue, Canada would earn a great deal of foreign exchange, and profit considerably from the employment created by construction of the required dams, dikes, canals, tunnels and pumping stations. But while proponents say little about the future once these works are built, the marginal benefits that might actually accrue to Canadians will be vastly outweighed by the costs of adverse economic, human and environmental consequences.

Land that Supports Its People

In the Canadian northlands, the indigenous Athabascan, Cree, Inuit and Anishinabe populations live primarily by time-honored methods of hunting, trapping and fishing, affording these occupations not only practical by central spiritual significance.[2] Those who hold wage jobs do so mainly in the three industries which support the resident non-Indian population: mining, forestry and tourism.[3] Each of these economies must be considered in any assessment of the overall impacts attending the projected hydrological rape of the Subarctic.

As developments in northern Quebec over the past quarter-century have amply demonstrated, massive water diversion is utterly devastating to the ecosystems upon which indigenous economies depend. The habitat of fur-bearing animals, without which there can be no trapping, is flooded out when free-flowing waters are dammed.[4] Similarly, much of the bottom land on which large mammals graze become submerged, killing or driving the animals away and destroying the basis for commercial or even subsistence hunting. Aquatic life is also disrupted by damming. Many of the varieties of fish natural to northern Canada require a current in which to thrive and disappear steadily once their rivers and streams have been converted into relatively motionless reservoirs.[5] The flooding caused by dams in turn tends to cause mercury contamination and other water pollution, rendering even those fish able to adapt poisonous to consume.[6]

Consummating the grand plan for water diversion in the Subarctic will have a catastrophic impact upon indigenous peoples there. It is certain to destroy their present economic self-sufficiency and, as discussed below, will foreclose on every economic alternative supposedly available to them. The net result may well be their rapid disappearance *as peoples*. In this sense, the effect of the "Water Plot" carries implications of genocide as well as ecocide.[7]

Permanent Deforestation

One aspect of this combined genocide and ecocide concerns the project's effects on forests. Although northern Canada is abundantly wooded, it takes more dollars' worth of equipment to generate a penny's worth of profit from the pulp and paper industry than nearly any other business in the world. Because trees in the Subarctic grow comparatively slowly, each paper mill must draw on a broad forest area to insure that the large and mobile capital investment involved receives a perpetual supply of raw materials.[8] In northwestern Ontario, for example, timber limits are almost fully allocated throughout the "harvesting" area south of Highway 11 and north of Lake Nipigon. Reservoirs already cover tens of thousands of square miles of former woodlands in the region, and it is easy to see that further hydrological "improvements" will certainly destabilize the forestry industry.[9] If the Water Plot were to achieve full fruition, forests and forestry, not only in Ontario but elsewhere in the north, would become relics of the past. Reduction of forestry would deny the indigenous people of the area both a primary source of what limited cash they now receive, and one of the major alternatives to their traditional economy that the dominant culture has always espoused.[10]

Shafting the Mining Industry

There is an estimated $1 billion worth of nickel in the new Inco mine on Shebandowan Lake in Ontario. The entrance to the mine shaft is barely twenty feet above the natural level of the lake. Shebandowan is but one of many similar sites, yielding rich mineral ores besides nickel, including copper, bauxite, manganese, uranium, iron, silver and, of course, gold.[11] Each of the mines is similarly located at or very near lake level. Projected areas of flooding if the Water Plot is consummated show that all of these will disappear beneath the waves, as will a number of Indian and non-Indian communities. Planners explain that construction of an elaborate system of coffer-dams, causeways and pumping facilities will be sufficient to save many existing mine sites. They are silent, however, concerning the expense involved; there are no estimates of the increase in costs of Canadian ores needed to pay the tab. In all likelihood, mining in much of northern Canada will be priced out of the market and correspondingly gutted. Further, planners have little to say about how their scheme would affect exploration and mining of presently undiscovered mineral deposits which will be buried, not tens, but often hundreds of feet under water.[12] Water diversion of the sort now envisioned would thus demolish the second supposed alternative to traditional native economies.

Submerging Tourism

Tourism, the third and final basis for an indigenous cash economy in the northlands, is also threatened. For more than forty years, a solid business of sport fishing, hunting, camping and the like has developed and provides a cash supplement to the subsistence activities of many native people.[13] This will be completely ruined if fast-moving pike streams, as well as pickerel lakes, are converted into a huge, largely stagnant inland sea in which only carp can live, and upon which one can barely cast a line without snagging the rotting remains of once-proud pine forests. Even where water still flows, navigation—as is readily demonstrated behind the sprawling Bennett Dam in British Columbia—will be severely impaired by floating timber, and landings will have to be made on mudflats, amidst the skeletal remains of miles upon miles of drowned trees.[14] The tourist industry in most of northern Canada will be obliterated if the Water Plot is realized. And with it would go the last hope of survival for the region's indigenous peoples.

Genocide as "National Sacrifice"

Once the dams and attendant paraphernalia are put in place, the entire "developed" area will quite literally be gone, leaving nothing by which a population—indigenous or otherwise—can support itself. Northern Canada will have become what in the United States has been described as a "national sacrifice area"; the human beings who reside there will have been converted into national sacrifice peoples.[15]

As the dimensions of this incipient disaster have dawned on people throughout Canada, and to a lesser extent in the U.S., questions have been raised. The response of the Canadian government in Ottawa, and of various provincial governments, has been to become increasingly secretive about their water diversion/hydroelectrical projects. Large-scale, detailed maps of the targeted locales—on which it might be possible to decipher the likely extent of flooding—have been withdrawn from circulation. Even general information and small-scale maps have become quite difficult to obtain in many instances.[16] Apparently, the government intends to deny the public's right to know what is being done to them and "their" resources until the dams have been erected and the damage done.[17]

But contrary to Ottawa's wishes, or the wishes of the cliques inhabiting a number of corporate board rooms and provincial capitals, such information is the property of the people, and not just of North America. Genocide is, after all, a crime against all humanity.[18] The same is true ecocide. As will be shown, existing and planned projects in the Canadian northlands entail significant negative implications for the biosphere of the entire planet.

The James Bay Projects

It all began early in the 20th century, when the "first

hydroelectric plants were built at those rare sites where large amounts of electric power could be generated, and where there were nearby cities to which it could be shipped, or the power so abundant and cheap that electricity-consuming industries could be enticed to build new plants near where it was generated."[19] Such endeavors were not especially disruptive of the environment, and remained concentrated in the heavily populated southeastern corridor of Canada. By the late 1930s, however:

> English-speaking capitalists and engineers [had] built the first major powerhouses in [Quebec], harnessing the Saint Lawrence River at rapids near Montreal, as well as tributaries of the Saint Lawrence where they tumbled off the central plateau of the Quebec-Labrador Peninsula. Montreal Light, Heat and Power Consolidated, for instance, supplied the large and growing market of Montreal with power generated nearby. It grew into one of the largest privately-owned electrical utilities in the world, and made Irish-born financier Henry Holt exceedingly wealthy. Shawnigan Water and Power Company, launched by American entrepreneurs, generated cheap and abundant electricity at Shawnigan Falls on the Saint Maurice River, a tributary of the Saint Lawrence. The company attracted aluminum refineries, pulp and paper mills, and other electricity-hungry industries to locate in what had been wilderness, and the surplus power flowed through North America's first long distance high-voltage transmission line to Montreal. On the Sanguenay River, another tributary of the Saint Lawrence, a subsidiary of the Aluminum Company of America (which later became the multinational firm Alcan) built its own hydroelectric plants to power its aluminum refineries.[20]

Toward the end of World War II, in April 1944, the provincial government began to lay the groundwork for a vast expansion of Quebec's hydroelectrical generation by "nationalizing" Montreal Light, Heat and Power. The resulting "public" utility, dubbed "Hydro-Quebec," began a rapid program of building "ever-bigger hydro projects on rivers ever-farther from the centres of population and industry, running transmission lines at ever-higher voltages over ever-greater distances."[21] The new utility doubled in size, and then doubled again. By 1963, it had become the largest employer in Quebec, and a source of ethnic pride among the province's large and francophone population. It had also begun to export a considerable portion of its electrical output to the U.S., and was eyeing schemes of development which transcended provincial boundaries altogether. It was in this context that René Lévesque—then serving as part of the Jean Lesage Liberal administration in 1962 and who would later become premier when the Parti Québécois was elected—oversaw the increase of Quebec's debt by $600 million in order to absorb all private utilities remaining within its borders.[22]

By 1967, "Québécois watched with pride [as an] army of workers and fleets of trucks [built] a dam—a giant, graceful structure of arched concrete—on the Manicougan River, some 700 kilometers away [from Montreal]. Technology usually advances in small steps, but to transmit power from the distant Manic hydroelectric complex, Hydro-Quebec made a large extrapolation; it more than doubled the standard voltage used for high voltage power transmission, and developed the first 735-kilovolt transmission line."[23] Next came the majestic falls of the Churchill River, more than 1,000 kilometers distant.

> Hydro-Quebec did not develop Churchill Falls, which is in Labrador, the mainland portion of the province of Newfoundland and Labrador. But Hydro-Quebec was its only potential customer. After marathon negotiations, Hydro-Quebec signed a deal with Brinco, the company developing the hydroelectric project. In return for securing the loans which paid for construction of the Churchill Falls hydroelectric plant, Hydro-Quebec, for 65 years, gets almost all its enormous output at what turns out to be extremely low prices—about one-fiftieth of those Hydro-Quebec charges its own customers in the United

States.[24]

With the election of Robert Bourassa as Premier of Quebec in April 1970, the pace of development increased exponentially. Having campaigned on a promise of delivering 100,000 new jobs in short order, the new premier demanded an immediate start-up of a massive project to dam three major rivers—the Nottaway, Broadback and Rupert—all of them draining into James Bay, an adjunct at the southern extreme of Hudson Bay.[25] Hydro-Quebec initially resisted the idea, which it had been exploring since at least as early as 1965, on the basis that anticipated expenses would be too great ($6 billion, at a minimum) and that demand for the quantity of power generation which would result did not yet exist.[26] Bourassa quickly overcame the financial objection by arranging an initial $300 million loan through David Rockefeller of the Chase Manhattan Bank. Concerns over weak demand were partially addressed via assurances from the banker's brother, New York Governor Nelson Rockefeller. He was in an excellent position to give these assurances: he served simultaneously as president of Consolidated Edison which supplies New York City.[27] A new subsidiary of Hydro-Quebec, the Société d'Energie de la Baie James (James Bay Energy Corporation) was established in 1971 to move things along.[28]

James Bay I
Canada as Energy Colony

By the time construction actually began in 1972, the scope of the project had been expanded to include a complex on the La Grande River. It was there that Canadian Bechtel, a subsidiary of the huge Bechtel International construction corporation, was contracted to engage in building "phase one," ultimately moving enough earth to recreate the Great Pyramid of Cheops 80 times over.[29] In the process, Bechtel also pushed through a network of roads where none had previously existed, installed airports and housing to accommodate 5,000 workers, beginning generally to "open up" the previously pristine James Bay wilderness to the ravages of "civilization."[30] And, as analyst Sean McCutcheon has pointed out, after such a dynamic is set in motion, it becomes well nigh impossible to stop it: "Once having paid a relatively fixed sum for infrastructure, then the more dams Hydro-Quebec builds, the lower the cost per kilowatt generated tends to be. Thus economies of scale encourage building on a large scale."[31]

The developers, however, encountered early, intense and unexpectedly effective opposition from the Mistissini Cree people indigenous to the area, a group the Bourassa administration had casually dismissed as "squalid savages."[32] Beginning in February 1972, a pair of young men, Philip Awashish and Billy Diamond, alerted by newspaper articles summarizing the government's plans, began a village-by-village campaign to organize a cohesive Indian resistance to the James Bay Project. By April, they had retained James O'Reilly, a specialist in environmental and Canadian Indian law, and filed a motion with the Superior Court of Quebec to enjoin all building pending the outcome of an independent environmental impact study they themselves had commissioned. (An earlier provincial study had been a sham, extrapolating from studies conducted in connection with the Aswan Dam in Egypt to give the James Bay plan a clean bill of health, and containing virtually no information related to Subarctic conditions.)[33]

After a number of site visits, a team of fifteen ecological scientists were prepared to take the stand in October and November of 1972. Their estimates of the impact were clear: not only would the proposed dams, roads and transmission lines precipitate an environmental catastrophe of the first magnitude, but its impact upon the Cree and more northerly Inuits would be "culturally genocidal."[34] Einar Skinnarland, who had been a ranking engineer in the Churchill Falls endeavor, also testified that he was having "second thoughts" about such projects, "especially [those involving] wholesale river diversions," which he described as being "the most disastrous decisions we can make." He termed the economic and energy rationales underlying construction "baloney."[35] More than sixty native people also took the stand, once their attorney had convinced the court that, even under Canadian law, those held a range of rights with regard to their lives and land.[36]

> Carefully coached by O'Reilly, speaking for the most part through translators, they explained themselves to the urban world which many of them had never before visited. They talked about fishing, hunting and trapping, about their reverence for the land, about their reliance upon it for what they call country food: for bear, beaver, caribou, moose, rabbit, seal, and whale; for geese and ptarmigan; for Arctic char, pike, salmon, sturgeon, trout, walleye, and whitefish.[37]

The defendants named in the action—Hydro-Quebec, the James Bay Development Corporation, and the James Bay Energy Corporation—"could not find a scientist in Canada to testify on their behalf and were astounded by the 'emotional fervour' of the opponents of the project." In the end, they were reduced to countering that

- the Indians and Inuits had "no right" to oppose destruction of their cultures by the dams because their cultures would "inevitably" be destroyed anyway;

- the threat to both people and environment was being greatly overstated because the initial phases of the project would flood "only" three percent of the affected portion of the province; and

- halting the project would be "inconvenient" to the

non-native majority of Quebec's population.[38]

The court was plainly unconvinced by such arguments.

In November 1973, Superior Court Judge Albert Malouf—who had spent the summer and fall crafting his opinion—ruled in favor of the plaintiffs, holding in effect that Bechtel and other developers were trespassing on native land. He then ordered all construction be halted until a hearing on a permanent injunction could be held.[39] A week later, the Quebec Court of Appeals overturned Malouf's decision, not on the basis of law, but because, it said, the interests of the "greater society" compelled it to do so. The appeals court, however, stipulated that the Crees and Inuits held a right to sue for damages, a circumstance which contained the prospect of dramatically increasing the costs of doing developmental business in the James Bay area.[40]

> Fearing a legal impasse, which in turn might give investors in the hydroelectric project cold feet, Bourassa had to settle with the Natives. He offered a treaty, the terms of which included, among other things, payment of $100 million. In March 1974, Cree hunting families were flown out of bush camps to vote on this offer. They rejected it. "The Indian lands are not for sale, not for millions and millions of dollars," said Billy Diamond.[41]

Ottawa then entered the fray, funding an entity called the "Grand Council of the Crees of Quebec," composed largely of representatives deemed acceptable to the government; Billy Diamond himself was coopted into becoming "Grand Chief."[42] A comparable group, the Northern Inuit Association of Quebec, headed by Charlie Watts, was created to "represent" that people.[43] The purpose was to negotiate an out-of-court settlement of some sort which would clear the way for a project completion unhampered by extensive litigation or other "obstructionist" acts by the natives. After eight months of intensive negotiation, what was called the "James Bay and Northern Quebec Agreement"—opposed by the bulk of grassroots Crees and Inuits—was signed in November 1975.[44]

> The Agreement divided just over one million square kilometers of land—not just the James Bay territory, but all of Quebec north of the 49th parallel, that is, two-thirds of the whole province—into three categories. About one percent of the land, in blocks around villages, is essentially Native-owned. The only resource of interest in this land is wildlife; before the Natives could select land in this category, the provincial government subtracted those areas with known hydroelectric or mineral potential, as well as land it would need for roads and power lines. About 14 percent is shared land; only Natives can hunt, trap, and fish here, but Quebec can develop mines, hydroelectric projects, and the like. The remaining 85 percent of the land is public, though certain species of wildlife are reserved for the Natives.[45]

Indian control over schools, health and social services and other government-funded programs was conceded, and members of the Cree Grand Council and Northern Inuit Association were placed on a range of environmental oversight boards. In addition, the Cree communities were awarded a total of $135 million, to be paid over twenty years as compensation; Inuit communities were awarded $90 million. A minimum annual income was guaranteed to the hunters of both groups, and additional funds were committed to underwrite the relocation of any village or band forced to relocate because of flooding or other factors. Altogether, the package came to some $500 million in payments and guarantees. In exchange, the native people had only to formally relinquish aboriginal rights to their homeland and, for the first time, accept ultimate federal and provincial authority over their affairs.[46]

The government could well afford its "generosity" in

the deal. In attaining native sanction—or an appearance of it—for its consolidation of power over indigenous territory, Canada and Quebec had finally placed themselves in a lawful position to renege on any portion of the agreement. All that was juridically required was that one or the other resort to such "domestic" or "internal" expedients as the exercise of "emminent domain" over native property.[47] Meanwhile, construction was proceeding full-tilt at not one, but *four* sites along the La Grande. At its peak, during 1978-79, the project employed more than 22,000 workers working nearly round-the-clock. By the time it was completed in 1984, it had cost approximately $20 billion, fifteen times the per capita expenditure of U.S. citizens in sending the Apollo space craft to the moon, more than three times what the Bourassa administration had originally predicted.[48] The La Grande, third largest river in Quebec, as well as two of its main tributaries—the Eastmain and the Caniapiscau—had been effectively "killed," transformed from free-flowing currents into a series of stagnant lakes and ponds incapable of supporting most life forms.[49]

Ironically, the huge cost overruns associated with James Bay I were in part responsible for Bourassa's defeat in the 1976 provincial election, and Lévesque's ascent to power (heading the Parti Québécois), just as the project began to show a return.[50] In 1978, Hydro-Quebec completed its first interconnection with the New York Power Authority and, by October 1979, was exporting electricity equivalent to burning 150,000 barrels of oil per day. By 1985, with James Bay I complete, the utility's aggregate production had outstripped total provincial usage even during the peak mid-winter months of consumption by at least 7,000 kilowatts.[51] With the grid capacity available to export much more than was needed by its U.S. customer, Hydro-Quebec began aggressively pursuing the development of electrically-intensive—and environmentally devastating—industries such as aluminum refining in the southern portion of the province itself.

> Electrical charges strong enough to erase credit cards, stop digital watches, or pull a wrench from your hands are what separate pure aluminum from its ore. An aluminum smelter uses as much power as a small city. So much electricity is used in making it that aluminum can be thought of as congealed electricity; the multinational firms who produce aluminum build their billion dollar smelters not where the ore is mined, but where they can be assured of getting abundant, cheap electricity. Hydro-Quebec offered rates low enough to induce several of these firms, notably Reynolds and Péchiney, to build or expand smelters in the Saint Lawrence Valley, and to induce other firms to build a magnesium smelter, and pulp and paper mills. All these plants use enormous quantities of electricity and, since their products are mainly exported, they are, in effect, exporting Quebec's electricity.[52]

Even as this was occurring, however, the grid "problem" of weak demand was being resolved. In March of 1982, Hydro-Quebec had entered into another long-term contract to provide greatly increased power to the New York Power Authority and, in 1984, the conduit was completed through which to fulfill its commitment. In 1983, the utility also signed the first of a two-part package with the New England Power Pool, an arrangement which committed it to providing a direct line to New Hampshire. The second part of the agreement, signed in 1985, called for erecting a 2,500 kilometer line, directly from the La Grande 2 generating facility to a point just outside Boston. A separate deal was negotiated in 1984 through which Hydro-Quebec would supply year-round power to Vermont.[53] By the early 1990s, James Bay was supplying approximately ten percent of the electricity consumed in the northeastern United States.[54]

None of this, of course, was sufficient to offset the huge debt incurred in the process of constructing James

Bay I, never mind render it profitable for the taxpayers who, in the final analysis, were its real investors.[55] On the other hand, it "proved the viability" of projects on the scale conceived by Bourassa and his colleagues, and appealed to the nationalist sensibilities of the Québécois, who reveled in the idea—pushed hard by provincial and utility propagandists alike—that by becoming the "sole provider" of a "crucial commodity" to Canada's powerful southerly neighbor, they had accomplished something "independent" of the Anglocentric government in Ottawa, on behalf of French-speaking culture.[56]

As Anishinabe activist Winona LaDuke, who spent several years at James Bay, puts it:

> These things take on a life of their own. Once you've gone in debt to start one, the only way to stay abreast of the debt service is to go even further in debt, borrowing more and more so you can build more and more and more, no matter what the consequences to land and people. You lose control of your destiny. In this sense, Canada is no different than most Third World countries. It owes its soul to U.S. corporate and financial élites, and so it must sacrifice everything it has, everything it is or claims to be, to satisfying the demands of those elites. For the power structure of Canada, especially in Quebec, there is no longer a way out of the trap it laid for itself thirty years ago. Canada is now little more than a U.S. satellite, an energy colony.[57]

Hence, even before James Bay I was finished, the groundwork was laid for undertaking James Bay II, a far more ambitious (and therefore destructive) project.

James Bay II and the Consolidation of Resistance

In 1983, Robert Bourassa and the Liberals returned to power in Quebec, bringing with him a plan to generate 12,000 megawatts of power to the northeastern U.S. by the turn of the century.[58] To this end, he almost immediately oversaw a revision of provincial legal codes in such a way that restrictions limiting sales of electricity to short-term contracts were eliminated. This allowed negotiation of contracts for "firm" provision of large blocks of hydroelectric current over periods ranging from fifteen to thirty years rather than the one to five year packages previously offered. As a result, by early 1988, Hydro-Quebec had signed agreements with Central Maine Power and Vermont Joint Owners, a utilities consortium in that state. A year later, the largest export contract ever—a deal to sell another thousand megawatts to the New York Power Authority every year for 21 years—was finalized.[59] Bourassa announced at about the same time that, in order to meet the requirements of these new contracts, as well as to accommodate burgeoning industrialization in the Saint Lawrence Valley, Quebec would need to possess a generating capacity of some 12,000 megawatts by 1998.[60] The amount was nearly triple the total Hydro-Quebec could muster with James Bay I and other projects, even considering its portion of Labrador's generation at Churchill Falls.

To acquire the necessary generating capacity, Bourassa stated, it would be necessary to move forward with a new three-stage project which made James Bay I seem tiny by comparison. The first stage, to begin immediately, was to construct two additional generating facilities in the existing La Grande River Complex. The second stage, to begin in 1991, would be to build a new complex involving five major dams along the Great Whale River—or Grande riviére de la Baleine, as it is called in French—about 160 kilometers north of the La Grande; another 4,400 square kilometers would be flooded at a projected construction cost of $12.6 billion. The third stage, by far the most extravagant, was set to begin not later than 1993. It was a return to the original concept of diverting the Nottaway and Rupert Rivers into the Broadback through construction of at least eleven major dams. No predictions were offered as to how much territory would be flooded in this, but construction costs were projected at $44 billion.[61] Together, the three complexes which would be in place when James Bay II was complete would effect a "replumbing" of virtually all of northern Quebec (see map).

For funding, Bourassa had already returned to New York in 1985, meeting with John Dyson, former president of the New York Power Authority, and James Schlesinger, U.S. Energy Secretary under Jimmy Carter and at the same time a vice president in the Lehman Brothers investment banking firm. The latter, in exchange for a 1.7 percent commission, organized the underwriting by an array of U.S. investment firms of an estimated $50 billion in bond issues over ten years in order to guarantee Hydro-Quebec's "solvency" during construction of the megaproject.[62] In 1989, Bourassa informed his public of these astronomical figures through resort to the usual nostrums of "progress": such expenditures would, he claimed, create 40,000 new jobs for Québécois, and "generate $40 billion in annual revenues by the year 2000."[63] By then, however, both the degree of error embodied in the government's earlier cost, profit and employment estimates, and the actual environmental and cultural consequences of James Bay I, were becoming well known.[64]

The environmental portrait is indeed bleak, the La Grande Complex having ultimately inundated about 12,000 square kilometers of forest land, including some 83,000 linear kilometers of shoreline.[65] As at Bennett Dam, "the rims of [the La Grande] reservoirs do not, and can not, replace any of the lost wetland habitat; they are broad, lifeless banks of mud, rock and dead trees."[66] In substance, the populations of aquatic mammals along the La Grande, Eastmain and Caniapiscau—beaver, muskrat, snowshoe hare, mink and otter, among others, all of which had still been abundant during the mid-70s—had been exterminated.[67] Submerged wood and floating de-

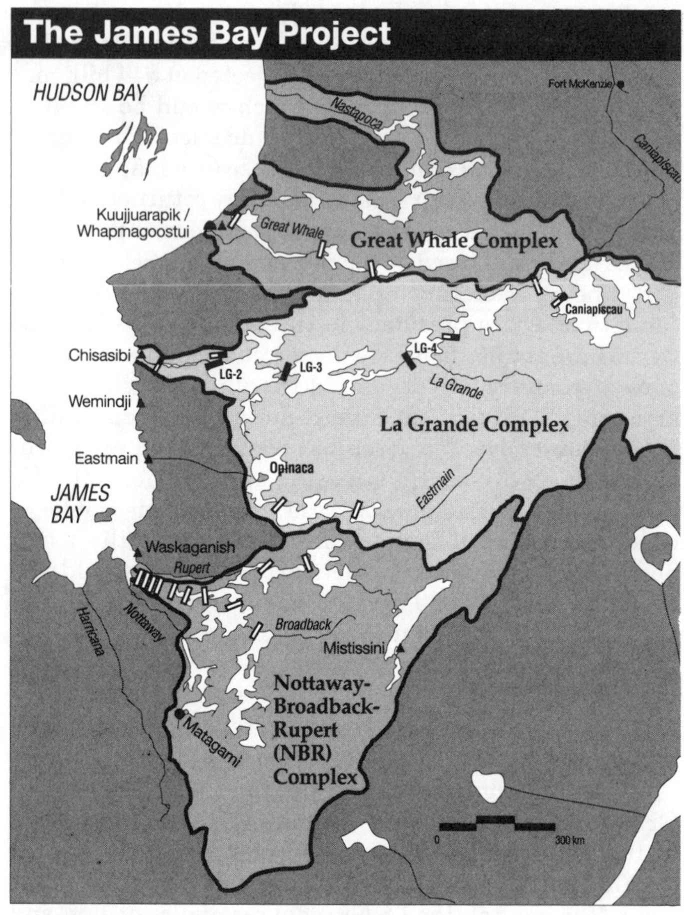

Sean McCutheon, *Electric Rivers.*

bris, as well as silt, have destroyed the water's capacity to oxygenate and have clogged spawning grounds, decimating most varieties of fish.[68]

> Millions of plants—mainly the pioneering, colonizing species, jack pine, willow and alder—have been planted

in an effort to reforest zones stripped by construction, as well as to reduce erosion on sections of the banks of desiccated rivers. This has been done, however, in only a fraction of damaged areas, those along the most well-used roads and around the most-visited installations. It will take a long time before the scattered plants reseed the barren spaces between them."[69]

Many Crees assert unequivocally that the damage has been terrible, much worse than anything they were led to expect: "there are fewer and fewer ducks and geese each year; the climate is changing; animals are confused because their migrations routes have been disrupted."[70] This last claim was amply borne out by a spectacular instance in late September 1984, when an estimated 10,000 caribou drowned during a single attempt by a large herd to cross the newly-transformed Caniapiscau.[71]

Among the people themselves, the permanent neurological damage caused by eating mercury-contaminated fish has become a substantial problem.[72] Fear of this, along with a steady diminution in available game animals, has led to a marked alteration in diet, an increase in the sugars and starches indicative of "civilized" consumption. Compounded by the increasingly sedentary way of life imposed upon them by the disappearance of traplines, and decreases in the hunting and fishing, all of which kept them physically active, these changes have led to a sudden appearance of diabetes, heart disease and obesity, maladies unknown in Cree communities until the 1980s. As traditional life has quickly disintegrated along the La Grande, social decay has come to be manifested in spiraling rates of alcoholism, glue sniffing among young people, and other forms of substance abuse. Concomitantly, domestic violence, child abandonment, and suicide—all virtually unheard of among the Crees until recently—have made their ugly appearance.[73] Like the habitat itself, the indigenous society impacted by James Bay I is plainly dying. Moreover, the sort of native participation in environmental oversight guaranteed in the James Bay and Northern Quebec Agreement of 1975, participation which might be used to alter favorably such an outcome, has proven illusory.

> Native leaders complain that they have not been able to exercise any significant control over decisions affecting their region. The mechanisms, such as joint committees, which were to give them power to participate actively in economic development of their land—not just as beneficiaries, but as controllers—do not work. For instance, the Crees have not been able to stop the loggers who, with Quebec's permission, are now clear-cutting most of the harvestable timber in the southern portion of the Cree homeland (including lands which Hydro-Quebec hopes to flood in the Nottaway-Broadback-Rupert complex).[74]

Under these conditions, Cree opposition to James Bay II was instantaneous and far more profound than was the case with the James Bay I proposals of the early '70s. In 1987, they decided to put the Grand Council, originally designed by the government to serve as a vehicle of cooptation, to work in forging a unified resistance to what was planned along the Great Whale, and in the "tri-river" area.[75] A young Mistissini named Matthew Coon-Come was elected to head this effort, and even Billy Diamond resumed his "radical" stance long enough to describe the agreement he himself had signed a dozen years earlier as "a trail of broken promises."[76] The bulk of the Inuits north of the project zone also renounced representation by the Quebec Inuit Association and the "leadership" of Charlie Watts—by then a member of the Canadian Senate and known as "Megawatts" by his ostensible constituents—and joined the Crees in opposing all further construction.[77] Both peoples flatly refused to negotiate with Hydro-Quebec about James Bay II, despite a $1 billion offer tabled by the utility in 1989, if they would endorse an updated version of the 1975 "understanding."[78]

This time they were not alone, reflecting increased

sophistication on the part of Coon-Come and others in the ways of attracting non-Indian support in both Canada and the U.S., as well as heightened sensitivity among many non-Indians with regard to native and environmental issues. In Montreal, long-time environmental activist Hélène Lajambe and Gordon Edwards, head of the Canadian Coalition for Nuclear Responsibility, utilized the 1989 conference of the Canadian Greens to establish what may have been the first anti-James Bay II organization outside of Indian Country.[79] This was soon followed by demands for a moratorium on construction by the Coalition for Public Debate on Energy, an organization in the City of Quebec claiming membership of one-sixth of the provincial population. The Arctic Resources Committee and Cultural Survival (Canada), both based in Ottawa, joined in, as did a new entity in Quebec, Prudent Residents Opposed To Electrical Cable Transmission (PROTECT).[80] Things developed similarly south of the border:

> In Vermont, for example, Jim Higgins, a social worker who has canoed in the James Bay area, helped found the New England Energy Efficiency Coalition. In New York City, Jeff Wollack of the Solidarity Foundation—which puts royalties earned by the Irish rock group U2 to work in defense of Native peoples—helped found the James Bay Defense Coalition, which comprises some twenty organizations, and began lobbying to cancel the New York Power Authority contracts. Major international environmental organizations became involved. In July 1989 the New York-based National Audubon Society publicized, in Quebec, its concerns that water resource developments would harm the large numbers of migratory birds that use the James Bay coast, and called for full, public environmental hearings. The Sierra Club created an umbrella organization, the James Bay and Northern Quebec Task Force [Mouvement au Courant], and channeled funds through a think-tank founded by Hélène Lajambe, the Centre d'analyse des politiques énergétiques, to establish an office in Montreal. The large

organizations have not swallowed up the grassroots movement. There are at least 30 anti-James Bay II groups on college campuses throughout New York State, and more elsewhere in the Northeast.[81]

The building of such a serious, multiethnic and multinational opposition movement had an almost immediate effect. In January 1989, a group calling itself No Thank Q Hydro-Quebec was successful in convincing the Maine Public Utilities Commission to deny approval of the Central Maine Power contract.[82] In New York, the Sierra Club, PROTECT, the Cree Grand Council and other groups joined in a suit against the New York Power Authority, arguing that it is required to insure that all electricity it imports is generated under conditions conforming to the state's own environmental protection standards. Although the legal action was unsuccessful, it was helpful in bringing pressure to bear on Governor Mario Cuomo and New York City Mayor David Dinkins. Consequently, in June of 1991, the state announced it was delaying ratification of its 1,000 megawatt contract with Hydro-Quebec for one year while the environmental implications of James Bay II were studied by New York's own experts.[83] In Vermont, the most recalcitrant of New England states, opponents also scored a partial victory in October; the state utilities board voted to approve 340 of the 450 megawatts called for in the Vermont Joint Owners contract with Hydro-Quebec, but only if the latter could guarantee that none of the electricity imported was generated at James Bay II facilities.[84]

Under these circumstances, Bourassa had little alternative but to postpone the beginning of construction for a year, until the summer of 1992. In April of that year, however, New York canceled its major contract altogether, and announced it was reviewing its previous arrangements with Hydro-Quebec as well. Left seriously in the lurch—the province was already guaranteeing $30 billion in long-term debt for its utility, which needed another $500 million in short-term funds to stay solvent—Bourassa was forced to announce a second year's postponement.[85] Meanwhile, public opinion polls showed that Québécois support for further development had plummeted for the first time.[86] Coon-Come and other Cree leaders reinforced this decline in civic morale by stating that they would meet any attempt to get building underway with physical resistance; the credibility of their warning was dramatically underscored by a confrontation between armed Mohawks, provincial police and the Canadian army at the town of Oka, near Montreal, in 1990.[87]

In April 1990, responding to rumblings from Bourassa energy minister Lise Bacon concerning use of the power of emminent domain to force the issue, O'Reilly and other attorneys for the Crees filed suit in Queen's Court challenging the provision of the James Bay and Northern Quebec Agreement whereby their clients allegedly relinquished aboriginal rights to their land, both north and south of the La Grande. After much governmental maneuvering, including repeated motions by Quebec that the case be dismissed, it was finally docketed for April 1992 and is in process as of this writing.[88] If the suit is successful, the province will be truly stymied, lacking so much as a pretense for the legal basis needed to undertake construction without indigenous consent.

Even as these actions were unfolding, in June 1991 Crees prevented an Inuit delegation aligned with Charlie Watts from leaving the Great Whale Airport to participate in a provincially-sponsored environmental impact hearing intended to secure some measure of native "ratification" for the James Bay II plan. Instead, the Grand Council filed another suit in Queen's Court, this one to compel implementation of the federal review process stipulated in the 1975 Agreement. The Court upheld the Crees' position in August and, although Quebec filed an appeal, it seems likely that federal oversight hearings will again be ordered, a process which could take as long as two years once it begins.[89] And, all the while, the clock keeps ticking on the massive loans Quebec has piled up against "future development." A default, or even the appearance of one, could well prove sufficient to topple Bourassa's sagging regime, and to stay hydroelectric projects in northern Quebec for decades to come.[90]

Other Water Diversion Schemes

Despite the prospect that a major victory may be in the offing against the Water Plot in northern Quebec, the balance of Canada remains in many ways up for grabs. This is readily evidenced by the damming of the Saint John River in New Brunswick, despite serious and sustained "protests by local residents that the benefits of this 'development' were vastly overrated, and that irreparable environmental damage was being done."[91] There are other illustrations, but the extent of the situation is best revealed in an official document of the Ottawa government, *Water Diversion Proposals of North America.*[92] Summarized are eight major schemes—the James Bay Projects account for only two—in which Canada's water and/or hydroelectricity are to be exported to the United States. The most grandiose of these, the Great Recycling and Northern Development (GRAND) Project and the North American Water and Power Alliance (NAWAPA) would, combined, turn literally the whole of the Subarctic west of Quebec into a single, interconnected "plumbing system."

The purpose of this would be primarily to provide truly gargantuan quantities of fresh water to the arid and semi-arid western plains and southwestern desert regions of the U.S. (and probably areas as far south as northern Mexico, given George Bush's recent "free trade" agreement to create agribusiness zones in the upper regions of Sonora and Chihuahua). Secondarily, planners suggest "adjustment" of water levels in the Great Lakes system (as a means of flushing industrial pollutants into the Atlantic Ocean), hydroelectric generation (as much as six times that which would be yielded by James Bay I and II combined), and provision of emergency water during droughts to the U.S. midwestern corn and industrial belts. Each of these gigantic projects is worthy of being examined in turn.

The GRAND Project

The GRAND Project, concentrated in northern Ontario, calls for construction of some 160 kilometers of dikes across James Bay to create a fresh water reservoir the size of Lake Superior. The water would be drawn off through the major rivers west of the bay—the Moose, Ogoki, Albany, Kenogami, Ramskau, Attawapiskat, and Skwaw—each of which would be extensively dammed in order to control water flow and afford a "fringe benefit" of allowing hydroelectric generation. To the north, along Ontario's portion of Hudson Bay's western shore, a comparable damming of major rivers—the Winisk, Severn, Sachigo, and Duck—would occur. Canals would join the northern complex to the northern portion of its southern counterpart by traversing the distance between Trout Lake and the Attawapiskat. From there, the joint flow would be diverted into Lake Nipigon and thence into Lake Superior. The lower portion of the southern complex would see water flow merged with the Aquasaubon River, emptying into Lake Superior.

The scope of the hydrological (re)engineering involved encompasses *all* of northern Ontario (see map). A minimum of 50 major dams, including at least three "megadams," are called for to make the scheme work. More than 250 kilometers of lined canal will be needed, not to mention thousands of kilometers of all-weather road, airports, housing for as many as 100,000 workers,

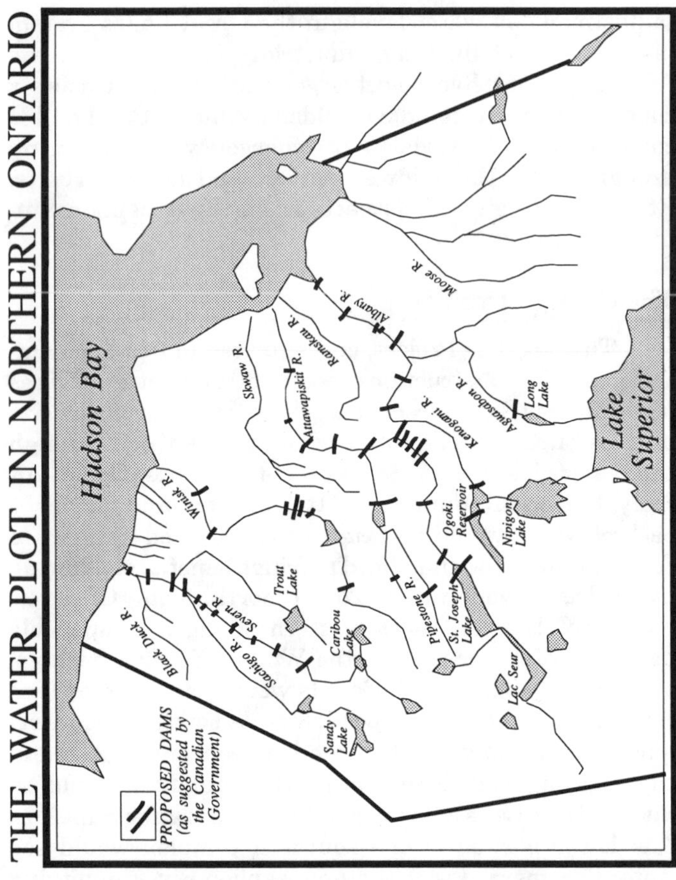

scores of pumping facilities, hydroelectric plants, and so on. No cost estimates of what would be required to complete the GRAND Project have been released, but a conservative estimate might be twice the aggregate expenditure calculated for both James Bay Projects, or about $150 billion. Moreover, little has been said with regard to what the environmental consequences of such an extravagant rearrangement of the natural order might

be. Where James Bay I destroyed the ecology of an area approximately the size of West Germany, the GRAND Project would flood about three times as much territory (at a minimum). The implications for the area's indigenous Anishinabe, Waswanipi Cree and Inuit populations are stark.[93]

The GRAND concept is not new. To the contrary, its origins may be discovered in some of the earliest large-scale water projects in Canada.

> North of Lake Superior, two diversions from the James Bay watershed into the Great Lakes were carried out during World War II. The headwaters of the Ogoki River were converted into a lake and now flow into Ombabika Bay on Lake Nipigon. The Long Lake watershed, which formerly drained north via the Kenogami River, was diverted into Lake Superior through the Aquasaubon River at Terrace Bay. The Ogoki diversion was implemented in 1940 to permit Ontario Hydro to increase the capacity of its Niagara River generating plants to meet Canadian wartime demand. The purpose of the Long Lake diversion was to supply power to the U.S.-owned Kimberly-Clark paper mill at Terrace Bay. At the time of these diversions, the U.S. was not yet at war and refused to reduce the quantity of hydro power Ottawa had committed to supply, or to allow Canada to withdraw more than its prewar "share" of Niagara River water.[94]

Serious planning for realization of something along the lines of the present GRAND Project can be traced back at least to October 1965, when "the Prime Minister of Canada and the Premier of Ontario announced that the governments of Canada and Ontario had agreed to undertake a series of coordinated studies on Ontario's northern water resources and related economic developments. Most of the work is being done in five river basins draining to Hudson Bay and James Bay. These are the Severn, Winisk, Attawapiskat, Albany and Moose River Basins."[95]

The Coordinating Committee prepared a statement of

objectives for the studies to be carried out by agencies of the two governments as follows: "with respect to waters draining into James Bay and Hudson Bay in Ontario, to assess the quantity and quality of water resources for all purposes; to determine present and future requirements for such waters; and to assess alternative possibilities for utilization of such waters locally or elsewhere through diversion.[96]

Thereafter, the "Federal Surveys and Mapping Branch...completed preliminary mapping of a possible diversion route between the Attawapiskat and Albany Rivers...A potential diversion route between Winisk Lake and the Attawapiskat River were [*sic*] also mapped by the [Engineering] Division."[97] And, in the process:

> Approximately four miles of leveling was carried out south of the Pipestone River to the north boundary of the Ogoki River and interconnecting structure sites along the Aguta glacial moraine. These sites were investigated in 1967 in connection with an engineering study of a scheme for using the Aguta Moraine as a diversion barrier. A topographic survey by the transit-stadia method was completed for a dam site on the Ogoki River at Whiteclay Lake to investigate the feasibility of providing additional storage required to regulate increased diversion flow to the Great Lakes. In addition, work described below was carried out in connection with engineering feasibility studies of power development on the Albany River from streams further north.[98]

Federal and provincial agencies, and private consulting engineering firms known to be actively involved in the Ontario development project are known to include Canada's Department of Mines, Energy and Resources (Inland Waters Branch); Canada's Department of Transport (Meteorology Branch); Water Survey of Canada (Federal Surveys and Mapping Branch); Federal Engineering Division; Ontario Water Resources Commission (Division of Water Resources, Hydrologic Branch, and Surveys and

Projects Branch); Ontario Department of Economics (Applied Economics Branch); Ontario Department of the Treasury (Economic Planning Branch); Ontario Department of Lands and Forests; Ontario Department of Mines; Ontario Hydro-Electric Power Commission; Gibb, Underwood and McClellan (a U.S. engineering firm); James F. McLaren (a U.S. engineer); J.D. Mollard (a Regina engineer); and Ripley, Klohn and Leonoff (a Winnipeg engineering firm).[99] The U.S. Army Corps of Engineers has also been directly involved at least once, conducting an "ice survey" during the period 1967-69.[100]

These agencies, particularly the branches of the Water Resources Commission and Energy, Mines and Resources Department, have steadily collected data on stream flow, snow-course, rainfall, water levels, chemical analyses of water, bathymetric contours of lakes and geological mapping. They have also conducted considerable core inspection and hydraulic testing of bore holes drilled along the Albany River, have levelled large areas, and have conducted feasibility studies of alternative diversion routes to those mentioned in the government documents quoted above, and have even gone to the lengths of making anthropological/sociological studies of the likely effects of development upon the region's native peoples.[101] The initial field work in Ontario appears to have begun in 1966, and to have accelerated steadily after 1969. At present, it looks as if the preliminary work has been accomplished, and that only the right public climate is necessary to put a program entailing full-scale actualization of the GRAND Project into motion.

NAWAPA

NAWAPA, once described by *Newsweek* magazine as "the greatest, most colossal, stupendous, supersplendificent public works project in history,"[102] was conceived by the Ralph M. Parsons engineering firm during the 1960s "to divert 36 trillion gallons of water [per year] from the Yukon River in Alaska [through the Great Bear and Great Slave Lakes southward] to thirty-three states, several Canadian provinces, the United States, and northern Mexico."[103] Under its provisions, the Yukon River, Rocky Mountain Trench, Peace River, Great Bear, Great Slave and Lesser Slave Lakes, Athabasca River, North Saskatchewan River, Fraser River, Nelson River, Qu'Appelle River, Columbia River and Lake Winnipeg, as well as many tributaries, would all be tied together. From Lake Winnipeg, a portion of the proceeds would be channeled into the western end of Lake Superior, the remainder into the dry zone of the U.S. west of the Mississippi River (see map).

As with the GRAND Project, there are signs that motions are being made toward fulfillment of the NAWAPA "vision." NAWAPA takes as its focus the western provinces of British Columbia, Saskatchewan, Alberta, Manitoba, the Yukon and the Northwest Territories. Beginning in British Columbia, where horror stories concerning the effects of the Bennett Dam and its attendant ninety Columbia River Treaty are well known, a Canadian Broadcasting Corporation (CBC) television program aired on the night of January 18, 1972 revealed plans to dam the Fraser River.[104] Nothing further was heard on the matter, and it was all but forgotten. This was a mistake.

> A second dam, completed at Moran Canyon on the Fraser River in 1976, backed up water into a 170 mile "lake." Since then, another score of dams have been built along the Columbia River, and twenty-five more along the Fraser. Another thirteen have been built along the Thompson River, and as many as thirty more are either in progress or planned in the immediate future.[105]

To the east, in the Prairie Provinces, the *Winnipeg Free Press* has reported that Manitoba Hydro intends to

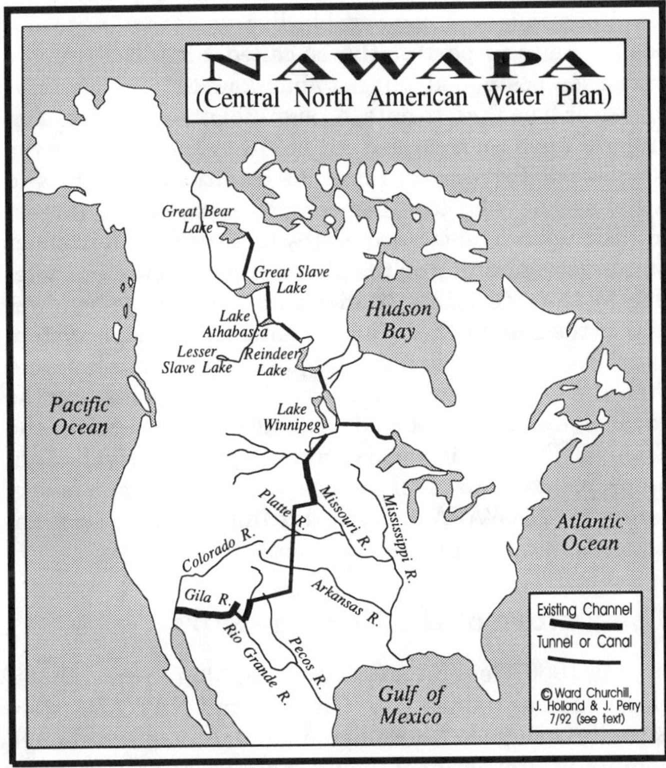

regulate water levels in Lake Winnipeg as part of its Nelson River power development project, before going ahead with a planned diversion of South Indian Lake. According to [CBC] filmmaker Dick Bocking, some water will be diverted directly to the U.S., and the Kettle Lake Dam and South Indian Lake hydro plant will, in combination, produce far more electricity than can possibly be used by Winnipeg. Barring installation of environmentally devastating industries such as the aluminum smelters installed in Quebec—and no such plans have been announced—the excess hydroelectric output is plainly slated for export southward. Because of the expense of the Manitoba endeavor, comparable diversions in Alberta and Saskatchewan—part of the so-called PRIME Project—have been postponed, but not abandoned.[106]

It is true that, to date, no significant water diversion projects have been carried out in either the Yukon or the Northwest Territories, home to traditional Inuits and Athabascans who together comprise one of the largest traditional indigenous groups (by territory, if not in sheer numbers) remaining on the planet. It is nonetheless noteworthy that feasibility studies on damming the headwaters of the Yukon River, and assembly of a canal system which would carry its fluids into first the Great Slave and then the Great Bear Lakes, *have* been conducted by the government and assorted contractors.[107] As with the GRAND Project, it seems that only the arrival of an "appropriate climate" of public opinion in Canada is necessary for NAWAPA to begin this final phase of its transition from drawing board to reality.

The Future of the North is Ours

In 1966, General A.G.L. McNaughton warned that if plans such as James Bay, GRAND and NAWAPA were actually effected, "Jurisdiction and control...although nominally international, would in reality be dominated by [the U.S., which] would thereby acquire a formidable vested interest in the national waters of Canada. It is obvious that if we make a bargain to divert water to the United States, we cannot ever discontinue or we shall face force to compel compliance." The general therefore concluded that ideas like those underlying each of the megaprojects represented "a monstrous concept, a diabolical thesis."[108]

Indeed, even without use of its military power, the U.S. has proven itself increasingly able to impose its will upon Canada as water diversion has increased since 1970.

As has been noted, Quebec has been forced to saddle itself with an astronomical debt load, much of it secretively assumed and virtually all of it held by Wall Street firms, since beginning its pursuit of "economic independence" at James Bay. This, in turn, has compelled provincial authorities such as Robert Bourassa to solicit an influx of "productive facilities" on terms favorable to the foreign corporations holding the reins, rather than to Canada; "by such deals, Quebec is locking itself into an almost third-world condition as a supplier of subsidized energy to an enormous, global, extractive industry."[109]

During the same year that General McNaughton issued his warning, the Parsons Company of Los Angeles, author of the NAWAPA plan, said that Canada would need to invest a minimum of $40 billion as "its part" in funding the project. It was noted that it would be necessary to borrow virtually all of this sum in the U.S. at a nominal interest rate of 8 percent, or $3.2 billion per year in debt service. The latter figure should be compared to the $4 billion per year Parsons estimated Canada might realize from export of hydroelectricity if NAWAPA were completed.[110] And, of course, inflation and other factors have conspired to drive the figure up by at least 400 percent over the subsequent quarter-century; the minimum price tag which could now be associated with just the "Canadian portion" of NAWAPA is somewhere around $160 billion, with annual debt service of about $14 billion.

Together—between James Bay II, the GRAND Project and NAWAPA—an array of "development interests" are moving along with plans which would encumber the Canadian public with about a third of a *trillion* dollars in debt, nearly $30 billion yearly in interest alone. This, in the context of a seriously deteriorating world economy and with the bulk of the profits flowing, one way or the other, to points south of the U.S./Canadian border. Yet both Ottawa and the provincial regimes appear to be proceeding full speed ahead, despite a range of consequences which should long since have become obvious to anyone who cared to examine the matter. History has yet to offer a single instance in which the patterns of debt assumption and external investment which have emerged in Canada turned out to have benefited the "host" country, either economically or in terms of sociopolitical self-determination.[111]

Environmentally, the prospects are even worse. Jan Beyea of the Audubon Society has compared James Bay to the Brazilian rainforest in terms of its importance to ecological equilibrium of the world, placing the James Bay II Project in a perspective never hinted at by developers.[112] Further:

> Quebec is not alone in disturbing this maritime ecosystem. Manitoba and Ontario, the provinces which share the western coasts of James Bay and Hudson Bay, are planning hydroelectric projects which will amplify the impacts of James Bay II. When the dams are built, far more fresh water will flow into James Bay in the winter than it did before, and far less in the spring. How will this affect the algae that grow under ice in the winter and bloom in the spring, and that form one of the bottom layers of a food pyramid whose upper layers include birds, seals, beluga [whales], and humans? How will the changes in salinity affect the dense beds of eelgrass on which the Brant geese feed, and which seem to require brackish conditions to flourish? Can the food-producing processes in this linked system or marshes, each with its own mix of plants and its own pattern of varying salinity over the year, adapt to alterations in the seasonal rhythm with which rivers have been pouring fresh water into salt water ever since the last Ice Age? How will the mercury injected into this ecosystem affect its creatures? Will ocean currents carry repercussions of disruptions in James Bay to Hudson Strait, the channel connecting Hudson Bay to the Atlantic, one of the most productive areas of the Arctic; will effects be felt to the south, on the Grand Banks of Newfoundland?[113]

And what of the ecologies of the river basins and intervening territory across the entire Subarctic expanse of northern Canada? Shall they all go the way of the La Grande? If so, then what? As the matter has been framed elsewhere, "What must be understood is that the Canadian North—like the Antarctic, the Amazon Basin in Brazil, and a few other portions of the globe—is absolutely essential to ecological survival. If it is destroyed, eventually everything else will be destroyed. We are all running out of 'alternatives' and places to hide from the grim reality which now stalks us, regardless of where and how we live."[114] In a very real sense, then, "The Crees [and other native peoples resisting the Water Plot] are not just defending their own cultures and environment; both in [Canada] and in the United States they and their advisers are challenging current energy and economic policies, and are proposing alternatives."[115]

In effect, by struggling to defend themselves against the ravages of genocide and ecocide, the indigenous peoples of the northlands have taken a position which could ultimately save their neighboring colonizers from themselves being colonized by a more powerful neighbor. In doing so, they have taken the sole position which stands to save the vital Subarctic ecosystem for all humanity. Theirs is thus a truly human position, perhaps the *only* genuinely human position to have emerged from the whole context of controversy and contention surrounding the Water Plot, and others are slowly but steadily waking up to the fact.

Non-Indians are at last discovering the truth that Indians have known, insights about the relationship of humans and nature that native people have been trying to share all along.[116] This is why the Crees and others have "gained many supporters, on both sides of the border" and around the world. The fundamental difference between the current dispute and that of twenty years ago is the extent to which thoughts and feelings that were dismissed a generation ago as the motley notions of counterculture cranks are now credible. Environmental concerns have moved from the margin towards the mainstream of politics. So, too, has sympathy with Native peoples."[117] In this new and evolving confluence of interest and understanding between Indian and non-Indian lie the seeds, not only of the demise of the Water Plot itself, but of many comparable enterprises underway in this "post-modern" age.

Herein, perhaps, lies the silver lining to the Water Plot's menacing cloud: in catalyzing an apprehension of the natural order antithetical to its own existence, it may well transcend itself, laying the groundwork for a universal negation of the beliefs, attitudes and outlooks which ushered it into being in the first place. If so, it will have turned out to be a blessing rather than a curse, the cornerstone of a sustainable and radically better future not only for ourselves, but for all who come after us.

Notes

1. This is not to say that everything is "okay" in the U.S. For a succinct treatment of the relevant issues in the "Lower 48," see Marianna Guerrero, "American Indian Water Rights: The Life Blood of Native North America," in M. Annette James, ed., *The State of Native America: Genocide, Colonization, and Resistance* (Boston: South End Press, 1992, pp. 189-216).
2. See, for example, Adrian Tanner, *Bringing Home Animals: Religious Ideology and Mode of Production Among Mistissini Cree Hunters* (Memorial University of Newfoundland: Institute of Social and Economic Research, No. 23, 1979).
3. This is brought out clearly in Morris Zaslow, *The Northward Expansion of Canada, 1914-1967* (Toronto: McClelland and Stewart Publishers, 1988).
4. See James VanStone, "Changing Patterns of Indian Trapping in the Canadian Subarctic," in William C. Wonders, ed., *Canada's Changing North* (Toronto: McClelland and Stewart Publishers, 1976, pp. 170-86). Also see A.M.A. Shkilnyk, *A Poison Stronger than Love: The Destruction of*

an Ojibway Community (New Haven: Yale University Press, 1985).

5. There are a number of good studies which reach such conclusions. See, for example, Peter Gorrie's "The James Bay Power Project," *Canadian Geographic*, February/March 1990, pp. 21-31. Also see the relevant portions of Harold Cardinal's *The Unjust Society: The Tragedy of Canada's Indians* (Edmonton: Hurtig Publishers, 1969).
6. Robert Hecky, "Methylmercury Contamination in Northern Canada," *Northern Perspectives*, October 1978, pp. 8-9. Also see George Hutchenson and Dick Wallace, *Grassy Narrows* (Toronto: Van Nostrand Reinhold Publishers, 1977). That the problem continues is readily evidenced in an article, "Indians eating contaminated fish," printed in the *Toronto Globe and Mail* on November 5, 1990.
7. For detailed elaboration of the way in which the term "genocide" is used herein, see Ward Churchill, "Genocide: Toward a Functional Definition," *Alternatives*, Vol. XI, No. 3, July 1986, pp. 403-430. On "ecocide," see Barry Weinberg, *Ecocide in Indochina: The Ecology of War* (San Francisco: The Canfield Press, 1970).
8. Such considerations are covered in Zaslow, *op. cit.*
9. These and related issues are covered in Kenneth S. Coats and William K. Morrison, ed., *For Purposes of Dominion* (Toronto: Captus University Publications, 1989).
10. Robert Paige, *Northern Development: The Canadian Dilemma* (Toronto: McClelland and Stewart Publishers, 1986). Also see William F. Sinclair, *Native Self-Reliance Through Resource Development* (Vancouver: Hemlock Publishers, 1984).
11. A good overview of the scale on which mineral resources are at issue in the sub-Arctic may be found in Robert Davis and Mark Zannis, *The Genocide Machine in Canada: The Pacification of the North* (Montreal: Black Rose Books, 1973). Mining, of course, carries with it its own set of environmental problems, as well as constraints against the bona fide expression of indigenous sovereignty; see J. Rick Ponting, ed., *Arduous Journey: Canadian Indians and Decolonization* (Toronto: McClelland and Stewart Publishers, 1986).
12. Paige, *op. cit.*

13. Sinclair, *op. cit.*
14. On the negative effects of the Bennett Dam, see Boyce Richardson, *Strangers Devour the Land: The Cree Hunters of the James Bay area versus Premier Bourassa and the James Bay Development Corporation* (Post Mills, VT: Chelsea Green Publishers, 1991, p. 148).
15. The term "National Sacrifice Area" accrues from Thadis Box, *et al.*, *Rehabilitation Potential for Western Coal Lands* (Cambridge, MA: Ballinger Publishing Co., 1974). The book is the published version of a study commissioned by the National Academy of Sciences and submitted to the Nixon administration for potential implementation as federal policy in 1972. At the 1980 Black Hills International Survival Gathering, AIM leader Russell Means spelled out the implications of the concept by linking it to the sacrifice of entire peoples. See Russell Means, "The Same Old Song," in Ward Churchill, ed., *Marxism and Native Americans* (Boston: South End Press, 1983, p. 25).
16. Dam the Dams Campaign and the Institute for Natural Progress, "The Water Plot: Hydrological Rape in Northern Canada," in Ward Churchill, ed., *Critical Issues in Native North America* (Copenhagen: International Work Group on Indigenous Affairs, 1989, pp. 137-51).
17. This sort of governmental/corporate secrecy has long been endemic to northern Canadian water development initiatives in general. See Boyce Richardson, *James Bay: The plot to drown the Northern Woods* (San Francisco: Sierra Club Books, 1972).
18. See the text of the United Nations 1948 Convention on Punishment and Prevention of the Crime of Genocide, contained in Ian Brownlie, *Basic Documents on Human Rights* (London/New York: Oxford University Press, 1981).
19. Sean McCutcheon, *Electric Rivers: The Story of the James Bay Project* (Montreal: Black Rose Books, 1991, p. 15).
20. *Ibid.*
21. *Ibid.*, p. 16. The impetus underlying this sort of rampant "infrastructural" expansion is detailed very well in Thomas P. Hughs, *Networks of Power: Electrification in Western Society, 1880-1930* (Baltimore: Johns Hopkins University Press, 1923).
22. See Graham Frasier, *PQ: René Lévesque and the Parti*

Québécois in Power (Toronto: Macmillan Publishers, 1984). Also see Jane Jacobs, *The Question of Separatism: Quebec and the Struggle over Sovereignty* (New York: Random House Publishers, 1980).

23. *Electric Rivers, op. cit.*, p. 16. The Manicougan and Churchill Falls projects are covered in Daniel Deudney, *Rivers of Energy: The Hydroelectric Potential* (Worldwatch Paper 44, June 1981).
24. *Ibid.*, p. 17. Also see Philip Smith, *Brinco: The Story of Churchill Falls* (Toronto: McClelland and Stewart Publishers, 1975).
25. L. Ian McDonald, *From Bourassa to Bourassa: A Pivotal Decade in Canadian History* (Montreal: Harvest House Publishers, 1984). Bourassa, who opposed separatism, won against the Parti Québécois, which had taken to advocating nuclear rather than hydroelectric development; see Roger Lecasse, *Baie James: une épopé* (Québec: Libre expression, 1983, p. 129).
26. *Ibid.*, p. 112-4. Also see Philippe Faucher and Johannes Bergeron, *Hydro-Quebec: la société de l'heure de pointe* (Montreal: Les Presses de l'Université de Montreal, 1986).
27. Alain Chanlat, with André Bolduc and Daniel Larouche, *Gestion et culture d'enterprise: le cheminement d'Hydro-Quebec* (Québec: Québec/Amérique, 1984).
28. Société d'energie de la Baie James, *Le Complexe hydroélectrique de la Grande Rivière: réalisation de la première phase* (Québec: Les Éditions de la Chenelière, 1987).
29. The utility is extraordinarily proud of this feat; see Hydro-Quebec, *James Bay: Development, Environment and the Native People of Quebec* (Montreal: Hydro-Quebec, 1989, 1984, p. 22).
30. Hydro-Quebec, *James Bay and the Environment: Hydro-Quebec Development Plan, 1989-1991—Horizon 1998* (Montreal: Hydro-Quebec, 1989, p. 3).
31. *Electric Rivers, op. cit.*, p. 35.
32. This view of native people is repeatedly expressed in so many words by Bourassa in his *James Bay* (Montreal: Harvest House Publishers, 1973). Such sentiments were also expressed by Gilles Massé, Minister of Natural Resources for Quebec, in the *Montreal Gazette* (November 8,

1972), and are well matched to those of James Bay Energy Corporation CEO Robert Boyd, quoted in McCutcheon (*op. cit.*, p. 45) as observing at the time, "I know the Crees well...They're all lazy."

33. The organizing is well-covered in *Strangers Devour the Land, op. cit.*
34. The team's findings were self-published by John and Gillian Spence as *Ecological Considerations of the James Bay Project* (Montreal, 1972). Also see Alan Penn, "Development of James Bay: the role of environmental assessment in determining the legal rights to an interlocutory injunction," *Journal of the Fisheries Research Board of Canada*, No. 32, 1975, pp. 136-60.
35. Quoted in *Electric Rivers, op. cit.*, pp. 50-1.
36. O'Reilly's legal argument was based primarily in the Indian Act, the provisions of which had not before really been applied to the indigenous peoples of the Hudson Bay region. See Indian Affairs Canada, *Indian Acts and Amendments, 1868-1950* (Ottawa: Research Branch: Indian and Northern Affairs Ministry of Canada, 1981). Also see *Ancestral Lands, Alien Laws: Judicial Perspectives on Aboriginal Title* (Saskatoon: University of Saskatchewan Law Centre, 1983).
37. *Electric Rivers, op. cit.*, p. 50.
38. *Ibid.*, p. 52.
39. Lacasse, *op. cit.*
40. See Albert Malouf, *La Baie James indienne: text intégral du judgement du Judge Albert Malouf* (Québec: Éditions du jour, 1973).
41. *Electric Rivers, op. cit.*, p. 55.
42. Although Diamond could never quite bring himself to admit the extent to which he was duped in the Grand Council scenario, he comes close in his "Aboriginal Rights: The James Bay Experience," in Menno Boldt and J. Anthony Long, *Aboriginal Peoples and Aboriginal Rights* (Toronto: University of Toronto Press, 1985, pp. 265-85). For an apologetic assessment, see Roy McGregor, *Chief: The Fearless Vision of Billy Diamond* (New York: Viking Press, 1989).
43. See Irwin Colin, "Lords of the Arctic, Wards of the State," *Northern Perspectives*, January-March 1989, pp. 2-20.

44. Harvey Feit, "Negotiating Recognition of Aboriginal Rights: History, Strategies and Reactions to the James Bay and Northern Quebec Agreement," *Canadian Journal of Anthropology*, Vol. 1, No. 2, Winter 1980, pp. 159-71. Also see Colin Scott, "Ideology of Reciprocity between the James Bay Cree and the Whiteman State," in Peter Skalnik, ed., *Outwitting the State* (New Brunswick, NJ: Transaction Books, 1989).
45. *Electric Rivers, op. cit.*, p. 59.
46. *James Bay and Northern Quebec Agreement Implementation Act Review* (Ottawa: Department of Indian and Northern Affairs, 1982).
47. The principles underlying the government's strategy are laid out rather clearly in *Under the Flag: Canadian Sovereignty and the Native People in Northern Canada* (Ottawa: Department of Indian and Northern Affairs, 1984). Also see Menno Boldt, "Social Correlates of Nationalism: A Study of Native Indian Leaders in a Canadian Internal Colony," *Comparative Political Studies*, Vol. 14, No. 2, Summer 1981, pp. 205-31.
48. Morisset, *op. cit.*, p. 151.
49. See Joyce Rosenthal and Jan Beyea, *Long-Term Threats to Canada's James Bay from Human Development* (New York: National Audubon Society Environmental Policy Analysis Department Report No. 29, July 1989).
50. Robert Bourassa, *Deux fois la Baie James* (Québec: Les Éditions La Presse, 1981).
51. Peter Haekle, "Power Politics," *Saturday Night*, June 1984, pp. 15-27. It should be noted that New York and New England generate their own electricity primarily by burning fuel oil.
52. *Electric Rivers, op. cit.*, p. 91.
53. Jane Kramer, "Power-ties link Canada, United States," *Focus*, Vol. 4, No. 2, Summer 1985, pp. 9-15. Also Amory Lovins, L. Hunter Lovins and Seth Zuckerman, *Energy Unbound: A Fable of America's Future* (San Francisco: Sierra Club Books, 1986) and Richard Munson, *The Power Makers: The Inside Story of America's Biggest Business and its Struggle to Control Tomorrow's Electricity* (Rodale Press, 1985).
54. Barrie McKenna, "James Bay plan: A Whale for the kill-

ing?" *Toronto Globe and Mail,* September 28, 1991.

55. The scale of loans and bonded indebtedness incurred during its construction, combined with a steady acceleration of normal operating and maintenance costs, suggests that James Bay I cannot under any circumstances become solvent in a conventional business sense for approximately 50 years. By then, aside from a need to replace major equipment components, the La Grande River dams will have become silted to the point where they are of marginal or sub-marginal utility for power generation. In economic terms, the entire project can be seen only as a net loss to the general public, profitable only for the elite strata which engineered it. See André Delisle, "Le Mirage des Hydro-Dollars," *Québec-Science,* April 1982, pp. 42-7.
56. See, for example, Hydro-Quebec, *Hydro-Quebec: Des premiers défis à l'aube de l'an 2000* (Quebec: Forces/Libre expression, 1984). Also see Robert Bourassa, *Power from the North* (Toronto: Prentice-Hall Publishers, 1985).
57. Winona LaDuke, lecture at the University of Colorado/Boulder, April 1992 (tape on file).
58. *Power from the North, op. cit.*
59. Jean-Marc Carpentier, "Electricity exports in a context of complementarity," *Forces,* No. 89, Spring 1990, pp. 40-42.
60. Gérard Belanger and Jean-Thomas Bernard, "Hydro-Quebec et les aluminairies," *Le Devoir,* October 20, 1989.
61. *Hydro-Quebec Development plan, 1989-1991, op. cit. Electric Rivers, op. cit.,* pp. 140-1.
62. *Ibid.,* pp. 142-3. Also see Jean-Jacques Simard, "Contrepoint: Une perspective québécoise du développement nordique," *Northern Perspectives,* March/April 1988, pp. 22-32.
63. Quoted in *Electric Rivers, op. cit.,* p. 138.
64. Using the approximate 300 percent cost multiplier which pertained with James Bay I, the expense embodied in the second and third stages of James Bay II would be $37.8 billion and $132 billion, respectively. Obviously, the public of Quebec could never hope to see such costs recovered within the lifetime of the facilities created.
65. Fikret Berkes, "Some Environmental and Social Impacts of the James Bay Hydroelectric Project, Canada," *Journal of Environmental Management,* No. 12, 1981, pp. 157-72.

66. *Electric Rivers, op. cit.*, p. 98.
67. Fikret Berkes, "The Intrinsic Difficulty of Predicting Impacts: Lessons from the James Bay Hydro Project," *Environmental Impact Assessment Review,* No. 8, 1988, pp. 201-20.
68. For graphic illustrations of the scale of destruction, see Rolf Wittenborn and Claus Biegert, eds., *James Bay Project: A River Drowned by Water* (Montreal: Montreal Museum of Fine Art, 1981).
69. *Electric Rivers, op. cit.*, p. 100.
70. *Ibid.*, p. 112.
71. See Ted Williams, "Who Killed 10,000 Caribou?" *Audubon Magazine,* March 1985, pp. 12-17. Also see Lawrence Jackson, "World's largest caribou herd mired in Quebec-Labrador boundary dispute, *Canadian Geographic,* June-July 1985, pp. 25-33.
72. "Intrinsic Difficulty of Predicting Impacts," *op. cit.*; "Methylmercury Contamination in Northern Canada," *op. cit.*
73. See Harvey Feit, "Legitimation and Autonomy in James Bay Cree Responses to Hydro-Electric Development," in Noel Dyck, ed., *Indigenous Peoples and the Nation-State: "Fourth World" Politics in Canada, Australia and Norway* (St. John's: Memorial University of Newfoundland, 1985).
74. *Electric Rivers, op. cit.*, pp. 129-30.
75. Catherine Leconte, "L'entrevue du lundi: Matthew Coon-Come," *Le Devoir,* September 23, 1991.
76. Billy Diamond, "Villages of the Dammed: The James Bay Agreement Leaves a Trail of Broken Promises," *Arctic Circle,* November/December 1990, pp. 24-34.
77. Conversation with Dalee Sambo, Inuit Circumpolar Conference, September 1988.
78. James O'Reilly, still lead attorney for the Crees, responded in behalf of his clients that, because of the nature of breaches to the previous agreement, the utility government already owed the Indians and Inuits more than $1 billion in damages (*Electric Rivers, op. cit.*, p. 155).
79. Lajambe had been involved in fighting against the James Bay projects almost since the outset. See her "D'une baie James à? l'autre," *La Presse,* March 23, 1987.
80. *Electric Rivers, op. cit.*, pp. 159-61.

81. *Ibid.*, pp. 161-2.
82. Paul Wells, "Most utilities must prove their proposal is cheapest," *Montreal Gazette*, July 24, 1991.
83. Stephen Hazell, "Battling Hydro: Taming Quebec's Runaway Corporate Beast is a Herculean Task," *Arctic Circle*, July/August 1991, pp. 40-1.
84. *Strangers Devour the Land, op. cit.*, p. 357.
85. "New York Cancels Contract with James Bay Project," *Women of All Red Nations*, June 1992.
86. Michelle Lalonde, "Soaring price tag raises serious doubts about Great Whale," *Toronto Globe and Mail*, April 30, 1991.
87. On the land dispute and other issues which led to the Oka confrontation, see Rick Hornung, *One Nation Under the Gun: Inside the Mohawk Civil War* (New York: Pantheon Books, 1991).
88. *Electric Rivers, op. cit.*, p. 184.
89. "L'industrie me en cause le sérieux des audiences publiques du BAPE," *Le Devoir*, September 20, 1991.
90. Lalonde, *op. cit.*
91. "The Water Plot," *op. cit.*, p. 143.
92. Canadian Board of Resource Ministers, *Water Diversion Proposals of North America* (Edmonton: Alberta Department of Agriculture, Water Resources Division, Development Planning Branch, 1968).
93. Conversation with Winona LaDuke, *op. cit.*
94. "The Water Plot," *op. cit.* For further background on the World War II period, see Richard Bocking, *Canada's Water for Sale* (Toronto: James Lewis and Samuel Publishers, 1972).
95. Ontario Water Resources Commission, *Data for Northern Ontario Water Resource Studies, 1966-68* (Toronto: Water Resources Bulletin 1-1, Gen. Series, 1969, p. 1).
96. *Ibid.*, p. 2.
97. Co-ordinating Committee on Northern Ontario Water Resource Studies, *Seventh Progress Report to the Governments of Ontario and Canada* (Toronto: Ontario Water Resources Commission, 1969, pp. 8-9).
98. Co-ordinating Committee on Northern Ontario Water Resource Studies, *Sixth Progress Report to the Governments of Ontario and Canada* (Toronto: Ontario Water

Resources Commission, 1968, pp. 6-7).

99. *Data for Northern Ontario Water Resource Studies, op. cit.*, pp. 2, 10; *Sixth Progress Report, op. cit.*, pp. 3-6; *Seventh Progress Report, op. cit.*, p. 6.

100. *House of Commons Debates* (Ottawa, 1967, p. 4007).

101. *Sixth Progress Report, op. cit.*, pp. 2, 6; *Seventh Progress Report, op. cit.*, pp. 7-8.

102. *Newsweek*, February 22, 1965, p. 53. In the same article, U.S. Secretary of the Interior Stewart Udall is quoted as saying, "I'm for this type of thinking. I'm glad engineers talk so much about it."

103. Daniel McCool, *Command of the Waters: Iron Triangles, Federal Water Development, and Indian Water* (Berkeley: University of California Press, 1987, pp. 107-8).

104. On the Columbia River Treaty, see Donald Waterfield, *Continental Waterboy* (Toronto: Free North Press, 1970). Also see Bocking, *op. cit.*

105. Guerrero, *op. cit.*, p. 210.

106. "The Water Plot," *op. cit.*, pp. 143-4.

107. *Water Diversion Proposals of North America, op. cit.*

108. McNaughton's statements are contained in *Water Resources of Canada* (Ottawa: Royal Society of Canada, 1968).

109. *Strangers Devour the Land, op. cit.*, p. 352. For detailed examination of the workings of the offending entities in other contexts, see Richard J. Barnett and Ronald E. Müller, *Global Reach: The Power of Multinational Corporations* (New York: Simon and Schuster Publishers, 1974).

110. *Water Diversion Proposals of North America, op. cit.*

111. For a succinct examination of the theoretical bases for this result, see Ian Roxborough, *Theories of Underdevelopment* (New York: Macmillan Education Ltd., 1979).

112. Beyea is quoted in Andrés Picard, "James Bay: A Power Play," *Toronto Globe and Mail*, April 13-17, 1990. Also see Rosenthal and Beyea, *op. cit.*

113. *Electric Rivers, op. cit.*, pp. 165-6.

114. "The Water Plot," *op. cit.*, p. 150.

115. *Electric Rivers, op. cit.*, p. 156. As concerns the sorts of alternatives being proposed, see Environmental Committee of the Sanikiluaq and Rawson Academy of Science, *Sustainable Development in the Hudson Bay/James Bay*

Bioregion: An Ecosystem Approach (Canadian Arctic Resources Committee, 1991).

116. A nice selection of statements along this line will be found in Virginia Irving Armstrong, comp. and ed., *I Have Spoken: American History Through the Voices of the Indians* (Athens, OH: The Swallow Press, 1971).

117. *Electric Rivers, op. cit.*, p. 157.

American Indian Self-Governance

Fact, Fantasy and Prospects for the Future

> I did a two year study on ratified and unratified treaties and agreements of all tribes with the white man. I can think of nothing from the studies I've done nor from [American Indian] oral history that would suggest that [Indians] ever gave, or ever intended to give, civil and criminal jurisdiction to the United States.
>
> —Vine Deloria, Jr.—
> 1974

The question of self-governance among American Indian nations encapsulated within what is now the United States of America is one of the more confused issues in modern politics. While there is a general understanding that the indigenous nations of North America once existed as fully self-governing entities, those concerned with the matter have proven spectacularly unable to arrive at even a common definition of what constitutes (or might constitute) contemporary Indian self-governance, whether it presently exists or, if it does not, how it might be achieved. What are the facts—and the fantasies—of self-governance and how do they affect relations between Indian nations and the United States? What are the possibilities for genuine Indian self-governance over

This essay is the polished version of a lecture presented at Evergreen State College, November 1988.

the coming decades? The following is a brief overview.

The Facts and the Paradox

As has been reviewed elsewhere in this volume:

- American Indian peoples are members of nations within even the strictest legal definition;
- they have been formally recognized as such through the U.S. government through the policy of entering into treaty agreements with them;
- this recognition of the existence of fully sovereign Indian nations is in accordance with international law;[1]
- it follows that American Indian nations possess every legal and moral right to conduct themselves as nations, unless they themselves have knowingly, willingly and formally given up such rights.

Today, representatives of the U.S. government contend that while this may be true in principle, and has been true in practice in certain historical instances, contemporary circumstances negate such facts. They point to a series of federal court decisions and statutes stipulating that American Indian peoples constitute "domestic dependent nations," less than completely sovereign entities, over which the federal government exercises superior sovereign prerogatives as well as a "fiduciary" or "trust" responsibility involving jurisdictional and administrative control.[2] Further, they argue, Indians are also citizens of the U.S. under provision of the 1887 General Allotment Act and the 1924 Indian Citizenship Act, and are thus doubly subordinate to the federal system of authority.[3]

The bottom line, from the federal perspective, is that American Indian nations enjoy a "limited sovereignty." That is, they retain all of their original national rights other than those specifically restricted or taken away by "Acts of Congress."[4] There are presently more than 5,000 federal statutes designed precisely to usurp sovereign native rights, a number indicative of the extent to which indigenous prerogatives of self-governance have been restricted by the 1990s.

Advocates of the federal view purposefully neglect to mention that each of these elements of "law" was unilaterally imposed by the United States in direct contradiction to the treaty understandings already (and, in most cases, still) in effect with North America's indigenous nations. There is no record of these nations having willingly accepted the notion that they were either domestic to or particularly dependent upon the United States. To the contrary, many of these nations spent the latter part of the 18th and the bulk of the 19th centuries engaged in armed resistance—incurring horrendous suffering—in concerted efforts to avoid being accorded this subordinate status. No one, not even the most stalwart federal bureaucrat, has been brazen enough to suggest that Indians were mutual participants in bringing about passage of the Allotment and Citizenship Acts, that they requested the extension of federal criminal and civil jurisdiction over their homelands, or that they in any way desired the rest of the measures upon which the argument of a superior U.S. sovereignty rests.

Without the willing consent of Indian nations to diminishment of their sovereign status, such maneuvers on the part of the federal government can be viewed only as abridgements (violations) of the treaties into which it entered with native people. The implications of this are readily apparent in Article VI of the U.S. Constitution, which states unequivocally that treaties represent the "Supreme Law of the Land," on par with the law embodied with the Constitution itself. The terms and provisions of a ratified and unabrogated treaty cannot be constitutionally contradicted or impugned by the passage of any subordinate legislation such as local ordinances, state laws or subsequent federal statutes.[5] As with legislation, the same principles prevent regulations of governmental agencies from usurping the treaty agreements.

Despite this seemingly ironclad case for soveriegnty, Indian nations have been unilaterally diminished to subordinate, "quasi-sovereign" status similar to that of the 50 states of the union. Increasingly, their status is being reduced even further, to that of counties or municipalities, subject to state jurisdiction and control. The situation poses an interesting paradox. To hold Indian peoples as less than fully sovereign nations implies that the entire treaty-making process undertaken by the United States with those peoples is and always was legally invalid. Either the treaties are valid or they are not. If the treaties are valid, Indian nations are fully sovereign states and can lay legitimate claim to the terms guaranteed by those treaties. On the other hand, if the treaties are invalid, then so are the land cession clauses in them on the United States bases its claim to "legal title" for about two-thirds of its present domestic territorality. Without the treaties, the legal basis for the United States ceases to exist.[6]

Absent its Indian treaties, the only options open to the United States by to explain the legitimacy of its occupancy in North America would be resort to the "Doctrine of Discovery" and its notorious sub-part, the "Rights of Conquest."[7] Such resort obviously presents no small doctrinal problem to a nation-state which—even in the wildest revisions of its history—can make no claim to having "discovered" its landbase. Any merit to that dubious assertion accrues not to the United States but to various European powers whose ships landed on these shores.[8] Moreover, the United States carefully foreswore conquest—both in its Articles of Confederation, and again, specifically with regards to American Indian nations, in the Northwest Ordinance of 1789—in order to attain a posture of supposed moral enlightenment upon which it has traded ever since.[9]

Faced with the dilemma that the United States will not abide by treaties yet depends on them for its legitimacy, federally-oriented legal apologists and policy-makers have been forced to insist on sheer logical impossibility. Namely, Indian nations are simultaneously fully sovereign (in the abstract sense) for purposes treaty-making and transferring land title to the United States, but less than sovereign (in the practical sense) for purposes of allowing "legitimate" federal control ("exercise of trust") over Indian land, water and other resources, regulation of trade and diplomatic relations, form of governance, recognition of citizenry, jurisprudence, and virtually anything else striking the federal fancy. This convoluted and absurd "doctrine" allows the United States to have it both ways. It can and does assert in the international arena that it has always acted on the basis of humane, treaty-anchored (i.e., nation-to-nation) understandings with "its" indigenous population(s). At the same time, it insists that "Indian Affairs" are a purely "internal" concern of the U.S., and thus not subject to international consideration, scrutiny or intervention (as would be the case in any true nation-to-nation relationship, under international law).[10]

The Colonial Reality

This two-faced view of American Indian nations is paralleled by other powers. The French, for example, offered similar arguments to justify their relationship to Indochina and Algeria during the 1950s. The Belgians advanced such rationales in an attempt to retain their hold on the Congo during the same decade. Portugal offered the same arguments concerning Mozambique and

Angola during the 1960s and '70s. The list could go on, but the common denominator of every example is that the relationship is one of colonialism.[11] That American Indian nations within the United States are held as colonies—internal colonies—of the United States is an inescapable conclusion. Viewed through the prism of anti-colonialist analysis, the apparent inconsistencies and contradictions of U.S. "Indian policy" disappear. Like other colonial relationships, the policy is illegal under international law, regardless of how it is framed. Federal "Indian law" is a misnomer and has always been an exercise in rationalizing the extension and maintenance of U.S. colonial domination over every indigenous nation it encountered.

Of primary importance to understanding the imperial context is recognizing that the notion of "self-governance" among the colonized—is an illusion. Like so many other colonial situations, this cruel hoax is deliberately fostered as a tactical expedient by the colonizer. Repeatedly, in advanced colonial settings, the colonized are convinced to administer and impose upon themselves the policies and regulations set forth by their colonizers. This self-administration in turn is so often cynically touted by the colonizers and their puppets among the colonized as "self-governance" and "democracy."

In sum, true self-governance by which sovereign states organize themselves does not currently exist in the American Indian colonies within the United States. Further, it cannot exist until the fundamental structural relationship between the U.S. and Indigenous nations is radically altered. American Indian nations, if they are ever to exercise self-governance, must embark on a decolonization struggle in the truest sense of the term.

Fantasy

The origins of what is passed off as the "model of modern American Indian self-governance" can probably be dated from 1919, when Standard Oil sent a group of geologists to the northern portion of the Navajo Reservation to investigate the possibilities of petroleum deposits in the area. In 1921, after explorers' reports were positive, Standard dispatched representatives to negotiate—in cooperation with the Bureau of Indian Affairs—a leasing arrangement to begin drilling operations. By provision of the 1868 treaty between the Diné (Navajo) Nation and the United States, it was necessary for Standard, in order to proceed legally, to secure both agreement from the Diné government and approval of the Secretary of Interior. Secretarial approval posed no problem. But the traditional Diné Council of Elders voted unanimously to reject the idea of allowing the corporation to exploit their land and resources.[12]

This outcome was unacceptable to Standard, and to the Department of Interior, under which responsibility for virtually all development of "government" lands and resources is lodged. Consequently, in 1923, the Interior Department unilaterally appointed what it called "The Navajo Grand Council," a small group of hand-picked and "educated" Indians (i.e., those indoctrinated in the values and morés of Euroamerica). Representatives of the traditional Diné government—the people with whom the United States had entered into a solemn treaty—were entirely excluded. Washington then announced that this new council, devoid as it was of any sort of Navajo support, would henceforth be recognized as the sole "legitimate" governmental representative body of the Navajo Nation. At the stroke of the federal pen and with no popular agreement of the Diné whatsoever, the traditional Diné form of governance was totally disenfranchised and supplanted. One of the very first acts of the Washington-appointed replacement group was, of course, to sign the federally/corporately desired leasing instruments, setting in motion and "legitimizing" a sustained process of mineral expropriation on the Navajo Reservation which has been extraordinarily profitable to a range of non-Diné businesses and individuals.[13] Correspondingly, the Diné have been forced into abject poverty, their traditional subsistence economy ruined, and their landbase destroyed to the point that it has become a serious candidate to become an official "National Sacrifice Area."[14]

Consistently since 1923, the forms of "democratic" governance at Navajo—inculcation of voting rather than consensus as a means of governmental selection, subdivision of the reservation into electoral districts, expansion of the council to include representatives from each district, the hypothetical division of governmental structure into executive; legislative and judicial spheres, and so on—have been carefully polished. The rhetoric of self-governance rests heavily on tribal council leaders having always affixed their signatures to business agreements made "on behalf of" their people. Further, a Navajo lobbying office is maintained in Washington. Both the signatures and the lobby are consistently advanced by Navajo and federal politicos alike as evidence that American Indians govern themselves. It is even possible that some of the actors on both sides of the equation actually believe what they are saying.[15]

But the reality is dramatically different from the rhetoric. During the entire half-century in which the Navajo council has been functioning in its mature form, it has never been allowed to negotiate a single business agreement on its own initiative. It has continued to be barred from entering into any agreement with "foreign governments" other than the United States, whether for purposes of trade or for any other reason. Consequently, it has never been able to negotiate mineral royalty rates on anything resembling favorable terms, to establish or enforce even minimal standards of cleanup and land reclamation upon transient extractive corporations doing business upon its land, or even to determine the number of livestock which can be grazed within its borders.[16] The

Navajo council has never—as the ongoing "Navajo-Hopi Land Disputes" in the 1882 Executive Order and so-called Bennett Freeze areas of the reservation readily attest—been able to exert an particular influence in the determination of exactly what the borders of the Navajo Nation actually are.[17] Even the citizenry of the Navajo Nation has been defined by the federal government, through imposition of a formal eugenics code termed "blood quantum" and nearly a century of direct control over tribal rolls described elsewhere in this volume. These methods of manipulating and arithmetically constricting the indigenous population have become so imbedded in the Indian consciousness and psyche that Washington can rely upon the "self-governance" mechanisms of Native America to abandon their own traditions and concern with sovereignty, adhering to federal definitions of Indian identity. The ugly burden of imposing racism is now carried by the oppressed themselves.[18]

Council members like to point out that they have a court system, police force and jails operating on the reservation, and submit that this is evidence of self-governance. But behind the smoke and mirrors of these institutions lies a complete lack of Navajo jurisdictional authority over non-Navajos committing crimes within the Navajo Nation.[19] They have little jurisdiction over their own citizenry when it comes to felony and serious misdemeanor crimes, and are limited as well in a number of important civil areas.[20] To resolve issues between themselves and any of their corporate lessees, they have no recourse but to pursue matters in U.S. courts rather than their own.[21] To resolve issues with the federal government, they must secure permission from that same government to litigate in that government's own courts.[22] To impose a severance tax upon their own mineral resources as these are extracted by transnational corporations—an uncontested right of every state in the union—they must secure permission from the federal government to seek (and, in a limited way, secure) a federal court opinion allowing them to do so.[23] Issues are now so confused that Navajo "tribal leaders," in apparent seriousness and in the same speech, can spout rhetoric about being head of a "sovereign, self-governing nation," yet propose that the Navajo Nation be elevated to the status of a state within the United States.[24]

This is national self-governance? Fantasies to the contrary, the Navajo council and its chair have exactly zero control over any aspect of Navajo affairs. Every shred of their policy is and always has been utterly contingent upon the approval of the U.S. Interior Secretary, the federal courts, corporate executives, and the governments of the three states (Arizona, New Mexico and Utah) within which the Navajo Reservation technically lies.

Today, the same colonial puppet "self governance" prevails on almost all reservations in the United States. The strength and utility of the Navajo Grand Council as a model in serving U.S. interests while offering useful illusions to the contrary has been so great that it was imposed across the face of Indian Country through the 1934 Indian Reorganization Act (IRA).[25] Although each American Indian nation which was "reorganized" under the statute—having its traditional governmental structure usurped and replaced by a council patterned directly after a corporate board—allegedly voted in a referendum to do so, the reality is rather different.[26] At the Pine Ridge Reservation (Oglala Lakota Nation), for example, a number of dead people somehow managed to crawl out of their graves to vote for reorganization; even after this was clearly documented, the referendum results were allowed to stand and reorganization proceeded.[27] At Hopi, to take another example, more than 85 percent of all (federally defined) eligible voters opposed and actively boycotted the referendum. Their abstentions were then counted as "aye" votes by the Bureau of Indian Affairs and reorganization proceeded.[28] The list of such examples in one or another degree of virulence, includes every Indian nation which was reorganized in accordance with the federal prescription.[29]

All fantasies of self-governing characteristics aside, the absolute predicate of any IRA government is its acceptance—indeed, reinforcement—of the emphatically subnational status accorded American Indian nations by the United States, to legitimize their peoples' subordination through their public endorsement of it, to toe the line of limitations decreed by the federal government and ultimately to barter the genuine interests of their people in exchange for the petty position and minor material compensation which serving as puppets of a foreign power affords them. This is advanced colonial administration in its very purest form, whether one wishes to draw one's parallel to the leadership of Vichy France or to the Thieu regime in what was once called the Republic of Vietnam ("South Vietnam").[30]

As any serious student of colonialism understands, such governments will not, indeed structurally *can*not, pursue actual self-determination, self-governance and sovereignty. They will never and can never attempt to consolidate real control over their remaining landbases, physically recover lands illegally taken from their people, throw the federal bureaucrats and supporting police off their reservations, try to physically bar the corporate rape of their territories, or enter into diplomatic and trade relations with other nations. They will not and they cannot, because in the final analysis they owe their fealty and their allegiance not to their own people (or even themselves) but to their colonizers. It is the colonizer, after all, not their people, who provides the positions they occupy, and the means for the continuation of these positions. The relationship is one of unbalanced symbiosis and mutual perpetuation in which U.S. élites are enriched, the "self-governing" puppets bought off with crumbs, and the vast majority left disenfranchised and destitute.[31]

Contrary to official propaganda, IRA governments are not the champions of American Indian self-governance, but must be counted among the barriers to it. Their very existence inherently engenders confusion over "who are the real representatives of Indian people." Further, these self-proclaimed and federally validated "responsible" (To whom? To what?) representatives of Native America have increasingly lent their energies and voices to discredit any Indian or group of Indians audacious enough to work for the resumption of national prerogatives by American Indian peoples.[32]

This latter condemnation of those seeking sovereignty is exemplified in former Rosebud Sioux Tribal President Webster Two Hawk. Wandering around on the federal dole like a clown, wearing a crew cut and "war bonnet," he parroted the views of the Nixon administration *vis-à-vis* the American Indian Movement's having called the BIA to account for its colonial arrogance and some of its more blatant transgressions at the expense of Indian people in 1972.[33]

More grimly, former Pine Ridge Tribal President Dick Wilson formed a cabal of gun-thugs known as the GOONs to act as surrogates for the FBI, engaging in outright mass murder to prevent an insurgent grassroots movement of traditional Oglalas pursuing their rights under the 1868 Fort Laramie Treaty from "spoiling" a planned secret expropriation of uranium deposits in the northwest quadrant of the reservation.[34] Two Hawk and Wilson are but two of many examples. At every level, rather than serving as models for the resumption and development of American Indian self-governance, the present IRA "governments" represent the exact opposite: institutionalized capitulation on virtually every significant issue of Indian rights. By and large, they are, in simplest terms, problems to be overcome as part of any genuine decolonization struggle and—if examples such as Wilson are any indication—they may be predicted to exact a nasty toll from their own ostensible constituents in a counter-struggle to avert any real dismantling of the colonial structure upon which they have come to depend for income and "prestige."

Strategic considerations for the Future

Native America is at a crossroads. If the present hegemony of IRA-style governance is maintained and continues its give-away program on American Indian resources and national rights, the outlook is bleak indeed. The future would consist of a permanent reduction of American Indian sovereignty and self-governance, or at best. In the case of many or even most of the smaller Indian nations, eventual termination—"auto-termination" may be a better term—and absorption directly into the "melting pot" seems the most likely outcome. The timeline for this final liquidation of Native America may be shorter than fifty years.

Fortunately, alternatives have emerged since 1970. These have related to a considerable degree to the momentum created by the actions and activities of the American Indian Movement and related "militant" organizations, particularly during the period 1972-78. The 1972 Trail of Broken Treaties occupation of the Bureau of Indian Affairs Building in Washington, for example, did more to bring Indians into the BIA than all the petitions and letters of "more responsible" and "legitimate" tribal officials over the preceding 50 years. The Twenty Point Program advanced by Trail participants as a cohesive American Indian sociopolitical agenda still represents a benchmark expression of indigenous sovereignty in North America.[35] Ironically, those Indians hired as a result—during the major BIA "integration" period lasting from 1973-76—seemed to take it as a matter of faith that they should conduct themselves in a manner which can only be described as anti-AIM.[36]

Similarly, AIM's actions at Gordon, Nebraska in 1972, and Custer, South Dakota in 1973—demanding that the Euroamerican murderers of Indian people be charged with their actual crimes rather than "manslaughter"—yielded an incalculable impact on Indian rights and the value of Indian life among non-Indians throughout the United States. These undertakings brought to a screeching halt a nation-wide rash of ritual or thrill killings of Indian people which had been mounting for some time.[37] This was vastly more than had been accomplished by a decade of "polite" discussions about the "problem" by the federally-approved Indian leadership with state, local and national law enforcement officials. Yet, predictably, "official" Native America did little in response but criticize and condemn AIM's "violent tactics." It is a testament to the strength of state propaganda that actions which resulted in the diminishing of a wave of homicides through utilization of methods involving no loss of life have been misconstrued as "violence."

AIM's stand on the Pine Ridge Reservation from 1973-76, refusing to swerve from its support of Oglala national rights—in the face of a hideously lethal federal repression—can only be viewed as a tremendously important point of departure for the general rebirth of American Indian pride, and an increasing Indian willingness to stand and attempt to (re)assert their broader rights to genuine self-determination.[38] As always, "duly elected" tribal officials tended overwhelmingly to attack AIM while defending the federal "right" to maintain "order" on the reservation, regardless of the cost and consequences of such order to Indians. It is a sublime paradox that many tribal council members have themselves begun to mimic AIM viewpoints and AIM pronouncements of a decade ago, never having abandoned their clever description of those who showed them the way as being "Assholes In Moccasins."

What the AIM "radicals" were (and in many cases

still are) demonstrating is that in order for Indians to make gains, to self-determine and self-govern, it is absolutely essential to proceed by something other than the self-serving "rules of the game" laid down by the U.S. government. Put another way, those who would claim sovereignty must endeavor to exercise it, to rely upon their *own* sense of legality and morality, and to act accordingly. By the 1980s, this dynamic had become clearly consolidated in the occupation of Yellow Thunder Camp near Rapid City, in the Black Hills, part of an overt program of reclaiming Lakota territory guaranteed under the Fort Laramie Treaty, but expropriated during the 1870s by the U.S.[39] The same may be said of the ongoing resistance to federally imposed relocation of traditional Diné from their land in the Big Mountain area of the Navajo and Hopi reservations in northeastern Arizona (see "Genocide in Arizona?", in this volume). There are many other examples, ranging from the continuing fishing rights struggles in the Pacific Northwest to the stands taken by the Haudenosaunee (Iroquois Six Nations Confederacy) along the U.S.-Canadian border,[40] to similar positions adopted by the O'Odham (Papago) along the U.S.-Mexican border, to the refusal of nearly half of all the Seminole people of Florida to accept federal recognition as a "validation" of their personal and national existence.[41] As noted elsewhere, the emergence of an American Indian presence in the international arena, through the United Nations Working Group on Indigenous Populations, has come from the same impetus outside the IRA governments.[42]

Perhaps the purest articulation of the AIM alternative to IRA colonialism may be found in the platform assembled under the title "TREATY" for use by Russell Means in his candidacy for the Pine Ridge tribal presidency in 1984. Here for the first time during the 20th Century, a truly comprehensive program was offered by which a given American Indian nation could undertake to recover control over its own affairs, abolishing the IRA system and restore political power to the traditional Councils of Elders, open up diplomatic and trade relations with nations other than the United States, begin a systematic effort at restoring its own landbase and revitalizing a traditionally-oriented economy thereon, assert jurisdictional prerogatives and control over the definition of its own membership/citizenry, and convert its educational system to its own uses rather than those of its opponents. These alternatives were conceived by way of using the IRA structure against itself in a sort of exercise in political ju jitsu.[43]

So effective and threatening was the TREATY concept seen by federal authorities and those Indians on Pine Ridge who owe their allegiance to that government, that they conspired to disqualify Means from the reservation ballot, not on the basis of any alleged offense against the Lakota people or Lakota law, but because he had been convicted of expressing contempt—by way of engaging in "criminal syndicalism"—toward an alien South Dakota court some years previously. Although never actualized on Pine Ridge, the TREATY bears extensive study for adaptation and implementation by other Indians in other places insofar as the IRA establishment was threatened enough to go to such lengths to suppress it.

This appears to be occurring, in both literal and more diffused fashions. The Haida Draft Constitution, generated by a people whose territory is split between the United States and Canada in the Alaska region, incorporates much of the same thinking brought forth in the TREATY Platform. Many of the gains posted by Pacific Northwest nations such as Quinault and Lummi in recent years also proceed in accordance with liberatory principles similar to those expressed in TREATY.[44] And, to a certain extent at least, most of the ideas concerning Lakota land recovery and self-governance contained in the S. 705 "Bradley Bill" were drawn from the TREATY framework.[45] These are all encouraging signs; a number of others might be cited.

It is time, if American Indian self-governance as nations rather than as integral components of the Euroamerican empire is to once again become a functioning reality, to begin to consciously destroy the IRA system, to discard "leaders" who profess loyalty to it, to reject the "federal trust relationship" and all interaction with the BIA, and to begin to (re)assert actual Indian alternatives. It will not be a quick or pleasant process. There will no doubt be severe costs and consequences associated with such a line of action and development. The adversaries of Native America have shown themselves consistently over more than two centuries to be utterly ruthless. But the costs and consequences attending subordination to the federal will are, and have always been, far higher. The choice before use is between extinction and resurgence.

Notes

1. The texts of 371 ratified treaty instruments appear in Kappler, Charles J., *Indian Treaties, 1778-1883,* Interland Publishing Co., New York, 1973. The Lakota scholar Vine Deloria, Jr., has uncovered several other texts of ratified treaties which are omitted in the Kappler compilation. Additionally, Deloria has collected more than 600 unratified treaties and agreements of various sorts, which the federal government considers to lack the same legal force as ratified instruments, but upon which it nonetheless predicates various portions of its aggregate land title. Concerning the recognition of sovereignty inherent to U.S. treaties with American Indian peoples, see Cohen, Felix S., *Handbook of American Indian Law,* University of New Mexico Press, Albuquerque, 1942 edition, pp. 33-6.
2. The "domestic dependent nation" concept was first articulated by Chief Justice of the Supreme Court John Marshall in *Worcester v. Georgia* (6 Pet. 515 (1832)). It set in motion the emergence of a legal doctrine wherein the United States contended it held "plenary [full] power" over indigenous nations, a notion elaborated most fully in *Cherokee*

Nation v. Hitchcock (187 U.S. 294 (1902)) and *Lonewolf v. Hitchcock* (187 U.S. 553 (1903)). The idea that the federal government, as the superior sovereignty in U.S./Indian relations, is obligated to exercise a "trust responsibility" over the affairs of its native "wards" stems from the plenary power doctrine. It was framed most clearly in *U.S. v. Kagama* (118 U.S. 375 (1886)) and *U.S. v. Thomas* (151 U.S. 557, 585 (1894)). Remarkably, there was never a shred of Indian consent to any of this. For an excellent overview, see Harvey, C., "Constitutional Law: Congressional Plenary Power over Indian Affairs—A Doctrine Rooted in Prejudice," *American Indian Law Review*, No. 5, 1977, pp. 117-50.

3. The 1887 General Allotment Act (25 U.S.C.A. 331) was primarily aimed at destroying traditional patterns of indigenous land tenure and transferring some two-thirds of all reservation acreage into the "public domain." It contained a clause, however, stipulating a *quid pro quo* by which each Indian seeking to retain a portion of his or her reservation through acceptance of a land parcel would concomitantly have to accept U.S. citizenship. In 1924, all native people who remained "unallotted" were decreed to be U.S. citizens under provision of the Indian Citizenship Act (8 U.S.C.A. 140 (a) (2)).
4. Incongruously, the supposed "source" of Congressional authority to strip away the sovereign prerogatives of indigenous nations by legislative fiat is the "commerce clause" of the U.S. Constitution, a passage clearly intended by the framers to regulate the behavior of their own citizenry—not Indians—in their dealings with native people. This is readily borne out in the series of federal "Trade and Intercourse Acts" beginning in 1790 and extending through 1834. The principle became inverted, as is evidenced in *United States v. Forty-Three Gallons of Whiskey* (93 U.S. 188 (1876)) and, ultimately, in *In re Mayfield, Petitioner* (141 U.S. 107, 115, 116 (1891)). As the matter was put in *United States v. McGowan* (302 U.S. 535 (1938)): "Congress alone has the right to determine the manner in which the country's guardianship [of Indians and their affairs] shall be carried out."
5. Although in *Lonewolf v. Hitchcock*, the Supreme Court

determined it was/is allowable for subsequent federal statutes to contravene treaty provisions, the original constitutional prohibition against such an "interpretation" had long been clear: "It [is] not competent for an act of Congress to alter the stipulations of [an Indian] treaty or to change the character of the agents appointed under it" (House Report No. 447, Commission on Indian Affairs, 23d Congress, 1st Session, Washington, D.C., May 20, 1834).

6. In effect, the United States holds title of other sorts only to the area of the original thirteen British colonies of the Atlantic seaboard, quit-claimed by King George III in the 1813 Treaty of Ghent, and to portions of northern Mexico quit-claimed by that republic through the 1848 Treaty of Guadalupe Hidalgo. In each case, the nation-state in question based its own title to the territory ceded upon earlier arrangements made with native inhabitants, usually through treaties and/or direct purchase. With such transactions as the Louisiana Purchase, the United States acquired, not territory, but the right to negotiate land cessions from native inhabitants within given areas. Hence, the United States entered into scores of treaties with Indian nations within the Louisiana Purchase territory. It is upon these treaties, most of which involved land cessions, that actual U.S. title rests. See Royce, Charles C., *Indian Land Cessions in the United States* (U.S. Bureau of Ethnology, Smithsonian Institution, Washington, D.C., 1899), for the most comprehensive delineation of the specific territorality involved.

7. Under the so-called "Rights of Conquest," a subpart of the Doctrine of Discovery, European Crowns were constrained to pursue territorial acquisition by force of arms only under the conditions required for the waging of a "just war." The latter doctrine was initially elaborated by St. Augustine during the early fifth century (see Brundage, James A., *Medieval Canon Law and the Crusader,* University of Wisconsin Press, Madison, 1969; also see Deane, Herbert Andrew, *The Political and Social Ideas of St. Augustine,* Columbia University Press, New York, 1963) and then codified by Thomas Aquinas during the 13th century (see Weinreb, Lloyd, *Natural Law and Justice,* Harvard University Press, 1987). Under the law, Crowns

could exercise conquest rights only when indigenous populations 1) refused to accept Christian missionaries among them, 2) refused to trade with representatives of the Crown, or 3) engaged in unprovoked attacks upon subjects of the Crown. None of these conditions applied in the U.S. portion of North America, either before or after decolonization occurred. This was plainly recognized by George II in his Proclamation of 1763, barring territorial expansion by his subjects into areas west of the Allegheny Mountains (see Knorr, K., *British Colonial Theories, 1570-1850,* University of Toronto Press, Toronto, 1944; also see Vaughan, Alden T., *Early American Indian Documents: Treaties and Laws, 1607-1789,* University Publications of America, Washington, D.C., 1979). Hence, conquest rights would not apply to U.S. legal standing in North America, even if discovery rights somehow did.

8. The "Doctrine of Discovery" is poorly understood in this country, having been horribly garbled in Chief Justice John Marshall's attempted appropriation of it in 1823 to rationalize U.S. legal standing in North America *(Johnson v. McIntosh,* 21 U.S. 8 (Wheat.) 543). In actuality, the doctrine, from the point it first began to emerge in the letters of Pope Innocent IV in 1271—and in the form it was ultimately codified by Franciscus de Victoria in his 1541 tract *De Indis et de Ivre Belli Reflectiones* (contained in Scott, James Brown, *The Spanish Origins of International Law,* Clarendon Press, Oxford University, 1934), and therefrom adopted by Great Britain (see Arber, Edward (ed.), *The First Three English Books on America: Being Chiefly Translations, Compilations, etc., by Richard Eden,* Constable Publishers, Westminster, England, 1895)—holds clearly that discovery rights accrue solely to European Crowns. Invocation of the doctrine did not convey land title to the monarch invoking it. Rather, it vested the given Crown only with a monopoly (excluding other European Crowns) within the area claimed to acquire title—via purchase agreements or other arrangements—from the indigenous population(s) already holding the territory at issue (see Lindley, Mark Frank, *The Acquisition and Government of Backward Territory in International Law,* Longmans, Green Publishers, London, 1926). Of course, a

Crown could, and often did, vest title to certain areas in its subjects (usually individual aristocrats or corporate entities), once legitimate acquisition from "the natives" had occurred. But George III made no such transfer of title to his former subjects in the Treaty of Paris, the instrument by which he quit-claimed his thirteen colonies along the present U.S. Atlantic seaboard at the end of the American Revolution. To the contrary, the revolutionists had deliberately created a complete legal rupture between themselves and the Crown to which discovery rights in their area of interest might be said to have accrued. Hence, the Doctrine of Discovery never applied to the legal standing of the United States, even if its content was what Justice Marshall claimed it was (see Bailyn, Bernard, *The Ideological Origins of the American Revolution,* Harvard University Press, Cambridge, MA, 1967).

9. See Jensen, Merrill, *The Articles of Confederation: An Interpretation of the Social-Constitutional History of the American Revolution, 1774-1778,* University of Wisconsin Press, Madison, 1940. Also see Horsman, Reginald, *Expansion and American Indian Policy, 1783-1812* (Michigan State University Press, East Lansing, 1967) and Prucha, Francis Paul, *American Indian Policy in the Formative Years: The Trade and Intercourse Acts, 1790-1834* (Harvard University Press, Cambridge, MA, 1962).
10. For one of the more influential attempts to forge this mutually exclusive set of elements into a single cohesive whole, see Wilkinson, Charles F., *American Indians, Time and the Law,* Yale University Press, New Haven, CT, 1987.
11. For a treatment tying all these apparently disparate settings together in terms of their conceptualization, see Verlinden, Charles, *The Beginnings of Modern Colonization,* Cornell University Press, Ithaca, NY, 1970.
12. This is covered very well in the first chapter of Jerry Kammer's *The Second Long Walk: The Navajo-Hopi Land Dispute* (University of New Mexico Press, Albuquerque, 1980). As to the source of the present Navajo government's source of authority, this was spelled out quite clearly by the Supreme Court of the Navajo Nation in a finding (A-CV-13-89) in response to certified questions (WR-CV-99-89) raised in the case *Navajo Nation, et al. v. Peter*

McDonald et al., on April 13, 1989. In the opinion of the Honorable Robert Yazzie, writing for the court, "There is nothing in either the history of the present Navajo government or in the Tribal Code to support the argument that the source of the Chairman's and Vice Chairman's governmental authority is the voting public."

13. *Ibid.* Also see Parlow, Anita, *Cry, Sacred Land: Big Mountain, U.S.A.*, Christic Institute, Washington, D.C., 1988.
14. The term accrues from Federal Energy Administration, *Project Independence: A Summary*, Washington, D.C., November 1, 1974.
15. Much of this is brought out in U.S. Senate, Select Committee on Indian Affairs, *The Federal Government's Relationship with American Indians: Hearings Before the Special Committee on Investigations of the Select Committee on Indian Affairs*, United States Senate, January 30,31, 1989 and February 1, 1990, 101st Congress, 1st Session, U.S. Government Printing Office, Washington, D.C., 1990. Also see Allan, R., "The Navajo Tribal Council: A Study of the American Indian Assimilation Process," unpublished report available from the *Arizona Law Review*.
16. U.S. Commission on Civil Rights, *The Navajo Nation: An American Colony*, U.S. Government Printing Office, Washington, D.C., 1975.
17. U.S. Senate, *Relocation of Certain Hopi and Navajo Indians*, 96th Congress, 1st Session, U.S. Government Printing Office, Washington, D.C., May 15, 1979. Also see U.S. Department of Interior Surveys and Investigations Staff, *A Report to the Committee on Appropriations*, U.S. House of Representatives, on the Navajo and Hopi Relocation Commission, U.S. Government Printing Office, Washington, D.C., January 22, 1985.
18. For detailed elaboration on this theme, see Jaimes, M. Annette, "Federal Indian Identification Policy: A Usurpation of Indigenous Sovereignty in North America," in Ward Churchill (ed.), *Critical Issues in Native North America, Volume I*, International Work Group on Indigenous Affairs, Copenhagen, Denmark, 1989, pp. 15-36.
19. That Indians have no authority to dispense justice to non-Indians committing crimes against them, even in Indian Country, has been a touchstone of U.S. jurisprudence

since the first of the Trade and Intercourse Acts (1 Stat. 137) on July 22, 1790. Crimes by non-Indians against non-Indians in Indian Country was left "a matter of common sense" for nearly a century, with native jurisdiction in such matters not being formally negated until *United States v. McBratney,* 104 U.S. 621 (1881).

20. This is pursuant to the Major Crimes Act (23 Stat. 362, 385, 18 U.S.C. 548) of March 3, 1885, tested and affirmed in *Gon-Hay-Ee, Petitioner,* 130 U.S. 343 (1889). The original seven felonies covered in the act were expanded to ten by amendment to the legislation (25 U.S.C. 217-218) in 1910. Crimes committed by Indians against non-Indians in Indian Country had been covered—with the U.S. preemptively assuming jurisdiction—since an act passed on March 3, 1817 (3 Stat. 383), subsequently incorporated into the last of the Trade and Intercourse Acts (4 Stat. 729, 733) on June 30, 1834.
21. As a federal court put it: "If the United States is entitled [within its self-defined "trust capacity"] to institute an action on its own behalf and on behalf of the Indians, the Indians cannot determine the course of the suit or settle it contrary to the position of the government. The Indians, being represented by the government, are not necessary parties [to their own litigation]" *(Heckman v. United States,* 224 U.S. 413 (1912)). Also see *State of New Mexico v. Abeyta,* 50 F.2d 12 (C.C.A. 10, 1931).
22. "Sovereign immunity" has always been a juridical principle of the U.S., first brought formally to bear against Indians in *Hy-yu-tse-mil-kin v. Smith,* 205 U.S. 458 (1907).
23. *Morris v. Hitchcock,* 21 App. D.C. 565, 593 (1903), aff'd 194 U.S. 384 (1904).
24. Speech by Navajo Tribal Chairman Peter McDonald at the University of Colorado at Boulder, October 9, 1988 (tape on file).
25. 25 U.S.C.A. 461 (1934). For the original federal intent underlying the act, see Nash, Jay B., Oliver LaFarge and W. Carson Ryan, *New Day for the Indians: A Survey of the Workings of the Indian Reorganization Act,* Academy Press, New York, 1938.
26. Extensive analysis of IRA governmental structure may be found in Deloria, Vine Jr., and Clifford M. Lytle, *The*

Nations Within: The Past and Future of American Indian Sovereignty, Pantheon Books, New York, 1984.

27. Concerning Lakota referenda and "the vote of the dead," see Kelly, Lawrence H. (ed.), *Indian Affairs and the Indian Reorganization Act: The Twenty Year Record,* University of Arizona Press, Tucson, 1954.
28. On the Hopi referendum and its outcome, see Lummis, Charles, *Bullying the Hopi,* Prescott College Press, Prescott, AZ, 1968. Also see Indian Law Resource Center, *Report to the Kikmongwe and Other Traditional Hopi Leaders on Docket 196 and Other Threats to Hopi Land and Sovereignty,* Washington, D.C., 1979.
29. See Kelly, *op. cit.*
30. For a superb examination of contemporary analogies, see Herman, Edward S., and Frank Brodhead, *Demonstration Elections: U.S.-Staged Elections in the Dominican Republic, Vietnam and El Salvador,* South End Press, Boston, 1984.
31. This is precisely the phenomenon addressed by Frantz Fanon in his *Black Skin/White Masks,* Grove Press, New York, 1965. Another view may be found in Memmi, Albert, *Domination,* Beacon Press, Boston, 1971.
32. For analysis of the psychology of this circumstance, see Memmi, Albert, *Colonizer and Colonized,* Beacon Press, Boston, 1967. Also see Fanon, Frantz, *The Wretched of the Earth,* Grove Press, Boston, 1964.
33. See Editors, *BIA, I'm Not Your Indian Anymore,* Akwesasne Notes, Rooseveltown, NY, 1973. Also see Deloria, Vine Jr., *Behind the Trail of Broken Treaties* (Delta Books, New York, 1974) and Burnette, Robert, with John Koster, *The Road to Wounded Knee* (Bantam Books, New York, 1974).
34. See Editors, *Voices From Wounded Knee, 1973,* Akwesasne Notes, Rooseveltown, NY, 1974. Also see Matthiessen, Peter, *In the Spirit of Crazy Horse,* Viking Press, New York, 1984.
35. The complete 20 Point Program, and official federal responses to each point, are included as an appendix to *BIA, I'm Not Your Indian Anymore, op. cit.*
36. This tendency is discussed to a certain extent in *Behind the Trail of Broken Treaties, op. cit.*

37. The AIM actions were focused upon the brothers, Melvin and Leslie Hare, non-Indians who had ritually murdered an Oglala Lakota named Raymond Yellow Thunder in Gordon, Nebraska in January of 1972, and Darld Schmitz, a non-Indian who had knifed to death another Oglala, Wesley Bad Heart Bull, in Buffalo Gap, South Dakota, in January 1973. The Hares were charged with nothing until AIM's intervention. Schmitz was charged with only "second degree manslaughter." Other major cases addressed by the movement during this period were the shooting death of an unarmed Papago youth named Philip Celay by a non-Indian sheriff's deputy, David Bosman, in Ajo, Arizona in July 1972 ("justifiable homicide"); the shooting death of unarmed Mohawk political leader Richard Oaks by Michael Morgan in September 1972 ("self-defense"); and the shooting death of unarmed Onondaga Special Forces veteran Leroy Shenandoah by non-Indian police in Philadelphia during November 1972 (another "justifiable homicide"). See Josephy, Alvin M. Jr., *Now That the Buffalo's Gone: A Study of Today's Indians,* Alfred M. Knopf Publishers, New York, 1982.
38. See Matthiessen, *op. cit.* Also see Johansen, Bruce, and Robert Maestas, *Wasi'chu: The Continuing Indian Wars* (Monthly Review Press, New York, 1979); and Churchill, Ward, and Jim Vander Wall, *Agents of Repression: The FBI's Secret Wars Against the Black Panther Party and the American Indian Movement* (South End Press, Boston, 1988).
39. On Yellow Thunder Camp, see Weyler, Rex, *Blood of the Land: The U.S. Government and Corporate War Against the American Indian Movement,* Everest House Publishers, New York, 1983, pp. 251-64.
40. With regard to the Haudenosaunee, see *ibid.*, pp. 245-50.
41. On O'Odham, see *Akwesasne Notes,* Late Summer 1973. Also see Moskowitz, Milton, Michael Katz, and Robert Levering (eds.), *Everybody's Business: An Irreverent Guide to Corporate America,* Harper and Row Publishers, San Francisco, 1980.
42. Independent Commission on International Humanitarian Issues, *Indigenous Peoples: A Global Quest for Justice,* Zed Press, London, 1987.

43. Means, Russell, and Ward Churchill, *TREATY: A Platform for Nationhood,* Fourth World Center for Study of Indigenous Law and Politics, University of Colorado at Denver (forthcoming).
44. In general, see Minugh, Carol J., Glenn T. Morris and Rudolph C. Ryser (eds.) *Indian Self-Governance: Perspectives on the Political Status of Indian Nations in the United States of America,* Center for World Indigenous Studies, Kenmore, WA, 1989.
45. The complete text of S. 705 may be found in *Wicazo Sa Review,* Vol. IV, No. 1, Spring 1988.

Part IV
I Am Indigenist

This time I almost wanted to believe you
when you said it would be alright
you wanted to end the suffering;
And the deliberateness of the wrongs
were only in my imagination
This time I almost wanted
to believe you
when you implied
the times of sorrow
were buried in the past
never would we
have to worry
about shadows and
memories clinging
and draining
the strength
from our souls

This time I almost wanted
to believe you
when you spoke
of peace and love
and caring and duty
and God and destiny

But somehow the
death in your eyes
and your bombs
and your taxes
and your greed

told me
this time
I cannot afford
to believe you.

—John Trudell—
from *Living in Reality*

I Am Indigenist

Notes on the Ideology of the Fourth World

> The growth of ethnic consciousness and the consequent mobilization of Indian communities in the Western hemisphere since the early 1960s have been welcomed neither by government forces nor by opposition parties and revolutionary movements. The "Indian Question" has been an almost forbidden subject of debate throughout the entire political spectrum, although racism, discrimination and exploitation are roundly denounced on all sides.
>
> —Roxanne Dunbar Ortiz—
> *Indians of the Americas*

Very often in my writings and lectures, I have identified myself as being "indigenist" in outlook. By this, I mean that I am one who not only takes the rights of indigenous peoples as the highest priority of my political life, but who draws upon the traditions—the bodies of knowledge and corresponding codes of values—evolved over many thousands of years by native peoples the world over. This is the basis upon which I not only advance critiques of, but conceptualize alternatives to the present social, political, economic and philosophical status quo. In turn, this gives shape not only to the sorts of goals and objectives I pursue, but the kinds of strategy and tactics I advocate, the variety of struggles I tend to support, the nature of the alliances I'm inclined to enter into, and so on.

This essay is a revised version of several recent lectures.

Let me say, before I go any further, that I am hardly unique or alone in adopting this perspective. It is a combination of ideas, sentiments and understandings which motivates the whole of the American Indian Movement, broadly defined, here in North America. This is true whether you call it AIM, or Indians of All Tribes (as was done during the 1969 occupation of Alcatraz), the Warriors Society (as was the case with the Mohawk rebellion at Oka in 1990), Women of All Red Nations, or whatever.[1] It is the spirit of resistance which shapes the struggles of traditional Indian people on the land, whether the struggle is down at Big Mountain, in the Black Hills or up at James Bay, in the Nevada desert or out along the Columbia River in what is now called Washington State.[2] In the sense that I use the term, indigenism is also, I think, the outlook which guided our great leaders of the past: King Philip and Pontiac, Tecumseh and Creek Mary and Osceola, Black Hawk, Nancy Ward and Satanta, Lone Wolf and Red Cloud, Satank and Quannah Parker, Left Hand and Crazy Horse, Dull Knife and Chief Joseph, Sitting Bull, Roman Nose and Captain Jack, Louis Riél and Poundmaker and Geronimo, Cochise and Mangus, Victorio, Chief Seattle, and on and on.[3]

In my view, those—Indian and non-Indian alike—who do not recognize these names and what they represent have no sense of the true history, the reality, of North America. They have no sense of where they've come from or where they are, and thus can have no genuine sense of who or what they are. By not looking at where they've come from, they cannot know where they're going, or where it is they should go. It follows that they cannot understand what it is they are to do, how to do it, or why. In their confusion, they identify with the wrong people, the wrong things, the wrong tradition. They therefore inevitably pursue the wrong goals and objectives, putting last things first and often forgetting the first things altogether, perpetuating the very structures of oppression and degradation they think they oppose. Obviously, if things are to be changed for the better in this world, then this particular problem must itself be changed as a matter of first priority.

In any event, all this is not to say that I think I'm one of the people I have named, or the host of others, equally worthy, who've gone unnamed. I have no "New Age" conception of myself as the reincarnation of someone who has come before. But it *is* to say that I take these ancestors as my inspiration, as the only historical examples of proper attitude and comportment on this continent, this place, this land on which I live and of which I am a part. I embrace them as my heritage, my role models, the standard by which I must measure myself. I try always to be worthy of the battles they fought, the sacrifices they made. For the record, I've always found myself wanting in this regard, but I subscribe to the notion that one is obligated to speak the truth, even if one cannot live up to or fully practice it. As Chief Dan George once put it, I "endeavor to persevere," and I suppose this is a circumstance which is shared more-or-less equally by everyone presently involved in what I refer to as "indigenism."

Others whose writings, speeches and actions may be familiar, and who fit the definition of indigenist—or "Fourth Worlder," as we are sometimes called—include Winona LaDuke and John Trudell, Simon Ortiz, Russell Means and Dennis Banks and Leonard Peltier, Annette Jaimes and Glenn Morris and Leslie Silko, Jimmie Durham, John Mohawk and Chief Oren Lyons, Bob Robideau and Dino Butler, Vine Deloria, Ingrid Washinawatok and Dagmar Thorpe. There are scholars and attorneys like Don Grinde, Pam Colorado, Sharon Venne, Tim Coulter, George Tinker, Bob Thomas, Jack Forbes, Rob Williams and Hank Adams. There are poets like Wendy Rose, Adrian Lewis, Dian Million, Chrystos, Elizabeth Woody and Barnie Bush. There are grassroots contemporary warriors, people like Roberto Cruz and Regina Brave,

Bernard Ominayak, Art Montour and Buddy Lamont, Madonna Thunderhawk, Anna Mae Aquash, Kenny Kane and Joe Stuntz, Minnie Garrow and Bobby Garcia, Dallas Thundershield, Phyllis Young, Andrea Smith and Richard Oaks, Margo Thunderbird, Tina Trudell and Roque Duenas. And, of course, there are the elders, those who have given, and continue to give continuity and direction to indigenist expression; I'm referring to people like Chief Fools Crow and Matthew King, Henry Crow Dog and Grampa David Sohappy, David Monongye and Janet McCloud and Thomas Banyacya, Roberta Blackgoat and Katherine Smith and Pauline Whitesinger, Marie Lego and Phillip Deer and Ellen Moves Camp, Raymond Yowell and Nellie Red Owl.[4]

Like the historical figures I mentioned earlier, these are names representing positions, struggles and aspirations which should be well-known to every socially-conscious person in North America. They embody the absolute antithesis of the order represented by the "Four Georges"—George Washington, George Custer, George Patton and George Bush—symbolizing the sweep of "American" history as it is conventionally taught in that system of indoctrination the United States passes off as "education." They also stand as the negation of that long stream of "Vichy Indians" spawned and deemed "respectable" by the process of predation, colonialism and genocide the Four Georges signify.[5]

The names I've named cannot be associated with the legacy of the "Hang Around the Fort" Indians, broken, disempowered and intimidated by their conquerors, the sellouts who undermined the integrity of their own cultures, appointed by the United States to sign away their peoples' homelands in exchange for trinkets, sugar and alcohol. They are not the figurative descendants of those who participated in the assassination of men like Crazy Horse and Sitting Bull, and who filled the ranks of the colonial police to enforce an illegitimate and alien order against their own. They are not among those who have queued up to roster the regimes installed by the U.S. to administer Indian Country from the 1930s onward, the craven puppets who to this day cling to and promote the "lawful authority" of federal force as a means of protecting their positions of petty privilege, imagined prestige, and often their very identities as native people. No, indigenists and indigenism have nothing to do with the sorts of Quisling impulses driving the Ross Swimmers, Dickie Wilsons, Webster Two Hawks, Peter McDonalds and David Bradleys of this world.[6]

Instead, indigenism offers an antidote to all that, a vision of how things might be which is based on how things have been since time immemorial, and how things must be once again if the human species, and perhaps the planet itself, is to survive much longer. Predicated in a synthesis of the wisdom attained over thousands of years by indigenous, land-based peoples around the globe—the Fourth World or, as Winona LaDuke puts it, "The Host World upon which the first, second and third worlds all sit at the present time"—indigenism stands in diametrical opposition to the totality of what might be termed "Eurocentric business as usual."[7]

Indigenism

The manifestation of indigenism in North America has much in common with the articulation of what in Latin America is called *indigenismo*. One of the major proponents of this, the Mexican anthropologist/activist Guillermo Bonfil Batalla, has framed its precepts this way: "[I]n America there exists only one unitary Indian civilization. All the Indian peoples participate in this civilization. The diversity of cultures and languages is not an obstacle to affirmation of the unity of this civilization. It is a fact that all civilizations, including Western civilization, have these sorts of internal differences. But the level of unity—the civilization—is more profound than the level of specificity (the cultures, the languages, the communities). The civilizing dimension transcends the concrete diversity."[8]

> The differences between these diverse peoples (or ethnic groups) have been accentuated by the colonizers as part of the strategy of domination. There have been attempts by some to fragment the Indian peoples...by establishing frontiers, deepening differences and provoking rivalries. This strategy follows a principle objective: domination, to which end it is attempted ideologically to demonstrate that in America, Western civilization is confronted by a magnitude of atomized peoples, differing from one another (every day more and more languages are "discovered"). Thus, in consequence, such peoples are believed incapable of forging a future of their own. In contrast to this, the Indian thinking affirms the existence of one—a unique and different—Indian civilization, from which extend as particular expressions the cultures of diverse peoples. Thus, the identification and solidarity among Indians. Their "Indianness" is not a simple tactic postulated, but rather the necessary expression of an historical unity, based in common civilization, which the colonizer has wanted to hide. Their Indianness, furthermore, is reinforced by the common experience of almost five centuries of [Eurocentric] domination.[9]

"The past is also unifying," Bonfil Batalla continues:

> The achievements of the classic Mayas, for instance, can be reclaimed as part of the Quechua foundation [in present-day Guatemala], much the same as the French affirm their Greek past. And even beyond the remote past which is shared, and beyond the colonial experience that makes all Indians similar, Indian peoples also have a common historic project for the future. The legitimacy of that project rests precisely in the existence of an Indian civilization, within which framework it could be realized, once the "chapter of colonialism ends." One's own civilization signifies the right and the possibility to create

one's own future, a different future, not Western.[10]

As has been noted elsewhere, the "new" indigenous movement Bonfil Batalla describes equates "colonialism/imperialism with the West; in opposing the West...[adherents] view themselves as anti-imperialist. Socialism, or Marxism, is viewed as just another Western manifestation."[11] A query is thus posed:

> What, then, distinguishes Indian from Western civilization? Fundamentally, the difference can be summed up in terms of [humanity's] relationship with the natural world. For the West...the concept of nature is that of an enemy to be overcome, with man as boss on a cosmic scale. Man in the West believes he must dominate everything including other [people around him] and other peoples. The converse is true in Indian civilization, where [humans are] part of an indivisible cosmos and fully aware of [their] harmonious relationship with the universal order of nature. [S]he neither dominates nor tries to dominate. On the contrary, she exists within nature as a moment of it...Traditionalism thus constitutes a potent weapon in the [indigenous] civilization's struggle for survival against colonial domination.[12]

Bonfil Batalla contends that the nature of the indigenist impulse is essentially socialist, insofar as socialism—or what Karl Marx described as "primitive communism"—was and remains the primary mode of indigenous social organization in the Americas.[13] Within this framework, he remarks that there are "six fundamental demands identified with the Indian movement," all of them associated with sociopolitical, cultural and economic autonomy (or sovereignty) and self-determination:

> First there is land. There are demands for occupied ancestral territories...demands for control of the use of the land and subsoil; and struggles against the invasion of...commercial interests. Defense of land held and recuperation of land lost are the central demands. Second, the

demand for recognition of the ethnic and cultural specificity of the Indian is identified. All [indigenist] organizations reaffirm the right to be distinct in culture, language and institutions, and to increase the value of their own technological, social and ideological practices. Third is the demand for [parity] of political rights in relation to the state...Fourth, there is a call for the end of repression and violence, particularly that against the leaders, activists and followers of the Indians' new political organizations. Fifth, Indians demand the end of family planning programmes which have brought widespread sterilization of Indian women and men. Finally, tourism and folklore are rejected, and there is a demand for true Indian cultural expression to be respected. The commercialization of Indian music and dance are often mentioned...and there is a particular dislike for the exploitation of those that have sacred content and purpose for Indians. An end to the exploitation of Indian culture in general is [demanded].[14]

In North America, these *indigenista* demands have been adopted virtually intact, and have been conceived as encompassing basic needs of native peoples wherever they have been subsumed by the sweep of Western expansionism. This is the idea of the Fourth World, explained by Cree author George Manuel, founding president of the World Council of Indigenous Peoples:

The 4th World is the name given to indigenous peoples descended from a country's aboriginal population and who today are completely or partly deprived of their own territory and its riches. The peoples of the 4th World have only limited influence or none at all in the nation states [in which we are now encapsulated]. The peoples to whom we refer are the Indians of North and South America, the Inuit (Eskimos), the Sami people [of northern Scandinavia], the Australian aborigines, as well as the various indigenous populations of Africa, Asia and Oceana.[15]

Manuel might well have included segments of the European population itself, as is evidenced by the ongoing struggles of the Irish, Welsh, Basques, and others to free themselves from the yoke of settler state oppression imposed upon them as long as 800 years ago.[16] In such areas of Europe, as well as in "the Americas and [large portions of] Africa, the goal is not the creation of a state, but the expulsion of alien rule and the reconstruction of societies."[17] That such efforts are entirely serious is readily evidenced by the fact that, in a global survey conducted by University of California cultural geographer Bernard Neitschmann during 1985-87, it was discovered that of the more than 100 armed conflicts then underway, some 85 percent were being waged by indigenous peoples against the state or states which had laid claim to and occupied their territories.[18] As Theo van Boven, former director of the United Nations Division (now Center) for Human Rights, put it in 1981: the circumstances precipitating armed struggle "may be seen with particular poignancy in relation to the indigenous peoples of the world, who have been described somewhat imaginatively—and perhaps not without justification—as representing the fourth world: the world on the margin, on the periphery."[19]

The issue of land in North America

What must be understood about the context of the Americas north of the Río Grande is that neither of the nation-states, the U.S. or Canada, which claim sovereignty over the territory involved has any legitimate basis at all in which to anchor its absorption of huge portions of that territory. I'm going to restrict my remarks in this connection mostly to the U.S., mainly because that's what I know best. Because both the U.S. and Canada have evolved on the basis of the Anglo-Saxon common law tradition,[20] I think much of what can be said about the U.S. is relevant to understanding the situation in Canada. Certain of the principles, of course, also extend to the situation in Latin America, but there you have an evolution of nation-states based in the Spanish legal tradition, so a greater transposition in terms is required.[21] Let's just say that the shape of things down south was summarized eloquently enough by the Peruvian freedom fighter Hugo Blanco with his slogan, "Land or Death!"[22]

During the first 90-odd years of its existence, the United States entered into and ratified more than 370 separate treaties with the peoples indigenous to the area of the 48 contiguous states.[23] There are a number of important dimensions to this, but two aspects will do for our purposes here. More detail is provided elsewhere in this book. First, by customary international law and provision of the U.S. Constitution itself, each treaty ratification represented a formal recognition by the federal government that the other parties to the treaties—the native peoples—were fully sovereign nations in their own right.[24] Second, the purpose of the treaties, from the U.S. point of view, was to serve as real estate documents through which it acquired legal title to specified portions of North American geography from the indigenous nations it was thereby acknowledging already owned it. From the viewpoint of the indigenous nations, of course, these treaties served other purposes: the securing of permanently guaranteed borders to what remained of their national territories, assurance of the continuation of their ongoing self-governance, trade and military alliances, and so forth. The treaty relationships were invariably reciprocal in nature: Indians ceded certain portions of their land to the U.S., and the U.S. incurred specific obligations in exchange.[25]

Even at that, there were seldom any outright sales of land by Indian nations to the U.S. Rather, the federal obligations incurred were usually couched in terms of perpetuity. The arrangements were set up by the Indians so that, as long as the U.S. honored its end of the bargains struck, it would have the right to occupy and use defined portions of Indian land. In this sense, the treaties more resemble rental or leasing instruments than actual deeds. And you know what happens under Anglo-Saxon common law when a tenant violates the provisions of a rental agreement, eh? The point here is that the U.S. has long since defaulted on its responsibilities under every single treaty obligation it ever incurred with regard to Indians. There is really no dispute about this. In fact, there's even a Supreme Court opinion—the 1903 *Lonewolf* case—in which the good "justices" held that the U.S. enjoyed a "right" to disregard any treaty obligation to Indians it found inconvenient, but that the remaining treaty provisions continued to be binding upon the Indians. This was, the high court said, because the U.S. was the stronger of the nations involved, and thus wielded "plenary" power—this means *full* power—over the affairs of the weaker indigenous nations. Therefore, the court felt itself free to unilaterally "interpret" each treaty as being a bill of sale rather than a rental agreement.[26]

Stripped of its fancy legal language, the Supreme Court's position was (and remains) astonishingly crude. There's an old adage that "possession is nine-tenths of the law." Well, in this case the court went a bit further, arguing that possession was *all* of the law. Further, the highest court in the land went on record arguing bold-faced that, where Indian property rights are concerned, might, and might alone, makes right. The U.S. held the power to simply take Indian land, they said, and therefore it had the "right" to do so. If you think about it, that's precisely what the nazis argued only thirty years later, and the United States had the unmitigated audacity to profess outrage and shock that Germany so blatantly transgressed against elementary standards of international law and the most basic requirements of human decency.[27] For that matter, this is all that Saddam Hussein was about when he took Kuwait—indeed, Iraq had a far stronger claim to rights over Kuwait than the U.S. has ever had with regard to Indian Country—with the result that George Bush began to babble about fighting a "just war" to "roll back naked aggression," "free occupied territory," and "reinstate a legitimate government." If he was in any way serious about that proposition, he'd have had to call air strikes in on *himself* before ordering the bombing of Baghdad.[28]

Be that as it may, there are a couple of other significant problems with the treaty constructions by which the U.S. allegedly assumed title over its landbase. On the one hand, a number of the ratified treaties can be shown to be fraudulent or coerced, and thus invalid. The nature of the coercion is fairly well known, so let's just say that perhaps a third of the ratified treaties involved direct coercion and shift over to the matter of fraud. This assumes the form of everything from the deliberate misinterpretation of proposed treaty provisions to Indian representatives during negotiations to the senate's alteration of treaty language after the fact and without the knowledge of the Indian signatories. On a number of occasions the U.S. appointed its own preferred Indian "leaders" to represent their nations in treaty negotiations.[29] In at least one instance—the 1861 Treaty of Fort Wise—U.S. negotiators appear to have forged the signatures of various Cheyenne and Arapaho leaders.[30] Additionally, there are about 400 treaties which were never ratified by the senate, and were therefore never legally binding, but upon which the U.S. now asserts its claims concerning lawful use and occupancy rights to, and jurisdiction over, appreciable portions of North America.[31]

When all is said and done, however, even these extremely dubious bases for U.S. title are insufficient to cover the gross territorality at issue. The federal government itself admitted as much during the 1970s, in the findings of the so-called Indian Claims Commission, an entity created to "quiet" title to all illegally taken Indian land within the "lower 48."[32] What the commission did over the ensuing 35 years was in significant part to research the ostensible documentary basis for U.S. title to literally every square foot of its claimed territory. It found, among other things, that the U.S. had no legal basis whatsoever—no treaty, no agreement, not even an arbitrary act of Congress—to fully one-third of the area within its boundaries.[33] At the same time, the data revealed that the reserved areas still nominally possessed by Indians had been reduced to about 2.5 percent of the same area.[34] What this means in plain English is that the United States cannot pretend to even a shred of legitimacy in its occupancy and control of upwards of 30 percent of its "home" territory. And, lest such matters be totally lost in the shuffle, I should note that it has even less legal basis for its claims to the land in Alaska and Hawaii.[35] Beyond that, it's "right" to assert dominion over Puerto Rico, the "U.S." Virgin Islands, "American" Samoa, Guam, and the Marshall Islands, tends to speak for itself, don't you think?

Priority of Indian Land Recovery in the U.S.

Leaving aside questions concerning the validity of various treaties, the beginning point for any indigenist endeavor in the United States centers, logically enough, in efforts to restore direct Indian control over the huge portion of the continental U.S. which was never ceded by native nations. Upon the bedrock of this foundation, a number of other problems integral to the present configuration of power and privilege in North American society can be resolved, not just for Indians, but for everyone else as well. It's probably impossible to solve, or even to begin meaningfully addressing, certain of these problems in any other way. But still, it is, as they say, "no easy sell" to convince anyone outside the more conscious sectors of the American Indian population itself of the truth of this very simple fact.

In part, uncomfortable as it may be to admit, this is because even the most progressive elements of the North American immigrant population shares a perceived commonality of interest with the more reactionary segments. This takes the form of a mutual insistence upon an imagined "right" to possess native property, merely because they are here, and because they desire it. The Great Fear is, within any settler state, that if indigenous land rights are ever openly acknowledged, and native people therefore begin to recover some significant portion of their land, the immigrants will correspondingly be dispossessed of what they've come to consider "theirs"; most notably, individually-held homes, small farms and ranches, and the like. Tellingly, every major Indian land recovery initiative in the U.S. during the second half of the 20th century—those in Maine, the Black Hills, the Oneida claims in New York State, and Western Shoshone are prime examples—has been met by a propaganda barrage from rightwing organizations ranging from the Ku Klux Klan to the John Birch Society to the Republican Party warning individual non-Indian property holders of exactly this "peril."[36]

I'll debunk some of this nonsense in a moment, but first I want to take up the posture of self-proclaimed left-wing radicals in the same connection. And I'll do so on the basis of principle, because justice is supposed to matter more to progressives than to rightwing hacks. Let me say that the pervasive and near-total silence of the left in this connection has been quite illuminating. Non-Indian activists, with only a handful of exceptions, persistently plead that they can't really take a coherent position on the matter of Indian land rights because, "unfortunately," they're "not really conversant with the issues" (as if these were tremendously complex). Meanwhile, they do virtually nothing, generation after generation, to inform themselves on the topic of who actually owns the ground they're standing on. Okay folks, the record can be played only so many times before it wears out and becomes just another variation of "hear no evil, see no evil." It doesn't take Einstein, at this point, to figure out that the left still doesn't know much about such things because it's never *wanted* to know, or that this is so because it's always had its own plans for utilizing land it has no more right to than does the status quo it claims to oppose.

The usual technique for explaining this away, has always been a sort of *pro forma* acknowledgement that Indian land rights are of course "really important stuff" (yawn), but that one "really doesn't have a lot of time" to get into it. (I'll buy your book though, and keep it on my shelf even if I never read it.) Reason? Well, one is just "overwhelmingly preoccupied" with working on what they consider to be "other important issues." (For "other" read "more important.") Typically enumerated are sexism, racism, homophobia, class inequities, militarism, the environment, or some combination. It's a pretty good evasion, all in all. Certainly, there's no denying any of these issues their due; they *are* all important, obviously so. But more important than the question of land rights? There are some serious problems of primacy and priority imbedded in the orthodox script.

To frame things clearly, let's hypothesize for a moment that all of the various non-Indian movements concentrating on each of these issues were suddenly successful in accomplishing their objectives. Let's imagine that the United States as a whole were somehow transformed into an entity defined by the parity of its race, class and gender relations, its embrace of unrestricted sexual preference, its rejection of militarism in all forms, and its abiding concern with environmental protection. (I know, I know, this is a sheer impossibility, but that's my point.) When all is said and done, the society resulting from this scenario is still, first and foremost, a colonialist society, an imperialist society in the most fundamental possible sense. This is true because the scenario does nothing at all to address the fact that whatever is happening happens on someone else's land, not only without their consent, but through an adamant disregard for their rights to the land. Hence, all it means is that the immigrant or invading population has rearranged its affairs in such a way as to make itself more comfortable at the continuing expense of indigenous people. The colonial equation remains intact and may even be reinforced by a greater degree of participation and vested interest in maintenance of the colonial order among the settler population at large.[37]

The dynamic here is not very different from that evident in the American Revolution of the late eighteenth century, is it? And we all know very well where that led, don't we? Should we therefore begin to refer to socialist imperialism, feminist imperialism, gay and lesbian imperialism, environmentalist imperialism, Afroamerican and la Raza imperialism? I would hope not.[38] I would hope this is all just a matter of confusion, of muddled priorities among people who really do mean well and who'd like to do better. If so, then all that is necessary to correct the situation is a basic rethinking of what it is that must be done, and in what order. Here, I'd advance the straightforward premise that the land rights of "First Americans" should serve as a first priority for attainment by *everyone* seriously committed to accomplishing positive change in North America.

But before I suggest everyone jump up and adopt this land rights priority, I suppose it's only fair that I examine its possible implications. If making things like class inequity and sexism the preeminent focus of progressive action in North America inevitably perpetuates the internal colonial structure of the U.S., would making land rights top priority perpetuate class and sexist domination? I assert unequivocally it would not. There is no indication whatsoever that a restoration of indigenous sovereignty in Indian Country would foster class stratification anywhere, least of all in Indian Country. In fact, all indications are that when left to their own devices, indigenous peoples have consistently organized their societies in the most class-free manner. Look to the example of the Haudenosaunee (Six Nations Iroquois Confederacy). Look to the Muscogee (Creek) Confederacy. Look to the confederations of the Yaqui and the Lakota, and those pursued and nearly perfected by Pontiac and Tecumseh. They represent the very essence of enlightened egalitarianism and democracy. Every imagined example to the contrary brought forth by even the most arcane anthropologist can be readily offset by a couple of dozen other illustrations along the lines of those I just mentioned.[39]

Would sexism be perpetuated? Ask one of the Haudenosaunee clan mothers, who continue to exercise political leadership in their societies through the present day. Ask Wilma Mankiller, current head of the Cherokee Nation, a people traditionally led by those called "Beloved Women." Ask a Lakota woman—or man, for that matter—about who owned all real property in traditional society, and what that meant in terms of parity in gender relations. Ask a traditional Navajo grandmother about her social and political role among her people. Women in most traditional native societies not only enjoy political, social and economic parity with men, they often hold a preponderance of power in one or more of these spheres.

Homophobia? Homosexuals of both genders were (and in many settings still are) deeply revered as special or extraordinary, and therefore spiritually significant, within most indigenous North American cultures. The extent to which these realities do not now pertain in native societies is exactly the extent to which Indians have been subordinated to the morés of the invading, dominating culture. Insofar as restoration of Indian land rights is tied directly to the reconstitution of traditional indigenous social, political and economic modes, you can see where this leads; the relations of sex and sexuality match rather well with the aspirations of feminism and gay rights activism.[40]

How about a restoration of native land rights precipitating some sort of "environmental holocaust?" Let's get at least a little bit real here. If you're not addicted to the fabrications of Smithsonian anthropologists,[41] or George Weurthner's Eurosupremicist *Earth First!* fantasies about how we beat all the woolly mammoths and mastodons and sabertoothed cats to death with sticks,[42] then this isn't even a question. I know it's become fashionable among *Washington Post* editorialists to make snide references to native people "strewing refuse in their wake" as they "wandered nomadically" about the "prehistoric" North American landscape.[43] What is that supposed to imply? That we, who were mostly "sedentary agriculturalists" in any event, were dropping plastic and aluminum cans as we went? Like I said, let's get real. Read the accounts of early European invaders about what they encountered: North America was invariably described as being a "pristine wilderness" at the point of European arrival, despite the fact that it had been occupied by 15 or 20 million people enjoying a remarkably high standard of living for nobody knows how long: 40,000 years? 50,000 years?[44] longer? Now contrast that reality to what's been done to this continent over the past couple of hundred years by the culture that Weurthner, the Smithsonian and the *Post* represent, and you tell *me* about environmental devastation.[45]

That leaves militarism and racism. How would concerns over these issues fare if land rights were a fundamental priority? Taking the last first, there really is no indication of racism in traditional Indian societies. To the contrary, the record reveals that Indians habitually intermarried between groups, and frequently adopted both children and adults from other groups. This occurred in precontact times between Indians, and the practice was broadened to include those of both African and European origin—and ultimately Asian origin as well—once contact occurred. Those who were naturalized by marriage or adoption were considered members of the group, pure and simple. This was always the Indian view.[46] The Europeans and subsequent Euroamerican settlers saw things rather differently, however, and foisted the notion that Indian identity should be determined primarily by "blood quantum" an outright eugenics code similar to those developed in places like nazi Germany and apartheid South Africa. Now, *that's* a racist set of policies and principles if there ever was one. Unfortunately, a lot of Indians have been conned into accepting this anti-Indian absurdity, and that's something to be overcome. But there's also solid indication that quite a number of native people continue to strongly resist such things as the quantum system.[47]

As to militarism, no one will deny that Indians fought wars among themselves both before and after the European invasion began. Probably half of all indigenous peoples in North America maintained permanent warrior societies. This could perhaps be reasonably construed as "militarism." But not, I think, in the sense it conveys when describing the European/Euroamerican tradition. There were never, so far as anyone can demonstrate, wars of annihilation fought in this hemisphere prior to the Columbian arrival. None. In fact, it seems that it was a more-or-less firm principle of indigenous warfare *not* to kill, the object being to demonstrate personal bravery, something which could be done only against a *live* opponent. There's no honor in killing another person, because a dead person can't hurt you. There's no risk. This is not to say that nobody ever died or was seriously injured in the fighting. They were, just as they are in contemporary full-contact sports like football and boxing. Actually, these kinds of Euroamerican games are what I would take to be the closest modern parallels to traditional inter-Indian warfare. For Indians, it was a way of burning excess testosterone out of young males, and not much more. Militarism in the way the term is used today is as alien to native tradition as smallpox and atomic bombs.[48]

So, not only is it perfectly reasonable to assert that a restoration of Indian control over unceded lands within the U.S. would do nothing to perpetuate such problems as sexism and classism, but the reconstitution of indigenous societies this would entail stands to free the affected portions of North America from such maladies altogether. Moreover, it can be said that the process should have a tangible impact in terms of diminishing such things elsewhere. The principle is this: sexism, racism, and all the rest arose here as a concomitant to the emergence and consolidation of the Eurocentric nation-state form of sociopolitical and economic organization. Everything the state does, everything it can do, is entirely contingent upon its maintaining its internal cohesion, a cohesion signified above all by its pretended territorial integrity, its ongoing domination of Indian Country. Given this, it seems obvious that the literal dismemberment of the nation-state inherent to Indian land recovery correspondingly reduces the ability of the state to sustain the imposition of objectionable relations within itself. Realization of indigenous land rights serves to undermine or destroy the ability of the status quo to continue imposing a racist, sexist, classist, homophobic, militaristic order upon non-Indians.

A brief aside. Anyone who doubts that it's possible to bring about the dismemberment of a superpower state using internal forces in this day and age, ought to sit down and have a long talk with a guy named Mikhail Gorbachev. It would be better yet if you could chew the fat with Leonid Breznev, a man we can be sure would have replied in all sincerity—only a decade ago—that this was the most outlandish idea he'd ever heard. Well, look on a map today, and see if you can find the Union of Soviet Socialist Republics. It ain't there, my friends. Instead, you're seeing, and you're seeing it more and more, the reemergence of the very nations Léon Trotsky and his colleagues consigned to the "dustbin of history" clear back at the beginning of the century. These megastates are not immutable. They can be taken apart. They can be destroyed. But first we have to decide that we can do it, and that we *will* do it.

All things considered, when indigenist movements like AIM advance slogans like "U.S. Out of North America," non-Indian radicals shouldn't react defensively. They should cheer. They should see what they might do to help. When they respond defensively to sentiments like those expressed by AIM, what they are ultimately defending is the very government, the very order they claim to oppose so resolutely. And if they manifest this contradiction often enough, consistently enough, pathologically enough, then we have no alternative but to take them at their word, that they really are at some deep level aligned—all protestations to the contrary notwithstanding—with the mentality which endorses our permanent dispossession and disenfranchisement, our continuing oppression, our ultimate genocidal obliteration as self-defining and self-determining peoples. To revive the old axiom, they make themselves part of the problem rather than becoming part of the solution.

Indian Land Restoration: Toward a North American Union of Indigenous Nations

There are certain implications to Indian control over Indian land which need to be clarified, beginning with a debunking of the "Great Fear," the reactionary myth that any substantive native land recovery would automatically lead to the mass dispossession and eviction of individual non-Indian homeowners. Maybe in the process I can reassure a couple of radicals that it's okay to be on the right side of this issue, that they won't have to give something up in order to part company with George Bush on this. It's hard, frankly, to talk about this without giggling because of some of the images it inspires. I mean, what *are* people worried about here? Do y'all really foresee Indians standing out on the piers of Boston and New York City, issuing sets of waterwings to long lines of non-Indians so they can all swim back to the Old World? Gimme a break.

Seriously, you can search high and low, and you'll never find an instance in which Indians have advocated that small property owners be pushed off the land in order to satisfy land claims. The thrust in every single case has been to recover land within national and state parks and forests, grasslands, military reservations, and the like. In a few instances, major corporate holdings have been targeted. A couple of times, as in the Black Hills, a sort of joint jurisdiction between Indians and the existing non-Indian government has been discussed with regard to an entire treaty area.[49] But even in the most hard-line of the indigenous positions concerning the Black Hills, that advanced by Russell Means in his TREATY Program, where resumption of exclusively Lakota jurisdiction is demanded, there is no mention of dispossessing or evicting non-Indians.[50] Instead, other alternatives—which I'll take up below—were carefully spelled out.

But first, I'd like to share with you something the rightwing propagandists never mention when they're busily whipping up non-Indian sentiment against Indian rights. You'll recall I said that the quantity of unceded land within the continental U.S. makes up about one-third of the landmass. Let's just round this off to 30 percent, because there's the matter of 2.5 percent of the overall landbase still being set aside as Indian reservations. Juxtaposed to that 30 percent is the approximately 35 percent of the same landmass the federal government presently holds in various kinds of trust status. Add the 10 or 12 percent of the land the 48 contiguous states hold in trust. The 30 percent Indian claim to the U.S. landmass is smaller than the 45 to 47 percent of the area held by the *government.*[51] Never mind the percentage of the land held by major corporations. The conclusion is clear: It is, and always has been, quite possible to accomplish the return of every square inch of unceded Indian Country in the United States without tossing a single non-Indian home-owner off the land on which they live.

Critics—that's the amazingly charitable term for themselves employed by those who ultimately oppose the assertion of indigenous rights in any form and as a matter of principle—are always quick to point out that the problem with this arithmetic is that the boundaries of the government trust areas do not necessarily conform in all cases to the boundaries of unceded areas. That's true enough, although I'd just as quickly point out that more often than not they *do* correspond. This "problem" is nowhere near as big as it's made out to be. And there's nothing intrinsic to the boundary question which couldn't be negotiated, once non-Indian America acknowledges that Indians have an absolute moral and legal right to the quantity of territory which was never ceded. Boundaries can be adjusted, often in ways which can be beneficial to those on both sides of the negotiation.[52]

Let me give you an example. Along about 1980, a couple of Rutgers University professors, Frank and Deborah Popper, undertook a comprehensive study of land-use patterns and economy in the Great Plains region. What they discovered is that 110 counties—a quarter of all the counties within the western portions of the states of North and South Dakota, Nebraska, Kansas, Oklahoma and Texas, as well as eastern Montana, Wyoming Colorado and New Mexico—have been fiscally insolvent since the moment they were taken from native people a century or more ago. This is an area of about 140,000 square miles, inhabited by a widely dispersed non-Indian population of only around 400,000 attempting to maintain school dis-

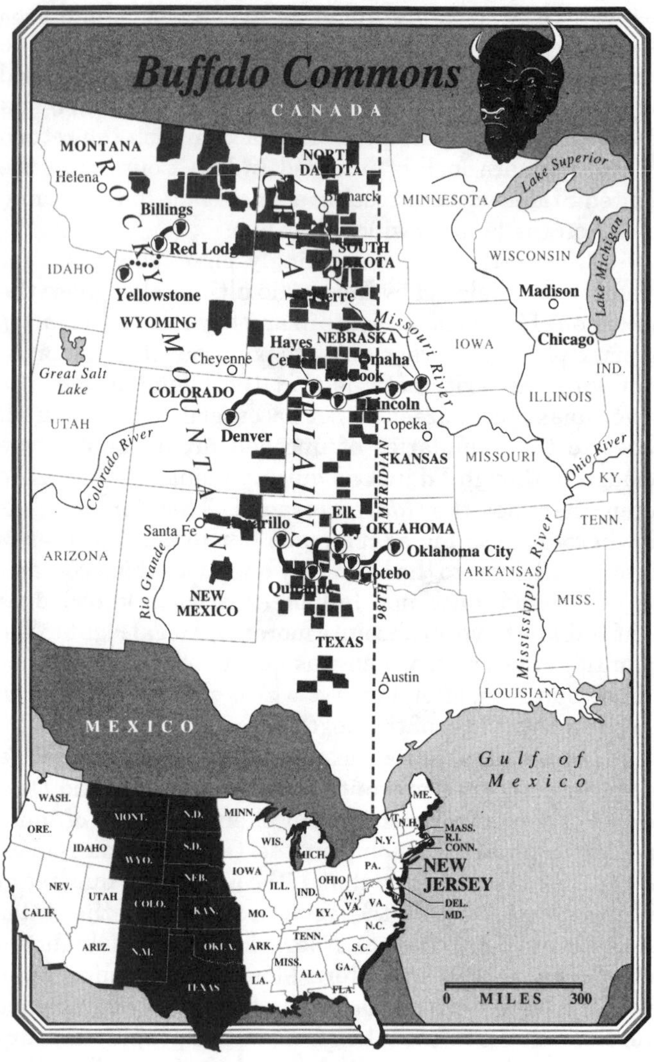

Anne Matthews, *Where the Buffalo Roam.*

tricts, police and fire departments, road beds and all the other basic accoutrements of "modern life" on the negligible incomes which can be eked from cattle grazing and wheat farming on land which is patently unsuited for either enterprise. The Poppers found that, without considerable federal subsidy each and every year, none of these counties would ever have been viable. Nor, on the face of it, will any of them ever be. Put bluntly, the pretense of bringing Euroamerican "civilization" to the Plains does little more than place a massive economic burden on the rest of the United States.

What the Poppers proposed on the basis of these findings is that the government cut its perpetual losses, buying out the individual land holdings within the target counties, and converting them into open space wildlife sanctuaries known as the "Buffalo Commons." The whole area would in effect be turned back to the bison which were very nearly exterminated by Phil Sheridan's buffalo hunters back in the nineteenth century as a means of starving "recalcitrant" Indians into surrendering. The result, they argue, would be both environmentally and economically beneficial to the nation as a whole. It is instructive that their thinking has gained increasing credibility and support from Indians and non-Indians alike during the second half of the '80s. I can't help but chuckle here: Indians have been trying to tell non-Indians that this would be the outcome of fencing in the Plains ever since 1850 or so, but some folks have a real hard time catching on. Anyway, it is entirely possible that we'll see some actual motion in this direction over the next few years.[53]

So, let's take the Poppers' idea to its next logical step. There are another 100 or so counties adjoining the "perpetual red ink" counties they've identified which are themselves economically marginal. These don't represent an actual drain on the U.S. economy, but they don't contribute much either. They could be "written off" and included into the Buffalo Commons scheme with no one feeling any appreciable ill effects. Now add in adjacent areas like the national grasslands in Wyoming, the national forest and parklands in the Black Hills, extraneous military reservations like Ellsworth Air Force Base, and existing Indian reservations. What you end up with is a huge territory lying east of Denver, west of Lawrence, Kansas, and extending from the Canadian border to southern Texas, all of it "outside the loop" of U.S. business as usual.

The bulk of this area is unceded territory owned by the Lakota, Pawnee, Arikara, Hidatsa, Mandan, Crow, Shoshone, Assiniboine, Cheyenne, Arapaho, Kiowa, Kiowa Apache, Comanche, Jicarilla and Mescalero Apache nations. There would be little cost to the United States, and virtually no arbitrary dispossession/dislocation of non-Indians, if the entire Commons were restored to these peoples. Further, it would establish a concrete basis from which genuine expressions of indigenous self-determination could begin to reemerge on this continent, allowing the indigenous nations involved to begin the process of reconstituting themselves socially and politically, and to begin to recreate their traditional economies in ways which make contemporary sense. This would provide alternative socioeconomic models for possible adaptation by non-Indians, and alleviate a range of not inconsiderable costs to the public treasury incurred by keeping the Indians in question in a state of abject and permanent dependency.

Alright, as critics will undoubtedly be quick to point out, a sizeable portion of the Buffalo Commons area I've sketched out—perhaps a million acres—lies outside the boundaries of unceded territory. That's the basis for the sorts of multilateral negotiations between the U.S. and indigenous nations I mentioned earlier. This land will need to be "charged off" in some fashion against unceded land elsewhere, and in such a way as to bring other native peoples into the mix. The Ponca, Omaha and Osage, whose traditional territories fall within the area in question, come immediately to mind; but the principle could extend as well to all native peoples willing to exchange land claims somewhere else for actual acreage in this locale. The idea is to consolidate a distinct indigenous territorality while providing a definable landbase to as many different Indian nations as possible in the process.

From there, the Buffalo Commons *cum* Indian Territory could be extended westwards into areas which adjoin or are at least immediately proximate to the Commons area itself. Vast areas of the Great Basin and Sonoran Desert regions of the U.S. are even more sparsely populated and economically insolvent than the Plains. A great deal of the area is also held in federal trust. Hence, it is reasonable—in my view at least—to expand the Commons territory to include most of Utah and Nevada, northern Montana and Idaho, quite a lot of eastern Washington and Oregon, most of New Mexico, and the lion's share of Arizona. This would encompass the unceded lands of the Blackfeet and Gros Ventre, Salish, Kootenai, Nez Percé, Yakima, Western Shoshone, Goshutes and Utes, Paiutes, Navajo, Hopi and other Pueblos, Mescalero and Chiricahua Apache, Havasupi, Yavapai and O'Odham. It would also set the stage for further exchange negotiations, in order to consolidate this additional territory, which would serve to establish a landbase for a number of other indigenous nations.

At this point, we've arrived at an area comprising roughly one third of the continental U.S., a territory which—regardless of the internal political and geographical subdivisions effected by the array of native peoples within it—could be defined as a sort of "North American Union of Indigenous Nations." Such an entity would be in a position to assist other indigenous nations outside its borders, but still within the remaining territorial corpus of the U.S., to resolve land claim issues accruing from

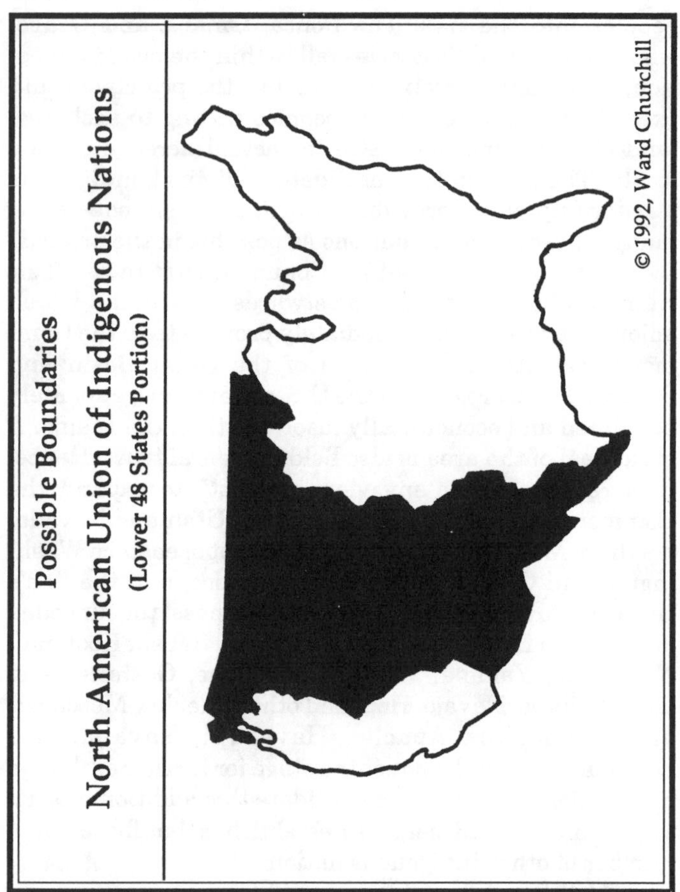

fraudulent or coerced treaties of cession (another 15 or 20 percent of the present 48 states). It would also be in a position to facilitate an accommodation of the needs of untreatied peoples within the U.S., the Abenaki of Vermont, for example, and the Native Hawaiians and Alaskan natives. Similarly, it would be able to help secure the self-determination of U.S. colonies like Puerto Rico. You can see the direction in which the dominoes begin to fall.

Nor does this end with the United States. Any sort of indigenous union of the kind I've described would be as eligible for admission as a fully participating member of the United Nations as, say, Croatia and the Ukraine have recently shown themselves to be. This would set a very important precedent, insofar as there's never been an American Indian entity of any sort accorded such political status on the world stage. The precedent could serve to pave the way for comparable recognition and attainments by other Native American nations, notably the confederation of Incan peoples of the Andean highlands and the Mayans of present-day Guatemala and southern Mexico. (Indians are the majority population, decisively so, in both locales.) And, from there, other indigenous nations, elsewhere around the world. Again, you can see some of the larger political implications. If we're going to have a "New World Order," let's make it something just a bit different from what George Bush and his friends had in mind. Right?

Sharing the Land

There are several closely related matters which should be touched upon before wrapping this up. One has to do with the idea of self-determination, what it is that is meant when indigenists demand the unrestricted right for native peoples. Most non-Indians, and even a lot of Indians, always seem confused by this and want to know whether it's not the same as complete separation from the U.S., or Canada, or whatever the colonizing power may be. The answer is, "not necessarily." The unqualified acknowledgement by the colonizer of the right of the colonized to total separation ("secession") from the colonial order, is the necessary point of departure for any exercise of self-determination to occur. Decolonization means the colonized can then exercise the right in whole or in part, as they see fit, in accordance with their own customs and traditions, and their own appreciation of their needs. They decide for themselves what degree of autonomy they wish to enjoy, and thus the nature of their political and economic relationship(s), not only with their former colonizers, but with all other nations as well.[54]

My own inclination, which is in some ways an emotional preference, tends to run toward complete sovereign independence, but that's not the point. I have no more right to impose my preferences on indigenous nations than do the colonizing powers; each indigenous nation will choose for itself the exact manner and extent to which it expresses its autonomy, its sovereignty. To be honest, I suspect very few would be inclined to adopt my sort of "go it alone" approach. (I must admit that part of my own insistence upon it often has more to do with forcing concession of the right from those who seek to deny it than it does with putting it into practice.) In the event, I expect you'd see the hammering out of a number of sets of international relations in the "free association" vein, a welter of variations of commonwealth and home rule governance.[55]

The intent here is not, no matter how much it may be deserved in an abstract sense, to visit some sort of retribution, real or symbolic, upon the colonizing or former colonizing powers. It is to arrive at new sets of relationships between peoples which effectively put an end to the era of international domination. The need is to gradually replace the existing world order with one which is predicated on collaboration and cooperation between nations. The only way to ever really accomplish that is to physically disassemble the gigantic state structures—structures which are literally predicated in systematic intergroup domination; they cannot in any sense exist without it—which are evolving in this the imperialist era. A concomitant of this disassembly is the inculcation of voluntary, consensual interdependence between formerly dominated and dominating nations, and a redefinition of the word "nation" itself to conform to its original meaning: bodies of people bound together by their bioregional and other natural cultural affinities.[56]

This last point is, it seems to me, crucially important. Partly, that's because of the persistent question of who it is who gets to remain in Indian Country once land restoration and consolidation has occurred. The answer, I think is anyone who wants to, up to a point. By "anyone who wants to," I mean anyone who wishes to apply for formal citizenship within an indigenous nation, thereby accepting the idea that s/he is placing him or herself under unrestricted Indian jurisdiction and will thus be required to abide by native law.[57] Funny thing, I hear a lot of non-Indians asserting that they reject nearly every aspect of U.S. law, but the idea of placing themselves under anyone else's jurisdiction seems to leave them pretty queasy. I have no idea how many non-Indians might actually opt for citizenship in an Indian nation when push comes to shove, but I expect there will be some. And I suspect some Indians have been so indoctrinated by the dominant society that they'll elect to remain within it rather than availing themselves of their own citizenship. So there'll be a bit of a tradeoff in this respect.

Now, there's the matter of the process working only "up to a point." That point is very real. It is defined, not by political or racial considerations, but by the carrying capacity of the land. The population of indigenous nations everywhere has always been determined by the number of people who could be sustained in a given environment or bioregion without overpowering and thereby destroying that environment.[58] A very carefully calculated balance—one which was calibrated knowing that in order to enjoy certain sorts of material comfort, human population had to be kept at some level below saturation per se—was always maintained between the number of humans and the rest of the habitat. In order to accomplish this, Indians incorporated into the very core of their spiritual traditions the concept that all life forms and the earth itself possess rights equal to those enjoyed by humans.

Rephrased, this means it would be a violation of a fundament of traditional Indian law to supplant or eradicate another species, whether animal or plant, in order to make way for some greater number of humans, or to increase the level of material comfort available to those who already exist. Conversely, it is a fundamental requirement of traditional law that each human accept his or her primary responsibility, that of maintaining the balance and harmony of the natural order *as it is encountered.*[59] One is essentially free to do anything one wants in an indigenous society so long as this cardinal rule is adhered to. The bottom line with regard to the maximum population limit of Indian Country as it has been sketched in this presentation is a very finite number. My best guess is that a couple of million people would be pushing the upper limit. Whatever. Citizens can be admitted until that point has been reached, and no more. And the population cannot increase beyond that number over time, no matter at what rate. Carrying capacity is a fairly constant reality; it tends to change over thousands of years, when it changes at all.

Population and Environment

What I'm going to say next will probably startle a few people (as if what's been said already hasn't). I think this principle of population restraint is the single most important example Native North America can set for the rest of humanity. It is *the* thing which it is most crucial for others to emulate. Check it out. I just read that Japan, a small island nation which has so many people that they're literally tumbling into the sea, and which has exported about half again as many people as live on the home islands, is expressing "official concern" that it's birth rate has declined very slightly over the last few years. The worry is that in 30 years there'll be fewer workers available to "produce," and to "consume" whatever it is that's manufactured.[60] Ever ask yourself what it is that's used in "producing" something? Or what it is that's being "consumed"? Yeah. You got it. Nature is being consumed, and with it the ingredients which allow ongoing human existence. It's true that nature can replenish some of what's consumed, but only at a certain rate. That rate has been vastly exceeded, and the excess is intensifying by the moment. An overburgeoning humanity is killing the natural world, and thus itself. It's no more complicated than that.[61]

Here we are in the midst of a rapidly worsening environmental crisis of truly global portions, every last bit of it attributable to a wildly accelerating human consumption of the planetary habitat, and you have one of the world's major offenders expressing grave concern that the rate at which it is able to consume might actually drop a notch or two. *Think* about it. I suggest that this attitude signifies nothing so much as stark, staring madness. It is insane, suicidally, homicidally and ecocidally insane. And, no I'm not being rhetorical. I mean these terms in clinically precise fashion. But I don't want to convey the misimpression that I'm singling out the Japanese. I only used them as an illustration of a far broader pathology called "industrialism"—or, lately, "post-industrialism"—a sickness centered on an utterly obsessive drive to dominate and destroy the natural order (words like "production," "consumption," "development" and "progress" are mere than code words masking this reality).[62]

It's not only the industrialized countries which are afflicted with this disease. One byproduct of the past 500 years of European expansionism and the resulting hegemony of Eurocentric ideology is that the latter has been drummed into the consciousness of most peoples to the point where it is now subconsciously internalized. Everywhere, you find people thinking it "natural" to view themselves as the incarnation of god on earth ("created in the image of God"), and thus dutybound to "exercise dominion over nature" in order that they can "multiply, grow plentiful, and populate the land" in ever increasing "abundance."[63] The legacy of the forced labor of the *latifundia* and inculcation of Catholicism in Latin America is a tremendous overburden of population devoutly believing that "wealth" can be achieved (or is defined) by having ever more children.[64] The legacy of Mao's implementation of the "reverse technology" policy—the official encouragement of breakneck childbearing rates in his already overpopulated country, solely as a means to deploy massive labor power to offset capitalism's "technological advantage" in production—resulted in a tripling of China's population in only two generations.[65] And then there is India...

Make absolutely no mistake about it. The planet was never designed to accommodate five billion human beings, much less the *ten* billion predicted to be here a mere 50 years hence.[66] If we are to be about turning power relations around between people, and between groups of people, we must also be about turning around the relationship between people and the rest of the natural order. If we don't, we'll die out as a species, just like any other species which irrevocably overshoots its habitat. The sheer number of humans on this planet needs to come down to about a quarter of what they are today, or maybe less, and the plain fact is that the bulk of these numbers are in the Third World.[67] So, I'll say this clearly: not only must the birth rate in the Third World come down, but the actual population levels must also start to come down dramatically, beginning right now.

Of course, there's another dimension to the population issue, one which is in some ways even more important, and I want to get into it in a minute. But first I have to say something else: I don't want a bunch of Third Worlders—or anyone else for that matter—jumping up in my face screaming that I'm advocating "genocide." Get *off* that bullshit. It's genocide when some centralized state, or some colonizing power, imposes sterilization or abortion on target groups. It's not genocide at all when we recognize that we have a problem, and take the logical steps *ourselves* to solve them. Voluntary sterilization is not a part of genocide. Voluntary abortion is not a part of genocide. And, most importantly, educating ourselves and our respective peoples to bring our birth rates under control through conscious resort to birth control measures is not a part of genocide.[68] What it *is* a part of is taking responsibility for ourselves again, of taking responsibility for our destiny and our children's destiny. It's about rooting the ghost of the Vatican out of our collective psyches, and the ghost of Adam Smith, and the ghost of Karl Marx. It's about getting back in touch with our *own* ways, our *own* traditions, our *own* knowledge, and it's long past time we got out of our own way in this respect. We've got an awful lot to unlearn, and an awful lot to relearn, not much time in which we can afford the luxury of avoidance, and we need to get on with it.

However, we are better off focusing on problems here at home where we have a better chance of succeeding, which brings me to the other aspect of population I wanted to take up: there's another way of counting. One way, the way I just did it, and the one its conventionally done, is to simply point to the number of bodies, or "people units." That's valid enough as far as it goes, so we need to look at it and act upon what we see, but it doesn't really go far enough. This brings up the second method, which is to count by relative rate of resource consumption per body—the relative degree of environmental impact per individual—and to extrapolate that into people units.

Using this method, which is actually more accurate in ecological terms, we arrive at conclusions that are a little different than the usual notion that the most overpopulated regions on earth are in the Third World. The average resident of the United States, for example, consumes about 30 times the resources of the average Ugandan or Laotian. Since a lot of poor folk reside in the U.S., this translates into the average yuppie consuming about 70 times the resources of an average Third Worlder.[69] Every yuppie born counts as much as another 70 Chinese. Lay *that* one on the next Izod-clad geek who approaches you with a baby stroller and an outraged look, telling you to put your cigarette out, eh? It's plainly absurd for anyone to complain about smoking when you consider the context of the damage done by American consumption patterns. Tell 'em you'll put it out when they snuff the kid, and not a moment before. Better yet, tell 'em they should snuff themselves, as well as the kid, and do the planet a *real* favor. Just "kidding" (heh-heh).[70]

Returning to the topic at hand, you have to multiply the U.S. population by a factor of 30—a noticeably higher ratio than either western Europe or Japan—in order to figure out how many Third Worlders it would take to have the same environmental impact. I make that to be 7.5 *billion* U.S. people units. I think I can thus safely say the most overpopulated portion of the globe is the United States. Either the consumption rates really have to be cut in this country, most especially in the more privileged social sectors, or the number of people must be drastically reduced, or both. I advocate both. How much? That's a bit subjective, but I'll tentatively accept the calculations of William Catton, a respected ecological demographer. He estimated that North America was thoroughly saturated with humans by 1840 with about 50 million, roughly one-fifth of the current population.[71] So we either need to get both population and consumption levels down to what they were in that year, or preferably a little earlier. Alternatively, we need to bring population down to an even lower level in order to sustain a correspondingly higher level of consumption.

Here's where I think the reconstitution of indigenous

territorality and sovereignty in the West can be useful with regard to population. You see, land isn't just land; it's also the resources within the land, things like coal, oil, natural gas, uranium, and maybe most important, water. How does that bear on U.S. overpopulation? Simple. Much of the population expansion in this country over the past quarter-century has been into the southwestern desert region. How many people have they got living in the valley down there at Phoenix, a place which might be reasonably expected to support 500? Look at L.A., 20 million people where there ought to be maybe a few thousand. How do they accomplish this? Well, for one thing, they've diverted the entire Colorado River from its natural purposes. They're syphoning off the Columbia River and piping it south. They've even got a project underway to divert the Yukon River all the way down from Alaska to support southwestern urban growth, and to irrigate George Bush's proposed agribusiness penetration of northern Sonora. Whole regions of our ecosphere are being destabilized in the process.

In the scenario I've described, the whole Colorado watershed will be in Indian Country, under Indian control. So will the source of the Columbia. And diversion of the Yukon would have to go right through Indian Country. Now, here's the deal. No more use of water to fill swimming pools and sprinkle golf courses in Phoenix and LA. No more watering Kentucky bluegrass lawns out on the yucca flats. No more drivethru car washes in Tucumcari. No more "Big Surf" amusement parks in the middle of the desert. Drinking water and such for the whole population, yes, Indians should deliver that. But water for this other insanity? No way. I guarantee that'll stop the inflow of population cold. Hell, I'll guarantee it'll start a pretty substantial out-flow. Most of these folks never wanted to live in the desert anyway. That's why they keep trying to make it look like Florida (another delicate environment which is buckling under the weight of population increases).[72]

And we can help move things along in other ways as well. Virtually all the electrical power for the southwestern urban sprawls comes from a combination of hydroelectric and coalfired generation in the Four Corners area. This is smack dab in the middle of Indian Country, along with all the uranium with which a "friendly atom" alternative might be attempted, and most of the low sulfur coal. Goodbye, the neon glitter of Las Vegas and San Diego. Adios to air conditioners in every room. Sorry about your hundred mile expanses of formerly streetlit expressway. Basic needs will be met, and that's it. Which means we can also start saying goodbye to western rivers being backed up like so many sewage lagoons behind massive hydro dams. The Glen Canyon and Hoover dams are coming down, boys and girls. And we can begin to experience things like a reduction in the acidity of southwestern rain water as facilities like the Four Corners Power Plant are cut back in generating time, and eventually eliminated altogether.

What I'm saying probably sounds extraordinarily cruel to a lot of people, particularly those imbued with the believe that they have a "God-given right" to play a round of golf on the well-watered green beneath the imported palm trees outside the air-conditioned casino at the base of the Superstition Mountains. Tough. Those days can be ended without hesitation or apology. A much more legitimate concern rests on the fact that a lot of people who've drifted into the southwest have no place to go to. The areas they came from are crammed. In many cases, that's why they left. To them, I say there's no need to panic; no one will abruptly pull the plug on you, or leave you to die of thirst. Nothing like that. But quantities of both water and power will be set at minimal levels. In order to have a surplus, you'll have to bring your number down to a certain level over a certain period. At that point, the levels will again be reduced, necessitating another population reduction. Things can be phased in over an extended period, several generations, if need be.[73]

Probably, provision of key items such as western water and coal should be negotiated on the basis of reductions in population and consumption by the U.S. as a whole rather than simply the region served in order to prevent population shifts from being substituted for actual reductions.[74] Any such negotiated arrangement should also include an agreement to alter the U.S. distribution of food surpluses and the like, so as to ease the transition to lower population and correspondingly greater self-sufficiency in hardpressed Third World areas.

While it's easy to raise objections over the particulars of the scenario sketched here, it's important to realize and act on the stark choice before us: on the one hand we could manage a phased retreat from gluttonous, individualistically organized consumption. The only alternative is a catastrophic drop off the ecological cliff that we are now perched on. The objective inherent to every aspect of this process should be, and can be, to let everyone down as gently as possible from the long and intoxicating high that has beset so much of the human species in its hallucination that it, and it alone, is the only thing of value and importance in the universe. In doing so, and I believe *only* in doing so, can we fulfill our obligation to bequeath our grandchildren, and our grandchildren's grandchildren, a world which is fit (or even possible) to live in.[75]

I Am Indigenist

There are any number of other matters which by rights should be discussed, but they will of necessity have to await another occasion. What has been presented has been only the barest outline, a glimpse of what might be called an "indigenist vision." Hopefully, it provides enough shape and clarity to allow anyone who wishes to pursue the thinking further, to fill in at least some of the gaps I've not had time to address, and to arrive at insights and conclusions of their own. Once the main tenets have been advanced, and I think to some extent that's been accomplished here, the perspective of indigenism is neither mystical nor mysterious.

In closing I would like to turn again to the critics, the skeptics, those who will decry what has been said as "unrealistic," or even "crazy." On the former score, my reply is that so long as we define realism, or reality itself, in conventional terms, the terms imposed by the order in which we now live, we will be locked forever into the trajectory in which we presently find ourselves. We will never break free, because any order, any structure, defines reality only in terms of itself. Consequently, allow me to echo the sentiments expressed in the French student revolt of 1968: "Be realistic, demand the impossible!"[76] If you read through a volume of American Indian oratory, and there are several available, you'll find that native people have been saying the same thing all along.[77]

As to my being crazy, I'd like to say, "Thanks for the compliment." Again, I follow my elders and my ancestors—and R.D. Laing, for that matter—in believing that when confronted with a society as obviously insane as this one, the only sane posture one can adopt is what that society would automatically designate as crazy.[78] It wasn't Indians who turned birthing into a religious fetish while butchering off a couple hundred million people with weapons of mass destruction and systematically starving another billion or so to death. Indians never had a Grand Inquisition, and we never came up with a plumbing plan to reroute the water flow on the entire continent. Nor did we ever produce "leaders" of the caliber of Ronald Reagan, Jean Kirkpatrick or Ross Perot. Hell, we never even figured out that turning prison construction into a major growth industry was an indication of social progress and enlightenment. Maybe we were never so much crazy as we were congenitally retarded by the dominant society's "standards."

Whatever the reason, and you'll excuse me for suspecting it might be something other than craziness or retardation, I'm indescribably thankful that our cultures turned out to be so different, no matter how much abuse and sacrifice it's entailed. I'm proud to stand inside the heritage of native struggle. I'm proud to say I'm an unreconstructable indigenist. For me, there's no other reasonable or realistic way to look at the world. And I invite anyone who shares that viewpoint to come aboard, regardless of your race, creed or national origin. Maybe Chief Seattle said it best back in 1854: "Tribe follows tribe, and nation follows nation, like the waves of the sea. Your time of decay may be distant, but it will surely come, for even the white man whose god walked with him and talked with him as friend with friend, cannot be exempt from the common destiny. We may be brothers after all. We will see."[79]

Notes

1. For what is probably the best available account of AIM, IAT, and WARN, see Peter Matthiessen's *In the Spirit of Crazy Horse* (New York: Viking Press, [2nd ed.] 1991). On Oka, see Rick Hornung's *One Nation Under the Gun: Inside the Mowhawk Civil War* (New York: Pantheon Books, 1991).
2. Most of these struggles are covered in M. Annette Jaimes, ed., *The State of Native America: Genocide, Colonization and Resistance* (Boston: South End Press, 1992). On James Bay, see Boyce Richardson's *Strangers Devour the Land* (Post Mills, VT: Chelsea Green Publishing, [2nd ed. 1991).
3. While it is hardly complete, a good point of departure for learning about many of the individuals named would be Alvin Josephy's *The Patriot Chiefs* (New York: Viking Press, 1961).
4. The bulk of those mentioned, and a number of others as well, appear in Jaimes, *op. cit.*
5. The term "Vichy Indians" comes from Russell Means. See his "The Same Old Song" in Ward Churchill, ed., *Marxism*

and Native Americans (Boston: South End Press, [2nd ed.] 1989, pp. 19-33).

6. Ross Swimmer is an alleged Cherokee and former Philips Petroleum executive who served as head of the U.S. Bureau of Indian Affairs under Ronald Reagan, and argued for suspension of federal obligations to Indians as a means of teaching native people "self-reliance." Dickie Wilson was head of the federal puppet government on Pine Ridge Reservation during the early 1970s, a capacity in which he formed an entity called the GOONs to physically assault and frequently kill members and supporters of AIM. Webster Two Hawk was head of the National Tribal Chairman's Association funded by the the Nixon administration. He used his federally-sponsored position to denounce Indian liberation struggles. Peter McDonald—often referred to as "McDollar" in Indian Country—utilized his position as head of the puppet government at Navajo to sell his people's interests to various mining corporations during the 1970s and '80s, greatly enriching himself in the process. David Bradley is a no-talent painter living in Santa Fe whose main claim to fame is having been made successful bid to have the federal government enforce "identification standards" against other Indian artists; he has subsequently set himself up as a self-anointed "Identity Police," a matter which, thankfully, leaves him little time to produce his typical graphic schlock. To hear them tell it, of course, each of these individuals acted in the service of "Indian sovereignty."
7. See LaDuke's "Natural to Synthetic and Back Again," the preface to *Marxism and Native Americans, op. cit.*, pp. i viii.
8. Guillermo Bonfil Batalla, *Utopia y Revolucíon: El Pensamiento Politico Contemporàneo de los Indios en América Latina* (Mexico: Editorial Nueva Imagen, SA., 1981, p. 37); translation by Roxanne Dunbar Ortiz.
9. *Ibid.*, pp. 378.
10. *Ibid.*, p. 38.
11. Roxanne Dunbar Ortiz, *Indians of the Americas: Human Rights and Self-Determination* (London: Zed Press, 1984, p. 83).
12. *Ibid.*, p. 84.

13. For an excellent overview on the implications of Marx's thinking in this regard, see the first couple of chapters in Walker Connor's *The National Question in Marxist-Leninist Theory and Strategy* (Princeton, NJ: Princeton University Press, 1984).
14. Dunbar Ortiz, *op. cit.*, p. 85.
15. George Manuel and Michael Posluns, *The Fourth World: An Indian Reality* (New York: Free Press, 1974).
16. On the Irish and Welsh struggles see Michael Hechter, *Internal Colonialism: The Celtic Fringe in British National Development, 1536-1966* (Berkeley: University of California Press, 1975). On the Basques, see Kenneth Medhurst, *The Basques and Catalans* (London: Minority Rights Group Report No. 9, September 1977).
17. Dunbar Ortiz, *op. cit.*, p. 89.
18. Bernard Neitschmann, "The Third World War," *Cultural Survival Quarterly*, Vol. 11, No. 3, 1987.
19. Geneva Offices of the United Nations, Press Release, August 17,1981 (Hr/1080).
20. For an excellent analysis of this tradition from an indigenist perspective, see Robert A. Williams, Jr., *The American Indian in Western Legal Thought: The Discourses of Conquest* (London/New York: Oxford University Press, 1990).
21. On the Iberian legal tradition, see James Brown Scott, *The Spanish Origin of International Law* (Oxford: Clarendon Press, 1934).
22. Hugo Blanco, *Land or Death: The Peasant Struggle in Peru* (New York: Pathfinder Press, 1972). Blanco was a marxist, and thus sought to pervert indigenous issues through rigid class analysis—defining Indians as "peasants" rather than by nationality—but his identification of land as the central issue was/is nonetheless valid.
23. The complete texts of 371 of these ratified treaties will be found in Charles J. Kappler, comp., *American Indian Treaties, 1778-1883* (New York Interland Publishers, 1973). The Lakota scholar Vine Deloria, Jr., has also collected the texts of several more ratified treaties which do not appear in Kappler, but which will be published in a forthcoming collection.
24. The constitutional provision comes at Article 1, Section 10. Codification of customary international law in this connec-

tion is explained in Sir lan Sinclair, *The Vienna Convention on the Law of Treaties* (Manchester: Manchester University Press, [2nd ed.] 1984).

25. See generally, Vine Deloria, Jr., and Clifford E. Lytle, *American Indians, American Justice* (Austin: University of Texas Press, 1983).
26. *Lonewolf v. Hitchcock,* 187 US. 553 (1903). For analysis, see Ann Laquer Estin, *"Lonewolf v. Hitchcock* The Long Shadow," in Sandra L. Gdwallader and Vine Deloria, Jr., eds., *The Aggressions of Civilization: Federal Indian Policy Since the 1880s* (Philadelphia: Temple University Press, 1984, pp. 21545).
27. Probably the best exposition of the legal principles articulated by the U.S. as being violated by the nazis may be found in Bradley F. Smith, *The Road to Nuremburg* (New York: Basic Books, 1981).
28. A fuller articulation of this thesis may be found in the author's "On Gaining 'Moral High Ground': An Ode to George Bush and the 'New World Order'," in Cynthia Peters, ed., *Collateral Damage: The New World Order at Home and Abroad* (Boston: South End Press, 1992, pp. 359-72).
29. For the origins of such practices, see Dorothy V. Jones, *License for Empire: Colonialism by Treaty in Early America* (Chicago: University of Chicago Press, 1982). For a good survey of U.S. adaptations, see Donald Worcester, ed., *Forked Tongues and Broken Treaties* (Caldwell, ID: Caxton Publishers, 1975).
30. The travesty at Fort Wise is adequately covered in Stan Hoig's *The Sand Geek Massacre* (Norman: University of Oklahoma Press, 1961).
31. Deloria compilation, forthcoming.
32. On the purpose of the commission, see Harvey D. Rosenthal, "Indian Claims and the American Conscience: A Brief History of the Indian Claims Commission," in Imre Sutton, ed., *Irredeemable America: The Indians' Estate and Land Tenure* (Albuquerque: University of New Mexico Press, 1985, pp. 35-86). You have to read between the lines a bit.
33. See Russel Barsh, "Indian Land Claims Policy in the United States," *North Dakota Law Review, No. 58, 1982,*

pp. 182.

34. The percentage is arrived at by juxtaposing the approximately fifty million acres within the current reservation landbase to the more than two billion acres of the lower 48. According to the Indian Claims Commission findings, Indians actually retain unfettered legal title to about 750 million acres of the continental U.S.
35. Concerning Alaska, see M.C. Berry, *The Alaska Pipeline: The Politics of Oil and Native Land Claims* (Bloomington/Indianapolis: Indiana University Press, 1975). On Hawai'i see Haunani-Kay Trask, *From a Native Daughter: Essays on Racism, Colonization and Sovereignty in Hawai'i* forthcoming, Monroe, ME: Common Courage Press, 1993.
36. A good exposition on this phenomenon may be found in Paul Brodeur, *Restitution: The Land Claims of the Mashpee. Passamaquoddy and Penobscot Indians of New England* (Boston: Northeastern University Press, 1985).
37. The problem is partially but insightfully examined in Ronald Weitzer, *Transforming Settler States: Communal Conflict and Internal Security in Zimbabwe and Northern Ireland* (Berkeley: University of California Press, 1992).
38. It is entirely possible to extend a logical analysis in this direction. See, for instance, J. Sakai, *Settlers: The Mythology of the White Proletariat* (Chicago: Morningstar Press, 1983).
39. For an outstanding survey of the forms of indigenous government in both the pre- and post-contact periods, see Rebecca L. Robbins, "Self-Determination and Subordination: The Past, Present, and Future of American Indian Governance," in *The State of Native America, op. cit.*, pp. 87-119.
40. These matters are covered quite well in M. Annette Jaimes and Theresa Halsey, "American Indian Women: At the Center of Indignous Resistance in Contemporary North America," in *The State of Native America, op. cit.*, pp. 311-44.
41. The Smithsonian view of Indians has been adopted even by some of the more self-consciously "revolutionary" organizations in the United States. For a classic example, see Revolutionary Communist Party, USA, "Searching for the

Second Harvest," in *Marxism and Native Americans, op. cit.*, pp. 355-8.

42. The thesis is, no kidding, that Indians were the first "environmental pillagers," and it took the invasion of enlightened Europeans like the author of the piece to save the American ecosphere from total destruction by its indigenous inhabitants; see George Weurthner, "An Ecological View of the Indian," *Earth First*, Vol. 7, No. 7, August 1987.
43. Paul W. Valentine, "Dances with Myths," *Arizona Republic*, April 7,1991 (Valentine is syndicated, but is on staff at the *Washington Post.)*
44. A fine selection of such early colonialist impressions will be found in the first few chapters of Richard Drinnon's *Facing West: The Metaphysics of Indian Hating and Empire Building* (New York: Schoken Books, 1980). On the length of indigenous occupancy in the Americas, see Jeffrey Goodman, *American Genesis* (New York: Summit Books, 1981). On precontact population, see Lenore A. Stiffamm and Phil Lane, Jr., "The Demography of Native North America: A Question of American Indian Survival," in *The State of Native America, op. cit.*, pp. 23-53.
45. For a succinct but reasonably comprehensive survey of actual precontact indignous material and intellectual realities, see M. Annette Jaimes, "The Stone Age Revisited: An Indigenist Examination of Labor," *New Studies On the Left*, Vol. XIV, No. 3, Spring 1991.
46. See Jack D. Forbes, *Black Africans and Native Americans: Race, Color and Caste in the Evolution of Red-Black Peoples* (London/New York: Oxford University Press, 1988).
47. On federal quantum policy, see M. Annette Jaimes, "Federal Indian Identification Policy: A Usurpation of Indigenous Sovereignty in North America," in *The State of Native America, op. cit*, pp. 123-38.
48. Probably the best examination of Indian warfare and "militaristic" tradition is Tom Holm's "Patriots and Pawns: State Use of American Indians in the Military and the Process of Nativization in the United States," in *The State of Native America, op. cit*, pp. 345-70.
49. Referred to here is the so called "Bradley Bill" (S.1453), introduced before the Senate by Bill Bradley in 1987. For

analysis, see the special issue of *Wicazo Sa Review* (Vol. XIV, No. 1, Spring 1988) devoted to the topic.

50. Russell Means and Ward Churchill, *TREATY: The Campaign of Russell Means for the Presidency of the Oglala Sioux Tribe* (Porcupine, S.D.: TREATY Campaign, 1982).
51. Barsh, *op. cit.*
52. A number of examples may be found in Mark Frank Lindley's *The Acquisition and Government of Backward Country in International Law: A Treatise on the Law and Practise Relating to Colonial Expansion* (London: Longmans Green Publishers, 1926).
53. Probably the only accessible material to date on the Buffalo Commons idea is unfortunately a rather frothy little volume. See Anne Matthews, *Where the Buffalo Roam: The Storm Over the Revolutionary Plan to Restore America's Great Plains* (New York: Grove Weidenfeld Publishers, 1992).
54. For one of the best elaborations of these principles, see Zed Nanda, "Self-Determination in International Law: Validity of Claims to Secede," *Case Western Reserve Journal of International Law,* No. 13, 1981.
55. A prototype for this sort of arrangement exists between Greenland (populated mainly by Inuits) and Denmark. See Gudmundur Alfredsson, "Greenland and the Law of Political Decolonization," *German Yearbook on International Law,* No. 25, 1982.
56. Although my argument comes at it from a very different angle, the conclusion here is essentially the same as that reached by Richard Falk in his *The End of World Order: Essays in Normative International Relations* (New York/London: Holmes and Meier Publishers, 1983).
57. This is the basic idea set forth in *TREATY, op. cit.*
58. The concepts at issue here are brought out very well in William R. Catton, Jr., *Overshoot: The Ecological Basis of Revolutionary Change* (Urbana: University of Illinois Press, 1982).
59. For further elaboration, see Vine Deloria, Jr., *God Is Red* (New York: Delta Books, 1973). The ideas have even caught on, at least as questions, among some Euroamerican legal practitioners; see Christopher D. Stone, *Should Trees Have Standing? Towards Legal Rights for*

Natural Objects (Los Altos, CA: William Kaufman Publishers, 1972).

60. CNN "Dollars and Cents" reportage, May 27,1992.
61. The idea is developed in detail in Jeremy Rifkin's *Entropy A New World View* (New York: Viking Press, 1980). It should be noted, however, that the world view in question is hardly new; indigenous peoples have held it all along.
62. One good summary of this, utilizing extensive native sources—albeit many of them go unattributed—is Jerry Mander's *In the Absence of the Sacred: The Failure of Technology and the Survival of Indian Nations* (San Francisco: Sierra Club Books, 1991).
63. If this sounds a bit scriptural, it's meant to. A number of us see a direct line of continuity from the these core imperatives of Judeo-Christian theology, through the capitalist secularization of church doctrine and its alleged marxian antithesis, right on through to the burgeoning technotopianism of today. This is a major conceptual cornerstone of what indigenists view as Eurocentrism (a virulently anthropocentric outlook in its essence).
64. The information is there, but the conclusion avoided, in Andre Gunder Frank's *Capitalism and Underdevelopment in Latin America* (New York: Monthly Review Press, 1967).
65. See Jerome Ch'en, *Mao and the Chinese Revolution* (London/New York: Oxford University Press, 1967).
66. Paul R. Ehrlich and Anne H. Ehrlich, *The Population Explosion* (New York: Simon and Schuster Publisher, 1990).
67. Extrapolating from the calculations of Catton in *Overshoot, op. cit.*
68. Sound arguments to this effect are advanced in Paul R. Ehrlich, *The Population Bomb* (San Francisco: W.H. Freeman Publishers, 1970).
69. Ehrlich and Ehrlich, from their book *Healing the Earth,* quoted in CNN series *The Population Bomb,* May 1992.
70. Lest my remarks be taken out of context, the point isn't to get people to commit suicide or take the lives of others. Rather, I'm tired of sanctimonious environmental ravagers seizing on smoking as an issue despite it's harm being virtually zero when stacked up against the impact the

complainers make simply by living their daily lives in the manner they do.

71. Catton, *op. cit.* p. 53.
72. This is essentially the same argument advanced, without ever quite arriving at the obvious conclusion, by Marc Reisner in his *Cadillac Desert* (New York: Penguin Books, 1986). For a better, though less comprehensive job, see Marianna Guerrero, "American Indian Water Rights: The Blood of Life in Native North America," in *The State of Native America, op. cit,* pp. 189-216.
73. A good deal of the impact could also be offset by implementing the ideas contained in John Todd and George Tukel, *Reinhabiting Cities and Towns: Designing for Sustainability* (San Francisco: Planet Drum Foundation, 1981).
74. For purposes of comparison, see *Funding Ecological and Social Destruction: The World Bank and International Monetary Fund* (Washington, D.C.: Bank Information Center, 1990). By contrast, the concept described in the text might be dubbed "Struggling for Ecological and Social Preservation."
75. Many indigenous peoples take the position that all social policies should be entered into only after consideration of their likely implications, both environmentally and culturally, for descendants seven generations in the future. Consequently a number of seemingly good ideas for solving short run problems are never entered into because no one can reasonably predict their longer term effects. See Sylvester M. Morey, ed., *Can the Red Man Help the White Man? A Denver Conference with Indian Elders* (New York: Myrin Institute Books, 1970).
76. Allan Priaulx and Sanford J. Ungar, *The Almost Revoution: France, 1968* (New York: Dell Books, 1969).
77. See, for example, Virginia Irving Armstrong, ed., *I have Spoken: American History Through the Voices of the Indians* (Chicago: The Swallow Press, 1971).
78. R.D. Laing, *The Politics of Experience* (New York: Ballentine Books, 1967).
79. Armstrong, *op. cit.*, p. 79.

Index

C

D

E

F

G

I

J

K

L

M

O

P

Q

T

U

XYZ